Lecture Notes in Computer Science 7111

Commenced Publication in 1973
Founding and Former Series Editors:
Gerhard Goos, Juris Hartmanis, and Jan van Leeuwen

Editorial Board

Thomas Erlebach   Sotiris Nikoletseas
Pekka Orponen (Eds.)

Algorithms for Sensor Systems

7th International Symposium on Algorithms
for Sensor Systems, Wireless Ad Hoc Networks
and Autonomous Mobile Entities, ALGOSENSORS 2011
Saarbrücken, Germany, September 8-9, 2011
Revised Selected Papers

 Springer

Volume Editors

Thomas Erlebach
University of Leicester, Department of Computer Science
University Road, Leicester, LE1 7RH, UK
E-mail: t.erlebach@leicester.ac.uk

Sotiris Nikoletseas
University of Patras and Computer Technology Institute
N. Kazantzaki Str. 1, Patras University Campus, 26504 Rion, Patras, Greece
E-mail: nikole@cti.gr

Pekka Orponen
Aalto University School of Science
Department of Information and Computer Science
P.O. Box 15400, 00076, Aalto, Finland
E-mail: pekka.orponen@aalto.fi

ISSN 0302-9743   e-ISSN 1611-3349
ISBN 978-3-642-28208-9   e-ISBN 978-3-642-28209-6
DOI 10.1007/978-3-642-28209-6
Springer Heidelberg Dordrecht London New York

Library of Congress Control Number: 2012930230

CR Subject Classification (1998): F.2, G.1.2, G.2.2, C.2, I.2.9, D.2, E.1

LNCS Sublibrary: SL 5 – Computer Communication Networks and Telecommunications

Typesetting: Camera-ready by author, data conversion by Scientific Publishing Services, Chennai, India

Printed on acid-free paper

Springer is part of Springer Science+Business Media (www.springer.com)

Preface

Wireless ad hoc sensor networks have recently become a very active research subject due to their great potential of providing diverse services to numerous important applications, including remote monitoring and tracking in environmental applications and low-maintenance ambient intelligence in everyday life. The effective and efficient realization of such large-scale, complex ad hoc networking environments requires intensive, coordinated technical research and development efforts, especially in power-aware, scalable, robust wireless distributed protocols, due to the unusual application requirements and the severe resource constraints of the sensor devices. On the other hand, a solid foundational background seems necessary for sensor networks to achieve their full potential. It is a challenge for abstract modeling, algorithmic design and analysis to achieve provably efficient, scalable and fault-tolerant realizations of such huge, highly dynamic, complex, unconventional networks. Features including the extremely large number of sensor devices in the network, the severe power, computing and memory limitations, their dense, random deployment and frequent failures pose new interesting abstract modeling, algorithmic design, analysis and implementation challenges of great practical impact. ALGOSENSORS aims to bring together research contributions related to diverse algorithmic and complexity theoretic aspects of wireless sensor networks.

Starting from 2011, ALGOSENSORS has broadened its thematic scope, keeping its focus on sensor networks but also including other related types of ad hoc wireless networks such as mobile networks, radio networks and distributed systems of robots. Papers were solicited into two tracks, one on Sensor Networks (Track A) and one on Ad Hoc Wireless and Mobile Systems (Track B). Furthermore, the status of the event was upgraded to "Symposium" and its length extended to two days. ALGOSENSORS 2011, the 7th International Symposium on Algorithms for Sensor Systems, Wireless Ad Hoc Networks and Autonomous Mobile Entities, was held in Saarbrücken, Germany, during September 8–9, 2011.

This year the event received a total of 31 submissions. After a careful selection procedure (involving at least two reviews for each paper and at least three reviews for the vast majority of papers, and fruitful discussions by the Program Committees), 16 papers were selected. This volume contains these papers as well as invited contributions for the two keynote talks.

The ten papers in Track A (Sensor Networks) present original research on topics such as localization, lifetime maximization, interference control, neighbor discovery, self-organization, detection, and aggregation. The topics covered by the six papers in Track B (Ad Hoc Wireless and Mobile Systems) include routing, scheduling and capacity optimization in the SINR model, continuous monitoring, and broadcasting.

We would like to warmly thank the ALGO/ESA 2011 organizers (and especially Kurt Mehlhorn) for kindly accepting the proposal of the Steering Committee to colocate ALGOSENSORS with these leading events on algorithms in Europe. Also, we thank the keynote speakers Shlomi Dolev and Friedhelm Meyer auf der Heide for accepting our invitation. Many thanks go to the Program Committee members for their dedicated contribution toward a strong program.

October 2011

Thomas Erlebach
Sotiris Nikoletseas
Pekka Orponen

Conference Organization

Steering Committee

Josep Diaz	Universitat Politècnica de Catalunya, Spain
Bhaskar Krishnamachari	University of Southern California, USA
P.R. Kumar	Texas A&M University, USA
Jan van Leeuwen	University of Utrecht, The Netherlands
Sotiris Nikoletseas	University of Patras and CTI, Greece
Jose Rolim	University of Geneva, Switzerland
Paul Spirakis	University of Patras and CTI, Greece

Program Committees

Chair

Sotitis Nikoletseas	University of Patras and CTI, Greece

Track A Chair

Pekka Orponen	Aalto University, Finland

Track B Chair

Thomas Erlebach	University of Leicester, UK

Track A: Sensor Networks

Mihaela Cardei	Florida Atlantic University, USA
Tassos Dimitriou	Athens Information Technology, Greece
Shlomi Dolev	Ben Gurion University, Israel
Alon Efrat	University of Arizona, USA
Jie Gao	SUNY Stony Brook, USA
Aubin Jarry	University of Geneva, Switzerland
Evangelos Kranakis	Carleton University, Canada
Alexander Kröller	TU Braunschweig, Germany
Fabian Kuhn	University of Lugano, Switzerland
Mingyan Liu	University of Michigan, USA
Sotiris Nikoletseas	University of Patras and CTI, Greece
Pekka Orponen (Chair)	Aalto University, Finland
Michael Rabbat	McGill University, Canada
Elad Schiller	Chalmers University of Technology, Sweden
Christian Schindelhauer	University of Freiburg, Germany
Stefan Schmid	T-Labs/TU Berlin, Germany

Jukka Suomela	University of Helsinki, Finland
Subhash Suri	University of California at Santa Barbara, USA
Sébastien Tixeuil	University of Paris 6, France
Dorothea Wagner	Karlsruhe Institute of Technology, Germany

Track B: Ad Hoc Wireless and Mobile Systems

Matthew Andrews	Alcatel-Lucent Bell Labs, USA
Costas Busch	Louisiana State University, USA
Xiaowen Chu	Hong Kong Baptist University, Hong Kong
Thomas Erlebach (Chair)	University of Leicester, UK
Stefan Funke	University of Stuttgart, Germany
Magnús M. Halldórsson	Reykjavik University, Iceland
David Ilcinkas	CNRS and Bordeaux University, France
Danny Krizanc	Wesleyan University, USA
Erik Jan van Leeuwen	University of Bergen, Norway
Xiang-Yang Li	Illinois Institute of Technology, USA
Sotiris Nikoletseas	University of Patras and CTI, Greece
Sriram Pemmaraju	University of Iowa, USA
Cristina M. Pinotti	University of Perugia, Italy
Rajmohan Rajaraman	Northeastern University, USA
Dror Rawitz	Tel-Aviv University, Israel
Nicola Santoro	Carleton University, Canada
My T Thai	University of Florida, USA
Anil Vullikanti	Virginia Tech, USA
Peter Widmayer	ETH Zürich, Switzerland
Prudence Wong	University of Liverpool, UK

Additional Referees

Andrew Berns	Nikola Milosavljevic	Dennis Schieferdecker
Asaf Cohen	Max Pagel	Markus Völker
Andreas Gemsa	Christoforos Raptopoulos	Vyacheslav Zalyubovskiy
Henning Hasemann	Rik Sarkar	

Table of Contents

Ad Hoc Wireless and Mobile Systems Track

Dynamic Multi-party Computation Forever for Swarm and Cloud Computing and Code Obfuscation*

Shlomi Dolev

Department of Computer Science,
Ben-Gurion University of the Negev, Beer-Sheva, 84105, Israel
dolev@cs.bgu.ac.il

Intuitive and Basic Description of Secure Multi-party Computation.
Secure multi-party computation [1,3] schemes allow participants to calculate a
function of their inputs, such that the inputs of the participants are not revealed
to each other.

An important building block in secure multi-party computation is secret sharing [11]. In secret sharing each participant (with identifier) i gets the value
$f(i) = y$ of a polynomial function f of degree t over a finite field. The secret is
the value of the function f in zero, namely $f(0)$, which is a value in the finite
field over which f is defined.

Since there is a need for at least $t+1$ (x, y) values for reconstructing f, it holds
that no information about the secret is revealed when t or less participants expose
their x and y values to each other. Thus, any coalition of t or less participants
cannot reveal the function f and therefore has no information about the secret.

Assuming private channels between every two participants, a participant can
distribute a secret s by choosing a random polynomial f among all the polynomials for which their value in 0 is s, and sending directly to each other participant
(with identifier) j the value of $f(j)$.

Verifiable secret sharing schemes are used to ensure a coherent distribution of a
secret, namely, that the distributer sends shares obtained by a single polynomial
[2]. A bivariate polynomial $f(x, y)$ is used in this case, so that the secret is the
value of $f(0, 0)$, the shares for the i'th participant is the polynomial for which the
first variable is fixed to i, namely $f(i, *)$, and the polynomial $f(*, i)$, for which
the second variable is fixed to i. Then participants i and j can check the shared
points of their four polynomial without revealing additional information to each
other, and broadcast contradicting values, if found. Thus, ensuring coherent
distribution of secrets.

The fact that two secret shares can be added and multiplied by the participants to obtain a global secret that is the result of the addition or multiplication,
respectively, allows a general secure multi-party computation of any function.
Note however that multiplications result in changing the degree of the polynomial. Multiplication can be followed by a procedure to reduce the degree to the

* Partially supported by the US Air-Force, Israel Science Foundation (grant number
  428/11), and Rita Altura Trust Chair in Computer Sciences.

T. Erlebach et al. (Eds.): ALGOSENSORS 2011, LNCS 7111, pp. 1–3, 2012.

original degree of the polynomial by a procedure that adds random polynomials of the desired degree, compute the obtained polynomial and subtract the values associated with the too high degrees, then subtract the random polynomials to get the desired secret sharing.

Dynamic Secure Multi-party Computation. Suppose participants can *leave* and *join* the group that got the shares of the secret [4]. When a participant leaves the rest of the participants may nullify the share of the leaving participant by randomly choosing a polynomial f of degree t, among the polynomials for which their value is zero at zero, $f(0) = 0$, and adding the shares of f to their shares. This is in fact a way to refresh the security of the secret sharing scheme. When a participant j joins $t + 1$ participants, $i_1, i_2, \cdots, i_{t+1}$, send the values $f(i, j)$ and $f(j, i)$ to j allowing j to construct the polynomials $f(j, *)$ and $f(*, j)$.

Additional dynamic operations among group of participants that share a secret may include *merge, clone* and *split*. In the case of merge of two groups of participants, each group member joins the other group. In the case of clone, new participants join and then the refresh security operation (adding a random polynomial that does not change the secret) in each group ensure that the cloned groups are independent. Split partitions the group of participants without performing the join to new member. All the dynamic operations may increase the secret threshold (number of shares needed to reveal the secret) by using a polynomial with the new threshold during the refresh security operation (the way to reduce the threshold has been described in the multiplication procedure above).

Secure Multi-party Computation Forever. Secure multi-party computation has been considered for a one-shot computation of a particular function. A circuit of additions and multiplications is performed to get the result. However, in reality some computations are non-terminating, such as operating systems, or web services, and some computations can be completed in a bounded time, but the bound is unknown. A general computation can be represented by a Turing machine where the current state is represented by the content of the tape of the Turing machine. If the Turing machine uses bounded memory then the computation can be implemented and continue forever.

Still the secure multi-party computation reveals information concerning the function being computed and the stage in the current state of the computation. Strongly oblivious Turing machine can be used to avoid such revealing [4]. The idea is to have a universal Turing machine that uses a circular working tape in which the head of the Turing machine seems to move to the same direction in every step. The computation of the next state and the symbol to be written is securely done using multiplications and additions.

Thus, we gain a provable information theoretic *code obfuscation*, where an adversary that compromises a subset of the participants does not get any information (but the upper bound on the space used) on the computation they perform. Note that inputs from the environment/operator can arrive to the members as shares of secrets.

Communication versus No-communication. Performing multi-party computation with no-communication is appealing since it can hide the participants in a crowd of computing entities, for example this crowd can be part of cloud processes or swarm computing entities [12,8]. One simple solution is to give to each participant a vector of several states such that only the current state appears in these vectors more than any other state [5]. State transitions are executed according to a common global input. In case distinct states in a vector of a user are transfered to the same state, all but one of them are randomly changed to different and distinct states.

A more sophisticated solution that avoids communication among the participants and assumes a common global input is based on Krohn-Rhodes composition. A composition of automata into a cascade of permutation and flip flop automata [9,10,6]. The solution is able to secure the current state in information theoretical fashion in unbounded computations in the presence of one-shot compromising adversary — an adversary that can only reveal the current state of less than a given threshold of participants.

Lastly fully homomorphic encryption [7] enables communication-less secure multi-party computational schemes, but still leaves the case of information theoretic schemes for future investigation.

References

1. Ben-OR, M., Goldwasser, S., Wigderson, A.: Completeness theorems for non-cryptographic fault-tolerant distributed computation. In: STOC, pp. 1–10 (1988)
2. Chor, B., Goldwasser, S., Micali, S., Awerbuch, B.: Verifiable Secret Sharing and Achieving Simultaneity in the Presence of Faults. In: FOCS, pp. 383–395 (1985)
3. Chaum, D., Crépeau, C., Damgård, I.: Multiparty unconditionally secure protocols (extended abstract). In: STOC, pp. 11–19 (1988)
4. Dolev, S., Garay, J., Gilboa, N., Kolesnikov, V.: Swarming secrets. In: 47th Annual Allerton Conference on Communication, Control, and Computing (2009)
5. Dolev, S., Lahiani, L., Yung, M.: Secret Swarm Unit Reactive k-Secret Sharing. In: Srinathan, K., Rangan, C.P., Yung, M. (eds.) INDOCRYPT 2007. LNCS, vol. 4859, pp. 123–137. Springer, Heidelberg (2007)
6. Dolev, S., Garay, J., Gilboa, N., Kolesnikov, V.: Secret Sharing Krohn-Rhodes: Private and Perennial Distributed Computation. In: Innovations in Computer Science (ICS) (January 2011); Also Private and Parennial Distributed Computation. In: Workshop on Cryptography and Security in Clouds (CSC) (2011)
7. Gentry, C.: Fully Homomorphic Encryption Using Ideal Lattices. In: STOC, pp. 169–178 (2009)
8. Higgins, F., Tomlinson, A., Martin, K.: Survey on Security Challenges for Swarm Robotics. In: ICAS 2009, pp. 307–312 (2009)
9. Krohn, K.R., Rhodes, J.L.: Algebraic theory of machines (1962)
10. Krohn, K.R., Rhodes, J.L.: Algebraic theory of machines i: prime decomposition theorems for finite semigroups and machines. Transactions of the American Mathematical Society 116, 450–464 (1965)
11. Shamir, A.: How to share a secret. Communications of the ACM 22, 612–613 (1979)
12. Weiser, M.: The Computer for the 21th Century. Scientific American (September 1991)

Local, Self-organizing Strategies
for Robotic Formation Problems

Barbara Kempkes and Friedhelm Meyer auf der Heide

Heinz Nixdorf Institute & Department of Computer Science,
University of Paderborn, 33102 Paderborn
{barbaras,fmadh}@uni-paderborn.de

Abstract. We consider a scenario with a set of autonomous mobile robots having initial positions in the plane. Their goal is to move in such a way that they eventually reach a prescribed formation. Such a formation may be a straight line between two given endpoints (Robot Chain Problem), a circle or any other geometric pattern, or just one point (Gathering Problem). In this survey, we assume that there is no central control that guides the robot's decisions, thus the robots have to self-organize in order to accomplish global tasks like the above-mentioned formation problems. Moreover, we restrict them to simple local strategies: the robots are limited to "see" only robots within a bounded viewing range; their decisions where to move next are solely based on the relative positions of robots within this range.

We survey recent results on local strategies for short robot chains and gathering, among them the first that come with upper and lower bounds on the number of rounds needed and the maximum distance traveled. Finally we present a continuous local strategy for short robot chains, and present a bound for the "price of locality": for every configuration of initial robot positions, the maximum distance traveled by the robots is at most by a logarithmic (in the number of robots) factor away from the maximum distance of the initial robot positions to the straight line.

1   Introduction

We envision a scenario, in which large swarms of small and cheap mobile robots cooperate in order to perform global tasks like the exploration of an unknown environment, or the support of evacuations in hazardous environments. A fundamental kind of tasks of such a swarm is to build geometric formations out of an arbitrary configuration of initial positions. It is especially interesting to figure out which sensor and actor capabilities are needed to do so. Naturally, the goal is to require as few capabilities as possible in order to be able to use robots which are as cheap as possible. Current research focuses on basic tasks such as building lines [1–5] or circles [6, 7], or simply gathering in a point [8–13].

In this talk, we present an approach to such formation problems that presents algorithms on a sufficiently abstract level, so that correctness and efficiency proofs are possible. For this, we consider very simple models of robots and their

T. Erlebach et al. (Eds.): ALGOSENSORS 2011, LNCS 7111, pp. 4–12, 2012.

environment: The environment is a plane without obstacles (for environments with obstacles see, e.g. [4, 14, 15]). The robots are considered as points in the plane (for robots with an extent see, e.g. [16, 17]). The main restriction we are focusing on is their bounded viewing range: robots can only "see" other robots within a fixed viewing radius around their current positions. In the sequel, this viewing radius is normalized to one. They have no compass, but can compute the exact relative positions of their neighbors within their viewing range, i.e. the distances and the angles between the rays to these neighbors (for inaccurate measurements see [18, 19]). Thus a robot has to base its decision where to move next solely on the relative positions of its neighbors within its current viewing range. A strategy consists of such so-called *local rules*. In this talk, we will distinguish among several execution modes, namely on discrete-synchronous, asynchronous, and continuous strategies.

A *discrete-synchronous strategy* consists of synchronous rounds. In each round, each robot senses the relative positions of its neighbors and computes a target position as a function of these relative positions. Then it moves to this target position. This type of strategies is often referred to as Look-Compute-Move (LCM) strategies. We further assume that the initial unit disk graph defined by the robot's position and their viewing ranges (the start configuration) is connected. All our strategies will always maintain the connectivity of their configurations. For a given strategy and a connected start configuration with n robots, we are interested in the *correctness* of the strategy, the *number of rounds* needed, and the *maximum distance traveled* by the robots. The number of rounds and especially the maximum distance traveled represent the major sources for energy consumption of such strategies.

In an *asynchronous strategy*, the robots are activated one at a time. When a robot is active, it performs a complete LCM cycle, before it is deactivated again and the next robot is activated. The order of activation can be determined by an adversary or alternatively by a randomized process. In order to measure progress and runtime of our stratgies, we use the following well-established notion of a round: a round ends as soon as every robot was active at least once. We also need a connected start configuration, and as above we are interested in the *correctness* of the strategy, the *number of rounds* needed, and the *maximum distance traveled* by the robots.

In a *continuous strategy*, the robots continuously sense their neighborhood and directly adjust their direction and speed. We only demand a speed limit which we normalize to one, the viewing radius. We abstract from several physical limitations of real robots; the most severe one is our assumption that there is no delay between sensing the neighborhood and reacting to the gathered information: The robots can adjust their direction and speed *at the same time* as they observe their neighborhood. As above we demand a connected start configuration; our strategies will maintain this connectivity. Besides correctness, we are interested in the *maximum distance traveled* by the robots.

The formation problems considered in this talk are the *gathering problem* and the *robot chain problem*.

The gathering problem is to let the n mobile robots $r_1, \ldots, r_n$ gather in one point. This point does not have to be prescribed.

The robot chain problem is defined as follows: In addition to n mobile robots $r_1, \ldots, r_n$, a base camp r_0 and an explorer r_{n+1} are given, which are both stationary. We assume that, in the beginning, r_{i-1} and r_{i+1} are in the viewing range of r_i for $i = 1, \ldots, n$. Moreover, the decisions of r_i are only based on the relative positions of its direct neighbors r_{i-1} and r_{i+1}. Thus, the robots form a maybe winding chain connecting the base camp with the explorer. The goal is to let all robots move towards the straight line connecting the base camp and the explorer, the so-called *target line*.

The next chapters survey the state of the art for the two above-mentioned formation problems.

2   The Gathering Problem

A local, self-organizing strategy for gathering is defined by a *local rule* that is executed by each robot. In the discrete setting, this local rule receives as an input the relative positions of its neighbors within its viewing range. Based on this local information, it computes a target position, and then moves to this position.

A very simple and intuitive local rule for the gathering problem is called *Go-To-The-Center*: the robots take the center of the smallest enclosing circle (SEC) around the robots in their viewing range as their target position. Unfortunately, this simple algorithm used in a synchronous setting does not necessarily keep the configuration connected. An example is shown in Fig. 1: The two robots in the middle will move to two points which are in distance more than one from each other, and so the configuration becomes disconnected.

We will therefore examine variants and extensions of *Go-To-The-Center*.

Asynchronous Go-To-The-Center. In the asynchronous setting, only one robot is active in a time step. (In fact it suffices to make sure that no neighboring robots are active concurrently.) In this case, it is shown in [8] that the robots gather in one point in finite time, but no time bound is proven.

The first local gathering algorithm with a proven time bound is

Asynchronous Extended Go-To-The-Center. This strategy, introduced in [9], is also executed asynchronously. Moreover, robots need the ability to assign a target position to their neighbors, and therefore the robots are not as simple as in [10]. The idea is that when a robot is active, it tries to reduce the size of the convex hull of the robots by moving itself and its neighbors far inside the convex hull of its local neighborhood. A detailed description of this more complicated strategy can be found in [9]. There it is also shown that the robots gather in expected $O(n^2)$ asynchronous rounds, if the order of activation is random.

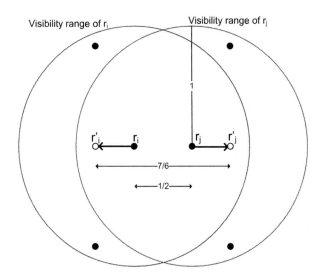

Fig. 1. A configuration which becomes disconnected when using the synchronous Go-To-The-Center algorithm

In order to modify the Go-To-The-Center rule so that it maintains connectivity of the underlying unit disk graph, a self evident idea is to let a robot only walk part of the distance towards its SEC. This yields the algorithm

Synchronous Extended Go-To-The-Center. In [10], the movement of each robot towards the center of the SEC is restricted in such a way that a robot stays within the circles with radius $1/2$ around the middle between itself and each of its neighbors (see Figure 2). The authors show that this rule maintains connectivity of the configuration and that the robots gather in finite time. In [20], a time bound of $\Theta(H^2 + n)$ for the number of synchronous rounds is shown. Here H denotes the diameter of the convex hull of the start configuration. As H is at most n, this yields a a worst case $\Theta(n^2)$ bound.

Ideas of the Analyses. Proving that connectivity is maintained is done using simple geometric arguments. In case of Synchronous extended Go-To-The-Center, this argument is illustrated in in Figure 2. Since two neighbors stay inside the same circle with radius $1/2$, they are within distance at most one of each other also in the next round, and therefore they remain neighbors.

The lower bound for Synchronous extended Go-To-The-Center uses a start configuration with n robots placed on a circle, so that neighbors have distance $\approx$ one.

The correctness proofs and time bounds for the three variants of Go-To-The-Center use a similar basic idea: Two measures for progress of a round are identified. (i): Two robots "fuse", i.e. they move to the same position. Our algorithms make sure that fused robots will never split again. Thus, there are at most n rounds

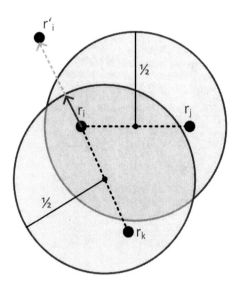

Fig. 2. The method to maintain connectivity with Synchronous extended Go-To-The-Center. r_i moves towards r'_i, the center of the SEC around its neighbors, but must stay inside the indicated circles.

with a fusion. (ii): The diameter (in case of Synchronous extended Go-To-The-Center) or the area of the convex hull (in case of Asynchronous extended Go-To-The-Center) of the robots is decreased. For correctness, it suffices to show that this diameter or area converges to zero. This implies that they even reach zero (i.e. gather in finite time), because our algorithms make sure that one round (plus maybe some of the fusion rounds in case of area) suffices to gather the robots, as soon as the diameter or the area of the convex hull is smaller than one.

In order to bound the number of rounds we need a lower bound for the reduction of the diameter or area. Geometric arguments are used to show that the for Asynchronous extended Go-To-The-Center, the area is in expectation reduced by a constant in each round without fusion, if the order of activation is at random. Since the area can be at most $O(n^2)$ in the beginning, this yields an expected runtime of $O(n^2)$. For the Synchronous extended Go-To-The-Center, the diameter is reduced by $\Omega(1/h)$ in a round that contains no fusion and starts with a configuration with diameter h. Thus, the algorithm gathers the robots in $\Theta(H^2 + n)$ rounds, when the start configuration has diameter H. Note that H is upper bounded by n, since the start configuration is connected. This yields the bound $\Theta(n^2)$. Further note that even in an optimal global algorithm some robots have to walk a distance of $\Theta(H)$. As, in the local algorithms mentioned above, the robots move only a constant distance per round, they travel at most a distance $O(H^2 + n)$. Thus, for sufficiently large H, the "price of locality" consists of at most squaring the distance traveled.

3   The Robot Chain Problem

A local, self-organizing strategy for the Robot Chain Problem is based on even less information about the overall configuration: the local rule gets as an input the relative positions only of its two direct neighbours in the chain. Based on this local information, it computes a target position, and then moves to this point. In this setting, the Go-To-The-Center strategy lets a robot move to the middle position between its neighbors. It is therefore called

Go-To-The-Middle. Unlike Go-To-The-Center, Go-To-The-Middle keeps the chain connected even in the synchronous setting [2]. On the other hand side, the robots can in general not reach the target line, but can only come arbitrarily close. In [2] an upper bound of $O(n^2 \log n/\epsilon)$ is shown for the number of synchronous rounds needed until all robots are in distance at most ϵ from the target line. The matching lower bound has only been found recently [5].

The Go-To-The-Middle strategy is an example for so-called

Linear Strategies. A synchronous round of such strategies can be expressed by a linear transformation of the spatial vectors connecting neighboring robots. This yields surprising correlations between several strategy properties and characteristics of these transformations. E.g., strategies that maintain connectivity of the chain and converge towards the target line correspond to transformations given by doubly stochastic, irreducible, and aperiodic matrices, see [5]. Based on these results, almost tight bounds on the strategies' convergence speed can be shown, by applying and extending results about the mixing time of Markov chains. Eventually, this framework enables us to define strategies that assume a weaker notion of locality: each relay bases its decision where to move only on the positions of its k next left and right neighbors. In [5], a convergence speed of $\Theta\left(\frac{n^2}{k^2} \log n\right)$ for these strategies is shown, establishing a trade-off between convergence time and locality.

The only known strategy which needs only $O(n)$ rounds (which is optimal) is the

Hopper Strategy. This asynchronous strategy, presented in [3], relies on a specific activation order where the robots are activated sequentially starting at the explorer. It is very fast in that it reduces the length of the chain to at most three times the distance between the base camp and the explorer in linear time. The strategy is more complicated, a detailed description can be found in [3].

The worst case distance traveled by the Go-To-The-Middle strategy is $\Theta(n^2)$, as shown in [21]. Therefore the question arises whether it is possible to reduce this bound. A positive answer to this question is given by the

δ-bounded Go-To-The-Middle Strategy. This strategy is introduced in [21]. In this modification of the Go-To-The-Middle strategy, the step size of the robots is reduced to δ, for $0 < \delta \leq 1$. A robot reaches its target position only if it is in distance at most δ from its current position. Otherwise, it moves towards its target position for a distance δ. Whereas the number of rounds only increases to $O(n^2 \log n/\epsilon + n/\delta)$ and $\Omega(n^2 + n/\delta)$, the distance traveled decreases to $\Theta(\delta n^2 + n)$. Thus, choosing $\delta \in \Theta(1/n)$, $O(n^2 \log n/\epsilon)$ and $\Omega(n^2)$ rounds are required in the worst case, and the maximum traveled distance is reduced to $\Theta(n)$.

Assuming δ tending to zero yields continuous versions of the Go-To-The-Middle strategy. The above results include a $O(n)$ bound for the maximum distance traveled. An even stronger result for continuous strategies yields the

Move-On-Bisector Strategy. This continuous strategy, introduced in [1], lets a robot move in direction of the bisector of the angle defined by the rays to its two neighbors. As soon as a robot reaches the straight line between its neighbors, it stays on this line. It is shown in [1] that the robots travel a maximum distance of $O(min\{n, (OPT + d) \log n\})$, where d denotes the distance between the base camp and the explorer. This strategy is $O(log(n))$-competitive compared to an optimal global algorithm, if the distance between the base camp and the explorer is not too large.

4 Outlook

We mention a few open problems closely related to the results shown above. Regarding the gathering problem, there exists no algorithm with tight upper and lower bounds for the traveled distance. Note that, since the robots only travel a constant distance in each round, the number of rounds also constitutes an upper bound for the traveled distance. But tighter upper bounds or (matching) lower bounds are unknown. Equally, the gathering problem has not been studied in a δ-bounded or continuous variant. A possibility would be to adapt the Move-On-Bisector Strategy to the gathering problem, by letting the a robot move in direction of the bisector of the angle of the robot's local convex hull. It should then be possible to adapt some of the proof ideas of Move-On-Bisector.

Some of the algorithms state a "price of locality", which compares the costs of the local algorithm with those of an optimal global one. But the bounds which are known so far are not tight. For Move-On-Bisector, the price of locality for the traveled distance is $O(\log n)$ for small d, but it is unknown whether it is even better. Simulations suggest that the price of locality is constant.

Furthermore, general lower bounds for local algorithms would be of interest. For example, assuming very simple robots, is it possible to show that gathering with bounded viewing range is not possible in linear time?

References

1. Degener, B., Kempkes, B., Kling, P., Meyer auf der Heide, F.: A Continuous, Local Strategy for Constructing a Short Chain of Mobile Robots. In: Patt-Shamir, B., Ekim, T. (eds.) SIROCCO 2010. LNCS, vol. 6058, pp. 168–182. Springer, Heidelberg (2010)

2. Dynia, M., Kutylowski, J., Lorek, P., Meyer auf der Heide, F.: Maintaining Communication Between an Explorer and a Base Station. In: IFIP 19th World Computer Congress, TC10: 1st IFIP International Conference on Biologically Inspired Computing (BICC 2006), pp. 137–146 (2006)
3. Kutylowski, J., Meyer auf der Heide, F.: Optimal strategies for maintaining a chain of relays between an explorer and a base camp. Theoretical Computer Science 410(36), 3391–3405 (2009)
4. Dynia, M., Kutylowski, J., Meyer auf der Heide, F., Schrieb, J.: Local Strategies for Maintaining a Chain of Relay Stations between an Explorer and a Base Station. In: SPAA 2007: Proceedings of the 19th Annual ACM Symposium on Parallel Algorithms and Architectures, pp. 260–269. ACM Press, New York (2007)
5. Kling, P., Meyer auf der Heide, F.: Convergence of Local Communication Chain Strategies via Linear Transformations. In: SPAA 2011: Proceedings of the 23rd ACM Symposium on Parallelism in Algorithms and Architectures, pp. 159–166 (2011)
6. Défago, X., Konagaya, A.: Circle formation for oblivious anonymous mobile robots with no common sense of orientation. In: Proceedings of the 2002 Workshop on Principles of Mobile Computing, POMC 2002, pp. 97–104 (2002)
7. Chatzigiannakis, I., Markou, M., Nikoletseas, S.: Distributed Circle Formation for Anonymous Oblivious Robots. In: Ribeiro, C.C., Martins, S.L. (eds.) WEA 2004. LNCS, vol. 3059, pp. 159–174. Springer, Heidelberg (2004)
8. Meyer auf der Heide, F., Schneider, B.: Local Strategies for connecting stations by small robotic networks. In: IFIP 20th World Computer Congress, TC10: 2nd IFIP International Conference on Biologically Inspired Computing (BICC 2008), pp. 95–104 (2008)
9. Degener, B., Kempkes, B., Meyer auf der Heide, F.: A local O(n^2) gathering algorithm. In: SPAA 2010: Proceedings of the 22nd ACM Symposium on Parallelism in Algorithms and Architectures, pp. 217–223 (2010)
10. Ando, H., Suzuki, Y., Yamashita, M.: Formation and agreement problems for synchronous mobile robots with limited visibility. In: Proceedings of the 1995 IEEE International Symposium on Intelligent Control, ISIC 1995, pp. 453–460 (August 1995)
11. Flocchini, P., Prencipe, G., Santoro, N., Widmayer, P.: Gathering of asynchronous robots with limited visibility. Theoretical Computer Science 337(1-3), 147–168 (2005)
12. Ando, H., Oasa, Y., Suzuki, I., Yamashita, M.: Distributed memoryless point convergence algorithm for mobile robots with limited visibility. IEEE Transactions on Robotics and Automation 15(5), 818–828 (1999)
13. Katreniak, B.: Convergence with Limited Visibility by Asynchronous Mobile Robots. In: Kosowski, A., Yamashita, M. (eds.) SIROCCO 2011. LNCS, vol. 6796, pp. 125–137. Springer, Heidelberg (2011)
14. Desai, J.P., Ostrowski, J.P., Kumar, V.: Controlling Formations of Multiple Mobile Robots. In: Proceedings of the IEEE International Conference on Robotics and Automation (ICRA 1998), vol. 4, pp. 2864–2869 (1998)
15. Fahimi, F., Nataraj, C., Ashrafiuon, H.: Real-time obstacle avoidance for multiple mobile robots. Robotica 27(2), 189–198 (2009)
16. Czyzowicz, J., Gasieniec, L., Pelc, A.: Gathering few fat mobile robots in the plane. Theoretical Computer Science 410(6-7), 481–499 (2009)

17. Cord-Landwehr, A., Degener, B., Fischer, M., Hüllmann, M., Kempkes, B., Klaas, A., Kling, P., Kurras, S., Märtens, M., Meyer auf der Heide, F., Raupach, C., Swierkot, K., Warner, D., Weddemann, C., Wonisch, D.: Collisionless Gathering of Robots with an Extent. In: Černá, I., Gyimóthy, T., Hromkovič, J., Jefferey, K., Královič, R., Vukolić, M., Wolf, S. (eds.) SOFSEM 2011. LNCS, vol. 6543, pp. 178–189. Springer, Heidelberg (2011)
18. Oasa, Y., Suzuki, I., Yamashita, M.: A robust distributed convergence algorithm for autonomous mobile robots. In: IEEE International Conference on Systems, Man, and Cybernetics (SMC 1997), vol. 1, pp. 287–292 (1997)
19. Cord-Landwehr, A., Degener, B., Fischer, M., Hüllmann, M., Kempkes, B., Klaas, A., Kling, P., Kurras, S., Märtens, M., Meyer auf der Heide, F., Raupach, C., Swierkot, K., Warner, D., Weddemann, C., Wonisch, D.: A New Approach for Analyzing Convergence Algorithms for Mobile Robots. In: Aceto, L., Henzinger, M., Sgall, J. (eds.) ICALP 2011, Part II. LNCS, vol. 6756, pp. 650–661. Springer, Heidelberg (2011)
20. Degener, B., Kempkes, B., Langner, T.: Meyer auf der Heide, F., Pietrzyk, P., Wattenhofer, R.: A tight runtime bound for synchronous gathering of autonomous robots with limited visibility. In: SPAA 2011: Proceedings of the 23rd Annual ACM Symposium on Parallel Algorithms and Architectures, pp. 139–147 (2011)
21. Brandes, P., Degener, B., Kempkes, B., Meyer auf der Heide, F.: Energy-Efficient Strategies for Building Short Chains of Mobile Robots Locally. In: Kosowski, A., Yamashita, M. (eds.) SIROCCO 2011. LNCS, vol. 6796, pp. 138–149. Springer, Heidelberg (2011)

Local Approximation Algorithms
for the Uncapacitated Metric Facility Location
Problem in Power-Aware Sensor Networks*

Sebastian Abshoff**, Andreas Cord-Landwehr, Bastian Degener**,
Barbara Kempkes, and Peter Pietrzyk

Heinz Nixdorf Institute & Computer Science Department,
University of Paderborn, 33095 Paderborn, Germany
{abshoff,cola,degener,kempkes,pietrzyk}@uni-paderborn.de

Abstract. We present two distributed, constant factor approximation algorithms for the metric facility location problem. Both algorithms have been designed with a strong emphasis on applicability in the area of wireless sensor networks: in order to execute them, each sensor node only requires limited local knowledge and simple computations. Also, the algorithms can cope with measurement errors and take into account that communication costs between sensor nodes do not necessarily increase linearly with the distance, but can be represented by a polynomial. Since it cannot always be expected that sensor nodes execute algorithms in a synchronized way, our algorithms are executed in an asynchronous model (but they are still able to break symmetry that might occur when two neighboring nodes act at exactly the same time). Furthermore, they can deal with dynamic scenarios: if a node moves, the solution is updated and the update affects only nodes in the local neighborhood. Finally, the algorithms are robust in the sense that incorrect behavior of some nodes during some round will, in the end, still result in a good approximation. The first algorithm runs in expected $\mathcal{O}(\log_{1+\epsilon} n)$ communication rounds and yields a $\mu^4(1 + 4\mu^2(1 + \epsilon)^{1/p})^p$ approximation, while the second has a running time of expected $\mathcal{O}(\log^2_{1+\epsilon} n)$ communication rounds and an approximation factor of $\mu^4(1 + 2(1 + \epsilon)^{1/p})^p$. Here, $\epsilon > 0$ is an arbitrarily small constant, p the exponent of the polynomial representing the communication costs, and μ the relative measurement error.

1 Introduction

Facility location is one of the most studied optimization problems in operations research and can be found as an important building block in a large variety of applications. A classical motivation is placing facilities (e.g., warehouses) in such a way that their combined costs of customer satisfaction and warehouse

---

* This work was partially supported by the Deutsche Forschungsgemeinschaft (DFG) within the Collaborative Research Centre "On-The-Fly Computing" (SFB 901).
** Fellow of the International Graduate School "Dynamic Intelligent Systems".

T. Erlebach et al. (Eds.): ALGOSENSORS 2011, LNCS 7111, pp. 13–27, 2012.
© Springer-Verlag Berlin Heidelberg 2012

construction are minimized. There are also plenty of applications in distributed scenarios. For instance, when dealing with wireless sensor networks it is often the case that a subset of nodes has to be chosen to provide some costly service. This can be the maintenance of a distributed database, the gathering of measurement data, the control of the remaining nodes or energy intensive computations. Making these services available incurs high costs at the *facility* nodes, while all remaining nodes act as *clients*. These clients use the services of the nearest facility node, and are charged a cost proportional to the corresponding distance. The objective is to find a set of nodes to assume the facility role such that the costs incurred by the clients and by setting up the facilities are as low as possible.

Problem Definition. We are given a complete, undirected, weighted graph $G = (V, E)$ as input. Each edge $\{i, j\}$ in G is weighted with a nonnegative value $c(i, j) \in \mathbb{R}_{\geq 0}$ that represents the distance between (or the costs of connecting) node i with node j. These weights satisfy the triangle inequality (i.e., $\forall\, i, j, k$ we have $c(i, j) \leq c(i, k) + c(k, j)$), are symmetric and $c(i, i) = 0$. Also, there are two values $d_i, f_i \in \mathbb{R}_{\geq 0}$ associated with each node i. The objective is to assign one of two roles to each node. A node must either become a *facility* or a *client*. We say that a node *opens* (resp. *closes*) if it changes its role to facility (resp. client). The value f_i represents the costs for opening node i and d_i represents the demand of a node with the client role. The assignment (partition of V into the sets F and C) has to be chosen in such a way that the objective function $\sum_{i \in F} f_i + \sum_{j \in C} d_j \cdot c(j, F)^p$ is minimized. Here, F (resp. C) represents the set of nodes with the facility (resp. client) role (thus, we have $C = V \setminus F$). The value $c(j, F) = \min_{i \in F}\{c(j, i)\}$ describes the distance between client j and its nearest facility i, while $p > 0$ is the exponent representing the communication costs. Since an arbitrary number of clients can use a single facility, we deal with the *uncapacitated* facility location problem.

The model used for the execution of our algorithm is based on the $\mathcal{CONGEST}$ model, which was introduced by Peleg (see [20]) and is commonly used to model the execution of distributed algorithms on graphs. Here, algorithms are executed in synchronous send-receive-compute cycles. In one cycle, each node sends a message to each of its neighbors in the graph. Note that the messages sent to each neighbor by a single node are not required to contain the same information. Once all nodes have sent their messages, they receive a single message from each of their neighbors. After all the messages have been received, every node is allowed to spend an arbitrary amount of time for computation (i.e., computation is for free and we are only interested in the number of communication rounds). The end of the computation by all nodes marks the start of a new send-receive-compute cycle.

The message size in the $\mathcal{CONGEST}$ model is bounded. We limit the size of the messages used in our algorithms to $\mathcal{O}(\log(n))$ bits, where $n = |V|$. The same limitations are also used in [9, 16, 19]. This bound is reasonable, because it allows the nodes to send their IDs in single messages. Due to this constraint, we restrict the values f_i, d_i, and $c(i, j)$ to be at most polynomial in n such that they can be represented with $\mathcal{O}(\log(n))$ bits (i.e., to be able to send them in a single message).

We generalize the $\mathcal{CONGEST}$ model as follows. First, we limit the communication range of the nodes by only allowing the nodes i and j to communicate with each other if the weight $c(i, j)$ of the edge $\{i, j\}$ is smaller than $\mathcal{O}(r_{max})$ where $r_{max} := \max_{i \in V}\{f_i/d_i\}$. One can assume that, with regard to sensor nodes, r_{max} is independent of the number of nodes, and thus nodes only need to be able to communicate within a constant distance when executing our algorithm. Second, again to better reflect the abilities and limitations of sensor nodes, we allow the nodes to execute the algorithm in asynchronous rounds. In such a round every node can be active multiple times. Nodes are not required to (but still can) act at the same time. A round is completed as soon as all nodes have been active at least once (note, that if all nodes would be required to act at the same time, a round in our model would be equal to a round in the standard $\mathcal{CONGEST}$ model). We abstract from message transmission delays and computation time. Here, a node that becomes active at time t receives all messages that have been sent before t (but not the message sent exactly at time t). Furthermore, all computation is done instantly and messages are sent immediately.

In order to represent errors that might occur when nodes measure distances between each other, we introduce relative measurement errors bounded by the parameter μ with $1 \leq \mu$. In other words, a node i's measurement may yield a distorted distance $\hat{c}(i, j)$ to node j instead of the exact distance $c(i, j)$ where $1/\mu \cdot c(i, j)^p \leq \hat{c}(i, j)^p = \hat{c}(j, i)^p \leq \mu \cdot c(i, j)^p$.

Based on the distance $\hat{c}(i, j)$ between i and neighboring nodes j, their demands d_j and its own opening costs f_i, each node i computes a value to which we will refer to as the *radius* of i. The exact value of a radius will be denoted as ρ_i, while r_i will denote a specific approximation done by a node including measurement errors. Finally, as a simplification for our decision rules, we introduce $\hat{r}_i := \mu^{2/p} \cdot r_i^{1/p}$ for all $i \in V$.

Our Contribution. We present two similar approximation algorithms for the facility location problem. Both algorithms are based on the approach by Mettu and Plaxton presented in [15]. The first algorithm runs in expected $\mathcal{O}(\log_{1+\epsilon} n)$ rounds and yields a $\mu^4(1 + 4\mu^2(1 + \epsilon)^{1/p})^p$ approximation, while the second has an expected running time of $\mathcal{O}(\log_{1+\epsilon}^2 n)$ rounds and an approximation factor of $\mu^4(1 + 2(1 + \epsilon)^{1/p})^p$, where $\epsilon > 0$ is an arbitrarily small constant.

These two algorithms are particularly suitable for sensor networks. They are fast (expected running time is polylogarithmic with high probability) and very simple to implement (once the radius value mentioned above is computed, the nodes only need to perform a relatively easy operation to ensure a specific property is satisfied). Since expecting the nodes to act in a synchronized manner might not always be appropriate, the model used allows for an asynchronous execution. To represent the fact that distances between nodes can not always be measured accurately, the parameter μ is introduced. It relates the resulting approximation factor to the relative measurement errors. Robustness is also added to the algorithms; if during the algorithms' execution some nodes do not execute the algorithms correctly for some rounds, the solution computed will (at the price of an increased number of rounds) still have the desired approximation factor (i.e., no restart of the algorithm is required). The algorithms can also deal with changes that might occur when nodes change their positions or are removed/added to the network. We show that such a change only forces our algorithms to update the role of nodes close by (i.e., nodes far away from this change are not affected).

Even though our algorithms were developed with sensor networks in mind (i.e., problem instances where the given metric is Euclidean), all results are valid for general metrics.

Related Work. During the last two decades, the uncapacitated metric facility location problem was of great interest, and a lot of progress has been made concerning upper bounds for the running time and approximation factor of sequential algorithms (see [5, 6, 11, 12, 14]).

Under the assumption that $\mathcal{NP} \not\subseteq \mathcal{DTIME}(n^{\log(\log(n))})$, Guha et al. showed in [10] that no polynomial time algorithm for the facility location problem with an approximation factor better than 1.463 exists.

The following results concerning the facility location problem can be found for the distributed scenario: In [19], Pandit et al. present an algorithm yielding a 7-approximation (which can be improved to $(3+\epsilon)$ by changing the incrementation factor used in their algorithm from 2 to $(1 + \epsilon)$ and bounding the difference between the highest and the lowest facility cost by a polynomial in n, where n is the number of nodes) and a running time of $\mathcal{O}(\log(n))$. Their algorithm is a parallel version of the primal-dual algorithm by Jain et al. [12]. A similar result to [19] was presented by Blelloch et al. in [3]. Instead of the $\mathcal{CONGEST}$, they use a PRAM model and achieve a $(3.722 + \epsilon)$ approximation with running time of $\mathcal{O}(\log^2_{1+\epsilon}(n))$ rounds by parallelizing the greedy algorithm by Jain et al. [11]. Building upon this they developed a parallel algorithm that yields a 1.861 approximation in $\mathcal{O}(\log^4_{1+\epsilon}(n))$ rounds in [4]. Although their algorithm has a better approximation factor than our algorithms, it has a higher running time than both of them. Also, the way our algorithms work is, in our opinion, more fitting for sensor nodes due to their simplicity and robustness when dealing with errors. In [18], Pandit et al. present a $\log^*(n)$ rounds algorithm that, contrary to ours, requires a *Unit Disc Graph* and the graph's geometrical representation for its execution.

The approach by Mettu and Plaxton [15], on which our algorithms are based on, has been successful in a lot of other settings as well: in the kinetic setting [7], in game theoretic settings [17], for algorithms working in sublinear time [2], for the uniform facility location problem [9] (i.e., opening each facility incurs the same costs), and when confronted with perpetual changes to the problem instance [8]. Regarding [8], which is a preceding paper of ours, we improve the approximation factor and introduce a more realistic model of computation.

2   Preliminaries

This section describes two building blocks that are used by our algorithms defined in Section 3. In the first part the concept of *invariants* is introduced. These are rules that are used to guarantee and to analyze the algorithms' approximation factors. The second part deals with the distributed computation of a maximal independent set, which is required to execute both algorithms.

The Invariant and the Radius. Here, we describe the basic intuition for our algorithms. Assuming that all neighbors of node i are clients, the radius value of i represents how advantageous it is to open i (a node's quality increases with a decreasing radius value). With the help of the invariant defined below, the algorithms try to find a balance between opening and closing nodes (preferring nodes with small radii to be opened).

Whenever node i becomes active during the algorithms' execution, it is responsible to assign a role (facility or client) to itself. This role might change in subsequent rounds. The invariant is a rule that describe how this role assignment works: in the case that i is a facility, it checks whether there are facilities that are more advantageous (i.e., have a smaller radius) than itself in its neighborhood. If this is true, then i is superfluous and becomes a client, otherwise it remains a facility. Now, in the case that i is a client, it checks whether there are facilities close by that have a smaller radius than its own radius. If this is the case, i remains a client (in the final solution i can be connected to one of those facilities). Otherwise, if there are no facilities i can use, it becomes a facility itself. Applying these rules will result in nodes changing their state over and over again. In Section 3 we show that at some point in time the invariant will hold for all nodes and thus no node will be required to change its role again. This section is dedicated to show that, once this point is reached, the solution induced by the nodes' roles is a solution with the claimed approximation factor.

Given $r \in \mathbb{R}$ and a node i we define the set $B(i, r)$ to contain all nodes j such that $c(i, j) \le r$. The radius ρ_i of a node i is the unique number satisfying

$$\sum_{j \in B(i, \rho_i^{1/p})} d_j \cdot (\rho_i - c(i, j)^p) = f_i \,,$$

while the distorted radius $\hat{\rho}_i$, which takes measurement errors into account, satisfies

$$\sum_{j \in B(i, \hat{\rho}_i^{1/p})} d_j \cdot (\hat{\rho}_i - \hat{c}(i, j)^p) = f_i \,.$$

Note that to define $B(i, \hat{\rho}_i^{1/p})$ the values $\hat{c}(i, j)$ are used. The value r_i is defined to be $\hat{\rho}_i$ rounded to the next power of $(1 + \epsilon)$ (where $\epsilon > 0$). This implies $\frac{1}{\mu(1+\epsilon)} \cdot r_i \le \rho_i \le \mu \cdot r_i$. In order to describe our algorithms we will only use $\hat{r}_i = \mu^{2/p} \cdot r_i^{1/p}$, while r_i will be used for the analysis of the approximation factors.

Proposition 1. *For every problem instance with n nodes, there exists a polynomial P such that $1/P(n) < r_i < P(n)$ for all nodes i.*

Therefore, the number of distinct rounded radius values is logarithmic in n and can be sent using at most $\mathcal{O}(\log_{1+\epsilon} n)$ bits (even $\mathcal{O}(\log\log_{1+\epsilon} n)$ is possible if only the exponent is encoded). Later on, we will use this property to bound the number of rounds that our algorithms require.

Now, we can state the invariant and the theorem describing the approximation factor of a solution where the invariant at each node is satisfied.

Definition 1 (Invariant). *The invariant is said to be fulfilled if and only if the following conditions that depend on the node's role are satisfied:*

Facility Role. *If node i is a facility (i.e., $i \in F$), then no other facility j, $j \neq i$ with $r_j \leq r_i$ and $\hat{c}(i,j) \leq 2 \cdot \mu^{2/p} \cdot r_i^{1/p}(= 2 \cdot \hat{r}_i)$ exists.*
Client Role. *If node i is a client (i.e., $i \in C$), then at least one facility j with $r_j \leq r_i$ and $\hat{c}(i,j) \leq 2 \cdot \mu^{2/p} \cdot r_i^{1/p}(= 2 \cdot \hat{r}_i)$ exists.*

Since we have $C = V \setminus F$, and the property that a client is connected to its closest facility, all that is necessary to describe a solution to any given instance of the facility location problem is the set F (i.e., the set of nodes with the facility role).

Theorem 1. *Let F_{opt} be an arbitrary optimal solution and F_{inv} be a solution where, for each facility and client, the invariant is satisfied. Then, the cost of F_{inv} can be bounded as follows,*

$$\text{cost}(F_{inv}) \leq \mu^4(1 + 2(1+\epsilon)^{1/p})^p \, \text{cost}(F_{opt}) \ .$$

Proof. Analogously to [15], we introduce a *charge* value for each node i which is dependent on a solution F, i.e.,

$$\text{charge}(i, F) = c(i, F)^p + \sum_{j \in F} \max\{0, \rho_j - c(i,j)^p\} \ .$$

Note that given a solution F, the sum over all charges is equal to the costs of the solution F, namely $\sum_{i \in V} d_i \text{charge}(i, F) = \sum_{i \in F} f_i + \sum_{j \in C} d_j \cdot c(j, F)^p$.

The theorem is proven by showing that for a solution F_{inv} satisfying the invariants (in particular a solution computed by our algorithms) and for any solution F (in particular an optimal solution) it holds that

$$\text{charge}(i, F_{inv}) \leq \mu^4(1 + 2(1+\epsilon)^{1/p})^p \, \text{charge}(i, F) \ .$$

This is done with the help of the following claims (the proofs of Claim 1 to Claim 3 can be found in the appendix):

Claim 1. *Let i be a node, let F be a set of facilities, and let j be a facility. If $c(i,j) = c(i, F)$, then $\text{charge}(i, F) \geq \max\{\rho_j, c(i,j)^p\}$.*

Claim 2. *Let i be a node and let F_{inv} be a set of facilities such that all invariants are satisfied. If $j \in F_{inv}$ with $i \in B(j, \rho_j^{1/p})$, then* charge$(i, F_{inv}) \leq \rho_j$.

Claim 3. *Let i be a node and let F_{inv} be a set of facilities such that all invariants are satisfied. For any facility $j \in F_{inv}$ with $i \notin B(j, \rho_j^{1/p})$ we have* charge$(i, F_{inv}) \leq c(i, j)^p$.

Using these claims, for each node we compare the charge of solution F_{inv} to its charge of an optimal solution F_{opt}:

Claim 4. *For any node i and any set of facilities F_{inv}, where all invariants are satisfied, we have* charge$(i, F_{inv}) \leq \mu^4 (1 + 2(1 + \epsilon)^{1/p})^p \cdot$ charge(i, F_{opt}).

Proof of Claim 4: Let $j \in F_{opt}$ such that $c(i, F_{opt}) = c(i, j)$. By the invariant there exists a facility $k \in F_{inv}$ such that $\hat{c}(j, k) \leq 2\mu^{2/p} r_j^{1/p}$ and $r_k \leq r_j$. We distinguish two cases, either $i \in B(k, \rho_k^{1/p})$, or $i \notin B(k, \rho_k^{1/p})$.

In the first case, by Claim 2, we have charge$(i, F_{inv}) \leq \rho_k$. Thus, by Claim 1, charge$(i, F_{inv}) \leq \rho_k \leq \mu r_k \leq \mu r_j \leq \mu^2 (1 + \epsilon)\rho_j \leq \mu^2 (1 + \epsilon) \cdot$ charge(i, F_{opt}). In the second case, by Claim 3, we have

$$\text{charge}(i, F_{inv}) \leq c(i, k)^p \leq \left(c(i, j) + \mu^{1/p} \hat{c}(j, k) \right)^p$$
$$\leq \left(c(i, j) + 2\mu^{3/p} r_j^{1/p} \right)^p \leq \left(c(i, j) + 2\mu^{4/p} (1 + \epsilon)^{1/p} \rho_j^{1/p} \right)^p$$
$$\leq \mu^4 (1 + 2(1 + \epsilon)^{1/p})^p \cdot \text{charge}(i, F_{opt}) .$$

The last estimation follows by distinguishing whether ρ_j or $c(i, j)^p$ is the biggest element of the term. □

Note that if all invariants hold, $\mu = 1$, and $p = 1$, then the solution is a $(3 + \epsilon)$ approximation, which is an improvement to the 17-approximation of [8].

Distributed Computation of a Maximal Independent Set. Here we re-state an inclusion maximal independent set (MIS) algorithm (see [1, 13, 20]) which was originally introduced by Luby. This distributed algorithm calculates a MIS in expected $\mathcal{O}(\log n)$ communication rounds and forms a building block of our approach.

The algorithm (given by Algorithm 1) works as follows on an arbitrary graph: When node i awakes, it *marks* itself with probability of $1/(2 \deg(i))$, where $\deg(i)$ is the number of i's neighbors. The next time i awakes, it checks whether a neighbor has *joined* the MIS in the meantime and decides to stay out of the MIS if this is the case. If not, then i decides to join the MIS if there is no other marked neighbor of a higher degree. When calculating the degree, only neighbors are considered which have not yet decided. If two neighboring nodes with same degree are marked, then the node with highest ID is selected. The decision to join or to stay out of the MIS is final and each node stops executing the algorithm as soon as it has decided.

Algorithm 1. CREATEMIS(G) executed by each node i (Luby's algorithm)

---

1 **if** $\exists$ neighbor j of i **with** $j \in$ MIS **then**
2   Not-in-MIS $\leftarrow$ Not-in-MIS $\cup \{j\}$;
3   stop execution;
4 **else**
5      $G' \leftarrow$ subgraph of G induced by $\{j \in V | j \notin$ Not-in-MIS$\}$;
6   **if** state(i) = marked **then**
7   **if** $\exists\, j \in G'$ **with** state(j) = marked **and** $(\deg_{G'}(j) > \deg_{G'}(i)$ **or**
           $\deg_{G'}(j) = \deg_{G'}(i)$ **and** id(j) > id(i)) **then**
8   state(i) $\leftarrow$ unmarked;
9   **else**
10   MIS $\leftarrow$ MIS $\cup \{i\}$;
11   stop execution;
12 **if** state(i) = unmarked **then**
13   with probability $\frac{1}{2\deg_{G'}(i)}$: state(i) $\leftarrow$ marked;

Please note that if some nodes start executing the algorithm belatedly, then the MIS is still calculated in expected $\mathcal{O}(\log n)$ communication rounds after the last node has started since previous decisions can only cause a faster termination. This is important for the interleaved calculation of an MIS in Algorithm 3.

3   Approximation Algorithms

Due to Theorem 1, we know that a solution, where the invariants are satisfied for every node, yields a good approximation. Also note that if the invariant of node i is violated, i can always remedy this by changing its own role. Thus, a straightforward idea for a distributed approximation algorithm would be to allow each node to change its role if its invariant is violated (and by doing so possibly violate the invariants of other nodes). As a result, all nodes would switch back and forth between being a client or a facility until they eventually reach a role assignment where all invariants are satisfied. This is essentially the idea used in [8]. The reason why this approach worked is that the model used in [8] only allowed a single node to be active (i.e., able to change its role) at any point in time. However, this approach is no longer feasible in our (more realistic and more general) model, where nodes can execute the algorithm simultaneously. For example, imagine a problem instance with only two nodes, both have the facility role and the same radius, and they are positioned in such a way that they mutually violate each other's invariant. If both become active at the same time, they will both become clients. Now, both their invariants are violated again so they both change their role to facility and everything is repeated. This process never reaches a state where all invariants are satisfied.

Therefore, we present two algorithms that can deal with this problem and show their approximation factors, expected running time in communication rounds and how they cope with dynamic scenarios. In oder to simplify the presentation we will set $\mu = p = 1$ and refer to the $(\mu^4(1 + 4\mu^2(1 + \epsilon)^{1/p})^p)$ (resp.,

$(\mu^4(1 + 2(1 + \epsilon)^{1/p})^p))$ approximation algorithm as the $(5 + \epsilon)$ (resp., $(3 + \epsilon)$) approximation algorithm. These two algorithms are presented in the following two sections.

3.1 $(5 + \epsilon)$-Approximation in $\mathcal{O}(\log_{1+\epsilon} n)$ Rounds

As we could see above, nodes with the same radius that are close to each other can cause undesired behavior if they act at the same time. To be able to avoid this, we introduce the *radius graph* as follows:

Definition 2. *A* radius graph $G_r = (V_r, E_r)$ *for radius* r *is defined by the nodes* $V_r = \{i \in V | \hat{r}_i = r\} \subseteq V$ *and edges* $E_r = \{\{i, j\} | i, j \in V_r \wedge \hat{c}(i, j) \leq 2r\}$.

A node belongs to exactly one radius graph. We will prevent the nodes with the same radius $\hat{r}$ to influence each other by calculating a MIS on each radius graph $G_{\hat{r}}$. The algorithm proceeds in three steps:

1. Every node i calculates its radius $\hat{r}_i$ and sends it to all neighbors (nodes at a distance of at most $2 \cdot \hat{r}_{max}$). Now, each node is aware of its neighbors and their radii in the specific radius graph $G_{\hat{r}}$ it belongs to.
2. For each radius graph the nodes compute a maximal independent set (MIS) using Algorithm 1.
3. If a node is not member of a MIS, it becomes a client. Otherwise, whenever a node becomes active, it checks whether its invariant is satisfied and, if necessary, changes its role such that its invariant is satisfied again.

As mentioned before, the radius (as well as all other information required to execute the algorithm) can be sent in a single message. A pseudocode description is given by Algorithm 2.

The expected number of rounds required to compute a solution, for which the invariant is satisfied for each node, is $\mathcal{O}(\log_{1+\epsilon} n)$. Step (1) requires a constant number of rounds, while step (2) is finished after $\mathcal{O}(\log n)$ communication rounds in expectation (see Section 2). Finally, step (3) requires $\mathcal{O}(\log_{1+\epsilon} n)$ rounds. To see this, note that a node i changing its status to facility can only violate invariants of nodes that have a strictly larger radius than $\hat{r}_i$ (nodes with strictly

---

Algorithm 2. FiveApproximation executed by each node $i \in V$

---
1 $\hat{r}_i \leftarrow$ CalculateRoundedRadius(i);
2 CreateMIS$(G_{\hat{r}_i})$
3 **if** $i \in$ Not-in-MIS **then**
4   become client;
5 **else if** $i \in$ MIS **then**
6   **if** i is client **and not** Invariant **then**
7   become facility;
8   **else if** i is facility **and not** Invariant **then**
9   become client;

---

smaller radius are never affected by node i's role changes and the MIS computation guarantees that nodes with equal radius are not affected either). With
each round, the invariants of the nodes with the next higher radius become (and
remain) satisfied, starting with the nodes with the smallest radius. Since there
are $\mathcal{O}(\log_{1+\epsilon} n)$ distinct radius values, the claim follows.

Theorem 2. *When the invariant holds for all nodes that are in the MIS and
all nodes not in the MIS are clients, then the resulting set of facilities yields a
$\mu^4(1 + 4\mu^2(1 + \epsilon)^{\frac{1}{p}})^p$-approximation.*

Proof. Since only a node that is a member of the MIS can be a facility, the
invariant is satisfied for every facility. The invariant of clients that are not in
the MIS is not necessarily satisfied. Consider a client i with a violated invariant.
There must be another client j with the same radius in distance $2\hat{r}_i$ which is part
of the MIS, otherwise i itself would be part of the MIS. Since the invariant of j is
satisfied, there is a facility k with a smaller or equal radius in distance $2\hat{r}_j$ of j.
Thus, due to the triangle inequality, facility k is at a distance of at most 4 times
$\mu^2\hat{r}_i$ of i. A small modification to Claim 4 yields the desired approximation. □

3.2 $(3 + \epsilon)$-Approximation in $\mathcal{O}(\log_{1+\epsilon}^2 n)$ Rounds

This section presents an algorithm with the improved approximation factor of
$\mu^4(1 + 2(1 + \epsilon)^{1/p})^p$, but increased running time of $\mathcal{O}(\log_{1+\epsilon}^2 n)$ communication
rounds. In contrast to the algorithm before, we want to guarantee that at every
single node the invariant is satisfied.

In order to describe the algorithm, the following states are introduced: undecided, marked, MIS/facility, or no-MIS/client. We say a node has *decided* if it
is either in state MIS/facility or no-MIS/client. Also, if a node i is in the state
undecided or marked and all neighbors j of i with a smaller radius and within
distance $c(i, j) \leq 2r_i$ have decided, then we say this node is *playing*.

The state diagram in Figure 1 and Algorithm 3 illustrate the nodes' behavior.
At the beginning, each node i is in the state undecided and calculates its radius $\hat{r}_i$.
Once a node enters the state MIS/facility (resp. no-MIS/client) it never changes
its state again and has the facility (resp. client) role in the final solution. A
node that is in the marked or undecided state changes its state to no-MIS/client
if by assuming the client role its invariant is fulfilled (i.e., the change of its role
to client satisfies its invariant). A node i, that cannot satisfy its invariant by
assuming the client role, starts computing a MIS once all nodes j with $\hat{r}_j < \hat{r}_i$
within distance $2 \cdot \hat{r}_i$ of i have decided. The MIS is computed on a *conflict graph*
consisting of all playing nodes which is a subgraph of the radius graph defined
in Section 3.1.

Definition 3. *A conflict graph $C_r(t) = (V_r(t), E_r(t))$ for radius r at the begin-
ning of round t is defined by the vertices $V_r = \{i \in V | r_i = r \wedge i \text{ is playing at}
\text{beginning of round } t\} \subseteq V$ and edges $E_r = \{\{i, j\} | i, j \in V_r \wedge c(i, j) \leq 2r\}$.*

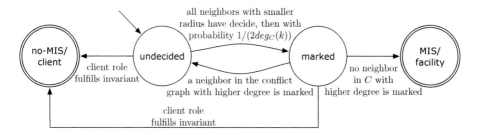

Fig. 1. A state diagram showing all possible states and their transitions in Algorithm 3

Once a node enters the MIS, it changes its state to MIS/facility. Otherwise (if one of its neighbors in the conflict graph joined the MIS and is therefore a facility), its state is changed to no-MIS/client.

Theorem 3. *After $\mathcal{O}(\log_{1+\epsilon} n \cdot \log n)$ communication rounds in expectation all nodes have decided. The resulting solution is a $\mu^4(1+2(1+\epsilon)^{1/p})^p$-approximation.*

Proof. We prove by induction over the radius values that once a node has decided to change its state to MIS/facility (i.e., it becomes a facility) or no-MIS/client (i.e., it becomes a client), its invariant will never be violated again.

All nodes with the smallest radius $\hat{r}_{small}$ start playing and compute a MIS (which takes $\mathcal{O}(\log n)$ expected rounds). If a node of this radius enters the MIS, it is a facility. No other node with this radius within distance $2r_{small}$ will ever enter the MIS, and therefore its invariant will always be fulfilled. Each node j which is not in the MIS is within distance $2\hat{r}_{small}$ of a node contained in the MIS and therefore within distance $2\hat{r}_{small}$ of a facility node. Thus, such a node's invariant is, and will remain, fulfilled.

Consider all nodes with radius $\hat{r}' > \hat{r}_{small}$. Assume that in some round the nodes with radius less than $\hat{r}'$ have decided and do not change their roles anymore. Then, we have two cases for node i with radius $\hat{r}'$. First, there is a facility j with radius less $\hat{r}'$ within distance $2\hat{r}'$ (i.e., assuming the client role satisfies the invariant of i). By the induction hypothesis facility j will never change its state again and thus the invariant of node i will not be violated in future rounds. Second, there is no facility j within distance $2\hat{r}'$. Here, using the same argumentation as for the nodes with the smallest radius (i.e., nodes with radius $\hat{r}'$ compute a MIS on their conflict graph), we can state that the invariant of i is satisfied after $\mathcal{O}(\log n)$ rounds. Since there are $\mathcal{O}(\log_{1+\epsilon} n)$ different radius values, the expected number of communication rounds is $\mathcal{O}(\log_{1+\epsilon} n \cdot \log n)$. $\square$

3.3 Dealing with Dynamics

Until now, we only considered a static scenario where the distances between nodes, facility costs and client demands do not change over time. Next, we introduce a dynamic scenario where such changes are possible. Starting with a

---

Algorithm 3. THREEAPPROXIMATION executed by each node $i \in V$

---

1 $\hat{r}_i \leftarrow$ CALCULATERADIUS(i);
2 **if** state$(i) =$ undefined **or** (state$(i) =$ client **and not** INVARIANT) **or**
   (state$(i) =$ facility **and not** INVARIANT) **then**
3   state$(i) \leftarrow$ undecided;
4 **if** INVARIANT **then**
5   state$(i) \leftarrow$ client;
6 $C \leftarrow$ conflict graph $G_{\hat{r}_i}(t)$;
7 **if** state$(i) =$ marked **then**
8   **if** $\exists\, j \in C$ **with** state$(j) =$ marked **and** $(\deg_C(j) > \deg_C(i)$ **or**
   $\deg_C(j) = \deg_C(i)$ **and** id$(j) >$ id$(i))$ **then**
9   state$(i) \leftarrow$ undecided;
10   **else**
11   state$(i) \leftarrow$ facility;
12 **if** state$(i) =$ undecided **and** $\forall\, j \in V$ **with** $\hat{r}_j < \hat{r}_i$ **and** $c(j, i) \leq 2\hat{r}_i$ **and**
   state$(j) \in \{$facility, client$\}$ **then**
13   with probability $\frac{1}{2\deg_C(i)}$: state$(i) \leftarrow$ marked;

---

problem instance and a role assignment where the invariant is satisfied for each node, we modify the instance (e.g., by changing the distance between two nodes) such that the invariant is violated at a single node (we call this "triggering an event at a node"). We want to enable our algorithm to deal with such a change and analyze the effect of this change on the roles of other nodes.

To be able to react to such changes, the algorithms have to be slightly extended. Regarding the $(5 + \epsilon)$-algorithm we have two cases to consider. First, assume the change did not invalidate the MIS on the nodes' radius graph. If the affected node is part of the MIS, the node needs just to correct its invariant (which will possibly trigger role changes of other MIS nodes). Otherwise, the node does nothing. Second, the change invalidates (by adding or removing edges in the radius graph) the MIS. Here, nodes at which the MIS property is violated change their states to unmarked (and thus start executing the $(5+\epsilon)$-algorithm). The modification of the $(3+\epsilon)$-algorithm is simpler: here, whenever the invariant of a *decided* node is violated, it just needs to change its state back to undecided.

The following lemma states that, given a solution satisfying the invariants of all nodes, both modified algorithms will compute a new solution with the desired approximation factor, and only nodes with a small distance to the node where the change occurred could have a different role in this new solution. Its proof, which is an adaptation of the proof in [8], can be found in the appendix.

Lemma 1. *A node i can only be affected by an event if it is triggered at a node which is at most in distance $4\mu^{3/p}(1 + \frac{1}{\epsilon})r_i$ from i.*

Notice that a node i can only be affected by a change occurring at node j, if $c(i, j) \in \mathcal{O}(\hat{r}_i)$. Also, $\hat{r}_i \in \mathcal{O}(f_i/d_i)$. This means that, if f_i and d_i are independent of the number of nodes (which might be reasonable in sensor networks) the area of effect of a change is independent of the number of nodes.

4 Conclusion

We converted the sequential algorithm by Mettu and Plaxton [15] to a distributed sensor nodes scenario by providing two constant factor approximation algorithms that require a polylogarithmic number of rounds. One of these algorithms retains the sequential algorithm's approximation factor up to an arbitrarily small constant ϵ. This is arbitrarily close to the best approximation factor one can achieve using this approach.

References

1. Alon, N., Babai, L., Itai, A.: A fast and simple randomized parallel algorithm for the maximal independent set problem. Journal of Algorithms 7(4), 567–583 (1986)
2. Bădoiu, M., Czumaj, A., Indyk, P., Sohler, C.: Facility Location in Sublinear Time. In: Caires, L., Italiano, G.F., Monteiro, L., Palamidessi, C., Yung, M. (eds.) ICALP 2005. LNCS, vol. 3580, pp. 866–877. Springer, Heidelberg (2005)
3. Blelloch, G.E., Tangwongsan, K.: Parallel approximation algorithms for facility-location problems. In: Proceedings of the 22nd Annual ACM Symposium on Parallelism in Algorithms and Architectures (SPAA), pp. 315–324 (2010)
4. Blelloch, G.E., Tangwongsan, K., Peng, R.: Linear-work greedy parallel approximation algorithms for set covering and variants. In: Proceedings of the 23rd Annual ACM Symposium on Parallelism in Algorithms and Architectures, SPAA (2011)
5. Byrka, J.: An Optimal Bifactor Approximation Algorithm for the Metric Uncapacitated Facility Location Problem. In: Charikar, M., Jansen, K., Reingold, O., Rolim, J.D.P. (eds.) RANDOM 2007 and APPROX 2007. LNCS, vol. 4627, pp. 29–43. Springer, Heidelberg (2007)
6. Chudak, F.A., Shmoys, D.B.: Improved approximation algorithms for a capacitated facility location problem. In: Proceedings of the 10th Annual ACM-SIAM Symposium on Discrete Algorithms (SODA), pp. 875–876 (1999)
7. Degener, B., Gehweiler, J., Lammersen, C.: Kinetic facility location. Algorithmica 57(3), 562–584 (2010)
8. Degener, B., Kempkes, B., Pietrzyk, P.: A local, distributed constant-factor approximation algorithm for the dynamic facility location problem. In: Proceedings of the 24th IEEE International Parallel & Distributed Processing Symposium (IPDPS), pp. 1–10. IEEE (2010)
9. Gehweiler, J., Lammersen, C., Sohler, C.: A distributed $\mathcal{O}(1)$-approximation algorithm for the uniform facility location problem. In: Proceedings of the 18th Annual ACM Symposium on Parallelism in Algorithms and Architectures (SPAA), pp. 237–243 (2006)
10. Guha, S., Khuller, S.: Greedy strikes back: improved facility location algorithms. Journal of Algorithms 31(1), 228–248 (1999)
11. Jain, K., Mahdian, M., Markakis, E., Saberi, A., Vazirani, V.V.: Greedy facility location algorithms analyzed using dual fitting with factor-revealing LP. Journal of the ACM 50(6), 795–824 (2003)
12. Jain, K., Vazirani, V.V.: Approximation algorithms for metric facility location and k-median problems using the primal-dual schema and lagrangian relaxation. Journal of the ACM 48(2), 274–296 (2001)

13. Luby, M.: A simple parallel algorithm for the maximal independent set problem. In: Proceedings of the Seventeenth Annual ACM Symposium on Theory of Computing, pp. 1–10 (1985)
14. Mahdian, M., Ye, Y., Zhang, J.: Improved Approximation Algorithms for Metric Facility Location Problems. In: Jansen, K., Leonardi, S., Vazirani, V.V. (eds.) APPROX 2002. LNCS, vol. 2462, pp. 229–242. Springer, Heidelberg (2002)
15. Mettu, R.R., Plaxton, C.G.: The online median problem. In: Proceedings of the 41st IEEE Annual Symposium on Foundations of Computer Science (FOCS), pp. 339–348 (2000)
16. Moscibroda, T., Wattenhofer, R.: Facility location: distributed approximation. In: Proceedings of the 24th Annual ACM Symposium on Principles of Distributed Computing (PODC), pp. 108–117 (2005)
17. Pal, M., Tardos, E.: Group strategy proof mechanisms via primal-dual algorithms. In: Proc. of the 44th Annual IEEE Symposium on Foundations of Computer Science, pp. 584–593 (2003)
18. Pandit, S., Pemmaraju, S.V.: Finding Facilities Fast. In: Garg, V., Wattenhofer, R., Kothapalli, K. (eds.) ICDCN 2009. LNCS, vol. 5408, pp. 11–24. Springer, Heidelberg (2008)
19. Pandit, S., Pemmaraju, S.V.: Return of the primal-dual: distributed metric facility location. In: Proceedings of the 28th Annual ACM Symposium on Principles of Distributed Computing (PODC), pp. 180–189 (2009)
20. Peleg, D.: Distributed computing: a locality-sensitive approach. Society for Industrial and Applied Mathematics, Philadelphia (2000)

Appendix

Proof of Claim 1:

Proof. We distinguish two cases: $i \in B(j, \rho_j^{1/p})$ and $i \notin B(j, \rho_j^{1/p})$. The first case gives $\text{charge}(i, F) \geq c(i,j)^p + \max\{0, \rho_j - c(i,j)^p\} \geq \rho_j \geq c(i,j)^p$, while the second case yields $\text{charge}(i, F) \geq c(i,j)^p \geq \rho_j$.   □

Proof of Claim 2:

Proof. First, we prove by contradiction that a node cannot be contained in the balls of two different facilities. Assume there are two facilities $j, k \in F_{inv}, j \neq k$, such that $i \in B(j, \rho_j^{1/p})$ and $i \in B(k, \rho_k^{1/p})$. Without loss of generality, assume $\rho_j^{1/p} \geq \rho_k^{1/p}$. Then, the invariant at j must be violated, since there is another facility k within distance $c(j,k) \leq c(j,i) + c(i,k)$ (by the triangle inequality) and $c(j,i) + c(i,k) \leq \rho_j^{1/p} + \rho_k^{1/p} \leq 2\rho_j^{1/p} \leq 2\mu^{1/p} \hat{r}_j^{1/p} = 2\hat{r}_j$.

Thus, $i \in B(j, \rho_j^{1/p})$ and i is in no other facility's ball. Then,

$$\text{charge}(i, F_{inv}) = c(i, F_{inv})^p + \sum_{j \in F_{inv}} \max\{0, \rho_j - c(i,j)^p\}$$

$$= c(i, F_{inv})^p + \rho_j - c(i,j)^p \leq \rho_j \,,$$

since $c(i, F_{inv})^p \leq c(i,j)^p$.   □

Proof of Claim 3:

Proof. We distinguish two cases. In the first case, let there be no facility $k \in F_{inv}$ with $i \in B(k, \rho_k^{1/p})$. It follows that for all facilities $l \in F_{inv}$: $c(i,l) \geq \rho_l^{1/p}$. Thus, $\text{charge}(i, F_{inv}) = c(i, F_{inv})^p \leq c(i,j)^p$.

In the second case, let $k \in F_{inv}$ be such that $i \in B(k, \rho_k^{1/p})$. This implies that $c(i,k) \leq \rho_k^{1/p}$. We know that $\hat{c}(j,k) > 2\mu^{2/p} \max\{r_j^{1/p}, r_k^{1/p}\}$ because of the invariants. This yields

$$c(i,j) \geq c(j,k) - c(k,i) \geq \frac{1}{\mu^{1/p}} \cdot \hat{c}(j,k) - \rho_k^{1/p} \geq \frac{1}{\mu^{1/p}} 2\mu^{2/p} r_k^{1/p} - \mu^{1/p} r_k^{1/p}$$

$$\geq \mu^{1/p} r_k^{1/p} \geq \rho_k^{1/p} \geq \text{charge}(i, F_{inv})^{1/p}.$$

$\square$

Proof of Lemma 1:

Proof. Let k be the node at which an event is triggered. Let $e_i \cdot r_i$ be the maximal range around k in which nodes with radii at most $r_i = (1+\epsilon)^i \cdot r_k$ are affected by the state change of k. First, we give an upper bound for e_0 which implies that $r_0 = (1+\epsilon)^0 \cdot r_k = r_k$. Nodes with radius $< r_0$ cannot be affected by the state change of k, as the invariant only depends on nodes with smaller or equal radii. If k changes its state from closed to opened, this cannot violate the invariant of nodes with radius r_0 because then the invariant of k would have been fulfilled (note that the distorted distances are symmetric). If k changes its state from opened to closed, then this change affects only nodes with radius r_0 within distance $\leq 2\mu^{3/p} r_k$ since they might underestimate their distance to k by a factor of $\mu^{1/p}$ when checking their invariant. Therefore, we have $e_0 = 2\mu^{3/p}$.

Now, we describe the step from e_{i-1} to e_i and claim $e_i \leq \frac{e_{i-1}}{1+\epsilon} + 4\mu^{3/p}$ for $i > 0$. By definition of e_{i-1}, nodes with radii at most $r_{i-1} = (1+\epsilon)^{i-1} \cdot r_k$ can be at a distance of at most $e_{i-1} \cdot r_k$ from k. Let m be such a node and let l be a node with radius $r_i = (1+\epsilon)^i \cdot k$ which changes its role due to a role change of m. This node l must be within distance $2\mu^{3/p} r_i$ of m. If l needs to be opened, then m must have closed. No invariant of nodes with radius r_i is affected. If l needs to be closed, then m must have opened. Another node n with the same radius r_i might have to open and n can be in distance of at $2\mu^{3/p} r_i$ of l. Again, the opening of n cannot violate the invariant of a node with the same radius. Therefore, $c(k,n) \leq e_{i-1} \cdot r_k + 2 \cdot 2\mu^{3/p} r_i \leq (\frac{e_{i-1}}{1+\epsilon} + 4\mu^{3/p}) r_i$ and thus $e_i \leq \frac{e_{i-1}}{1+\epsilon} + 4\mu^{3/p}$. Finally, the recurrence can be solved,

$$e_i \leq \frac{e_{i-1}}{1+\epsilon} + 4\mu^{3/p} = \frac{e_0}{(1+\epsilon)^j} + \sum_{j=0}^{i-1} \frac{4\mu^{3/p}}{(1+\epsilon)^j} = \frac{e_0}{(1+\epsilon)^i} + 4\mu^{3/p} \frac{1 - \frac{1}{(1+\epsilon)^i}}{1 - \frac{1}{1+\epsilon}}$$

$$= 4\mu^{3/p} \cdot \frac{1+\epsilon}{\epsilon} - \frac{4\mu^{3/p} \frac{1+\epsilon}{\epsilon} - e_0}{(1+\epsilon)^i} \leq 4\mu^{3/p} \left(1 + \frac{1}{\epsilon}\right).$$

$\square$

Maximizing Network Lifetime
on the Line with Adjustable Sensing Ranges

Amotz Bar-Noy and Ben Baumer

The Graduate Center of the City University of New York
365 Fifth Avenue, New York, NY 10016
amotz@sci.brooklyn.cuny.edu, bbaumer@gc.cuny.edu

Abstract. Given n sensors on a line, each of which is equipped with a
unit battery charge and an adjustable sensing radius, what schedule will
maximize the lifetime of a network that covers the entire line? Trivially,
any reasonable algorithm is at least a $\frac{1}{2}$-approximation, but we prove
tighter bounds for several natural algorithms. We focus on developing
a linear time algorithm that maximizes the expected lifetime under a
random uniform model of sensor distribution. We demonstrate one such
algorithm that achieves an average-case approximation ratio of almost
0.9. Most of the algorithms that we consider come from a family based
on RoundRobin coverage, in which sensors take turns covering predefined
areas until their battery runs out.

Keywords: wireless sensor networks, adjustable range, restricted strip
cover, lifetime, area coverage.

1   Introduction

We consider the following disaster-relief scenario: Suppose you have a highway,
supply line, or fence that you want to cover with a wireless sensor network (WSN)
for as long as possible. Each sensor has a fixed location along the highway and a
unit battery charge that drains in inverse proportion to its sensing radius, which
you control. Given a deployment of sensors, what schedule will maximize the
lifetime of the network? We analyze both the case where the sensors are placed
by an adversary, and the case where they are deployed uniformly at random (e.g.
- perhaps they have been dropped from an airplane).

Formally, let $U = [0, 1]$ be a line, and suppose that n sensors are deployed
on U with locations $X = \{x_1, ..., x_n\}$. For any time $t \geq 0$, we associate with
each sensor i a sensing radius $r_i(t) \in [0, 1]$ and a corresponding coverage interval
$R_i(t) = [x_i - r_i(t), x_i + r_i(t)]$, and say that U is covered at time t if for every
$x \in U$, there exists an $1 \leq i \leq n$ such that $x \in R_i(t)$. We impose the constraint
that each sensor has a unit battery charge that drains at the rate $(r_i(t))^{1/\alpha}$ for
some fixed $\alpha > 0$. Our goal is to construct a sensing schedule $S = \{r_i(t)\}_{i=1}^{n}$ that
covers U for as long as possible, and call this value the *lifetime* of the network.
That is, the lifetime T of a network is the largest time value t such that for every
point $(x, t) \in U \times [0, T]$, there exists some sensor i such that $x \in R_i(t)$.

T. Erlebach et al. (Eds.): ALGOSENSORS 2011, LNCS 7111, pp. 28–41, 2012.

*Problem 1 (*ADJUSTABLE RANGE RESTRICTED STRIP COVER*)*. Given a set of sensor locations X and a battery drainage rate α, compute a schedule $S = \{r_i(t)\}_{i=1}^n$, where $r_i(t)$ is the sensing radius of sensor i at time t, that maximizes T, subject to the constraints that for all pairs $(x, t) \in U \times [0, T]$, there exists an i such that $x \in R_i(t)$, and for all i, $\int_0^T (r_i(t))^{1/\alpha} dt \leq 1$.

In this paper, we provide both worst case (adversarial deployment) and average case (random deployment) analysis of several natural algorithms, for the particular situation in which $\alpha = 1$.

1.1 Previous Research

A closely related (and known NP-hard) problem is RESTRICTED STRIP COVER (RSC) [4], in which each sensor has a fixed sensing radius and a fixed duration indicating the length of time that it can be active. Our problem extends RSC by replacing the notion of duration with a that of a finite battery charge, and converting the sensing radius from a fixed input to a variable to be optimized. This introduces considerable complexity to the problem.

To see this, note that in RSC, each sensor can be represented in space-time by a single rectangle of fixed dimensions whose center has a fixed x-coordinate. The only variable to consider is the time (t-coordinate) at which the sensor becomes activated (e.g. - the rectangles can only be moved up and down). In our problem, the regions of space-time occupied by each sensor still have a fixed central x-coordinate and a fixed area, but the height and width may vary as a continuous function of time, so they are not even necessarily rectangles. Furthermore, in general we allow *pre-emptive scheduling*, meaning that a sensor can activate and deactivate more than once, splitting a region into multiple non-contiguous parts. In some cases, pre-emptive scheduling can increase the achievable lifetime. We show one such example in Figure 1.

Buchsbaum et al. [4] proved the NP-hardness of RSC and gave an $O(\log \log \log n)$-approximation algorithm. Recently, a constant factor approximation algorithm for RSC was discovered by Gibson and Varadarajan [7].

Much of the related work on network lifetime has focused on *duty cycling*, wherein the goal is to maximize the number of covers k, rather than explicitly maximizing the network lifetime T. The notion of decomposability of multiple coverings can be found in Pach [10]. The connection to sensor networks was made more recently, but it has brought with it increased attention and results. Pach and Tóth [11] showed that a k-fold cover of translates of a centrally-symmetric open convex polygon can be decomposed into $\Omega(\sqrt{k})$ covers. This result was improved to the optimal $\Omega(k)$ covers by Aloupis et al. [1]. Gibson and Varadarajan [7] showed the same result without the centrally-symmetric restriction.

In the plane, Berman et al. [3] gave the first provably good $O(\log n)$-approximation algorithm for the Maximum Lifetime problem with fixed sensing ranges. Wu and Yang [12] initiated the study of area coverage with adjustable sensing ranges, and Cardei et al. [5] pursued a duty cycling approach involving set covers. Dhawan et al. [6] extended the work of [3] to the adjustable range setting.

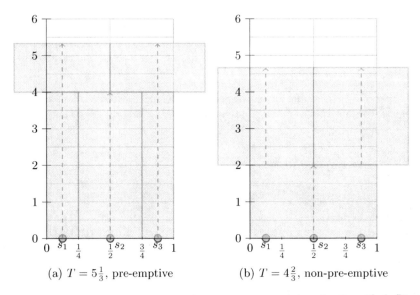

(a) $T = 5\frac{1}{3}$, pre-emptive   (b) $T = 4\frac{2}{3}$, non-pre-emptive

Fig. 1. Illustration of the advantages of pre-emptive scheduling for $X = \{\frac{1}{8}, \frac{1}{2}, \frac{7}{8}\}$. The lifetime of the network is shown on the vertical axis, while location is shown on the horizontal axis. Each sensor is indicated by a red dot, and each rectangle represents a coverage assignment. The dashed arrows indicate periods of activity. Note that the total area of space-time consumed by each sensor is exactly 2.

In the one-dimensional setting, Peleg and Lev-Tov [8] found an optimal polynomial time solution to the one-time *target coverage* problem using dynamic programming. However, this question was about coverage efficiency, and not explicitly about network lifetime. The running time of the one-dimensional target coverage algorithm was later improved to $O(n + m)$, where m is the number of target points to be covered [2]. A PTAS is known for the area coverage version of the problem (again, for coverage efficiency, not lifetime), but no NP-hardness result is known. These results may offer optimal solutions for one moment in time, but do not necessarily lead to an optimal lifetime.

1.2 Our Contribution

Our extension of RESTRICTED STRIP COVER is the first to consider the true lifetime for area coverage on the line with adjustable sensing ranges. For the special case where $\alpha = 1$, any reasonable algorithm is at least a $\frac{1}{2}$-approximation, but we prove tigher bounds for several natural algorithms. However, since a constant factor approximation is trivial, most of our efforts are focused on raising the approximation ratio in the *average case*, which in an application scenario, is likely to be of greater value. Our main result is a constructive proof that a linear time algorithm exists that achieves an approximation ratio of nearly 0.9 in the average case. We accomplish this by employing RoundRobin coverage on a hierarchical system of pre-defined coverage areas. Although we allow pre-emptive scheduling, we do not explicitly use it in our algorithms. Thus, our results are also valid for the special case in which pre-emptive scheduling is not allowed. A summary of our results is shown in Table 1.

Table 1. Summary of lifetime results for `RoundRobin` algorithms. T is a random variable describing the per sensor lifetime under uniform random deployment. AC and WC show lower bounds for the average-case and upper bounds for the worst-case approximation ratios, respectively.

Algorithm	$\mathbb{E}[T]$	$Var[T]$	AC	WC
`RoundRobin`	1.386	0.078	0.693	2/3
k-`RoundRobin`	1.386	0.078	0.693	2/3
$\log_2$-`RoundRobin`	1.738	0.022	0.869	2/3
Optimized $\log_2$-`RoundRobin`	1.791		0.896	2/3

2 Preliminaries

For any set of sensor locations X, we assume that there exists some optimal schedule $S = \{r_i(t)\}_{i=1}^n$ that will produce the longest possible lifetime T_{OPT}. As the battery charges are finite, we can bound this value.

Proposition 1. *If n sensors are deployed, then $n \leq T_{OPT} \leq 2n$.*

Proof. The lower bound is immediate since *any* reasonable algorithm achieves $T \geq n$. Consider the case where all of the sensors were located at 0; each could cover U for exactly 1 time unit.

For any time t, each sensor i covers a subinterval of U of width $2r_i(t)$. The total energy consumed is given by $\int_0^\infty r_i(t)\,dt$, which is at most 1 since the battery has unit capacity. Thus, if V_i is the region of space-time consumed by the sensor i, then $|V_i| = \int_0^\infty 2r_i(t)\,dt \leq 2$. The total area of space-time consumed then satisfies

$$\left| \bigcup_{i=1}^n V_i \right| \leq \sum_{i=1}^n |V_i| \leq 2n \,.$$

It is easy to see in this geometric setting that the goal of maximizing T is equivalent to the goal of minimizing coverage overlap (i.e. - intersections $V_i \cap V_j$), and any extraneous coverage outside of U.

In some cases, we can bound T_{OPT} away from $2n$. For any subset $Y = \{x_1, ..., x_m\} \subseteq X$, let $f(Y) = -\frac{1}{2} + \sum_{j=1}^m (-1)^{m-j} x_j$. We show (see the Appendix for a full proof) that if $f(Y) = 0$, then the sensors in Y have the proper spacing to create a *pinned disk* coverage assignment, which has no wasted coverage.

Proposition 2. *A radial assignment that gives perfect coverage over $[0, 1]$ at time t exists if and only if there is a subset $Y \subseteq X$ such that $f(Y) = 0$.*

Corollary 1. *If no subset $Y \subseteq X$ satisfies $f(Y) = 0$, then $T_{OPT}(X) < 2n$.*

Our work in this paper is focused on RoundRobin algorithms, but we show a worst-case approximation bound for Greedy, which iteratively schedules the least-wasteful assignment of radii until a sensor runs out of battery life.

Observation 1. *The approximation ratio of Greedy is at most $\frac{5}{6}$.*

Proof. Consider $X = \{\frac{1}{6} - \epsilon, \frac{1}{2}, \frac{5}{6}\}$, for some $\epsilon > 0$. Greedy chooses to activate the middle sensor by itself on U first, since that is the only perfect assigment possible. This produces a T approaching 5 as $\epsilon \to 0$, but $T_{OPT} = 6$ is achievable in the limit (see Figure 2).

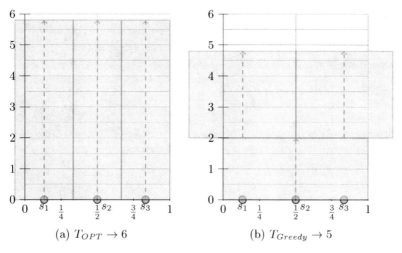

(a) $T_{OPT} \to 6$ (b) $T_{Greedy} \to 5$

Fig. 2. Proof that Greedy is at best a $\frac{5}{6}$-approximation. Both diagrams show what happens as $\epsilon \to 0$.

3   Analysis of RoundRobin Algorithms

Let $\bar{T} = T/n \in [0, 2]$ be the average network lifetime per sensor. For a group of sensors working simultaneously, it is often convenient to discuss the *normalized* lifetime $\hat{T}$, which is scaled so that $\hat{T} \in [0, 2]$.[1]

3.1   RoundRobin

In its simplest incarnation, RoundRobin simply forces each sensor to successively cover all of U for as long as possible. That is, each sensor i is assigned a radius of $r_i = \max(x_i, 1 - x_i)$, and is pushed onto a single queue. It is easy to show that this algorithm is at best a $\frac{2}{3}$-approximation of T_{OPT}.

Lemma 1. *RoundRobin is at best a $\frac{2}{3}$-approximation.*

---

[1] This distinction will be made clear in Section 3.2.

Proof. Consider $X = \{\frac{1}{4}, \frac{3}{4}\}$. The only two sensible assignments are shown in Figure 3. But while $T_{OPT} = 4$, RoundRobin achieves a lifetime of only $2\frac{2}{3}$.

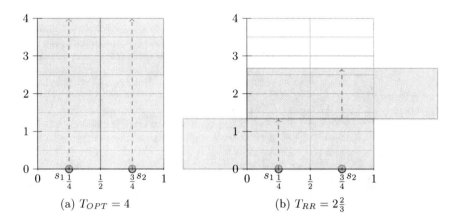

$\qquad$ (a) $T_{OPT} = 4$ $\qquad\qquad\qquad\qquad$ (b) $T_{RR} = 2\frac{2}{3}$

Fig. 3. Proof that RoundRobin is at best a $\frac{2}{3}$-approximation

A more complicated argument (presented in the Appendix) shows that RoundRobin is at least a 0.548-approximation of T_{OPT}.

Clearly, RoundRobin performs best when sensors are located close to 1/2, where the lifetime is close to 2, and poorly for sensors near 0 and 1, where the lifetime is 1. We analyze the average case by assuming that X is a uniform random variable over $[0, 1]$. Then the function $T_{0,1}(X) = \frac{1}{\max (X, 1-X)}$ yields a new r.v. giving the lifetime of an *individual sensor*. It is easy to calculate its mean

$$\mu_T \triangleq \mathbb{E}[T_{0,1}(X)] = \int_0^1 \frac{dx}{\max(x, 1-x)} = 2\int_{\frac{1}{2}}^1 \frac{dx}{x} = 2\ln x \Big|_{\frac{1}{2}}^1 = 2\ln 2, \qquad (1)$$

and variance

$$\sigma_T^2 \triangleq \mathbb{E}[T_{0,1}^2(X)] - \mu_T^2 = \int_0^1 \frac{dx}{(\max(x, 1-x))^2} - \mu_T^2 = 2 - 4\ln^2 2. \qquad (2)$$

We will develop algorithms that improve on this expected lifetime of μ_T.

Central Limit Theorem. Of course, with n sensors, we are more interested in the distribution of $\bar{T}$, as opposed to that of T. Since we know μ_T and σ_T^2, the Central Limit Theorem implies that the distribution of $\bar{T}$ approaches a normal distribution with mean μ_T and variance σ_T^2/n as $n \to \infty$. For this reason we report the variance but focus most of our attention on the expected average lifetime of each algorithm.

Theorem 1. *The approximation ratio of RoundRobin is between 0.548 and 2/3, but it achieves at least a 0.693-approximation ratio in the average case.*

3.2 k-RoundRobin

A natural extension of RoundRobin is to partition U into k equally-spaced subin-tervals, and run it independently on each of those. Somewhat surprisingly, the performance is no better in either the worst or the average case.

Let k be a fixed positive integer, and let $U_k(i) = [\frac{i-1}{k}, \frac{i}{k}]$ for $i = 1, ..., k$ de-fine a partition of U. We define k-RoundRobin to be the algorithm that runs RoundRobin independently on each subinterval $U_k(i)$; maintaining k parallel queues. However, over any subinterval $[a, b] \subseteq U$, the r.v. giving the lifetime of a sensor in $U_k(i)$ is simply a rescaling of T from the original RoundRobin.

Remark 1. For any interval $[a, b] \subseteq U$, the expected lifetime $T_{a,b}(X)$ of a sensor running RoundRobin on $[a, b]$ is $\frac{\mu_T}{b-a}$ with variance $(\frac{\sigma_T}{b-a})^2$.

With $b - a = 1/k$, the expected lifetime of each sensor in k-RoundRobin is $\mathbb{E}[T] = k\mu_T$, with a maximum lifetime of $2k$. However, in order to cover the whole line, we have to run k parallel queues, so that the expected *normalized* lifetime of each sensor is $\mathbb{E}[\hat{T}] = \mu_T$. For a set of n sensors, the total expected lifetime is $n\mu_T$, so the expected *average* network lifetime $\mathbb{E}[\bar{T}]$ is μ_T. Similar calculations show that the variance of each sensor's lifetime is $(k\sigma_T)^2$, while the normalized variance is σ_T^2 and the variance of the mean is $Var(\bar{T}) = \sigma_T^2/n$.

Load Balancing. Since we are maintaining k parallel queues that must work together to cover U, our calculations are sensitive to the requirement that the lifetime be the same in each queue.

Following [9], we can think of the observation of each sensor location as an independent Poisson trial, and use a Chernoff bound to ensure that the prob-ability of a sub-interval $U_k(i)$ getting too few sensors is $o(1)$. Let N_i be a r.v. denoting the number of sensors in $U_k(i)$. Then for any $k < \frac{n}{3 \ln n}$, we have that

$$\Pr\left[\left|N_i - \frac{n}{k}\right| \geq \sqrt{\frac{3n \ln n}{k}}\right] \leq 2 \exp\left\{-\frac{1}{3}\frac{n}{k}\frac{3k \ln n}{n}\right\} = \frac{2}{n}.$$

In our case, we need to bound the probability that *some* $U_k(i)$ has too few sensors in it, but using a union bound, the probability of this is at most $\frac{2k}{n}$, which still goes to 0 as $n \to \infty$ for a fixed k. This shows that with high probability, the deviations from the mean number of sensors in each interval are on the order of $O(\sqrt{n \ln n})$ for a fixed k.

Set $n = n_1 + n_2$, where $n_1 = k \cdot \min_{1 \leq i \leq k} N_i$. Our scheduler allows the n_1 sensors to run k-RoundRobin on perfectly balanced stacks, and then throws the n_2 leftover sensors away. Thus, the actual expected average lifetime of the algorithm is

$$\mathbb{E}[\bar{T}_{actual}] = \frac{n_1}{n} \cdot \mathbb{E}[\bar{T}] + \frac{n_2}{n} \cdot 0 \to \mathbb{E}[\bar{T}] = \mu_T, \quad \text{as } n \to \infty,$$

since $n_2 = O(\sqrt{n \ln n})$ and thus $\frac{n_2}{n} \to 0$ as $n \to \infty$.

Observation 2. *k-RoundRobin provides the same worst-case and average-case performance as RoundRobin.*

3.3 $\log_2$-RoundRobin

Nevertheless, clever applications of RoundRobin can yield efficient algorithms. While the expected lifetime of a sensor in RoundRobin is independent of the length of the interval it covers, it still performs better when it is near the center of the interval. Specifically, the expected lifetime of a sensor covering an interval $[a, b]$, that is located within a subinterval $U_{a,b}(c) = [\frac{b+a}{2} - c, \frac{b+a}{2} + c] \subseteq [a, b]$ for some $c \in [0, \frac{b-a}{2}]$, is given by

$$\mathbb{E}[T_{a,b}(X;c)] = \frac{1}{2c} \int_{\frac{b+a}{2}-c}^{\frac{b+a}{2}+c} \frac{dx}{\max(x - a, b - x)} = \frac{1}{c} \ln\left(1 + \frac{2c}{b - a}\right). \quad (3)$$

Since the maximum lifetime is $2/(b - a)$, the expected normalized lifetime is $\mathbb{E}[\hat{T}_{a,b}(X;c)] = \frac{b-a}{c} \ln\left(1 + \frac{2c}{b-a}\right)$, and the normalized variance is:

$$Var(\hat{T}_{a,b}(X;c)) = 4\left[1 - \frac{1}{1 + \frac{b-a}{2c}} - \left(\frac{b - a}{2c} \cdot \ln\left(1 + \frac{2c}{b - a}\right)\right)^2\right]. \quad (4)$$

Within the framework of using RoundRobin on subintervals $[a, b]$, but selecting only those sensors that are closest to the midpoints of those intervals, an algorithm emerges naturally: partition U into subintervals, but employ RoundRobin only on those sensors that are close to the midpoint of each subinterval. To make efficient use of each sensor, we construct a hierarchical series of such partitions. We call this algorithm log_2-RoundRobin, and it is indexed by a depth parameter k, which indicates the number of partitions it employs.

Formally, for a fixed positive integer k, we partition U into $2^k + 1$ subintervals $U_k(i) = [\frac{i}{2^k} - \frac{1}{2^{k+1}}, \frac{i}{2^k} + \frac{1}{2^{k+1}}] \cap U$ for $i = 0, 1, ..., 2^k$. [2] If sensor $x \in U_k(i)$, then x is responsible for covering the interval around $i/2^k$ with radius $\frac{gcd(i,2^k)}{2^k}$. For example, any sensor that lies within 2^{-k-1} of $\frac{1}{2}$ is assigned to cover all of U. Similarly, sensors within 2^{-k-1} of either $\frac{1}{4}$ or $\frac{3}{4}$ are assigned to cover the subintervals $[0, \frac{1}{2}]$ and $[\frac{1}{2}, 1]$, respectively. A graphical depiction of the normalized sensor network lifetime as a function of location in shown in Figure 4.

For $j = 1, ..., k$, we define $\Gamma_k(j)$ to the be the set of intervals that comprise the jth level of the algorithm. Formally, we denote

$$\Gamma_k(j) = \left\{ \bigcup_{i=1}^{2^k-1} U_k(i) : \log_2\left(gcd(i, 2^k)\right) = k - j \right\}.$$

---

[2] Note that the first and last intervals, $U_k(0) = [0, 2^{-k-1}]$ and $U_k(2^k) = [1 - 2^{-k-1}, 1]$, respectively, are only half as wide as the others, all of which have width 2^{-k}.

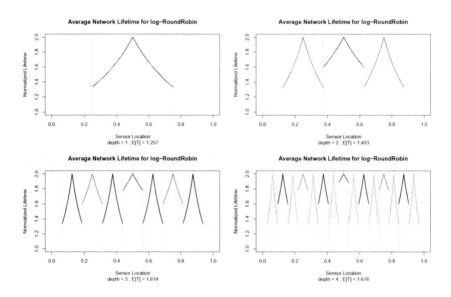

Fig. 4. Normalized Sensor Network Lifetime for $k = 1, 2, 3, 4$ using the log_2-RoundRobin algorithm. Each color represents the lifetime of the sensors in $\Gamma_k(j)$. Note that while the actual lifetime of a sensor in $\Gamma_k(j)$ may reach 2^j, it must run in parallel with 2^{j-1} partners, so the normalized lifetime *of the group* is at most 2. The expected average lifetime of the network approaches 1.737752 as $k \to \infty$.

Note that $\Gamma_k(j)$ consists of 2^{j-1} disjoint intervals, each of width 2^{-k}.[3] Thus $\Gamma_k(j)$ occupies 2^{j-k-1} of U. We can compute the expected normalized lifetime for $\Gamma_k(j)$ using Equation 3

$$\mathbb{E}[\hat{T}_k(j)] = \mathbb{E}[\hat{T}_{0,2^{-j+1}}(X; 2^{-k-1})] = 2^{k-j+2} \ln\left(1 + 2^{j-k-1}\right),$$

and the variance using Equation 4:

$$Var(\hat{T}_k(j)) = 4\left[1 - \frac{1}{1 + 2^{k-j+1}} - \left(2^{k-j+1} \cdot \ln\left(1 + 2^{j-k-1}\right)\right)^2\right].$$

Summing over the $\Gamma_k(j)$'s to find the total expected normalized lifetime, we obtain

$$\mathbb{E}[\hat{T}_k] = \sum_{j=1}^{k} \frac{\mathbb{E}[\hat{T}_k(j)]}{2^{k-j+1}} = 2\ln\prod_{j=1}^{k}\left(1 + 2^{j-k-1}\right) = 2\ln\prod_{\ell=1}^{k}\left(1 + 2^{-\ell}\right). \qquad (5)$$

---

[3] We let $\Gamma_k(0)$ be the set of sensors assigned to $U_k(0)$ or $U_k(2^k)$, and have those cover their respective half-intervals. Their contribution to the network lifetime becomes negligible as $k \to \infty$, so we omit it from our calculations.

The analogous infinite product is a q-series [13], denoted here by $\left(-1; \frac{1}{2}\right)_\infty$, for which we can compute an approximate limiting value. This leads directly to the expected average lifetime:

$$\mu_T^* \triangleq \mathbb{E}[\hat{T}] = \lim_{k \to \infty} \mathbb{E}[\hat{T}_k] = 2\ln\left(\prod_{\ell=1}^{\infty} 1 + 2^{-\ell}\right) \approx 1.737752\,.$$

The mean normalized variance satisfies

$$\mathbb{E}[Var(\hat{T}_k)] = \sum_{j=1}^{k} \frac{Var(\hat{T}_k(j))}{2^{k-j+1}} = 4\left[\sum_{\ell=1}^{k} \frac{1}{1+2^\ell} - 2^\ell \cdot \ln^2\left(1 + 2^{-\ell}\right)\right]\,,$$

which has the approximate limit of 0.02202547 as $k \to \infty$. Computation of the total variance is omitted, but it will converge to the above as $k \to \infty$.

Furthermore, it is clear from Figure 4 that the worst-case lifetime occurs when a sensor in $\Gamma_k(k)$ lies near one of the endpoints of the interval on which it is active. The normalized lifetime at this point is $4/3$, a constant. This provides the same worst-case performance as RoundRobin.

Load Balancing, Revisited. In $\log_2$-RoundRobin, each set $\Gamma_k(j)$ for $j = 1, ..., k$ maintains 2^{j-1} parallel queues. Proper functioning of our algorithm requires balanced loads across these queues, but the hierarchical structure of $\log_2$-RoundRobin alleviates the load balancing issue if the $\Gamma_k(j)$'s are pushed onto a central stack in ascending order of j. To see this, suppse that the left half of $\Gamma_k(2)$ runs out, while the right half is still going. U remains covered if the left half of $\Gamma_k(3)$ starts running alongside the right half of $\Gamma_k(2)$. In this manner load imbalances are averaged out over the k levels of the algorithm.

Nevertheless, a Chernoff bound analogous to the one used above for k-RoundRobin will show that for $k < \ln n$, with high probability N_i will deviate from its mean of $\frac{n}{2^k}$ by $O(\sqrt{n \ln n})$. Setting $n_1 = 2^k \cdot \min_{1 \leq i \leq 2^k - 1} N_i$ yields

$$\mathbb{E}[\bar{T}_{actual}] \geq \frac{n_1}{n} \cdot \mu_T^* + \frac{n_2}{n} \cdot 0 \to \mu_T^*, \text{ as } n \to \infty.^4$$

Theorem 2. *The $\log_2$-RoundRobin algorithm is at best a $\frac{2}{3}$-approximation of T_{OPT}, but for sufficiently large n, achieves an average-case 0.869-approximation ratio with high probability.*

3.4 Optimizations

Still, it is clear from Figure 4 that efficiency is highest in $\Gamma_k(1)$ and lowest in $\Gamma_k(k)$. We can show that in fact, the relative efficiency of $\Gamma_k(k)$ is the constant

---

[4] The inequality is justified by the preceding argument that in practice, the actual load balancing will work at least this well.

$2 \ln \frac{3}{2} \approx 0.81$. On the other hand, it is easy to see that the relative efficiency of $\Gamma_k(1)$ approaches 1 as $k \to \infty$. Therefore, we can improve the efficiency of $\log_2$-RoundRobin by shrinking the intervals over which $\Gamma_k(k)$ is active. Note that since every $\Gamma_k(j)$ for $j = 1, ..., k-1$ borders $\Gamma_k(k)$ on both sides, we maintain balanced loads across each $\Gamma_k(j)$ even as we shrink the width of $\Gamma_k(k)$. Let $\epsilon(k) \in [0, 1]$ be a parameter measuring the inward shift of the boundaries of $\Gamma_k(k)$. Then using Equation 3, the expected normalized lifetime becomes

$$\mathbb{E}[\hat{T}_k(j, \epsilon)] = \mathbb{E}\left[\hat{T}_{0,2^{-j+1}}\left(X; \frac{1+\epsilon}{2^{k+1}}\right)\right] = \frac{2^{k-j+2}}{1+\epsilon} \ln\left(1 + (1+\epsilon)2^{j-k-1}\right)$$

for $j = 1, ..., k-1$, and

$$\mathbb{E}[\hat{T}_k(k, \epsilon)] = \mathbb{E}\left[\hat{T}_{0,2^{-k+1}}\left(X; \frac{1-\epsilon}{2^{k+1}}\right)\right] = \frac{4}{1-\epsilon} \ln\left(\frac{3-\epsilon}{2}\right).$$

Taking the weighted average again, we have a generalization of Equation 5 that can be expressed as another q-series:

$$\mathbb{E}[\hat{T}_k(k, \epsilon)] = 2 \ln\left(\frac{3-\epsilon}{2}\right) \prod_{i=2}^{\infty} 1 + (1+\epsilon)2^{-i} = 2 \ln \frac{(3-\epsilon)\left(-(1+\epsilon); \frac{1}{2}\right)_\infty}{(\epsilon+3)(\epsilon+2)}.$$

We can find the optimal $\epsilon(k)$ using elementary calculus, but unfortunately a general solution requires factoring a polynomial of degree $k-1$:

$$T_k'(\epsilon) = 0 \Rightarrow \frac{1}{3-\epsilon} = \sum_{j=1}^{k-1} \frac{1}{2^{j+1}+1+\epsilon}. \tag{6}$$

However, since $T_k'(0) > 0$ for $k > 3$, and $T_k'(1) < 0$ for $k > 0$, the derivative has a root between 0 and 1 for $k > 3$ by the Intermediate Value Theorem. Moreover the Second Derivative Test confirms that for $k > 1$, each of these roots is a local maximum.

Numerical approximations of some relevant roots of this polynomial are shown in Table 2, alongside the expected network lifetime of the optimized algorithm. Our optimizations improve the expected average network lifetime by more than 3% above that of $\log_2$-RoundRobin.

Theorem 3. *For sufficiently large n, the optimized $\log_2$-RoundRobin algorithm achieves an average-case approximation ratio of 0.895 with high probability.*

Convergence. The Ratio Test, combined with L'Hôpital's Rule, will show that both series $T_k(\epsilon)$ and $T_k'(\epsilon)$ converge as $k \to \infty$ for any fixed $\epsilon \in [0, 1]$. As we have not found a closed functional form for either limit, we cannot prove that the optimal ϵ converges to a limit.

Table 2. Numerical Approximations for Optimal Choice of ϵ. Note that $T_{20}(0)$ equals $T_\infty(0) = \mu_T^*$ to six digits. The rightmost column shows the percentage of U that is covered by $\Gamma_k(k; \epsilon)$.

k	ϵ	$T_k(0)$	$T_k(\epsilon)$	Gain %	$|U_k(k;\epsilon)|\%$
2	0	1.492783	1.492783	0	50.00
3	0	1.614033	1.614033	0	50.00
4	0.211103	1.675576	1.696157	1.23	39.44
5	0.371297	1.706584	1.743439	2.16	31.44
6	0.448178	1.722149	1.767123	2.61	27.59
7	0.485871	1.729946	1.778990	2.84	25.71
8	0.504537	1.733848	1.784931	2.95	24.77
10	0.518459	1.736777	1.789391	3.03	24.08
12	0.521929	1.737509	1.790506	3.05	23.90
15	0.522941	1.737723	1.790831	3.06	23.85
20	0.523081	1.737752	1.790876	3.06	23.85

4 Open Problems

One obvious variation on this problem is to change the battery drainage rate. If $\alpha > 1$ then larger coverage regions become more expensive, so that, for example, the performance of Γ_1 would decline. Secondly, the average-case analysis could be studied for any probability distribution with finite support.

Another avenue for exploration would be to extend the analysis to higher dimensions, including one in which the sensors are not necessarily located on the line, but rather in the plane, and one in which the sensors remain on the line, but the coverage region extends into the plane.

Lastly, while we allow for pre-emptive scheduling in our definition, we did not actually use it in the case of random deployment. We hope to tackle some of these questions in future research.

References

1. Aloupis, G., Cardinal, J., Collette, S., Langerman, S., Orden, D., Ramos, P.: Decomposition of Multiple Coverings into More Parts. Discrete & Computational Geometry 44(3), 706–723 (2010)
2. Bar-Noy, A., Brown, T., Johnson, M.P., Liu, O.: Cheap or Flexible Sensor Coverage. In: Krishnamachari, B., Suri, S., Heinzelman, W., Mitra, U. (eds.) DCOSS 2009. LNCS, vol. 5516, pp. 245–258. Springer, Heidelberg (2009)
3. Berman, P., Calinescu, G., Shah, C., Zelikovsky, A.: Efficient Energy Management in Sensor Networks. Ad Hoc and Sensor Networks 2, 71–90 (2005)
4. Buchsbaum, A.L., Efrat, A., Jain, S., Venkatasubramanian, S., Yi, K.: Restricted Strip Covering and the Sensor Cover Problem. In: Proceedings of the 18th Annual ACM-SIAM Symposium on Discrete Algorithms, pp. 1056–1065 (2007)
5. Cardei, M., Wu, J., Lu, M.: Improving Network Lifetime Using Sensors with Adjustable Sensing Ranges. Int. J. Sensor Networks 1(1), 41–49 (2006)

6. Dhawan, A., Vu, C.T., Zelikovsky, A., Li, Y., Prasad, S.K.: Maximum Lifetime of Sensor Networks with Adjustable Sensing Range. In: Proceedings of the International Conference on Software Engineering, Artificial Intelligence, Networking, and Parallel/Distributed Computing (SNPD), pp. 285–289 (2006)
7. Gibson, M., Varadarajan, K.: Decomposing Coverings and the Planar Sensor Cover Problem. In: 50th Annual IEEE Symposium on Foundations of Computer Science, pp. 159–168 (2009)
8. Lev-Tov, N., Peleg, D.: Polynomial Time Approximation Schemes for Base Station Coverage with Minimum Total Radii. Computer Networks 47(4), 489–501 (2005)
9. Mitzenmacher, M., Upfal, E.: Probability and Computing: Randomized Algorithms and Probabilistic Analysis. Cambridge University Press, New York (2005)
10. Pach, J.: Covering the Plane with Convex Polygons. Discrete & Computational Geometry 1(1), 73–81 (1986)
11. Pach, J., Tóth, G.: Decomposition of Multiple Coverings into Many Parts. Computational Geometry 42(2), 127–133 (2009)
12. Wu, J., Yang, S.: CoverageIissue in Sensor Networks with Adjustable Ranges. In: Proceedings of the 2004 Intl. Conference on Parallel Processing Workshops, pp. 61–68 (2004)
13. Weisstein, E.W.: "q-Series." From MathWorld–A Wolfram Web Resource, http://mathworld.wolfram.com/q-Series.html

Appendix

Pinned Disks. For a fixed time t, let $Y = \{x_1, ..., x_m\} \subseteq X$ be the locations of active sensors, so that $r_i > 0$ for all $1 \leq i \leq m$. The unique radial assignment function $R^*(Y)$ corresponding to pinned disks is then given recursively by

$$(R^*(Y))_i = r_i = \begin{cases} x_1 & \text{if } i = 1 \\ x_i - (x_{i-1} + r_{i-1}) & \text{if } 2 \leq i \leq m \end{cases}.$$

Setting $x_m + r_m = 1$ to ensure a perfect fit yields

$$1 = 2 \sum_{j=1}^{m} (-1)^{m-j} x_j.$$

We then define the polynomial $f(Y) = -\frac{1}{2} + \sum_{j=1}^{m} (-1)^{m-j} x_j$, and use it in the proof of Lemma 2.

Proof. (of Proposition 2) $\Rightarrow$ From our previous argument, a radial assignment that gives perfect coverage necessarily consists of pinned disks that satisfy $f(Y) = 0$.
    $\Leftarrow$ Suppose that there exists $Y \subseteq X$ satisfying $f(Y) = 0$. Then $R^*(Y)$ gives perfect coverage.

RoundRobin. We present the proof of the lower appoximation bound for RoundRobin given in Lemma 1.

Proof. (of Lemma 1) To prove the lower bound, let $\beta \in (0, \frac{1}{4})$ be a parameter to be determined later. Let $A = [0, \beta], B = [\beta, 1 - \beta]$, and $C = [1 - \beta, 1]$ be a division of I into three closed intervals. Let $t_{(1,0,0)}$ denote any block of time in OPT in which sensors from A are active (i.e. - have non-zero radius), but no sensors from B or C are active. Note that in $t_{(1,0,0)}$ (respectively $t_{(0,0,1)}$), exactly one sensor is active in A (resp. C). Thus, for any such time block, RoundRobin gives the same solution as OPT. Furthermore, any non-empty time interval in OPT in which only one sensor is active gives the same solution as RoundRobin.

It remains to consider the following situations:

- $t_{(0,1,0)}$: The worst position for the sensors are at β and $1 - \beta$, where the radii must be set to at least $1 - \beta$. So the total network lifetime of RoundRobin in this situation is $T \geq \frac{n}{1-\beta}$. Since the maximum network lifetime is $2n$, we know that RoundRobin is at least a $\frac{1}{2(1-\beta)}$-approximation in this case.
- $t_{(1,1,0)} \sim t_{(0,1,1)}$: The worst case here is to have $\frac{n}{2}$ pairs of sensors at 0 and β, which then must be assigned radii of 1 and $1 - \beta$, respectively, under RoundRobin. The lifetime of RoundRobin is thus at least $T \geq \frac{n}{2} \cdot 1 + \frac{n}{2} \cdot \frac{1}{1-\beta} = \frac{2-\beta}{2(1-\beta)} n$. The approximation ratio of RoundRobin is thus at least $\frac{2-\beta}{4(1-\beta)}$.
- $t_{(1,0,1)}$: With no sensors active in B, the worst case scenario for RoundRobin is a lifetime of n, with all n sensors at either 0 or 1. However, note that since $\beta < \frac{1}{4}$, OPT cannot achieve a lifetime of $2n$ under these conditions. [Note in light of Corollary 1, that no subset $Y \subseteq X$ satisfies $f_k(Y) = 0$.] In fact, the maximum network lifetime for OPT occurs when there are $\frac{n}{2}$ pairs of sensors at β and $1 - \beta$, each with radii set to $\frac{1}{2} - \beta$. Thus, the lifetime of OPT is at most $\frac{n}{2} \cdot \frac{1}{\frac{1}{2}-\beta} = \frac{n}{1-2\beta}$. The approximation ratio of RoundRobin is thus at least $1 - 2\beta$.
- $t_{(1,1,1)}$: Here the worst case is to have $\frac{n}{3}$ sensors at β or $1 - \beta$, and corresponding pairs at 0 and 1. The lifetime of RoundRobin under this scenario is $T \geq \frac{n}{3} \cdot \frac{1}{1-\beta} + \frac{2n}{3} \cdot 1 = \frac{3-2\beta}{3(1-\beta)} n$. The approximation ratio of RoundRobin is then at least $\frac{3-2\beta}{6(1-\beta)}$.

Thus, for any possible arrangement of active sensors, the approximation ratio of RoundRobin is at least

$$\rho(\beta) \geq min \left\{ 1, \frac{1}{2(1-\beta)}, \frac{2-\beta}{4(1-\beta)}, 1 - 2\beta, \frac{3-2\beta}{6(1-\beta)} \right\}$$

Since $1 \geq \frac{1}{2(1-\beta)} \geq \frac{2-\beta}{4(1-\beta)} \geq \frac{3-2\beta}{6(1-\beta)}$ for any $0 < \beta < \frac{1}{4}$, the optimal choice of β occurs when $1 - 2\beta = \frac{3-2\beta}{6(1-\beta)} \Rightarrow \beta = \frac{4-\sqrt{7}}{6} \approx 0.226$. The minimum value of ρ is thus $\frac{\sqrt{7}-1}{3} \approx 0.54857$.

Sensor Fusion: From Dependence Analysis via Matroid Bases to Online Synthesis

Asaf Cohen[1], Shlomi Dolev[2], and Guy Leshem[2,3]

[1] Department of Communication System Engineering
[2] Department of Computer Science,
Ben-Gurion University of the Negev, Beer-Sheva 84105 Israel
[3] Department of Computer Science, Ashkelon Academic Collage, Israel
`coasaf@bgu.ac.il`, {`dolev,leshemg`}`@cs.bgu.ac.il`

Abstract. Consider the two related problems of sensor selection and sensor fusion. In the first, given a set of sensors, one wishes to identify a subset of the sensors, which while small in size, captures the essence of the data gathered by the sensors. In the second, one wishes to construct a fused sensor, which utilizes the data from the sensors (possibly after discarding dependent ones) in order to create a single sensor which is more reliable than each of the individual ones.

In this work, we rigorously define the dependence among sensors in terms of joint empirical measures and incremental parsing. We show that these measures adhere to a polymatroid structure, which in turn facilitates the application of efficient algorithms for sensor selection. We suggest both a random and a greedy algorithm for sensor selection. Given an independent set, we then turn to the fusion problem, and suggest a novel variant of the exponential weighting algorithm. In the suggested algorithm, one competes against an augmented set of sensors, which allows it to converge to the best fused sensor in a family of sensors, without having any prior data on the sensors' performance.

1   Introduction

Sensor networks are used to gather and analyze data in a variety of applications. In this model, numerous sensors are either spread in a wide area, or simply measure different aspects of a certain phenomenon. The goal of a central processor which gathers the data is, in general, to infer about the environment the sensors measure and make various decisions. An example to be kept in mind can be a set of sensors monitoring various networking aspects in an organization (incoming and outgoing traffic, addresses, remote procedure calls, http requests to servers and such). In many cases, an anomalous behavior detected by a single sensor may not be reliable enough to announce the system is under attack. Moreover, different sensors might have correlated data, as they measure related phenomenons. Hence, the central processor faces two problems. First, how to identify the set of sensors which sense independent data, and discard the rest, which only clutter the decision process. The second, how to intelligently combine the data from the sensors it selected in order to decide whether to raise an alarm or not.

T. Erlebach et al. (Eds.): ALGOSENSORS 2011, LNCS 7111, pp. 42–56, 2012.

In this work, we target both problems. First, we consider the problem of sensor selection. Clearly, as data aggregated by different sensors may be highly dependent, due to, for example, co-location or other similarities in the environment, it is desirable to identify the largest set of independent (or nearly independent) sensors. This way, sensor fusion algorithms can be much more efficient. For example, in the fusion algorithm we present, identifying the set of independent sensors allows us to create families of fused sensors based on fewer sensors, hence having a significantly smaller parameter space. Moreover, identifying independent sensors is of benefit also to various control methods, were a few representative independent inputs facilitate easier analysis. Note that the sensor selection problem is different from the data compression problem, where the independence among the data sets is reduced via some kind of Slepian-Wolf coding [17]. Herein, we do not wish all data to be reconstructed at the center, but focus only identify good sets of independent sensors, such that *their* data can be sent and analyzed, disregarding other sensors. Note that, in this context, we do not wish to replace Slepian-Wolf coding by sending data of independent sensors, only identify the independent subsets. For example, the randomized algorithm we suggest gathers data only from small subsets of the sensors, yet is assured to identify independent sets with high probability. A greed algorithm we suggest can identify subset of sensors with relatively high independence among them (compared to other subsets), even in cases we do not wish to identify a subset containing all the information.

Given two data sets, a favored method to measure their dependence is through various *mutual information estimates*. Such estimates arise from calculating marginal and joint empirical entropies, or the more efficient method of incremental (Lempel-Ziv) parsing [22]. Indeed, LZ parsing was used, for example, for multidimensional data analysis [23], neural computation [2] and numerous other applications. However, although the ability of the parsing rule to approximate the true entropy of the source, and hence, as one possible consequence, identify dependencies in the data, applications reported in the current literature were ad-hoc, using the resulting measures to compare between mainly *pairs of sources*.

To date, there is no rigorous method to analyze independence among large sets, and handle cases where one sensor's data may depend on measurements from many others, including various delays. In this work, we give the mathematical framework which enables us to both rigorously define the problem of identifying sets of independent sources in a large set of sensors and give highly efficient approximations algorithms based on the observations we gain.

Still, when no single sensor is reliable enough to give an accurate estimate of the phenomenon it measures, sensor fusion is used [5,14,19]. In the second part of this work, we consider the problem of sensor fusion. In this case, for a given set of sensors, one wishes to generate a *new sensor*, whose performance over time is (under some measure) better than any single sensor in the set. Note, however, that in most cases, choosing the best-performing sensor in the set might not be enough. We wish, in general, to create a sensor whose performance is strictly better than any given sensor in the original set, by utilizing data from several sensors simultaneously and intelligently combining it.

Contribution. Our main contributions are the following. First, we show how to harness the wide variety of algorithms for identifying largest independent sets in matroids, or the very related problems of minimum cycle bases and spanning trees in graphs to our problem of identifying sets of independent sensors in a sensor network. Our approach is based on highly efficient (linear time in the size of the data) methods to estimate the dependence among the sensors, such as the Lempel-Ziv parsing rule [22]. The key step is in showing how these estimates can either yield a polymatroid, or at least approximate a one, facilitating the use of polynomial time algorithms to identify the independent sets, such as [7,1]. We construct both random and a greedy selection algorithms, and analyze their performance.

We then turn to the problem of (non-correlated) sensor fusion. In particular, we describe an online fusion algorithm based on exponential weighting [18]. While weighted majority algorithms were used in the context of sensor networks [6,21,12], in these works, the exponential weighting was used only to identify good sensors and order them by performance. Hence, applied directly, this algorithm does not yield a good *fused* sensor. In this part of our work, we suggest a novel extension by creating parametric families of synthesised sensors. This way, we are able to *span a huge set of fused sensors*, and choose online the best fused sensor. That is, given a set of sensors $\mathcal{S}$, this algorithm *constructs synthesised sensors*, from which it selects a sensor whose performance converges to that of the best sensor in both $\mathcal{S}$ and the constructed parametric family of synthesised sensors. Hence, the algorithm results in online sensor fusion.

We rigorously quantify the regret of the suggested algorithm compared to the best fused sensor. In this way, a designer of a sensor fusion algorithm has a well-quantified trade-off: choosing a large number of parameters, thus covering more families of fusion possibilities, at the price of higher regret.

Due to space limitations, proofs are not included in this proceedings.

2   Preliminaries

The basic setting we consider is the following. A set of sensors, $\mathcal{S} = \{S_1, \ldots, S_K\}$ is measuring a set of values in a certain environment. Each sensor may depend on a different set of values, and may base its decision on these values in a different way. However, each sensor, at each time instance, estimates whether a target exists in the environment or not. Thus, the input to sensor S_j at time t is some vector of measurements V_t^j, based on which it will output a value $p_t^j \in [0, 1]$, which is his estimate for the probability a target exists at time t. Throughout, capital letters denote random variables while lower case denotes realizations. Hence, P_t^j denotes the possibly random output of sensor S_j, $j = 1, 2, \ldots, K$ at time t, $t = 1, 2, \ldots, n$.

Let $\{x_t\}_{t=1}^n$ be the binary sequence indicating whether a target actually appeared at time t or not. The normalized cumulative loss of the sensor S_j over n time instances is defined as $L_{S_j}(x_1^n) = \frac{1}{n}\sum_{t=1}^n d(p_t^j, x_t)$, for some distance function $d : [0,1] \times \{0,1\} \mapsto \mathbb{R}$. If the sensor's output is binary (a sensor either decides a target exists or not), then $p_t^j \in \{0,1\}$ and a reasonable distance measure is the Hamming distance, that is, $d(a,b) = 0$ if $a = b$ and 1 otherwise. If the sensor's output is in $[0,1]$, then we think of it as the sensor's estimate for the probability a target exists, and a reasonable d is the *log-loss*, $d(p,x) = -x\log(p) - (1-x)\log(1-p)$. In any case, the goal of a good sensor S is to minimize the normalized cumulative loss $L_S(x_1^n)$.

Polymatroids, Matroids and Entropic Vectors. Let $\mathcal{K}$ be an index set of size K and $\mathcal{N}$ be the power set of $\mathcal{K}$. A function $g : \mathcal{N} \mapsto \mathbb{R}$ defines a *polymatroid* $(\mathcal{K}, g)$ with a ground set $\mathcal{K}$ and rank function g if it satisfies the following conditions [11]:

$$g(\emptyset) = 0, \tag{1}$$
$$g(I) \leq g(J) \text{ for } I \subseteq J \subseteq \mathcal{K}, \tag{2}$$
$$g(I) + g(J) \geq g(I \cup J) + g(I \cap J) \text{ for } I, J \subseteq \mathcal{K}. \tag{3}$$

For a polymatroid g with ground set $\mathcal{K}$, we represent g by the vector $(g(I) : I \subseteq \mathcal{K}) \in \mathbb{R}^{2^K-1}$ defined on the ordered, non-empty subsets of $\mathcal{K}$. We denote the set of all polymatroids with a ground set of size K by Γ_K. Thus $\mathbf{w} \in \Gamma_K$ if and only if $w(I)$ and $w(J)$ satisfy equations (1)–(3) for all $I, J \subseteq \mathcal{K}$, where $w(I)$ is the value of $\mathbf{w}$ at the entry corresponding to the subset I. If, in addition to (1)–(3), $g(\cdot) \in \mathbb{Z}^+$ and $g(I) \leq |I|$, then $(\mathcal{K}, g)$ is called a *matroid*.

Now, assume $\mathcal{K}$ is some set of discrete random variables. For any $A \subseteq \mathcal{K}$, let $H(A)$ denote the joint entropy function. An entropy vector $\mathbf{w}$ is a $(2^K - 1)$-dimensional vector whose entries are the joint entropies of all non-empty subsets of $\mathcal{K}$. It is well-known that the entropy function is a polymatroid over this ground set $\mathcal{K}$. Indeed, (1)–(3) are equivalent to the Shannon information inequalities [20]. However, there exists points $\mathbf{w} \in \Gamma_K$ ($K > 3$) for which there is no set of K discrete random variables whose joint entropies equal $\mathbf{w}$. We denote by Γ_K^* the set of all $\mathbf{w} \in \Gamma_K$ for which there exists at least one random vector whose joint entropies equal $\mathbf{w}$. A $\mathbf{w} \in \Gamma_K^*$ is called *entropic*. Finally, denote by $\bar{\Gamma}_K^*$ the convex closure of Γ_K^*. Then $\bar{\Gamma}_K^* = \Gamma_K$ for $K \leq 3$ but $\bar{\Gamma}_K^* \neq \Gamma_K$ for $K > 3$ [20].

3   A Matroid-Based Framework for Identifying Non-correlated Sensors

In this section, we use the incremental parsing rule of Lempel and Ziv [22] to estimate the *joint empirical entropies* of the sensors' data. We then show that when the sensors data is stationary and ergodic, the vector of joint empirical entropies can be approximated some point in the polyhedral cone Γ_K. In fact, this point is actually in $\bar{\Gamma}_K^*$. As asymptotically entropic polymatroids are well approximated by asymptotically entropic matroids [13, Theorem 5], the point in $\mathbb{R}^n$ which corresponds to the joint empirical entropies of the sensors is approximated by the *ranks of some matroid*. This enables us to identify independent sets of sensors, and, in particular, largest independent sets, by identifying the bases (or circuits) of the matroid. Doing this, the most complex dependence structures among sensors, including both dependence between past/future data and dependence among values at the same time instant can be identified. Non-linear dependencies are also captured.

We now show how to approximate an entropy vector (hence, a polymatroid) for the sensor data. We prove that indeed for large enough data and ergodic sources the approximation error is arbitrarily small. This polymatroid will be the input from which we will identify the independent sensors.

We first consider the most simple case in which one treats the sensors as having memoryless data. That is, sensors for which each reading (in time) is independent of the previous or future readings. Note, however, that this model still allows the reading of a sensor to depend on the readings of other sensors *at that time instant*. The dependence might be a simple (maybe linear) dependence between two sensors, or a more complex one, where one sensor's output is a random function of the outputs of a few others. It is important to note that it is inconsequential if the sensors are indeed memoryless or not. Using this simplified method, only dependencies across a single time instant will be identified.

For the sake of simplicity, assume now all P_t^j are binary. Given a sequence $\{p_i\}_{i=1}^n$, denote by $N(0|\{p_i\}_{i=1}^n)$ and $N(1|\{p_i\}_{i=1}^n)$ the number of zeros and ones in $\{p_i\}_{i=1}^n$, respectively. That is, $N(0|\{p_i\}_{i=1}^n) = \sum_{i=1}^n \mathbf{1}_{\{p_i=0\}}$, where $\mathbf{1}_{\{\cdot\}}$ is the indicator function. When the sequence indices are clear from the context, we will abbreviate this by $N(0|p)$. Hence, $T_p^n = \left(\frac{1}{n}N(0|p), \frac{1}{n}N(1|p)\right)$ denotes the *type* of the sequence p, that is, its empirical frequencies [4].

In a similar manner, we define the empirical frequencies of several sequences together, e.g. pairs. For example, $N\left(0,1|p^1,p^2\right) = \sum_{i=1}^n \mathbf{1}_{\{p_i^1=0, p_i^2=1\}}$. In this case, the 4-tuple

$$T_{p^1,p^2}^n = \left(\frac{1}{n}N\left(0,0|p^1,p^2\right), \frac{1}{n}N\left(0,1|p^1,p^2\right), \frac{1}{n}N\left(1,0|p^1,p^2\right), \frac{1}{n}N\left(1,1|p^1,p^2\right)\right)$$

denotes the *joint type* of p^1, p^2, hence, it includes the empirical frequencies of the two sequences *together*, over their product alphabet $\{0,1\} \times \{0,1\}$. For more than two sequences, we denote by $T_{p^1,\ldots,p^s}^n$ the joint type of the sequences $p^j, j \in \mathcal{S}$.

For a probability vector $\mathbf{q} = (q_1, \ldots, q_m)$, let $H(\mathbf{q})$ denote its entropy, that is, $H(\mathbf{q}) = -\sum_{i=1}^m q_i \log(q_i)$. Let $\mathbf{w}_n$ be the $(2^K - 1)$-dimensional vector whose entries are all the joint *empirical entropies* calculated from $\{(p_t^j)_{j \in \mathcal{S}}\}_{t=1}^n$. I.e,

$$\mathbf{w}_n = \left(H(T_{p^1}^n), \ldots, H(T_{p^K}^n), H(T_{p^1,p^2}^n), H(T_{p^1,p^3}^n), \ldots, H(T_{p^1,\ldots,p^K}^n)\right)$$

Under these definitions, we have the following.

Proposition 1. *For every realization of the sensors' data, $\mathbf{w}_n \in \Gamma_K^*$.*

Let $\mathbf{w}$ denote the true (memoryless) entropy vector of the sources. That is,

$$\mathbf{w} = \left(H(P_1^1), \ldots, H(P_1^K), H(P_1^1, P_1^2), H(P_1^1, P_1^3), \ldots, H(P_1^1, \ldots, P_1^K)\right).$$

For stationary and ergodic sources, the following Proposition is a direct application of Birkhoff's ergodic theorem.

Proposition 2. *Let $\{(p_t^j)_{j \in \mathcal{S}}\}_{t=1}^n$ be drawn from a stationary and ergodic source $\{(P_t^j)_{j \in \mathcal{S}}\}_{t=1}^\infty$ with some probability measure Q. Then, for any subset $\mathcal{S}' \subseteq \mathcal{S}$, we have $\lim_{n \to \infty} H(T_{p^j, j \in \mathcal{S}'}^n) = H\left((P_1^j)_{j \in \mathcal{S}'}\right)$ Q-a.s. (almost surely). As a result, $\Pr\left(\lim_{n \to \infty} \mathbf{w}_n = \mathbf{w}\right) = 1$.*

That is, the entropy calculated from the empirical distribution converges to the true entropy. Moreover, the vector of empirical entropies converges almost-surely (a.s.) to the true entropy vector, which is, of course, an entropic polymatroid. To be able to harness the diverse algorithmic literature on matroids (such as matroid optimization relevant for our independence analysis application), we mention that by [13, Theorem 5], describing the cone of asymptotically entropic polymatroids, $\bar{\Gamma}_K^*$, is reduced to the problem of describing asymptotically entropic *matroids*.

Dependence Measures for Sensors with Memory. Till now, we considered sensors for which the data for any *individual* sensor is a stationary and ergodic process, yet, through first-order empirical entropies, only the dependence along a single time instant was estimated. While being very easy to implement (linear in the size of the data), this method fails to capture complex dependence structures. For example, consider a sensor whose current data depends heavily on *previous data* acquired by *one or several other* sensors.

To capture dependence in time, we offer the incremental parsing rule [22] as a basis for an empirical measure. We show that indeed such a measure will converge almost surely to a polymatroid, from which maximal independent sets can be approximated. We start with a few definitions.

Let $\{p_i\}_{i=1}^n$ be some sequence over a finite alphabet of size α. The ZL78 [22] parsing rule is a sequential procedure which parses the sequence p in a way where a new phrase is created as soon as the still unparsed part of the string differs from all preceding phrases. For example, the string $01000110110000001010011\ldots$ is parsed as $0, 1, 00, 01, 10, 11, 000, 001, 010, 011, \ldots$. Let $c(\{p_i\}_{i=1}^n)$ denote the number of distinct phrases whose concatenation generates $\{p_i\}_{i=1}^n$. Furthermore, let $\rho_E(s)(\{p_i\}_{i=1}^n)$ denote the compression ratio achieved by the best finite-state encoder with at most s state, and define

$$\rho(p) = \lim_{s \to \infty} \limsup_{n \to \infty} \rho_{E(s)}(\{p_i\}_{i=1}^n).$$

In a nutshell, the main results of [22] states that

$$H^{LZ}(\{p_i^1\}_{i=1}^n) = \frac{c(\{p_i^1\}_{i=1}^n) \log c(\{p_i^1\}_{i=1}^n)}{n\alpha}$$

is an asymptotically attainable lower bound on the compression ratio $\rho(p)$. Denote by $\bar{H}(P)$ the *entropy rate* of a stationary source P, that is, $\lim_{n\to\infty} \frac{1}{n} H(P_1, \ldots, P_n)$. For K sources $P^1, \ldots, P^K$, the entropy rate vector $\bar{\mathbf{w}}$ is defined as

$$\bar{\mathbf{w}} = \left(\bar{H}(P^1), \ldots, \bar{H}(P^K), \bar{H}(P^1, P^2), \bar{H}(P^1, P^3), \ldots, \bar{H}(P^1, \ldots, P^K)\right).$$

It is not hard to show that $\bar{\mathbf{w}} \in \bar{\Gamma}_K^*$.

Analogously to the memoryless case, herein we also define the joint parsing rule in the trivial way, that is, parsing any subset of $1 < k \leq K$ sequences as a single sequence over the product alphabet. Define the LZ-based estimated entropy vector $\mathbf{w}_n^{LZ}$ as (suppressing the dependence on n)

$$\mathbf{w}_n^{LZ} = \left(H^{LZ}(p^1), \ldots, H^{LZ}(p^K), H^{LZ}(p^1, p^2), \ldots, H^{LZ}(p^1, \ldots, p^K)\right).$$

The following is the analogue of Proposition 2 for the non-memoryless case.

Proposition 3. *Let* $\{(p_t^j)_{j\in\mathcal{S}}\}_{t=1}^n$ *be drawn from a stationary and ergodic source* $\{(P_t^j)_{j\in\mathcal{S}}\}_{t=1}^\infty$. *Then,* $\Pr\left(\lim_{n\to\infty} \mathbf{w}_n^{LZ} = \bar{\mathbf{w}}\right) = 1$.

To see that $\bar{\mathbf{w}} \in \bar{\Gamma}_K^*$, remember that $H(\{P_i^j\}_{i=1}^n, j \in I)$, ranging over all subsets $I \subseteq \mathcal{S}$ forms an entropic polymatroid [20]. Hence $\frac{1}{n} H(\{P_i^j\}_{i=1}^n, j \in I)$ forms an asymptotically entropic polymatroid (as the closure of the entropic region is convex), hence $\bar{\mathbf{w}} \in \bar{\Gamma}_K^*$.

Note, however, that the analogue of Proposition 1 is not true in this case. That is, for finite n, $\mathbf{w}_n^{LZ}$ might not satisfy the polymatroid axioms at all. Nevertheless, by Proposition 3, for large enough n, $\mathbf{w}_n^{LZ}$ is sufficiently close to $\bar{\Gamma}_K^*$. A fortiori, it is sufficiently close to Γ_K. Moreover, for ergodic sources with finite memory, namely, sources for which

$$\Pr(P_n = a_n | P_{n-1} = a_{n-1}, P_{n-2} = a_{n-2}, \ldots)$$
$$= \Pr(P_n = a_n | P_{n-1} = a_{n-1}, \ldots, P_{n-m} = a_{n-m})$$

for some finite m, there exist a few strong tail bounds on the probability that the LZ compression ratio exceeds a certain threshold. For example, if $\|\mathbf{w}\|_0$ denotes the maximal entry in $\mathbf{w}$, we have the following proposition.

Proposition 4. *Let* $\{(p_t^j)_{j\in\mathcal{S}}\}_{t=1}^n$ *be drawn from a stationary and ergodic Markov source* $\{(P_t^j)_{j\in\mathcal{S}}\}_{t=1}^\infty$. *Then, with probability at least* $1 - O(\frac{2^K-1}{\sqrt{n}})$,

$$\|\mathbf{w}_n^{LZ} - \bar{\mathbf{w}}\|_0 \leq \frac{\bar{H}(P^j, j\in\mathcal{S})}{\log n}.$$

The usefulness of Proposition 4 is twofold. First, it gives a practical bound on the approximation the vector $\mathbf{w}_n^{LZ}$ gives to $\bar{\mathbf{w}}$. However, assume $\bar{\mathbf{w}}$ is a matroid. This is the case, for example, when bits in the sensors' data are either independent or completely dependent (in fact, in this case $\bar{\mathbf{w}}$ is a *linearly representable* binary matroid). Since $\mathbf{w}_n^{LZ}$ might not satisfy the polymatroid axioms at all, using Proposition 4 one can then easily check when can the entries of $\mathbf{w}_n^{LZ}$ be rounded to the nearest integer in order to achieve $\bar{\mathbf{w}}$ exactly. Finally, note that if the number of sensors is small, and the complexity of calculating all entries of $\mathbf{w}_n^{LZ}$ is not an issue, then the problem caused by $\mathbf{w}_n^{LZ}$ not satisfying the polymatroid axioms is a non-issue as well - to find a subset with high enough entropy (strong independence) simply take the smallest set of sensors with high enough $\frac{c \log c}{n\alpha}$.

Identifying Independent Sensors. Having set the ground, it is now possible to utilize optimization algorithms for submodular functions, and matroids in particular, in order to find maximal independent sets of sensors. Herein, we include two examples: a random selection algorithm, which fits cases where true data forms a matroid, for which possibly many subsets of sensors include the desired data, and a greedy algorithm, which easily fits any dependence structure (while matroids asymptotically span the entropic cone, an additional approximation step is required [13]). It is important to note that, unlike the greedy selection (also used in [16] in the context of maximum a posteriori estimates) which approximates the optimum value *up to a constant factor*, the random selection process we suggest here can guarantee exact approximation.

Algorithm RandomSelection
% Input: A set of $\mathcal{S}$ sensors. A parameter $0 \leq q \leq 1$.
% Output: A subset $I \subseteq \mathcal{S}$, of expected size qK, which with high probability contains a maximal independent set of $\mathcal{S}$ (see conditions in Corollary 1).

– Include a sensor j in subset I with probability q, independently of the other sensors.

The randomized algorithm is given in Algorithm RandomSelection. As simple as it looks, by [7, Theorem 5.2] and Proposition 4, under mild assumptions on the true distribution of the data, it guarantees that indeed with high probability such a random selection produces a subset of sensors which is a q-fraction of the original, yet if the original contains enough bases (maximal independent sets), then the subset contains a base as well. This is summarized in the following corollary.

Corollary 1. *Let* $\{(p_t^j)_{j \in \mathcal{S}}\}_{t=1}^n$ *be drawn from a stationary and ergodic Markov source. Assume that* $\bar{\mathbf{w}}$ *is a matroid of rank* r *which contains* $a + 2 + \frac{1}{q} \ln r$ *disjoint bases. Then, with probability at least* $1 - e^{-aq} - O(\frac{2^K - 1}{\sqrt{n}})$, *the subset* I *produced by Algorithm* RandomSelection *contains a maximal independent set of sensors.*

At first sight, Algorithm RandomSelection does not depend on any of the discussed dependence measures in this paper. Yet, it power *is drawn from them*: once we have established the estimated entropy vector as the key variable in determining dependence, we know that this asymptotic matroid is the one we should analyze for independent sets, *according to its features we should choose the parameters* in RandomSelection and these features will indeed eventually determine the success probability of RandomSelection.

Algorithm GreedySelection

% Input: Data of K sensors, $\{p_t^1, \ldots, p_t^K\}_{t=1}^n$.

% Output: At each time instant, a set I of sensors.

- Initialization: $I = \phi, \hat{H} = 0$.

1. $j^* = \mathrm{argmax}_{j \notin I} \mathbf{w}_n^{LZ}(I \cup \{j\})$
2. if $\mathbf{w}_n^{LZ}(I \cup \{j^*\}) > \hat{H}$
   - $I \leftarrow I \cup \{j^*\}$, then $\hat{H} \leftarrow \mathbf{w}_n^{LZ}(I)$
   - Go to step 1.

On the other hand, algorithm GreedySelection takes a different course of action, to answer a slightly different question: how to choose a small set of sensors with a relatively hight entropy (hence, independence)? How bad can one subset of sensors be compared to another of the same size? What is a good method to choose the better one? The algorithm sequentially increases the size of the sensors set I until its entropy estimate $\mathbf{w}_n^{LZ}(I)$ does not grow. In a similar manner, one can choose empirical entropies. Due to the polymatroid properties we proved, a bound on the performance compared to the optimum can be given. In practice, it might be beneficial to stop the algorithm if the entropy estimate does not grow above a certain threshold, to avoid steps which may include only a marginal improvement. In fact, this is exactly where the polymatroid properties we proved earlier in the section kick in, and we have the following (proof is omitted due to space limitation).

Proposition 5. *Assume Algorithm* GreedySelection *is stopped after the first time* $\mathbf{w}_n^{LZ}(I)$ *was incremented by less than some* $\epsilon > 0$. *Then, for stationary and ergodic sources, the difference between the entropy of the currently selected subset of sensors and the entropy that could have been reached if the algorithm concluded is upper bounded by* $K\epsilon + o(1)$.

The LZ parsing rule on an alphabet of size α can be implemented in $O(n \log \alpha)$ time (using an adequate tree and a binary enumeration of the alphabet). Hence, the complexity of GreedySelection is $O(nK^3)$. [10] analyzed the performance of greedy schemes for submodular functions. As noted in [16] also for such algorithms, they achieve a factor of $1 - \frac{1}{e}$ of the optimum.

4   A Sensor Fusion Algorithm via Exponential Weighting

In this section, we present an online algorithm for sensor fusion. In [18], Vovk considered a general set of experts and introduced the *exponential weighting* algorithm. In this algorithm, each expert is assigned a weight according to its past performance. By decreasing the weight of poorly performing experts, hence preferring the ones proved to perform well thus far, one is able to compete with the best expert, having neither any *a priori* knowledge on the input sequence nor which expert will perform the best. This result was further extended in [8], where various aspects of a "weighted majority" algorithm were discussed. It is important to note that the exponential weighting algorithm assumes nothing on the set of experts, neither their distribution in the space of all possible experts nor their structure. Consequently, all the results are of the "worst case" type.

Given a set of sensors $\mathcal{S}$, our goal, however, is to construct a *new sensor, $\hat{S}$*, whose output depends on the outputs of the given sensors, yet its performance is better than the best sensor in the set $\mathcal{S}$. We call $\hat{S}$ a *synthesised (fused) sensor*. Clearly, when the true target appearance sequence x_1^n is known in advance, suggesting such a sensor is trivial. However, we are interested in an *online* algorithm, which receives the sensors' outputs at each time instant t, together with their *performance in the past* (calculated by having access to $x_{t'}$ for $t' < t$ or estimating it), and computes a synthesised output. We expect the sequence of synthesised outputs given by the algorithm at times $t = 1, \ldots, n$ to have a lower cumulative loss than the best sensor in $\mathcal{S}$, for *any possible sequence x_1^n and any set of sensors $\mathcal{S}$*.

Towards this goal, we will define a parametric set of synthesised sensors. Once such a set is constructed, say $\mathcal{S}_\Theta$ for some set of parameters Θ ($|\Theta|$ possible new sensors), we will use the online algorithm to compete with the *best sensor in $\mathcal{S} \cup \mathcal{S}_\Theta$*. Clearly, a good choice for $\mathcal{S}_\Theta$ is such that on the one hand $|\mathcal{S} \cup \mathcal{S}_\Theta|$ is not too large, yet on the other hand $\mathcal{S}_\Theta$ includes "enough" good synthesised sensors, so the best sensor in $\mathcal{S} \cup \mathcal{S}_\Theta$ will indeed perform well.

Example 1. An example to be kept in mind is a case where the set of sensors, $S_1, \ldots, S_K$, has the property such that all under-estimate the probability that a target exists (for example, since each sensor measures a different aspect of the target, which might not be visible each time the target appears). In this case, a sensor $\hat{S}$ whose output at time t is $\max_j\{p_t^j, 1 \le j \le K\}$ will have a much smaller cumulative loss $L_{\hat{S}}(x_1^n)$ compared to any individual sensor, $L_{S_j}(x_1^n)$. As a result, when designing families of synthesised sensors for such a set of K sensors, one can think of a set synthesised family $\mathcal{S}_m$, which includes, for example, all sensors of the type $\max\{p_t^{j_1}, \ldots, p_t^{j_m}\}$ for some subset $\{j_1, \ldots, j_m\} \subset \{1, \ldots K\}$. If the miss-detection probabilities of the sensors are not all equal, clearly some synthesised set of m sensors will perform better than the others.

This example can be easily extended to a case where sensors either under-estimate or over-estimate. Following a single sensor will give a non-negligible error, while a simple median filter (sensor-wise) on a sufficiently large set of sensors might give asymptotically zero error.

Exponential Weighting for a Parametric Family of Sensors. Recall that for any time instant $t \le n$, $L_{S_j}(x_1^t)$ denotes the intermediate normalized cumulative loss of sensor S_j. Hence, $t L_{S_j}(x_1^t)$ is simply the unnormalized cumulative loss until (and including) time instant t. For simplicity, we denote this loss by $L_{j,t}$. Furthermore, note that for each $1 \le j \le K + |\Theta|$, $L_{j,0} = 0$. At each time instant t, the exponential weighing algorithm assigns each sensor $S_j \in \mathcal{S} \cup \mathcal{S}_\Theta$ a probability $P_t(j|\{L_{j,t}\}_{j=1}^{K+|\Theta|})$. That is, it assumes the cumulative losses of all sensors up to time t are known. Then, at each time instant t, after computing $P_t(j|\{L_{j,t}\}_{j=1}^{K+|\Theta|})$, the algorithm selects a sensor in $\mathcal{S} \cup \mathcal{S}_\Theta$ according to that distribution. The selected sensor is used to compute the *algorithm output at time* $t + 1$, namely, the algorithm uses the selected sensor as the synthesised sensor $\hat{S}$ at time $t + 1$. Note that this indeed results in a synthesised sensor, as even if it turns out that the best sensor at some time instant is in $\mathcal{S}$, it is not necessarily always the same sensor, hence the algorithm output will probably not equal any fixed sensor for all time instances $1 \leq t \leq n$. The suggested algorithm in summarized in Algorithm OnlineFusion below. The main advantage in this algorithm

---

Algorithm OnlineFusion

% Input: $K + |\Theta|$ sensors, $\mathcal{S} \cup \mathcal{S}_\Theta$; Data x_1^n, arriving sequentially.

% Output: At each time instance, a synthesised sensor $\hat{S} \in \mathcal{S} \cup \mathcal{S}_\Theta$, chosen at random, such that the excess cumulative loss compared to the best synthesised sensor is almost surely asymptotically (in n) negligible (see Proposition 6 and the discussion which follows).

- Initialization:
  $W = K + |\Theta|$; $\forall_{1 \leq j \leq K+|\Theta|}$ $L_j = 0$, $P(j|\{\}) = \frac{1}{W}$; $\eta = \sqrt{\frac{8 \log(K+|\Theta|)}{nd_{max}^2}}$.
- For each $t = 1, \ldots, n$:
  - Choose $\hat{S}$ according to $P(j|\{\})$.
  - For each $j = 1, \ldots, K + |\Theta|$:
    * $L_j \leftarrow L_j + d(p_t^j, x_t)$.
  - $W \leftarrow \sum_{j=1}^{K+|\Theta|} e^{-\eta L_j}$.
  - For each $j = 1, \ldots, K + |\Theta|$:
    * $P(j|\{\}) \leftarrow \frac{e^{-\eta L_j}}{W}$.

---

is that, under mild conditions, the normalized cumulative loss of the synthesised sensor $\hat{S}$ it produces is approaching that of the best sensor in $\mathcal{S} \cup \mathcal{S}_\Theta$, hence it converges to the best synthesised sensor in a family of sensors, without knowing in advance which sensor that might be. By the standard analysis of exponential weighing, similar to [9], the following proposition holds.

Proposition 6. *For any sequence x_1^n, any set of sensors $\mathcal{S}$ of size K and any set of synthesised sensors $\mathcal{S}_\Theta$, the expected performance of Algorithm* OnlineFusion *is given by* $E[L_{\hat{S}}(x_1^n)] \leq \min_{S \in \mathcal{S} \cup \mathcal{S}_\Theta} L_S(x_1^n) + d_{max}\sqrt{\frac{\log(K+|\Theta|)}{2n}}$, *where the expectation is over the randomized decisions in the algorithm and d_{max} is some upper bound on the instantaneous loss.*

As a result, as long as $\log(K + |\Theta|) = o(n)$ the synthesised sensor $\hat{S}$ has a vanishing redundancy compared to the best sensor in $\mathcal{S} \cup \mathcal{S}_\Theta$. This gives us an enormous freedom in choosing the parametrized set of sensors $\mathcal{S}_\Theta$, and even sets whose size grows polynomially with the size of the data are acceptable.

The performance of the exponential weighting algorithm can be summarized as follows. For any set of stationary sources with probability measure Q, as long as the number of synthesised sensors does not grow exponentially with the data, we have $\liminf_{n\to\infty} E_Q EL_{\hat{S}}(X_1^n) \leq \liminf_{n\to\infty} \min_{S\in\mathcal{S}\cup\mathcal{S}_\Theta} E_Q L_S(X_1^n)$, where the inner expectation in the left hand side is due to the possible randomization in $\hat{S}$. When the algorithm bases its decisions on independent drawings, we have $\lim_{n\to\infty} L_{\hat{S}}(x_1^n) \leq \lim_{n\to\infty} \min_{S\in\mathcal{S}\cup\mathcal{S}_\Theta} L_S(x_1^n)$ almost surely (in terms of the randomization in the algorithm). If, furthermore, the sources are strongly mixing, almost sure convergence in terms of the sources distribution is guaranteed as well [3]: $\liminf_{n\to\infty} L_{\hat{S}}(X_1^n) \leq \liminf_{n\to\infty} \min_{S\in\mathcal{S}\cup\mathcal{S}_\Theta} L_S(X_1^n)$, Q-a.s.

A by product of the algorithm is the set of weights it maintains while running. These weights are, in fact, good estimates of the *sensors' reputation*. Moreover, such weights can help us make intelligent decisions for synthesised control and fine-tuning of the sensor selection process, namely, we are able to clearly see which families of synthesised sensors perform better, and within a family, which set of parameters should be described in higher granularity compared to the others (since sensors with these values perform well).

5   Results on Real and Artificial Data

To validate the proposed methods in practice, simulations were carried out on both real and synthetic data. We present here some of the results.

To demonstrate Algorithm OnlineFusion, We used real sensors data collected from 54 sensors deployed in the Intel Berkeley Research Lab between February 28th and April 5th, 2004.[1] To avoid too complex computations, we used only the first 15 real sensors (corresponding to a wing in the lab) and artificially created from them 225 fused (synthesised) sensors. For this basic example, the fused sensors were created by simply averaging the data of any two real sensors. Yet, the results clearly show how the best fused sensor outperforms the best real sensor, with very fast convergence times. Figure 1(a) demonstrates the convergence of the weight vectors created by the algorithm. At start (top row), all weights are equal. Very fast, the two best sensors have a relatively high weight (approximately 0.5), while the weight of the others decrease exponentially. Hence, the algorithm identifies the two best sensors very fast. The two best sensors are indeed synthesised ones, with the real sensors performing much worse. Note that there was no real data (x_t) for this sample. The real data was artificially created from *all 15 sensors* with a more complex function than simple average (first, artifacts where removed, then an average was taken). Thus, an average over simply two sensors, yet the best two sensors, outperforms any single one, and handles the artifacts in the data automatically. Figure 1(b) depicts the data of two random real sensors (to avoid cluttering the graph), the artificially created true data x_t and the best synthesised sensor.

To demonstrate the greedy and random selection algorithms, we used the same data. Table 1 includes the results. The entropy of the maximal triplet of

---

[1] For details, see http://db.csail.mit.edu/labdata/labdata.html.

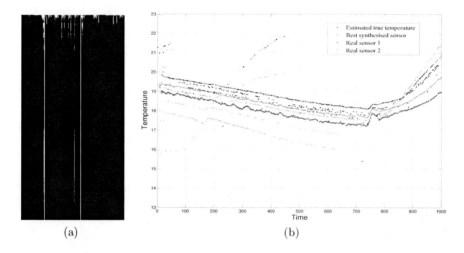

(a)   (b)

Fig. 1. (a) Weight vectors generated by OnlineFusion for 240 sensors - 15 real sensors and 225 synthesised ones. While at first (top row) all sensors have equal weight, as time evolves (downwards) some sensors gain reputation (white color), while others loose it exponentially fast (dark color). Very soon, the two best sensors are identified. (b) Real temperature data from the Intel Research Lab, Berkeley.

sensors can be compared to that of random selections of triplets. Note that since many sensors are spread in a relatively small aria, there are several triplets which include an amount of information very close to the maximal (for a triplet). To get a sense of how correlated sensors can be, the entropy of a minimal triplet (also achieved by a greedy algorithm) is also depicted.

We also demonstrate the random sensor selection algorithm on artificial data. To do this, we artificially created randomized data for 5 independent sensors, and used them to create 5 additional depend ones, which are a function of the original sensor. Sensors with even numbers are independent of each other, while sensors with odd number are linearly dependent on the even number sensors. Note that this is a very simplified model, which is included here only to demonstrate in practice the number of rounds the random selection algorithm requires in order to find an independent set. Furthermore, note that dependent sensors may still be independent of each other, depending on the other sensors in the group. For example, if P^1 and P^2 are independent bits (with entropy 1 each), and $P^3 = P^1 \oplus P^2$, then P^2 and P^3 are still independent, with joint entropy 2, while the three are dependent, with joint entropy 2 as well.

The algorithm then chose sets of 5 sensors at random. Entropy estimates of the 5 selected sensors are computed according to the joint first order probability estimate, that is, $H(T^n_{p^{j_1},\ldots,p^{j_5}})$, where $p^{j_1},\ldots,p^{j_5}$ is the data for the five selected sensors. It is easy to see from Table 2 that 5 independent sensors were drawn very fast, with 4 out of 20 trials succeeding.

Table 1. Entropy estimates for sensors from the Intel Research Lab, Berkeley

METHOD	SENSOR NUMBERS	ENTROPY ESTIMATE
MAX. TRIPLET	1, 2, 8	4.0732
RANDOM	15, 7, 2	2.9340
RANDOM	2, 4, 13	3.3720
RANDOM	10, 11, 6	3.4966
RANDOM	2, 10, 8	3.5630
RANDOM	5, 7, 1	3.7798
RANDOM	7, 9, 15	3.8290
RANDOM	1, 9, 14	3.8511
RANDOM	2, 9, 4	3.8528
RANDOM	11, 10, 1	3.8570
RANDOM	12, 7, 2	3.8730
MIN. TRIPLET	15, 5, 7	2.4758

Table 2. Entropy estimate results of 20 independent drawings of 5 out of 10 sensors

DRAW NUMBER	ENTROPY ESTIMATE	DRAW NUMBER	ENTROPY ESTIMATE
1	3.9938	11	3.9899
2	3.9938	12	2.9966
3	3.9938	13	4.9829
4	3.9915	14	3.9938
5	3.9938	15	3.9938
6	2.9970	16	4.9829
7	1.9976	17	4.9829
8	4.9829	18	2.9966
9	3.9895	19	2.9943
10	3.9938	20	3.9938

References

1. Berger, F., Gritzmann, P., de Vries, S.: Minimum cycle bases for network graphs. Algorithmica 40(1), 51–62 (2004)
2. Blanc, J.L., Schmidt, N., Bonnier, L., Pezard, L., Lesne, A.: Quantifying neural correlations using lempel-ziv complexity. In: Neurocomp (2008)
3. Cohen, A., Merhav, N., Weissman, T.: Scanning and sequential decision making for multi-dimensional data - part I: the noiseless case. IEEE Trans. Inform. Theory 53(9), 3001–3020 (2007)
4. Cover, T.M., Thomas, J.: Elements of information theory. Wiley (2006)
5. Hall, D.L., Llinas, J.: An introduction to multisensor data fusion. Proceedings of the IEEE 85(1), 6–23 (1997)
6. Jeon, B., Landgrebe, D.A.: Decision fusion approach for multitemporal classification. IEEE Transactions on Geoscience and Remote Sensing 37(3), 1227–1233 (1999)

7. Karger, D.R.: Random sampling in matroids, with applications to graph connectivity and minimum spanning trees. In: Proceedings of 34th Annual Symposium on Foundations of Computer Science, pp. 84–93. IEEE (1993)

8. Littlestone, N., Warmuth, M.K.: The weighted majority algorithm. Inform. Comput. 108, 212–261 (1994)

9. Merhav, N., Ordentlich, E., Seroussi, G., Weinberger, M.J.: On sequential strategies for loss functions with memory. IEEE Trans. Inform. Theory 48, 1947–1958 (2002)

10. Nemhauser, G.L., Wolsey, L.A.: Best algorithms for approximating the maximum of a submodular set function. Mathematics of Operations Research, 177–188 (1978)

11. Oxley, J.G.: Matroid Theory. Oxford Univ. Press, Oxford (1992)

12. Polikar, R., Parikh, D., Mandayam, S.: Multiple classifier systems for multisensor data fusion. In: Proceedings of the 2006 IEEE Sensors Applications Symposium, pp. 180–184 (2006)

13. Matúš, F.: Two constructions on limits of entropy functions. IEEE Trans. Inform. Theory 53(1), 320–330 (2007)

14. Sasiadek, J.Z.: Sensor fusion. Annual Reviews in Control 26(2), 203–228 (2002)

15. Savari, S.A.: Redundancy of the lempel-ziv incremental parsing rule. IEEE Transactions on Information Theory 43(1), 9–21 (1997)

16. Shamaiah, M., Banerjee, S., Vikalo, H.: Greedy sensor selection: Leveraging submodularity. In: 49th IEEE Conference on Decision and Control (CDC), pp. 2572–2577 (2010)

17. Slepian, D., Wolf, J.: Noiseless coding of correlated information sources. IEEE Trans. Inform. Theory 19(4), 471–480 (1973)

18. Vovk, V.G.: Aggregating strategies. In: Proc. 3rd Annu. Workshop Computational Learning Theory, San Mateo, CA, pp. 372–383 (1990)

19. Waltz, E.: Data fusion for c3i: A tutorial. In: Command, Control, Communications Intelligence (C3I) Handbook, pp. 217–226 (1986)

20. Yeung, R.W.: A First Course in Information Theory. Springer, Heidelberg (2002)

21. Yu, B., Sycara, K.: Learning the quality of sensor data in distributed decision fusion. In: 9th International Conference on Information Fusion, pp. 1–8. IEEE (2006)

22. Ziv, J., Lempel, A.: Compression of individual sequences via variable-rate coding. IEEE Trans. Inform. Theory IT-24, 530–536 (1978)

23. Zozor, S., Ravier, P., Buttelli, O.: On lempel-ziv complexity for multidimensional data analysis. Physica A: Statistical Mechanics and its Applications 345(1-2), 285–302 (2005)

Neighbor Discovery in a Sensor Network with Directional Antennae

Jingzhe Du[1,*], Evangelos Kranakis[1,**], Oscar Morales Ponce[1,*], and Sergio Rajsbaum[2,***]

[1] School of Computer Science, Carleton University
K1S 5B6, Ottawa, Ontario, Canada
[2] Instituto de Matemáticas, Universidad Nacional Autónoma de México,
Mexico City, Mexico

Abstract. Consider a network of n directional antennae in the plane. We consider the problem of efficient neighbor discovery in a (synchronous) network of sensors employing directional antennae. In this setting sensors send messages and listen for messages by directing their antennae towards a specific direction (which is not necessarily known in advance). In our model the directional antennae can be rotated by the sensors as required so as to discover all neighbors in their vicinity. In this paper we will limit ourselves to the (D, D) communication model whereby sensors employ directional antennae with identical transmission/reception beam widths. Our methodology is based on techniques for symmetry breaking so as to enable sender/receiver communication. We provide 1) deterministic algorithms that introduce delay in the rotation of the antennae and exploit knowledge of the existence of a vertex coloring of the network, and 2) randomized algorithms that require knowledge only of an upper bound on the size of the network so as to accomplish neighbor discovery. In both instances we study tradeoffs on the efficiency of the algorithms proposed.

Keywords and Phrases: Deterministic, Randomized algorithms, Neighbor discovery, Rotating directional antennae, Sensor network.

1 Introduction

Directional antennae are known to reduce energy consumption because they can reach further for the same amount of energy consumed. However, unlike sensors with omnidirectional antennae sensors with directional antennae take longer to discover their neighbors. This is due to the fact that although sensors may be within transmission range the sender (respectively, receiver) sensor may not necessarily be located within the given sector determined by the beaming antenna of the transmitting sensor. This raises the question of what algorithms to employ so as to attain efficient communication (e.g., routing, broadcasting, etc.) using only directional antennae. This approach can be particularly beneficial

* Research supported in part by NSERC.
** Research supported in part by NSERC and MITACS grants.
*** Research supported in part by Conacyt.

T. Erlebach et al. (Eds.): ALGOSENSORS 2011, LNCS 7111, pp. 57–71, 2012.
© Springer-Verlag Berlin Heidelberg 2012

in delay tolerant sensor networks, for example, whereby sensors may be able to take advantage of opportunistic appearances of sensors due to mobility and other factors.

For a given radius $r > 0$, assume that a given sensor, say S, can reach all other sensors within the disc having centre S and radius r. There are several directional antenna models, but for our study it will suffice to consider the following directional antenna model. We assume that either 1) the sensors are standing on a swivel and can rotate in any desired direction or 2) the sensors' coverage area can be divided into non-overlapping sectors that can be activated by an antenna switch so as to reach other sensors within a particular region. It is clear that in the former mode of operation the rotation of the antenna is continuous around the circle while in the latter the circular sectors are in discrete predefined sectors around the circle. We will not elaborate further in this paper the differences and similarities between these two modes of operation for directional antennae.

1.1   Preliminaries and Notation

In this subsection we discuss several related antenna models that are related to our study.

Communication Models with Directional Antennae. Several communication models are possible for a pair of sensors with omnidirectional and directional antennae. Consider the pair (X, Y), where the first parameter X indicates the capability of the sender sensor and the second parameter Y the capability of the receiver sensor. To be more precise, X, Y may take either of the values O, D, where O means omnidirectional and D directional antenna. Thus, the (X, Y) *communication model* for a pair of communicating sensors means that the sender uses antenna of type X and the receiver of type Y. We also assume a *duplex* communication model whereby sensors can send and receive messages at the same time ignoring collisions. It is clear from the previous discussion that

- in the (O, O) model two sensors can communicate if they are within transmission range of each other,
- in the (D, O) (respectively, (O, D)) model, the sender (respectively, receiver) must turn its antenna so as to reach its neighbor, and
- in the (D, D) model both sender and receiver must direct their antennae towards each other at the same time.

More specifically, in all four models the sensors must be within range of each other so as to communicate. However, in the (D, O) and (O, D) models the sensor with the directional antenna must also turn its antenna toward the other sensor, while in the (D, D) model both sensors' antennae must face against each other. Therefore it follows that (D, D) is the weakest and (O, O) is the strongest among the four communication models.

More general models are also possible whereby a sensor's transmission beam width is not necessarily the same with its reception beam width. To simplify notation and terminology, in this paper we will limit ourselves to the (D, D) communication model with identical transmission/reception beam widths. Our results generalize without much difficulty to this more general setting.

The *neighbor discovery* process usually entails the exchange of identities (e.g., MAC addresses) between two adjacent nodes. It will not be necessary to go into the details of such an exchange and for our purposes it will be sufficient to assume that this is a one step process whereby one sensor sends its identity and the other acknowledges by sending back its own. Throughout this paper we will assume that the sensors have distinct identities but their corresponding locations (i.e., (x, y)-coordinates) in the plane are not known to each other.

Antenna Models. The transmission area of an omnidirectional antennae is modelled by a circular disk in the plane while the transmission area of a directional antennae is modelled by a circular sector in the disk. We assume that sensors have the capability to rotate their directional antenna and change sectors. so as to establish communication.

Consider a set of n sensors in the plane. Each sensor u is equipped with a directional antenna having beam width ϕ_u. Further we will assume that $\phi_u = \frac{2\pi}{k_u}$, for some integer k_u.[1] In particular, if $k_u = 1$ then we have an omnidirectional antenna at u. The sensors are synchronous and can rotate their antennae counter-clockwise (see Figure 1). Assume that the UDG formed by the sensors

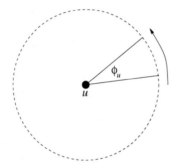

Fig. 1. An antenna at u rotating counter-clockwise

is connected and c-colorable, i.e., there is a coloring of its vertices $\chi : V \to \{0, 1, \ldots, c - 1\}$ such that if sensors u, v are adjacent in the UDG then u and v have different colors, i.e., $\chi(u) \neq \chi(v)$. Observe any "integer based" identity scheme, e.g., the n sensors are numbered $0, 1, 2, \ldots, n - 1$, that provides different numbering to different sensors satisfies this property (albeit it is not efficient).

1.2 Related Work

There are protocols using directional antennas in neighbor discovery processes. In [4], the authors proposed the gradual increase of directional communication range levels for neighbor discovery purposes. Nearby neighbors are discovered first and faraway neighbors will be discovered at later stages. Directional transmission and reception are used in this work. In [5], a direct discovery protocol and a gossip based neighbor discovery protocol using directional antennas in a

---

[1] It turns out that this assumption is not required for the subsequent results; we use it because it makes the proofs simpler.

static wireless network were proposed. During direct discovery process, a node discovers a neighbor node only when information is received from this neighbor, while nodes exchange their neighbors' location information to enable faster discovery in gossip based algorithm. The protocol tries to optimize the discovery probability in a randomized neighbor discovery process using directional transmission and reception. In [1], a neighbor discovery protocol which considers node movements was proposed where directions with less possibility of discovering new nodes will be bypassed during neighbor scanning and neighbor discovery frequency is adjusted according to node mobility. It uses directional antenna for transmissions and omnidirectional antenna for receptions. In [6], two Scan Based Algorithms (SBA-D, SBA-R) and one Completely Random Algorithm (CRA-DD) were proposed, which use only directional antennae. In SBA-D, a node decides whether to scan or listen depending on node ID, while a node transmits at one direction or receives at the opposite direction with probability $\frac{1}{2}$ in SBA-R. SBA-D and SBA-R algorithms require perfectly synchronized antenna rotation direction, time and instantaneous antenna rotation to any direction, which are very strong assumptions. In CRA-DD, at each time slot, nodes decide whether to transmit/receive and which direction to transmit/receive completely randomly, which is the simplest algorithm one can imagine and it also requires instantaneous antenna rotation to any direction. In [3], an analytical model was proposed for synchronized 2D neighbor discovery protocols. The model is based on directional transmission and directional reception and a node transmits in one direction and receives in the opposite direction simultaneously.

1.3   Outline and Results of the Paper

In this paper, we propose novel neighbor discovery algorithms in a (D, D) communication model whereby sensors employ directional antennae with identical transmission/reception beam widths and each sensor has only one directional antenna. Our methodology is based on techniques for symmetry breaking so as to enable sender/receiver communication. We provide 1) deterministic algorithms that introduce delay in the rotation of the antennae and exploit knowledge of the existence of a vertex coloring of the network, and 2) randomized algorithms that require knowledge only of an upper bound on the size of the network so as to accomplish neighbor discovery. In both instances we study tradeoffs on the efficiency of the algorithms proposed. Through experimentation, we also show that the algorithms achieve desirable neighbor discovery delays with efficiency in energy consumption. Details can be found in the full version of the paper [2].

The rest of the paper is organized as follows. Deterministic algorithms on neighbor discovery are presented in Section 2. As an alternative scenario, Section 3 gives out the randomized algorithm and its analysis. We conclude with possible future directions in Section 4.

2   Deterministic Algorithms for Neighbor Discovery

In this section we give algorithms for neighbor discovery in the (D, D) communication model and analyze their complexity. First we give a simple lower bound that indicates the complexity of the neighbor discovery problem.

In all the results below as measure of complexity for neighbor discovery we will use the time required for sensors to discover each other and we will ignore collisions during simultaneous transmissions. For two sensors, this is the number of steps until the first successful send/receive exchange. For a sensor network, this is the minimum for any algorithm taken over the maximum time required for any two adjacent sensors in the network to communicate.

2.1 Lower Bound

In a setting whereby two adjacent sensors know each other's location all they need to do is turn their antennae towards each other in the specified locations. Therefore the observation below is useful when sensors do not know each other's location.

Theorem 1. *Consider two sensors u, v within communication range of each other and respective antenna beam widths $\frac{2\pi}{k_u}$ and $\frac{2\pi}{k_v}$, respectively. If the sensors do not know each other's location then any algorithm for solving the neighbor discovery problem in the (D, D) communication model requires at least $\Omega(k_u k_v)$ time steps.*

Proof. For a successful communication to occur each sensor must be within the beam of the other sensor's antenna at the same time. Since the sensors do not know each other's location they must attempt transmissions in all their respective sectors. This completes the proof of Theorem 1.

2.2 Antenna Rotation Algorithms

Given these preliminary definitions we consider the following class of *antenna rotation* algorithms. For each sensor u, let d_u be an integer delay parameter and k_u be defined so that $\phi_u = \frac{2\pi}{k_u}$. Given u, d_u, k_u the sensor executes the following algorithm.

Algorithm 1. Antenna Rotation Algorithm $ARA(d_u, k_u)$

1 Start at a given orientation;
2 **while** *true* **do**
3   **for** $i \leftarrow 0$ to $d_u - 1$ **do**
        //For d_u steps stay in chosen sector
4   Send message to neighbor(s);
5   Listen for messages from neighbor(s) (if any);
6   Rotate antenna beam one sector counter-clockwise;
    //rotate by an angle equal to ϕ_u

Remarks and Observations on the *ARA* Algorithm. There are several issues concerning interpretations of the execution of the rotation algorithm which are worth discussing.

- In Step 1 the initial antenna orientation is selected. There are many consistent ways to define this but for simplicity in this paper it is taken to be the

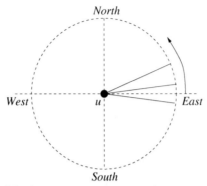

(a) An antenna at u with sectors counted counter-clockwise.

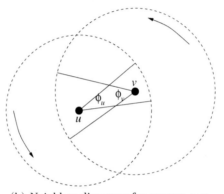

(b) Neighbor discovery for sensors u, v.

Fig. 2. Directional antennae

bisector of the angle which defines the antenna beam. Also, if the sensors are equipped with a compass then we may assume that they all start with identical orientations, say East (see Figure 2a). Otherwise, the initial orientation may be chosen in an arbitrary manner. It turns out that our analysis is valid in this more general setting.

- The main neighbor discovery algorithm is executed in Step 2. We are interested in measuring the number of steps until all (available) neighbors are discovered. For the duplex communication model being considered here, it is clear that two sensors u, v will be able to discover each other if (see Figure 2b)

  1. each sensor is within each other's range, and
  2. the corresponding antennae of the two sensors are oriented so that each sensor is within the other sensor's beam at the same time.

  These are the basic requirements we employ in order to prove the correctness and running time of our algorithm.

- In Step 3, the algorithm imposes a *rotation delay*, i.e., for d_u (equal to the delay imposed) steps the sensor sends messages and also listens for messages

from neighbors. The delay imposed in Step 3 is required so as to break symmetry and ensure that neighboring sensors' antennae are within each other's beam range and will eventually communicate using the (D, D) communication model. There are several possibilities here. The sensor may elect to send/receive messages 1) at each step during the delay interval $[0, d_u - 1]$, 2) select a time within the delay interval $[0, d_u - 1]$ at random. In our analysis we will assume the former.
- Step 6 involves rotation of the antenna by ϕ_u which is also equal to the beam width of the antenna. This ensures that after each rotation a new region (located counter-clockwise from the old region) is covered. Several possibilities exist, for example 1) allow overlap between the new and old antenna beaming location, 2) select the new antenna beaming location at a sector chosen at random among the k_u possible sectors in the disk.[2]

2.3   Complexity of Deterministic Antenna Orientation Algorithm

Now we consider the complexity of the various antenna orientation algorithms. Assume the sensor network is synchronous. Recall our basic assumption that there is a coloring $\chi : V \to \{0, 1, \ldots, c - 1\}$ of the vertices of the sensor network using c colors. Table 1 summarizes the results of this section.

Table 1. List of theorems and running times of deterministic algorithms

Antenna at u	Knowledge	Running Time	Theorems
$2\pi/k$	Identical	$O(k^{c-1})$	Theorem 2
$2\pi/k$	Identical	$O(k(c\ln c)^3)$	Theorem 3

The simplest possible delay model is for a sensor to wait "sufficient amount of time" so as to send to (receive from) the desired node.

However, there are choices of delay under which sensors with directional antennae will never be able to communicate as illustrated in Figure 3.

Example 1. Assume the antenna beam width is $\frac{2\pi}{4} = \frac{\pi}{2}$ and the four sectors are labelled $0, 1, 2, 3$. Both sensors depicted in Figure 3 start beaming East. Sensor u employs delay $d_u = 2$ and sensor v delay $d_v = 1$. Sensors can communicate only if u's antenna faces East and v's antenna faces West at the same time. Observe that sensor u faces East only at time $t = 0, 1, 8, 9, 16, 17, \ldots$ while sensor v faces West only when $t = 2, 6, 10, \ldots$. Therefore u, v can never communicate.

The previous example indicates that sensor delays must be chosen judiciously so as to enable communication. The first theorem considers the simplest model whereby a sensor delays the rotation of its antenna sufficient time so as to allow all its neighbors' antennae to perform a complete rotation.

---

[2] The point of these assumptions is to consider collision models. In this paper we assume that the sensors send/receive messages at each step during the delay interval. Further, if we were to analyze a collision model we would have to assume that the corresponding intervals of adjacent nodes are disjoint.

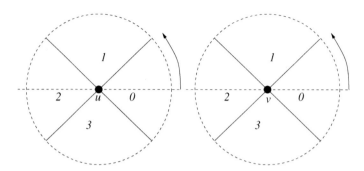

Fig. 3. Neighbor discovery for sensors u, v is not possible

Theorem 2. *Consider a set of sensors in the plane with identical antenna beam widths equal to $\phi = \frac{2\pi}{k}$. For each sensor u let the delay be defined by $d_u := k^{\chi(u)}$. If each sensor u executes algorithm $ARA(d_u, k)$ then every sensor in the network will discover all its neighbors in at most k^{c-1} time steps.*

Proof. Consider two adjacent sensors u, v. Clearly, $\chi(u) \neq \chi(v)$ since they must have different colors. By assumption, $d_u = k^{\chi(u)}$ and $d_v = k^{\chi(v)}$. Without loss of generality assume that $\chi(u) < \chi(v)$. Observe that for each chosen sector the sensor v beams its antenna in this sector for $k^{\chi(v)}$ steps. But $k^{\chi(v)} = k^{\chi(v)-\chi(u)}k^{\chi(u)}$ and hence $k^{\chi(v)}$ is a multiple of $k^{\chi(u)}$. In particular, while sensor v waits in a given sector the other sensor u will execute $k^{\chi(v)-\chi(u)}$ rotations around the circle before returning to its original sector. It follows that sensors u, v will discover each other within the specified number of steps. This completes the proof of Theorem 2.

The running time of the algorithm depends on the coloring being used in Theorem 2. If no knowledge on the network is available then any integer identity scheme will work, however this will typically be of size $\Omega(n)$ thus giving an exponential running time $k^{\Omega(n)}$. If the sensor network is bipartite (e.g., tree) then it is easy to see that $c = 2$ is sufficient. For random UDGs with range at the connectivity threshold the number of colors required is $c = \Theta(\log n)$ in which case the running time of the algorithm is about $k^{\log n} = n^{\log_2 k}$, which is polynomial in n with exponent $\log_2 k$ (In many applications a typical value of k is 6.)

Nevertheless we would be interested to provide algorithms with running time not dependent on the size n of the network but rather on the number of colors of a vertex coloring. Indeed, this is the case as shown by the next theorem.

Theorem 3. *Consider a set of sensors in the plane with identical antenna beam widths equal to $\phi = \frac{2\pi}{k}$. Assume the sensor network is synchronous. Suppose that the delays d_u at the nodes are chosen so that*

1. $\gcd(k, d_u) = 1$, and $d_u > k$, for all u, and
2. if u, v are adjacent then $\gcd(d_u, d_v) = 1$.

If each sensor u executes algorithm $ARA(d_u, k)$ then every sensor in the network will discover all its neighbors in at most $O\left(k(\max_u d_u)^3\right)$ time steps. In addition, the delays d_u can be chosen so that every sensor in the network will discover all its neighbors in at most $O(k(c \ln c)^3)$ time steps. In particular, this is at most $O\left((c \ln c)^3\right)$ time steps provided that $k \in O(1)$.

Proof. Without loss of generality, in the proofs below we assume that the sensors can determine a fixed starting antenna sector facing East, say (see Figure 2a). Proofs carry over to the more general case and the necessary modifications are omitted. Consider two adjacent sensors u, v. Without loss of generality assume that

1. sensor u is to the left of sensor v, and
2. that both antennae orientations are initially set to *East*, say.

First we consider the case when the line segment connecting u to v is horizontal. Observe that u, v can communicate when v's antenna is facing *West* which is sector $\lfloor \frac{k}{2} \rfloor$. Since $\gcd(d_u, d_v) = 1$, by Euclid's algorithm there exist integers $0 < a_u < d_u, 0 < a_v < d_v$ such that

$$a_u d_u = a_v d_v + 1. \tag{1}$$

Lets look at sensor u first. Recall that because of the delay constrains of the algorithm, the sensor stays in the same sector for d_u steps before it rotates its antenna. After $d_u k$ steps sensor u will be in its starting position and, clearly, the same applies for any time duration that is a multiple of $d_u k$. Thus sensor u is in its initial position (facing East) at time $j a_u d_u k$, for any $j > 0$. If we multiply both sides of Equation $a_u d_u = a_v d_v + 1$ by jk we have that

$$j a_u d_u k = j a_v d_v k + jk$$

It follows that at time $t = j a_u d_u k$ the sensor at u is facing *East*. If there is a j such that $jk = \lfloor \frac{k}{2} \rfloor d_v + r$ for $0 \le r < d_v$, then sensor v is facing West and therefore the sensors u, v can discover each other. Starting from $j = 1$, with $k \le \lfloor \frac{k}{2} \rfloor d_v$, we can find a j such that,

$$jk \le \lfloor \frac{k}{2} \rfloor d_v < jk + k \tag{2}$$

which means that $jk + k = \lfloor \frac{k}{2} \rfloor d_v + r$, with $r \le k < d_v$. A simple modification of the proof will prove the result when the two sensors are not necessarily on a horizontal line.

The number of rotations required is $j a_u d_u k$, where j satisfies Inequality (2). Since $j a_u d_u k \le k(\max_u d_u)^3$ it follows that $k(\max_u d_u)^3$ is an upper bound on the time required by all pairs of sensors to discover each other.

If $k \in O(1)$ (this is a reasonable assumption since in practice $k = 6$) then we can satisfy the conditions of Theorem 3 by choosing the d_us to be prime numbers. Since the number of colors is c, we will need c prime numbers (one for each color class of vertices of the graph). Hence by the prime number theorem the largest prime needed in order to define the delays $\{d_u : u \in V\}$ will be in the order of the c-th prime number, which is in $O(c \ln c)$. Therefore every sensor in the network will discover all its neighbors in at most $O\left((c \ln c)^3\right)$ time steps. This completes the proof of Theorem 3.   □

Theorem 3 can be improved further with only slight modifications in the proof even in the case where $\frac{2\pi}{\phi}$ is not necessarily an integer. To this end define $k := \lfloor \frac{2\pi}{\phi} \rfloor$. We can modify algorithm $ARA(d_u, k)$ to a new algorithm $ARA'(d_u, \phi)$ as follows: we still have k sectors and we can modify Step 6 in algorithm $ARA(d_u, k)$ so that the antenna at u rotates along the corresponding sectors $0, 1, \ldots, k-1$ (thus there is overlap between the new and the old sector). It is easy to prove the following generalization of Theorem 3.

Theorem 4. *Consider a set of sensors in the plane such that the antenna beam width of sensor u is equal to ϕ. Define $k := \lfloor \frac{2\pi}{\phi} \rfloor$ Assume the sensor network is synchronous. Suppose that the delays d_u at the nodes are chosen so that*

1. *$gcd(d_u, k) = 1$ and $d_u > k$, for all u, and*
2. *if u, v are adjacent then $\gcd(d_u, d_v) = 1$.*

If each sensor u executes algorithm $ARA'(d_u, \phi)$ then every sensor in the network will discover all its neighbors in at most $k \left(\max_u d_u\right)^3$ time steps. In addition, the delays d_u can be chosen so that every sensor in the network will discover all its neighbors in at most $O(k(c \ln c)^3)$ time steps. In particular, this is at most $O\left((c \ln c)^3\right)$ time steps provided that $k \in O(1)$.

Proof. With some simple modifications, this is identical to the proof of Theorem 3. Details are left to the reader.

Observe that for a random UDG at the connectivity threshold we have that $c = \Theta(\ln n)$ and therefore the running time of the algorithms in Theorems 3 and 4 will be $O((\ln n \ln \ln n)^3)$.

3   Randomized Neighbor Discovery Algorithms

In this section we consider several randomized algorithms. The main advantage of the algorithms in Theorems 5 and 6 is that no a priori knowledge of coloring or of any proper identity scheme is required; just an upper bound n on the size of the network. Moreover, the algorithm in Theorem 7 requires only a bound on the antennae beam widths. Table 2 summarizes the results of this section.

Table 2. List of theorems and running times of randomized algorithms

Antenna at u	Knowledge	Running Time	Theorems
$2\pi/k$	Identical	$kn^{O(1)}$	Theorem 5
$2\pi/k$	Identical	$O(k^2 \log n)$	Theorem 6
$2\pi/k_u$	$\max_u k_u \leq k$	$O(k^4 \log n)$	Theorem 7

3.1   Deterministic Algorithm with Selection of Random Delay

In this algorithm each sensor u selects a random prime number as delay d_u (in a range $k..R$ to be specified) and runs the deterministic algorithm $ARA(d_u, k)$.

Algorithm 2. Randomized Antenna Rotation Algorithm $RARA(d_u, k)$

1 Select $d_u \leftarrow RANDOMPRIME(k..R)$;
2 Execute $ARA(d_u, k)$;

Theorem 5. *Consider a set of sensors in the plane such that the antenna beam width of sensor u is equal to $\phi = \frac{2\pi}{k}$. Assume the sensor network is synchronous. If each sensor u executes algorithm $RARA(k; R)$, where $R = n^{O(1)}$ and n is an upper bound on the number of sensors, then every sensor in the network will discover all its neighbors in at most $kn^{O(1)}$ expected time steps, with high probability.*

Proof. For every node u, let $N(u)$ denote the neighborhood of u and $\deg(u)$ the degree of u. Further, let $D = \max_u \deg(u)$ denote the maximum degree of a node of the sensor network. By the prime number theorem, the number of primes $\leq R$ and $> k$ is approximately equal to $\frac{R}{\ln R} - \frac{k}{\ln k}$ and therefore the probability that the primes chosen by two adjacent nodes, say u and v, are different is $1 - \frac{1}{\frac{R}{\ln R} - \frac{k}{\ln k}}$.

Let E_u be the event that the prime chosen at u is different from all the primes chosen by its neighbors. It is easily seen that

$$
\begin{aligned}
\Pr[E_u] &= 1 - \Pr[\neg E_u] \\
&= 1 - \Pr\left[\exists v \in N(u)(d_u = d_v)\right] \\
&\geq 1 - \sum_{v \in N(u)} \Pr\left[d_u = d_v\right] \\
&\approx 1 - \deg(u)\frac{1}{\frac{R}{\ln R} - \frac{k}{\ln k}} \\
&\geq 1 - D\frac{1}{\frac{R}{\ln R} - \frac{k}{\ln k}}.
\end{aligned}
$$

Similarly, we can prove that

$$
\begin{aligned}
\Pr\left[\bigcap_u E_u\right] &= 1 - \Pr\left[\bigcup_u \neg E_u\right] \\
&\geq 1 - \sum_u \Pr[\neg E_u] \\
&\geq 1 - nD\frac{1}{\frac{R}{\ln R} - \frac{k}{\ln k}} \\
&\geq 1 - \frac{1}{n}.
\end{aligned}
$$

By choosing R in $n^{O(1)}$ and recalling that $D \leq n$ we see that all the primes chosen by all the nodes in the network are pairwise distinct, with high probability. The claim concerning the expected number of time steps follows immediately from the analysis of the antenna rotation algorithm in Theorem 3. This completes the proof of Theorem 5.

3.2   Algorithm with Random Selection of Rotation Mechanism

In the algorithms below we assume that the antenna beam width of u is equal to $\frac{2\pi}{k}$. In the main algorithm a sensor chooses a "rotation mechanism" between two given rotation mechanisms independently at random. In the first mechanism, the antenna cycles k rounds with no sector delay, while in the second the antenna cycles only one round but with delay k per sector. The two rotation mechanisms can be described formally as follows.

Algorithm 3. Rotate with no Sector Delay $Mech_0(k, d)$

```
//Cycle k rounds with no sector delay
```
1 **for** $j \leftarrow 1$ **to** d **do**
2   **for** $i \leftarrow 0$ **to** $k - 1$ **do**
3   Send message to neighbor(s) in sector i;
4   Listen for messages from neighbor(s) (if any) in sector i;
5   Rotate antenna one sector;

Algorithm 4. Rotate with Delay k per Sector $Mech_1(k, d)$

```
//Cycle one round with delay k per sector
```
1 **for** $i \leftarrow 0$ **to** $k - 1$ **do**
2   **for** $j \leftarrow 0$ **to** d **do**
3   Send message to neighbor(s) in sector i;
4   Listen for messages from neighbor(s) (if any) in sector i;
5   Rotate antenna one sector;

Algorithm 5. Random Selection Rotation Mechanism Algorithm $RSRMA(k)$

```
//Choose rotation mechanism at random.
```
1 Select $bit \leftarrow RANDOM(\{0, 1\})$;
2 **if** $bit = 0$ **then** Execute $Mech_0(k, k)$;
3 **if** $bit = 1$ **then** Execute $Mech_1(k, k)$;

Thus algorithm $RSRMA(u, k)$ selects the rotation mechanism at random. We can prove the following theorem.

Theorem 6. *Consider a set of n sensors in the plane with identical antenna beam width equal to $\phi = \frac{2\pi}{k}$. Assume the sensor network is synchronous. If each sensor u executes algorithm $RSRMA(u; k)$ for $O(\log n)$ times then every sensor in the network will discover all its neighbors in at most $O(k^2 \log n)$ expected time steps, with high probability.*

Proof. The proof of correctness is not difficult. The sensor flips a coin. If the outcome is $bit = 0$ (Step 2) then it rotates the antenna k rounds around the circle; in each round it rotates the antenna with no delay and sends messages and listens for messages. However, if the outcome is $bit = 1$ (Step 3) then it rotates the antenna once around the circle; in each sector it sends messages and listens for messages k times and then rotates the antenna one sector. Now consider two sensors u, v within range of each other and assume, without loss of generality, that u is to the left of v (The same proof will work regardless of the direction of the line segment uv connecting u to v). Both sensors start beaming *East*. We know that a necessary and sufficient condition to establish communication is for u's antenna to beam *East* and v's antenna to beam *West* at the same time. If both sensors' coin-flips give the same bit then the sensors will select the same rotation mechanism and their antennae will not face "against" each other. However, if their coin-flips give different bits then it is clear that their corresponding antennae will face *East* and *West*, respectively, at the same time.

Let $m = 3 \log n$ and suppose that all sensors run algorithm $RSRMA(k)$ for m times. The only case that two adjacent sensors u, v cannot communicate in m steps is that the coin flips yield identical outcomes m times. In particular we have two random binary strings of length m each one drawn from u and another from v. The probability that the strings are identical is equal to $2^{-m} = n^{-3}$ since $m = 3 \log n$.

Finally, we can prove the main result of the theorem. Let $E_{u,v}$ denote the event that sensors u, v can communicate (at some time). Consequently, from the discussion above we conclude that

$$\Pr[\neg E_{u,v}] \leq n^{-3}, \text{ for any pair } u, v \text{ of sensors.} \tag{3}$$

Therefore we obtain that the probability that any two adjacent sensors communicate is at least

$$\begin{aligned}
\Pr[\forall u, v E_{u,v}] &= 1 - \Pr[\neg(\forall u, v E_{u,v})] \\
&= 1 - \Pr[\exists u, v \neg E_{u,v}] \\
&= 1 - \Pr\left[\bigcup_{u,v} \neg E_{u,v}\right] \\
&\geq 1 - \sum_{u,v} \Pr[\neg E_{u,v}] \\
&\geq 1 - n^2 \frac{1}{n^3} \\
&= 1 - \frac{1}{n}.
\end{aligned}$$

This proves our assertion and completes the proof of Theorem 6.

3.3 Algorithm If Bound on Antenna Beam Widths Is Known

We now indicate how to extend Theorem 6 to the case of sensors with arbitrary antenna beam widths. First of all, we modify the rotation mechanisms by introducing the delay as a parameter.

Following the proof of Theorem 6, observe that if two adjacent sensors u, v execute the following algorithm for $m = 3 \ln n$ times then they will discover each other with high probability.

Algorithm 6. Random Selection Rotation Mechanism Algorithm $RSRMA'(k_u, d)$

```
//Choose rotation mechanism at random
```
1 Select $bit \leftarrow RANDOM(\{0, 1\})$;
2 **if** $bit = 0$ **then**   Execute $Mech_0(k_u, d)$;
3 **if** $bit = 1$ **then**   Execute $Mech_1(k_u, d)$;

This idea is for each sensor to use the neighbor sensor's antenna beam width to determine an appropriate delay. However, this will not work because sensor u (respectively, v) does not necessarily know the beam width of v's (respectively, u's) antenna. However, this difficulty is easy to resolve if an upper bound, say k, on $\max\{k_u, k_v\}$ is known by both u and v. Namely, sensor u executes algorithm $RSRMA'(k'_u, k'_v)$ and sensor v executes algorithm $RSRMA'(k'_v, k'_u)$, for all pairs (k'_u, k'_v) such $k'_u, k'_v \leq k$. To maintain synchronicity all k^2 pairs of algorithms are executed in the same lexicographic order by all pairs of sensors each algorithm for $m = 3\ln n$ times. Clearly, the running time of the algorithm is $O(k^4 \log n)$ with high probability.

Putting these ideas together and repeating the proof of Theorem 6 it is easy to prove the following theorem.

Theorem 7. *Consider a set of n sensors in the plane such that sensor u has antenna beam width equal to $\phi_u = \frac{2\pi}{k_u}$. Assume the sensor network is synchronous and that an upper bound k is known to all sensors so that $\max_u k_u \leq k$. If each sensor u executes algorithm $RSRMA'(a, b)$, for each pair (a, b), with $a, b \leq k$, for $O(\log n)$ times then every sensor in the network will discover all its neighbors in at most $O(k^4 \log n)$ expected time steps, with high probability.* □

4   Conclusion and Open Problems

An interesting class of problems arises in considering the efficiency of broadcasting in the single channel UDG model, i.e., if first there is a single send/receive channel and multiple transmissions on the same node produce packet collisions, and second a link between two sensors u, v exists if and only if $d(u, v) \leq 1$. In general, broadcasting with omnidirectional antennae requires scheduling of transmissions (typically using *group testing* techniques) so as to avoid collisions. Clearly, if broadcasting time with omnidirectional antennae without collisions is B then the result of Theorem 3 indicates that broadcasting in the directional antennae model can be accomplished in time $O(B(c \ln c)^3)$, where c is the number of colors of a vertex coloring of the sensor network. The main question arising is whether we can improve on this time bound when using directional antennae.

References

1. An, X., Hekmat, R.: Self-adaptive neighbor discovery in ad hoc networks with directional antennas. In: 16th IST Mobile and Wireless Communications Summit, pp. 1–5. IEEE (2007)

2. Du, J., Kranakis, E., Morales, O., Rajsbaum, S.: Neighbor Discovery in a Sensor Network with Directional Antennae (2011), http://www.scs.carleton.ca/~jdu3/algorithm/algosensors11.pdf (accessed October 5, 2011)
3. Park, J.S., Cho, S.W., Sanadidi, M.Y., Gerla, M.: An analytical framework for neighbor discovery strategies in ad hoc networks with sectorized antennas. IEEE Communications Letters 13(11), 832–834 (2009)
4. Pei, G., Albuquerque, M.A., Kim, J.H., Nast, D.P., Norris, P.R.: A neighbor discovery protocol for directional antenna networks. In: IEEE Military Communications Conference, MILCOM 2005, pp. 487–492. IEEE (2006)
5. Vasudevan, S., Kurose, J., Towsley, D.: On neighbor discovery in wireless networks with directional antennas. In: INFOCOM 2005. 24th Annual Joint Conference of the IEEE Computer and Communications Societies. Proceedings IEEE, vol. 4, pp. 2502–2512. IEEE (2005)
6. Zhang, Z., Li, B.: Neighbor discovery in mobile ad hoc self-configuring networks with directional antennas: algorithms and comparisons. IEEE Transactions on Wireless Communications 7(5), 1540–1549 (2008)

LiMoSense – Live Monitoring
in Dynamic Sensor Networks

Ittay Eyal, Idit Keidar, and Raphael Rom

Department of Electrical Engineering,
Technion — Israel Institute of Technology
{ittay@tx,idish@ee,rom@ee}.technion.ac.il

Abstract. We present LiMoSense, a fault-tolerant live monitoring algorithm for dynamic sensor networks. This is the first asynchronous robust average aggregation algorithm that performs live monitoring, i.e., it constantly obtains a timely and accurate picture of dynamically changing data. LiMoSense uses gossip to dynamically track and aggregate a large collection of ever-changing sensor reads. It overcomes message loss, node failures and recoveries, and dynamic network topology changes. We formally prove the correctness of LiMoSense; we use simulations to illustrate its ability to quickly react to changes of both the network topology and the sensor reads, and to provide accurate information.

1 Introduction

To perform monitoring of large environments, we can expect to see in years to come sensor networks with thousands of light-weight nodes monitoring conditions like seismic activity, humidity or temperature [2,14]. Each of these nodes is comprised of a sensor, a wireless communication module to connect with close-by nodes, a processing unit and some storage. The nature of these widely spread networks prohibits a centralized solution in which the raw monitored data is accumulated at a single location. Specifically, all sensors cannot directly communicate with a central unit. Fortunately, often the raw data is not necessary. Rather, an *aggregate* that can be computed *inside the network*, such as the sum or average of sensor reads, is of interest. For example, when measuring rainfall, one is interested only in the total amount of rain, and not in the individual reads at each of the sensors. Similarly, one may be interested in the average humidity or temperature rather than minor local irregularities.

In dynamic settings, it is particularly important to perform *live monitoring*, i.e., to constantly obtain a timely and accurate picture of the ever-changing data. However, most previous solutions have focused on a static (single-shot) version of the problem, where the average of a single input-set is calculated [10,4,12,11]. Though it is in principle possible to perform live monitoring using multiple iterations of such algorithms, this approach is not adequate, due to the inherent tradeoff it induces between accuracy and speed of detection. For further details on previous work, see Section 2. In this paper we tackle the problem of live

T. Erlebach et al. (Eds.): ALGOSENSORS 2011, LNCS 7111, pp. 72–85, 2012.

monitoring in a dynamic sensor network. This problem is particularly challenging due to the dynamic nature of sensor networks, where nodes may fail and may be added on the fly (churn), and the network topology may change due to battery decay or weather change. The formal model and problem definition appear in Section 3.

In Section 4 we present our new **Li**ve **Mo**nitoring for **Sens**or networks algorithm, LiMoSense. Our algorithm computes the average over a dynamically changing collection of sensor reads. The algorithm has each node calculate an estimate of the average, which continuously converges to the current average. The space complexity at each node is linear in the number of its neighbors, and message complexity is that of the sensed values plus a constant. At its core, LiMoSense employs gossip-based aggregation [10,12], with a new approach to accommodate data changes while the aggregation is on-going. This is tricky, because when a sensor read changes, its old value should be removed from the system after it has propagated to other nodes. LiMoSense further employs a new technique to accommodate message loss, failures, and dynamic network behavior in asynchronous settings. This is again difficult, since a node cannot know whether a previous message it had sent over a faulty link has arrived or not.

In Section 5, we review the correctness proof of the algorithm, showing that once the network stabilizes, in the sense that no more value or topology changes occur, LiMoSense eventually converges to the correct average, despite message loss. The complete analysis can be found in the technical report [5].

We evaluate the algorithm's behavior in general (unstable) settings in Section 6. As convergence time is inherently unbounded in asynchronous systems, we analyze convergence time in a *synchronous uniform* run, where all nodes take steps at the same average frequency. We show that in such runs, once the system stabilizes, the estimates nodes have of the desired value converge exponentially fast (i.e., in logarithmic time). Furthermore, to demonstrate the effectiveness of LiMoSense in various dynamic scenarios, we present results of extensive simulations, showing its quick reaction to dynamic data read changes and fault tolerance. In order to preserve energy, communication rates may be decreased, and nodes may switch to sleep mode for limited periods. These issues are outside the scope of this work.

In summary, this paper makes the following contributions: (1) It presents LiMoSense, a live monitoring algorithm for highly dynamic and error-prone environments. (2) It proves correctness of the algorithm, namely robustness and eventual convergence. (3) It shows, through analysis and simulation, that LiMoSense converges exponentially fast and demonstrates its efficiency and fault-tolerance in dynamic scenarios.

2   Related Work

To gather information in a sensor network, one typically relies on in-network *aggregation* of sensor reads. The vast majority of the literature on aggregation has focused on obtaining a *single* summary of sensed data, assuming these reads do not change while the aggregation protocol is running [11,10,4,12]. The only exception we are aware of is work on aggregation with dynamic inputs by Birk et al. [3]; however, this solution is limited to unrealistic settings, namely a static topology with reliable communication links, failure freedom, and synchronous operation.

For obtaining a single aggregate, two main approaches were employed. The first is hierarchical gathering to a single base station [11]. The hierarchical method incurs considerable resource waste for tree maintenance, and results in aggregation errors in dynamic environments, as shown in [7].

The second approach is gossip-based aggregation at all nodes. To avoid counting the same data multiple times, Nath et al. [13] employ order and duplicate insensitive (ODI) functions to aggregate inputs in the face of message loss and a dynamic topology. However, these functions do not support dynamic inputs or node failures. Moreover, due to the nature of the ODI functions used, the algorithms' accuracy is inherently limited – they do not converge to an accurate value [6].

An alternative approach to gossip-based aggregation is presented by Kempe et al. [10]. They introduce Push-Sum, an aggregation algorithm, and show that it converges exponentially fast in fully connected networks where nodes operate in lock-step. Shah et al. analyze this algorithm in an arbitrary topology [4]. Jelasity et al. periodically restart the push-sum algorithm to handle dynamic settings, trading off accuracy and bandwidth. Although these algorithms do not deal with dynamic inputs and topology as we do, we borrow some techniques from them. In particular, our algorithm is inspired by the Push-Sum construct, and operates in a similar manner in static settings. We analyze its convergence speed when the nodes operate independently. Jesus et al. [9,1] also solve aggregation in dynamic settings, overcoming message loss, dynamic topology and churn. However, they consider synchronous settings, and they do not prove correctness nor analyze the behaviour of their algorithm with dynamic inputs.

Note that aggregation in sensor networks is distinct from other aggregation problems, such as stream aggregation, where the data in a sliding window is summarized. In the latter, a single system component has the entire data, and the distributed aspects do not exist.

3   Model and Problem Definition

3.1   Model

The system is comprised of a dynamic set of nodes (sensors), partially connected by dynamic undirected communication links. Two nodes connected by a link are called *neighbors*, and they can send messages to each other. These messages either arrive at some later time, or are lost. Messages that are not lost on each link arrive in FIFO order. Links do not generate or duplicate messages.

The system is asynchronous and progresses in steps, where in each step an event happens and the appropriate node is notified, or a node acts spontaneously. In a step, a node may change its internal state and send messages to its neighbors.

Nodes can be dynamically added to the system, and may fail or be removed from the system. The set of nodes at time t is denoted $\mathcal{N}_t$. The *system state* at time t consists of the internal states of all nodes in $\mathcal{N}_t$, and the links among them. When a node is added (init event), it is notified, and its internal state becomes a part of the system state. When it is removed (remove event), it is not allowed to perform any action, and its internal state is removed from the system state.

Each sensor has a time varying *data read* in $\mathbb{R}$. A node's initial data read is provided as a parameter when it is notified of its init event. This value may later change (change event) and the node is notified with the newly read value. For a node i in $\mathcal{N}_i$, we denote[1] by r_i^t, the latest data read provided by an init or change event at that node before time t.

Communication links may be added or removed from the system. A node is notified of link addition (addNeighbor event) and removal (removeNeighbor event), given the identity of the link that was added/removed. We call these *topology events*. For convenience of presentation, we assume that initially, nodes have no links, and they are notified of their neighbors by a series of addNeighbor events. We say that a link (i, j) is *up* at step t if by step t, both nodes i and j had received an appropriate addNeighbor notification and no later removeNeighbor notification. Note that a link (i, j) may be "half up" in the sense that the node i was notified of its addition but node j was not, or if node j had failed.

A node may send messages on a link only if the last message it had received regarding the state of the link is addNeighbor. If this is the case, the node may also receive a message on the link (receive event).

Global Stabilization Time. In every run, there exists a time called *global stabilization time*, GST, from which onward the following properties hold: (1) The system is *static*, i.e., there are no change, init, remove, addNeighbor or removeNeighbor events. (2) If the latest topology event a node $i \in \mathcal{N}_{\text{GST}}$ has received for another node j is addNeighbor, then node j is alive, and the latest topology event j has received for i is also addNeighbor (i.e. there are no "half up" links). (3) The network is connected. (4) If a link is up after GST, and infinitely many messages are sent on it, then infinitely many of them arrive.

3.2 The Live Average Monitoring Problem

We define the *read average* of the system at time t as $R^t \triangleq \frac{1}{|\mathcal{N}_t|} \sum_{i \in \mathcal{N}_t} r_i^t$. Note that the read average does not change after GST. Our goal is to have all nodes

---

[1] For any variable, the node it belongs to is written in subscript and, when relevant, the time is written in superscript.

estimate the read average after GST. More formally, an algorithm solving the *Live Average Monitoring Problem* gets time-varying data reads as its inputs, and has nodes continuously output their *estimates* of the average, such that at every node in $\mathcal{N}_{\mathrm{GST}}$, the output estimate converges to the read average after GST.

Metrics. We evaluate live average monitoring algorithms using the following metrics: (1) *Mean square error, MSE,* which is the mean of the squares of the distances between the node estimates and the read average; and (2) ε-*inaccuracy,* which is the percentage of nodes whose estimate is off by more than ε.

4   The LiMoSense Algorithm

In Section 4.1 we describe a simplified version of the algorithm for dynamic inputs but static topology and no failures. Then, in Section 4.2, we describe the complete robust algorithm.

4.1   Failure-Free Algorithm

We begin by describing a version of the algorithm that handles dynamically changing inputs, but assumes no message loss, and no link or node failures. This algorithm is shown in Algorithm 1.

The base of the algorithm operates like Push-Sum[10,4]: Each node maintains a weighted estimate of the read average (a pair containing the estimate and a weight), which is updated as a result of the node's communication with its neighbors. As the algorithm progresses, the estimate converges to the read average.

A node whose read value changes must notify the other nodes. It needs not only to introduce the new value, but also to undo the effect of its previous read value, which by now has partially propagated through the network.

The algorithm often requires nodes to merge two weighted values into one. They do so using the *weighted value sum* operation, which we define below and concisely denote by $\oplus$. Subtraction operations will be used later, they are denoted by $\ominus$ and are defined below.

$$\langle v_a, w_a \rangle \oplus \langle v_b, w_b \rangle \overset{\Delta}{=} \langle \frac{v_a w_a + v_b w_b}{w_a + w_b}, w_a + w_b \rangle . \tag{1}$$

$$\langle v_a, w_a \rangle \ominus \langle v_b, w_b \rangle \overset{\Delta}{=} \langle v_a, w_a \rangle \oplus \langle v_b, -w_b \rangle . \tag{2}$$

The state of a node (lines 2–3)consists of a weighted value, $\langle est_i, w_i \rangle$, where est_i is an output variable holding the node's estimate of the read average, and the value $prevRead_i$ of the latest data read. We assume at this stage that each node knows its static set of neighbors. We shall remove this assumption later, in the robust LiMoSense algorithm.

Algorithm 1. Failure Free

---

1 **state**
2    $\langle est_i, w_i \rangle \in \mathbb{R}^2$
3    $prevRead_i \in \mathbb{R}$

4 **on** $\mathrm{init}_i(initVal)$
5    $\langle est_i, w_i \rangle \leftarrow \langle initVal, 1 \rangle$
6    $prevRead_i \leftarrow initVal$

7 **on** $\mathrm{receive}_i(\langle v_{\mathrm{in}}, w_{\mathrm{in}} \rangle)$ from j
8    $\langle est_i, w_i \rangle \leftarrow \langle est_i, w_i \rangle \oplus \langle v_{\mathrm{in}}, w_{\mathrm{in}} \rangle$

9 **periodically send**$_i()$
10   Choose a neighbor j uniformly at random.
11    $w_i \leftarrow w_i/2$
12   send $(\langle est_i, w_i \rangle)$ to j

13 **on change**$_i(newRead)$
14    $est_i \leftarrow est_i + \frac{1}{w_i} \cdot (newRead - prevRead_i)$
15    $prevRead_i \leftarrow newRead$

Node i initializes its state on its `init` event. The data read is initialized to the given value *initVal*, and the estimate is $\langle initVal, 1 \rangle$ (lines 5–6).

The algorithm is implemented with the functions `receive` and `change`, which are called in response to events, and the function `send`, which is called periodically.

Periodically, a node i shares its estimate with a neighbor j chosen uniformly at random (line 10). It transfers half of its estimate to node j by halving the weight w_i of its locally stored estimate and sending the same weighted value to that neighbor (lines 11-12). When the neighbor receives the message, it merges the accepted weighted value with its own (line 8).

Correctness of the algorithm in static settings follows from two key observations. First, *safety* of the algorithm is preserved, because the system-wide weighted average over all weighted-value estimate pairs at all nodes and all communication links is always the correct read average; this invariant is preserved by send and receive operations. Thus, no information is "lost". Second, the algorithm's *convergence* follows from the fact that when a nodes merges its estimate with that received from a neighbor, the result is closer to the read average.

We proceed to discuss the dynamic operation of the algorithm. When a node's data read changes, the read average changes, and so the estimate should change as well. Let us denote the previous read of node i by r_i^{t-1} and the new read at step t by r_i^t. In essence, the new read, r_i^t, should be added to the system-wide estimate with weight 1, while the old read, r_i^{t-1}, ought to be deducted from it, also with weight 1. But since the old value has been distributed to an unknown set of nodes, we cannot simply "recall" it. Instead, we make the appropriate adjustment locally, allowing the natural flow of the algorithm to propagate it.

We now explain how we compute the local adjustment. The system-wide estimate should move by the difference between the read values, factored by the relative influence of a single sensor, i.e., $1/n$. To achieve this, we could shift a weight of 1 by $r_i^t - r_i^{t-1}$. Alternatively, we can shift a weight of w by this difference factored by $1/w$. Therefore, in response to a `change` event at time t, if the node's estimate before the change was est_i^{t-1} and its weight was w_i^{t-1}, then the estimate is updated to (lines 14-15)

$$est_i^t = est_i^{t-1} + (r_i^t - r_i^{t-1})/w_i^{t-1} \ .$$

Algorithm 2. LiMoSense

---

1 **state**
2     $\langle est_i, w_i \rangle \in \mathbb{R}^2$
3     $prevRead_i \in \mathbb{R}$
4     $neighbors_i \subset \mathbb{N}$
5     $sent_i : n \to (\mathbb{R}^2 \times \mathbb{R}^2) \cup \bot$
6     $received_i : n \to (\mathbb{R}^2 \times \mathbb{R}^2) \cup \bot$

7 **on** init$_i$($initVal$)
8     $\langle est_i, w_i \rangle \leftarrow \langle initVal, 1 \rangle$
9     $prevRead_i \leftarrow initVal$
10    $neighbors_i \leftarrow \emptyset$
11    $\forall j : sent_i(j) = \bot$
12    $\forall j : received_i(j) = \bot$

13 **function** pushSend$_i$($sendVal$)
14    $\langle est_i, w_i \rangle \leftarrow \langle est_i, w_i \rangle \ominus sendVal$
15    $sent_i(j) \leftarrow sent_i(j) \oplus sendVal$
16   send $(sent_i(j), \text{PUSH})$, to j

17 **periodically** send$_i$()
18   **if** $w_i < 2q$ **then** return   (weight min.)
19   Choose a neighbor j uniformly at random.
20    $type \leftarrow$ choose at random from $\{\text{PUSH}, \text{PULL}\}$
21   **if** $type = \text{PUSH}$ **then**
22   pushSend($\langle est_i, w_i/2 \rangle$)
23   **else**   ($type = \text{PULL}$)
24   send $(\langle est_i, w_i/2 \rangle, \text{PULL})$ to j

25 **on** receive$_i$($\langle v_{\text{in}}, w_{\text{in}} \rangle, type$) from j
26   **if** $type = \text{PUSH}$ **then**
27        $diff \leftarrow \langle v_{\text{in}}, w_{\text{in}} \rangle \ominus received_i(j)$
28        $\langle est_i, w_i \rangle \leftarrow \langle est_i, w_i \rangle \oplus diff$
29        $received_i(j) \leftarrow \langle v_{\text{in}}, w_{\text{in}} \rangle$
30   **else**   ($type = \text{PULL}$)
31   pushSend($\langle v_{\text{in}}, -w_{\text{in}} \rangle$)

32 **on** change$_i$(r_{new})
33    $est_i \leftarrow est_i + \frac{1}{w_i} \cdot (r_{\text{new}} - prevRead_i)$
34    $prevRead_i \leftarrow r_{\text{new}}$

35 **on** addNeighbor$_i$(j)
36    $neighbors_i \leftarrow neighbors_i \cup \{j\}$
37    $sent_i(j) \leftarrow \langle 0, 0 \rangle$
38    $received_i(j) \leftarrow \langle 0, 0 \rangle$

39 **on** removeNeighbor$_i$(j)
40    $\langle est_i, w_i \rangle \leftarrow \langle est_i, w_i \rangle \oplus sent_i(j) \ominus received_i(j)$
41    $neighbors_i \leftarrow neighbors_i \setminus \{j\}$
42    $sent_i(j) \leftarrow \bot$
43    $received_i(j) \leftarrow \bot$

4.2   Adding Robustness

Overcoming failures is challenging in an asynchronous system, where a node cannot determine whether a message it has sent was successfully received. In order to overcome message loss and link and node failure, each node maintains a summary of its conversations with its neighbors. Nodes interact by sending and receiving these summaries, rather than the weighted values they have sent in the failure-free algorithm. The data in each message subsumes all previous value exchanges on the same link. Thus, if a message is lost, the lost data is recovered once an ensuing message arrives. When a link fails, the nodes at both of its ends use the summaries to retroactively cancel the effect of all the messages transferred over it. A node failure is treated as the failure of all its links. There is a rich literature dealing with the means of detecting failures, usually with timeouts. This subject is outside the scope of this work.

Implementing the summary approach naïvely would cause summary sizes to increase unboundedly as the algorithm progresses. To avoid that, we devised a hybrid approach of push and pull gossip that negates this effect without resorting to synchronization assumptions.

The full LiMoSense algorithm, shown as Algorithm 2, is based on the failure-free algorithm. In addition to the state information of the failure-free algorithm, is also maintains the list of its neighbors, and a summary of the data it has sent to and received from each of them (lines 5-6). On initialization, a node has no neighbors (lines 10–12).

The **change** function is identical to the one of the failure-free algorithm. The functions **receive** and **send**, however, instead of transferring the weighted values as in the failure-free case, transfer the summaries maintained for the links. In addition, when a node i wishes to send a weighted value to a node j, it may do so using either *push* or *pull*.

When pushing, node i adds the new weighted value to $sent_i(j)$ and sends $sent_i(j)$ to j (lines 14–16). When receiving this summary, node j calculates the received weighted value by subtracting the appropriate *received* variable from the newly received summary (line 27). After acting on the received message (line 28), node j replaces its *received* variable with the new weighted value (line 29). Thus, if a message is lost, the next received message compensates for the loss and brings the receiving neighbor to the same state it would have reached had it received the lost messages as well. Whenever the last message on a link (i, j) is correctly received and there are no messages in transit, the value of $sent_i^j$ is identical to the value of $received_j^i$.

Since the weights are (usually) positive, push operations, if used by themselves, cause the *sent* and *received* variables to grow to infinity. In order to overcome that, LiMoSense uses a hybrid push/pull approach, which keeps these weights small without requiring bilateral coordination. A node uses pull operations to decrease the *sent* variables of its neighbors, and thereby its own *received*. The pull message is a request from a neighbor to push an inverse weighted value, and does not change any state variables; these are only changed when the neighbor performs the requested push. The effect of a node pushing a value is equivalent to that of a node pulling (requesting) the inverse value and its neighbor pushing the inverse. Therefore, the use of pull messages does not hamper correctness.

In line 20, the algorithm randomly decides whether to perform push or pull[2]. When pulling, i sends the weighted value to j with the PULL flag. Once node j receives the message, it merges it with its own value, and relays i the same weighted pair using the standard push mechanism, but with a *negative* weight (line 31). Thus, the weights of the *sent* and *received* records fluctuate around 0 rather than grow to infinity. To prevent infinitesimal weights, a node does not perform a **send** step if the result would bring its weight to be smaller than a quantization constant q.

Upon notification of topology events, nodes act as follows. When notified of an **addNeighbor** event, a node initializes its transfer records *sent* and *received* for this link, noting that 0 weight was transferred in both directions. It also adds the new neighbor to its *neighbors* list (lines 36-38). When notified of a **removeNeighbor** event, a node reacts by nullifying the effect of this link. Pull messages that were sent and/or received on this link had no effect. Nodes therefore need to undo only the effects of sent and received push messages, which are summarized in the respective *sent* and *received* variables. When a node i discovers that link (i, j) has failed, it adds the outgoing link summary $sent_i^j$ to its

---

[2] We use random choice for ease of presentation. One may choose to perform pull less frequently to conserve bandwidth.

estimate, thus cancelling the effect of ever having sent anything on the link, and subtracts the incoming link summary *received$_i^j$* from its estimate, thereby cancelling the effect of everything it has received (line 40). The node also removes the neighbor from its *neighbors* list and discards its link records (lines 41–43).

After a node joins the system or leaves it, its neighbors are notified of the appropriate topology events, adding links to the new node, or removing links to the failed one. Thus, when a node fails, any parts of its read value that had propagated through the system are annulled, and it no longer contributes to the system-wide estimate.

5   Correctness Overview

We defer the correctness proof of LiMoSense to the full version of this paper. We overview here the key theorems.

First, define the invariant $\mathcal{I}$. The *estimate average* at time t, E^t, is the weighted average over all nodes of their weighted values, their outgoing link summaries in their *sent* variables and the inverse of their incoming logs in their *received* variables. We denote the *read average* at time t by R^t. We define the *read sum* to be $\langle R^t, n \rangle \triangleq \bigoplus_{i=1}^n \langle r_i^t, 1 \rangle$ and the *estimate sum* to be:

$$\langle E^t, n \rangle \triangleq \bigoplus_{i=1}^n \left(\langle est_i^t, w_i^t \rangle \oplus \bigoplus_{j \in neighbors_i^t} \left(sent_i^t(j) \ominus received_i^t(j) \right) \right) .$$

The invariant $\mathcal{I}$ states that the estimate sum equals the read sum: $\langle R^t, n \rangle = \langle E^t, n \rangle$.

We prove the following theorem, which states that the invariant is maintained throughout the system's asynchronous operation, despite message loss, topology changes and churn.

Theorem 1. *In a run of the system, the read average equals the estimate average at all times.*

Then, we prove the following theorem, that shows that after GST the estimates of the nodes eventually mix, i.e., all node estimates converge to the estimate average, which, as the invariant states, equals the read average.

Theorem 2 (Liveness). *After GST, the estimate error at all nodes converges to zero.*

6   Evaluation

6.1   Static

We say that the suffix of a run is *uniform synchronous* if (1) the choice of which node runs and choice of which neighbor it chooses for data exchange is uniformly random, and (2) the latency of all operations and links is 0 (negligible with respect to the time between periodic sends). This assumption means that there are no asynchrony issues; it is still weaker than the lock-step assumption often used to evaluate sensor networks.

In uniform synchronous runs, we argue that the nodes' estimates are normally distributed, and it is possible to show analytically that after each push operation, the expected variance decreases by $1 - \frac{1}{n}$. The details of this discussion may be found in the technical report [5].

We have conducted simulations to verify the predicted convergence rate of LiMoSense. We simulated a fully connected network of 100 sensors. The samples were taken from a standard normal distribution. Figure 1 shows mean square error of the nodes and the value predicted by the analysis. The simulation value is averaged over 100 instances of the simulation. The result perfectly fits the predicted behavior. This result also corresponds to those obtained in [8], where a similar static algorithm is analyzed with the nodes running in lock step.

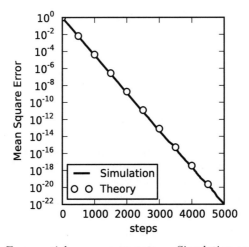

Fig. 1. Exponential convergence rate — Simulation and theory

6.2 Dynamic

In order to evaluate LiMoSense in the dynamic settings it was designed for, we have conducted simulations of various scenarios. Our goal is to asses how fast the algorithm reacts to changes, and succeeds to provide accurate information. Some of the results are described below. Further details can be found in the technical report [5].

We performed the simulations using a custom made Python event driven simulation that simulated the underlying network and the nodes' operation. Unless specified otherwise, all simulations are of a fully connected network of

100 nodes, with initial values taken from the standard normal distribution. We have seen that in well connected networks, the convergence behavior is similar to that of a fully connected network. The simulation proceeds in steps, where in each step, the topology and read values may change according to the simulated scenario, and one node performs a pull or push action. Scheduling is uniform synchronous, i.e., the node performing the action is chosen uniformly at random.

Unless specified otherwise, each scenario is simulated 1000 times. In all simulations, we track the algorithms' output and accuracy over time. In all of our graphs, the X axis represents steps in the execution. We depict the following three metrics for each scenario:

(a) **base station**. We assume that a base station collects the estimated read average from some arbitrary node. We show the median of the values obtained in the runs at each step.
(b) **ε-inaccuracy**. For a chosen ε, we depict the percentage of nodes whose estimate is off by more than ε after each step. The average of the runs is depicted.
(c) **MSE**. We depict the average square distance between the estimates at all nodes and the read average at each step. The average of all runs is depicted.

We compare LiMoSense, which does not need restarts, to a Push-Sum algorithm that restarts at a constant frequency — every 5000 steps unless specified otherwise. This number is an arbitrary choice, balancing between convergence accuracy and dynamic response. In base station results, we also show the read average, i.e., the value the algorithms are trying to estimate.

Slow Monotonic Increase. This simulation investigates the behavior of the algorithm when the values read by the sensors slowly increase. This may happen if the sensors are measuring rainfall that is slowly increasing. Every 10 steps, the read values of a random set of 5 nodes increase by 0.01. The results are shown in Figures 2a–2c. LiMoSense closely follows the correct dynamically changing average, whereas a restarting Push-Sum is unable to get close to the moving target.

Step Function. This simulation investigates the behavior of the algorithm when the values read by some sensors are shifted. This may occur due to a fire outbreak in a limited area, as close-by temperature nodes suddenly read high values. At step 2500, the read values of a random set of 10 nodes increase by 10. The results, shown in Figures 2d–2f, demonstrate how the LiMoSense algorithm updates immediately after the shift, whereas the periodic Push-Sum algorithm updates at its first restart only.

Robustness. To investigate the effect of link and node failures, we construct the following scenario. The sensors are spread in the unit square, and they have a transmission range of 0.7 distance units. The neighbors of a sensor are the sensors in its range. The system is run for 3000 steps, at which point, due to

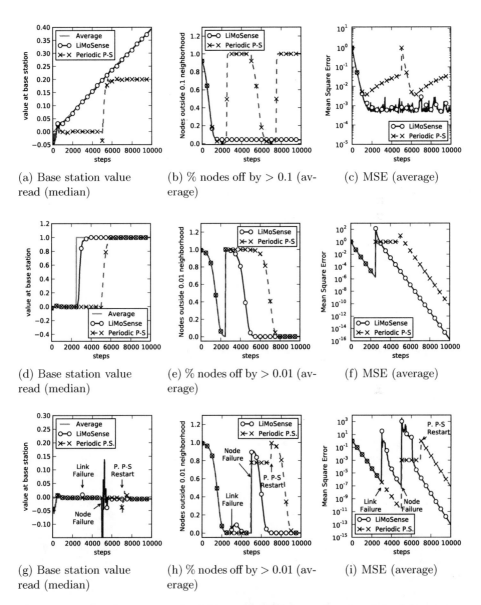

(a) Base station value read (median)

(b) % nodes off by > 0.1 (average)

(c) MSE (average)

(d) Base station value read (median)

(e) % nodes off by > 0.01 (average)

(f) MSE (average)

(g) Base station value read (median)

(h) % nodes off by > 0.01 (average)

(i) MSE (average)

Fig. 2. **(a)–(c) Creeping value change:** LiMoSense promptly tracks the creeping change, providing an accurate estimates at 95% of the nodes. **(d)–(f) Response to a step function:** LiMoSense immediately reacts, quickly propagating the new values. **(g)–(i) Failure robustness:** LiMoSense quickly overcomes link loss and node crash.

battery decay, the transmission range of 10 sensors decreases by 0.99. Due to this decay, about 7 links are lost in the entire system, and the relevant nodes employ their `removeNeighbor` functions. In step 5000, a node fails, removing its read value from the read average. Upon node failure, all its neighbors call their `removeNeighbor` functions.

The results, shown in Figures 2g–2i, shows the small error caused at some of the nodes due to the link failure. A much stronger interruption is caused by the node failure, which actually changes the read average. While the restarting Push-Sum algorithm is oblivious to the link failure, it is unable to recover from the node failure until its next restart.

7   Conclusion

We presented LiMoSense, a fault-tolerant live monitoring algorithm for dynamic sensor networks. This is the first asynchronous robust average aggregation algorithm to accommodate dynamic inputs. LiMoSense employs a hybrid push/pull gossip mechanism to dynamically track and aggregate a large collection of ever-changing sensor reads. It overcomes message loss, node failures and recoveries, and dynamic network topology changes. We have proven the correctness of LiMoSense and illustrated by simulation its ability to quickly react to network and value changes and provide accurate information.

Acknowledgements. This work was partially supported by the Hasso-Plattner Institute for Software Systems Engineering.

References

1. Almeida, P.S., Baquero, C., Farach-Colton, M., Jesus, P., Mosteiro, M.A.: Fault-Tolerant Aggregation: Flow-Updating Meets Mass-Distribution. In: Fernàndez Anta, A., Lipari, G., Roy, M. (eds.) OPODIS 2011. LNCS, vol. 7109, pp. 513–527. Springer, Heidelberg (2011)
2. Asada, G., Dong, M., Lin, T., Newberg, F., Pottie, G., Kaiser, W., Marcy, H.: Wireless integrated network sensors: Low power systems on a chip. In: ESSCIRC (1998)
3. Birk, Y., Keidar, I., Liss, L., Schuster, A.: Efficient Dynamic Aggregation. In: Dolev, S. (ed.) DISC 2006. LNCS, vol. 4167, pp. 90–104. Springer, Heidelberg (2006)
4. Boyd, S.P., Ghosh, A., Prabhakar, B., Shah, D.: Gossip algorithms: design, analysis and applications. In: INFOCOM (2005)
5. Eyal, I., Keidar, I., Rom, R.: LiMoSense – live monitoring in dynamic sensor networks. Tech. Rep. CCIT 786, Technion, Israel Institute of Technology (2011)
6. Flajolet, P., Martin, G.N.: Probabilistic counting algorithms for data base applications. J. Comput. Syst. Sci. 31(2) (1985)
7. Jain, N., Mahajan, P., Kit, D., Yalagandula, P., Dahlin, M., Zhang, Y.: Network imprecision: A new consistency metric for scalable monitoring. In: OSDI (2008)

8. Jelasity, M., Montresor, A., Babaoglu, O.: Gossip-based aggregation in large dynamic networks. ACM Transactions on Computer Systems (TOCS) 23(3) (2005)
9. Jesus, P., Baquero, C., Almeida, P.: Fault-tolerant aggregation for dynamic networks. In: SRDS (2010)
10. Kempe, D., Dobra, A., Gehrke, J.: Gossip-based computation of aggregate information. In: FOCS (2003)
11. Madden, S., Franklin, M.J., Hellerstein, J.M., Hong, W.: Tag: A tiny aggregation service for ad-hoc sensor networks. In: OSDI (2002)
12. Mosk-Aoyama, D., Shah, D.: Computing separable functions via gossip. In: PODC (2006)
13. Nath, S., Gibbons, P.B., Seshan, S., Anderson, Z.R.: Synopsis diffusion for robust aggregation in sensor networks. In: SenSys (2004)
14. Warneke, B., Last, M., Liebowitz, B., Pister, K.: Smart dust: communicating with a cubic-millimeter computer. Computer 34(1) (2001)

Evader Interdiction and Collateral Damage

Matthew P. Johnson[1,*] and Alexander Gutfraind[2]

[1] Pennsylvania State University
[2] Theoretical Division, Los Alamos National Laboratory

Abstract. In network interdiction problems, evaders (e.g., hostile agents or data packets) may be moving through a network towards targets and we wish to choose locations for sensors in order to intercept the evaders before they reach their destinations. The evaders might follow deterministic routes or Markov chains, or they may be *reactive*, i.e., able to change their routes in order to avoid sensors placed to detect them. The challenge in such problems is to choose sensor locations economically, balancing security gains with costs, including the inconvenience sensors inflict upon innocent travelers. We study the objectives of 1) maximizing the number of evaders captured when limited by a budget on sensing cost and 2) capturing all evaders as cheaply as possible.

We give optimal sensor placement algorithms for several classes of special graphs and hardness and approximation results for general graphs, including for deterministic or Markov chain-based and reactive or oblivious evaders. In a similar-sounding but fundamentally different problem setting posed by [7] where both evaders *and* innocent travelers are reactive, we again give optimal algorithms for special cases and hardness and approximation results on general graphs.

1   Introduction

In network interdiction problems, one or more *evaders* (e.g., smugglers or terrorists, or hostile data packets) travel through a network, beginning at some initial locations and attempting to reach some targets. Our goal is to stop them. We do so by placing *sensors* on nodes in hopes that most or all the evaders will pass by a sensor and thus be captured (or *intercepted*) before reaching their destinations. We take as given the evader movement dynamics, which may be either deterministic (each evader specified by a path from source to target) or stochastic, e.g. each evader specified by a Markov chain whose states are the nodes of the network. Evader e_i induces a subgraph $G_i \subseteq G$ in which she roams, according to the probabilities specified by her Markov chain. An unreactive or *oblivious* evader [10] behaves the same regardless of the choice of sensor locations (or *interdiction* sites), and so her set of possible routes can be construed as objects we wish to pierce.

We try to make economical use of the sensors—i.e., to balance the benefits of security (the interdiction of many or all evaders) with the total cost (widely defined) of doing so. The cost of placing a sensor at a given node can incorporate

---

* This work was performed in part while visiting Los Alamos National Laboratory.

T. Erlebach et al. (Eds.): ALGOSENSORS 2011, LNCS 7111, pp. 86–100, 2012.

the cost of the device itself, the effort or danger involved in performing the placement, and the inconvenience it causes to any innocent travelers subjected to it. If traffic flow estimates on the graph's edges are known for both evaders and innocent travelers, then it is natural to try to place sensors where they will intercept many evaders but inconvenience few innocents. If a sensor acts as a checkpoint, capturing the evaders but examining and then letting pass the innocents, then the inconvenience cost can be incorporated directly into the node's sensor placement cost since placing two sensors on an innocent's path inconveniences her twice. In this model we study two natural objectives: 1) maximizing the (expected, weighted) number of evaders captured while respecting a budget on sensing cost, and 2) capturing *all* evaders (with probability 1) as cheaply as possible. In the latter case evaders may be *reactive*, i.e., able to observe the sensor locations and choose a different path in G_i. Regardless, e_i is guaranteed to be captured only if her target node is separated from all her source nodes *within subgraph* G_i. We solve these problems optimally in several special graph settings and give hardness and approximation results in general settings.

In contrast, allowing the innocents *also* to re-act to sensor locations changes the character of the problem significantly. In this setting we study a special case of the problem which was posed by Glazer & Rubinstein [7], motivated by the following scenario: there are a collection of bridges crossing a river, with each traveler p restricted to using some set $\sigma(p)$ of bridges (because of p's preferences or geography, say), and the task is to decide which bridges to open and close. This can be viewed as a special case of our network setting in which every travel path is of length 2 but with the restriction that sensors cannot be placed on a traveler's start node (see Fig. 1). Note that in this special case, sensors can also be viewed as roadblocks, in the sense that placing a sensor on a node effectively means deleting the node from the network for evader and innocent alike.

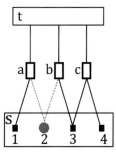

Fig. 1. A bridges problem instance represented as network interdiction with three intermediate nodes corresponding to bridges. An innocent begins at node 2 and evaders begin at nodes 1,3,4.

This change yields a setting in which the problem instance is specified by a set system with real-valued elements that may be either positive or negative, corresponding to the value or cost (respectively) of capturing evaders or blocking innocents. Several possible objective functions could be considered, such as capturing all evaders while blocking as few innocents as possible or capturing as many evaders as possible given a budget allowing a certain number of blocked innocents. Unfortunately, the former is precisely the Red-Blue Set Cover problem, which is "strongly inapproximable" (hard to approximate with factor $\Omega(2^{\log^{1-\epsilon} m})$ for any $\epsilon > 0$ (where m is the number of sets, or bridges) unless $NP \subseteq DTIME(m^{\mathrm{polylog}(m)}))$ [20]; the latter turns out to be harder still (see Appendix B). Instead, we next study objectives suggested by [7] that combine the two goals into a single score, where captured (i.e. unsuccessful) innocents and uncaptured (i.e. successful) evaders can be construed as false positives (FP) and false negatives (FN), respectively: maximize the "net flow" ($TN - FN$) or minimize the total errors ($FP + FN$). Although the $TN - FN$ model turns out to be hard to approximate with factor $n^{1-\epsilon}$ (once again, see Appendix B), we obtain nontrivial approximation results for the $FP + FN$ setting.

Contributions. With oblivious evaders and innocents, we solve the budgeted problem optimally in path and cycle graphs. With oblivious innocents (and evaders either oblivious or not), we solve the full interdiction problem optimally in paths, cycles, and trees. (In the edge sensor model, full interdiction is 2-approximable, which is the optimal approximation factor assuming UGC.)

In general graphs, we give hardness results including showing that the budgeted problem is NP-hard with even one Markovian evader, strengthening the hardness result of [8] which held only for two or more such evaders. In contrast, we show that full interdiction with a single evader is in P. With m possible evader paths, the problem is H_m-approximable (where $H_m = \sum_{i=1}^{m} \frac{1}{i}$), which is essentially optimal, given certain complexity-theoretic assumptions.

When both evaders and innocents are reactive, we optimally solve a special case in which the graph and travelers' sets of paths can be represented by *bridges* and *convex bridge sets*, respectively. We also show that $FP + FN$ is approximable with factor one plus the maximum size of any innocent's bridge set.

Due to space limitations, a number of proofs appear in Appendix A.

Related Work. The problems analyzed here belong to a large class of discrete optimization problems, collectively termed Network Interdiction [16, 2, 19, 9]. They are motivated by applications such as supply chains, electronic sensing, and counter-terrorism and relate to classical optimization problems like Set Cover and Max Coverage. Our setting of budgeted interdiction with deterministic evaders on the path graph can be solved by a complicated algorithm given by [17], but we present a much simpler algorithm. Recent work on Set Cover with submodular costs [15, 12] applies to some of our settings. Previous work on the Unreactive Markovian Evader (UME) interdiction problem (maximizing the expected number of Markov chain-based evaders captured with B sensors) showed that it is already NP-hard with just two evaders [8] and that it is $\frac{e}{e-1}$-approximable by the natural greedy algorithm [10], which is the optimal approximation factor (we prove this for completeness in Proposition 4).

Other evader models have been studied such as the Most Vital Nodes Problem, in which the task is to delete a set of nodes in order to maximize the weight of the shortest path from source to destination [2, 1] or to decrease the maximum flow [11, 21], both of which could be construed as frustrating an evader's progress. Such evaders are *reactive* in the sense that the routes they take are modified based on the set of available edges or nodes. In [9], an intermediate model was studied in which the evader follows a parametrized generalization of shortest path and random walk.

The Bridges problem was introduced by Glazer & Rubinstein [7] in an economics context, primarily motivated in terms of strategies for a listener to accept good arguments and reject bad arguments. In this setting, (positive/negative) states correspond to (positive/negative) people and allowing oneself to be persuaded by a statement corresponds to opening a bridge.

2   Preliminaries

Given is a graph $G(V, E)$ with $|V| = n$ unless otherwise noted, used by travelers (or *people*) of two types: evaders (or *bads*) and innocents (or *goods*). (These terms are used interchangeably.) Each person p can travel within some subgraph $G_p \subseteq G$. Depending on the setting, sensors can be placed on nodes or edges to capture the *flow* passing through. A user p's Markov chain determines the probability weight $f_{p,v}$ of p's traffic through each node v. If oblivious, p is unable to shift her flow $f_{p,v}$ from the path going through v to some other path, so placing a sensor at v captures all of $f_{p,v}$ (or at least whatever portion of it was not captured upstream). In some settings we assume all innocents, all evaders, or both are *oblivious*, as discussed below.

We emphasize that *reactive* indicates a two-stage setting in which all the sensors are placed and then p can choose an unblocked path in G_p if one exists. Sensors are *not* deployed in sequence over time.We also emphasize that person p is restricted to subgraph G_p regardless of whether p is oblivious or reactive, an evader or an innocent.

Edge and Node Interdiction. In *edge interdiction*, sensors are installed on edges and are represented by a matrix of decision variables $\mathbf{r}$: $r_{uv} = 1$ if (u, v) has a sensor placed at it (with cost c_{uv}) and 0 otherwise. If an evader crosses an edge with a sensor she is detected with probability 1. In *node interdiction*, placing a sensor on node u (with cost c_u) means setting $r_{uv} = 1$ for every edge (u, v), that is, interdicting all evaders *leaving* u). A sensor on a target node does *not* protect that node itself but will stop evaders as they pass through it.

The node and edge settings are equivalent in *general, directed graphs with location-varying costs*, in the sense that a problem in one setting can be transformed into the other [10]. Although the UME model is defined for convenience in terms of edge interdiction, unless otherwise stated we assume node interdiction.

Oblivious Evaders. An evader is specified in terms of the probabilities of her taking various routes, where a route is a walk (possibly containing cycles) ending at a target node. A Markovian evader is represented by a Markov chain given by an initial *source* distribution $\mathbf{a}$ over nodes and a transition probability matrix $\mathbf{M}$. The matrix $\mathbf{M}$ has the property that a specified target node t is an absorbing state: upon reaching t the evader is removed from the network. Under mild restrictions on the Markov chain such as this, the probability of capturing the evader can be expressed in closed form [10]:

$$J(\mathbf{a}, \mathbf{M}, \mathbf{r}) = 1 - \left(\mathbf{a} \left[\mathbf{I} - (\mathbf{M} - \mathbf{M} \odot \mathbf{r}) \right]^{-1} \right)_t \qquad (1)$$

where the symbol $\odot$ indicates element-wise (Hadamard) multiplication. This formulation generalizes to a setting of multiple simultaneous evaders, each realized with probability w_e, or equivalently having weight w_i representing the importance of capturing her. The probability of capturing e_i is denoted by $J_i(\mathbf{r})$.

Definition 1. *An evader e_i is specified by a $(\mathbf{M_i}, \mathbf{a_i})$ pair. Evader e_i is deterministic if from each of her possible starting nodes, $\mathbf{M_i}$ specifies a single next node with probability 1, and is* nondeterministic *otherwise. In both cases, $\mathbf{a_i}$ may specify multiple starting points with positive probability.*

Budgeted Interdiction (BI). The BI objective is to capture as many evaders as possible, given a budget on sensors. More precisely, suppose we have a bound on the number of nodes we can monitor (or on their total cost, with costs always scaled to be integral). Any choice of some subset of nodes to observe determines a probability that a given evader will be captured (i.e., that she will pass through at least one observed node) prior to reaching her target t. The task in Budgeted Interdiction is to maximize the expected (weighted) number of evaders interdicted, subject to a budget B on sensor costs:

$$\text{maximize} \sum_i w_i J_i(\mathbf{r}) \text{ such that } \sum_u r_u c_u \leq B$$

Full Interdiction (FI). This problem seeks a minimum-cost set of nodes to observe in order to capture all evaders (denoted by D) with probability one.

$$\text{minimize} \sum_u r_u c_u \text{ such that } \sum_i J_i(\mathbf{r}) = |D|$$

Reactive Evaders and Innocents. In this setting both types of travelers are reactive, which means a traveler is captured only if *all* her paths *within* G_p from source nodes to target node have received a sensor placed on some node prior to the target. Let $\hat{w}_p$ indicate the cost of having person p succeed, which is negative if p is good, and let binary variables $x_p = 1$ indicate p's success and $y_s = 1$ indicate that bridge s is open. Let N indicate the goods and D the bads. Then in the following formulation of the Bridges Problem the constraints code for the requirement that $x_p = \max_{s \in \sigma(p)} y_s$, i.e., traveler p can cross iff at least one of her bridges is open, and the objective is to minimize the sum of errors (failed goods + successful bads).

$$\text{minimize} \sum_{p \in D} \hat{w}_p x_p + \sum_{p \in N} \hat{w}_p (1 - x_p) \text{ such that } x_p \leq \sum_{s \in \sigma(p)} y_s \; \forall p \text{ and } x_p \geq y_s \; \forall p, \forall s \in \sigma(p)$$

Let TP, FP, TN, FN indicate the weighted numbers of true positives (bads failing to cross), false positives (goods failing), true negatives (goods succeeding), and false negatives (bads succeeding), respectively. We focus on the objective of minimizing $FP + FN$, in the problem setting in which each traveler's path from source to target passes through exactly one other node, a *bridge*. Since the bridges are the decision points, with *closed* corresponding to receiving a sensor and *open* corresponding to not, in this problem we use n to denote the number of bridges. The problem setting as defined generalizes to graphs in the roadblock model by replacing each bridge set $\sigma(p)$ with a set of paths to some target node. A traveler p (either bad or good) is then captured if her target is disconnected from all her starting nodes in G_p as for evaders before (where placing a sensor on a node means deleting it), and otherwise inflicts cost $\hat{w}_p$. Since each path is essentially a single edge, sensors can (as mentioned above) be thought of as either checkpoints or roadblocks.

3   Oblivious Innocents and Evaders Oblivious or Not

3.1   Paths, Trees, and Cycles

In this section we consider the Budgeted (BI) and Full Interdiction (FI) problems where the graph G (on n nodes) is one of several special topologies.

Definition 2. *In a path graph P with nodes numbered 1 through n, an* interval $[x, y]$ *indicates the sequence of nodes numbered x through y (with $x \leq y$) the interval's* startpoint *and* endpoint, *respectively. Half-open intervals $[x, y) = [x, y - 1]$ and $(x, y] = [x + 1, y]$ are defined similarly. For nodes x, y we write $x < y$ to indicate that x precedes y in P. Similarly, in a tree T, an* interval $[x, y]$ *is the sequence of nodes lying on the path in T from x to y. A node v* pierces *interval $[x, y]$ if $v \in [x, y]$. An* interval sequence *is a set of intervals that can be ordered so that each interval is strictly contained by the previous one. All the intervals in a* suffix sequence *share the same endpoint; all the intervals in a* prefix sequence *share the same start point.*

The budgeted problem is solvable in polynomial time as we show below. It will follow that FI is also solvable by searching for the smallest budget B that permits full interdiction. The problem can be solved more efficiently, however.

Theorem 1. *When $c_v = 1 \ \forall v$, Full Interdiction is optimally solvable in $O(n \log n)$ time on paths.*

We then obtain the following.

Theorem 2. *When $c_v = 1 \ \forall v$, Full Interdiction is optimally solvable in $O(n^3)$ time on trees.*

Proof. The $O(n^2)$ intervals are now paths in the tree, whose intersection graph (constructable in $O(n^3)$) is a *chordal graph*, on which Minimum Clique Cover can also be solved in linear time [6].   □

For the setting of edge sensors, Full Interdiction is closely related to the Minimum Directed Multicut (MDM) problem, in which the task is to find a minimum cut that separates each of k source-sink pairs (s_i, t_i).

Proposition 1. *In the edge interdiction setting, Full Interdiction is 2-approximable on trees, which is the optimal factor (assuming the Unique Games Conjecture [14]).*

Proof. When restricted to an underlying tree graph, the Full Interdiction problem is identical to Directed Multicut. □

Definition 3. *For a possible route r traveled by some evader, let V_r indicate the nodes visited along route r before reaching its target, or the* route set *of r. Let m be the number of distinct route sets among all evaders.*

Note that multiple distinct routes can give rise to the same route set, and that a route set in a path graph is always an interval with an end point at the target node. We now turn to Budgeted Interdiction.

Theorem 3. *Let m be the total number of different evader route sets. Budgeted Interdiction with deterministic evaders and (integer) budget B is optimally solvable on the path graph in time $O(Bnm) = O(Bn^3)$.*

Proof. We give a dynamic programming solution in Algorithm 1. We compute an optimal solution using a table $opt[\ell, \hat{v}, b]$ that stores the optimal solution restricted to the ℓ left-most intervals, nodes $1...\hat{v}$ and budget b. We first compute the value of node v restricted to the first ℓ intervals, i.e., $val[\ell, v]$ is the sum of the weights of those intervals when the only sensor is node v. Each subproblem solution is computed in constant time: given inputs ℓ, v, b, if v is not chosen, then the optimal solution value is the same as inputs $\ell, v - 1, b$; if v is chosen, then the optimal solution value is the value of choosing v in this situation, plus optimal solution on the intervals lying to the left of v, using the first $v - 1$ nodes and a budget of $b - c_v$ (or 0 if $b - c_v < 0$).

Proof of correctness is by induction: if node v is chosen, then due to the linear ordering, nodes prior to v only contribute to piercing intervals 1 through $pr(v)$. Note that correctness holds also when interval weights may be negative. □

The case of nondeterministic evaders is more complicated since, as noted above, it gives rise to sequences of suffix intervals and sequences of prefix intervals. For each such sequence corresponding to a single nondeterministic evader, the computation of $val[\ell, v]$ will be based on all the intervals in the sequence that v pierces. More precisely, let $\{[1, t), [2, t), ..., [s, t)\}$ be a suffix sequence for some nondeterministic evader e_i with source s and target t. For each node $v < t$ there is some probability p_v that placing a sensor at node v *suffices* for capturing e_i. Namely, p_v is 1 for any $v \in [s, t)$, while for each node $v < s$ the probability p_v can be computed based on the Markov chain of e_i, that is, just the probability that her Markov chain visits v and is computed as follows. For e_i's Markov chain $(\mathbf{a}, \mathbf{M})$, let $\mathbf{M}_{-\mathbf{v}}$ denote a transition matrix where row v has been replaced by zeros, i.e. the chain with v as a killing state. Then $p_v = \left(\mathbf{a}\left[\mathbf{I} - \mathbf{M}_{-\mathbf{v}}\right]^{-1}\right)_v$.

For each interval in the sequence, we now define a *marginal* probability $\hat{p}_v$ as follows: $\hat{p}_1 = p_1$; $\hat{p}_v = p_v - p_{v-1}$ for $1 < v \leq s$, and $\hat{p}_v = 1 - p_{s-1}$ for

---

Algorithm 1. Budgeted Interdiction DP for Evaders on the Path Graph

---

1: sort the $O(n^2)$ intervals by right endpoint
2: $pr[v]$ = index of the last interval lying before node v, or 0 if none **for** every v
3: $val[\ell, v]$ = value of node v, restricted to intervals 1 to ℓ, **for** every v, ℓ
4: $opt[0, v, b] = 0$ **for** every v, b
5: $opt[\ell, 0, b] = 0$ **for** every ℓ, b
6: $opt[\ell, v, 0] = 0$ **for** every ℓ, v
7: **for** $b = 1$ to B **do**
8:     **for** $\ell = 1$ to m **do**
9:        **for** $v = 1$ to n **do**
10:           $opt[\ell, v, b] = \max\{opt[\ell, v - 1, b], \ val[\ell, v] + opt[pr[v], v - 1, \max(0, b - c_v)]\}$
11:        **end for**
12:     **end for**
13: **end for**
14: **return** $opt[m, n, B]$

$s \leq v < t$. By construction, the $\hat{p}_v$ values for all intervals containing a given node u will sum to exactly the probability of evader e_i reaching node u, and hence of such a sensor placement sufficing to capture evader e_i. (The values labeling the intervals in Fig. 2 are the marginal probabilities, weighted by the probability of choosing their starting points.) Marginal probabilities are assigned to prefix intervals similarly. Therefore the value of a set of sensor locations for a given instance of the problem with nondeterministic evaders is exactly the value of those locations for the resulting problem instance with interval sequences of deterministic evaders; that is, the nondeterministic problem reduces to the deterministic problem (albeit with up to a factor n more intervals). Thus we have the following.

Theorem 4. *Budgeted Interdiction with nondeterministic evaders is optimally solvable on the path graph, in time $O(Bn^2 m) = O(Bn^4)$.*

These problems can also be solved on the cycle by reduction to path graphs.

Theorem 5. *Full Interdiction is optimally solvable in $O(n^2)$ time on the cycle graph. Budgeted Interdiction with deterministic or nondeterministic evaders and budget B is optimally solvable on the cycle graph in time $O(Bn^4)$ or $O(Bn^5)$, respectively.*

Proof. For the minimization problem, we reduce to a collection of n path graph instances, corresponding to n ways to "cut" the cycle graph, as follows. For each node $v \in V$, consider placing a sensor at node v. It will pierce some set of intervals, with the effect that none of the remaining intervals to pierce include node v, yielding a path graph instance with nodes $v + 1, ..., n, 1, ..., v - 1$. Solve each resulting path graph instance in linear time, and return the cheapest solution (combined with v). The budgeted problems are solved by a similar reduction. □

The process can be generalized to arbitrary graphs containing c cycles, though at a cost of $O(n^c)$: find all the cycles [13] and then explore all possible cuts.

3.2   General Graphs

We show in Appendix A that Budgeted Interdiction (BI) is hard already with one Markovian evader. This improves on the result in [8] which held for two or more evaders.

Theorem 6. *Budgeted Interdiction is NP-hard even with a single Markovian evader.*

It follows from the hardness proof of [8] that Full Interdiction is NP-hard with 2 evaders. It does not remain hard when limited to a single evader, however.

Theorem 7. *Full Interdiction with one evader is solvable in polynomial time.*

We now turn to approximation algorithms for the general setting, by relating interdiction to the Set Cover and Maximum Coverage problems. It was shown in [10] that weighted Budgeted Interdiction with any number of Markovian evaders is 1-1/e-approximable, which is the optimal factor (see Appendix B).

Identifying nodes and route sets with elements and sets in the Hitting Set problem yields a reversible reduction, and hence the following immediately resulrs:

Corollary 1. *Full Interdiction is hard to approximate with factor $(1 - \epsilon)\ln m$ for any $\epsilon > 0$, assuming $NP \subseteq DTIME(m^{O(\log\log m)})$ but can be approximated with factor H_m in time polynomial in $n + m$.*

Proof. We reduce from Set Cover, as in [10], creating a node for each set and a route set (with a corresponding deterministic evader) for each element.   □

4   Reactive Innocents and the Bridges Problem

Since maximizing the "net flow" $TN - FN$ [7] turns out to be as hard to approximate as Maximum Independent Set (see Appendix B), we focus primarily on the the min-error $FP + FN$ setting. A geometric or "convex" version of the min-error problem is optimally solvable, however. Since the two objective functions differ only by a constant and a negation ($TN - FN = (w_N - FP) - FN$, where w_N indicates the total value of all goods), the same holds for the net flow problem.

4.1   Convex Bridge Sets

Definition 4. *An instance of the Bridges Problem is convex if the bridges can be ordered so that if two bridges x and y are accessible to a person p then any bridge z with $x < z < y$ is accessible to p as well.*

The problem example shown in Figure 1 in the introduction is convex. We assume that the indices of people are sorted in order of their positions from left to right and the bridge indices are sorted in order of their rightmost accessing person. This setting can be solved by mapping it to Budgeted Interdiction on the path graph and adapting Algorithm 1.

Corollary 2. *The convex Bridges problem is solvable in time* $O(n|N| + n|D|)$ $= O(n^3)$.

Proof. Given a Bridges problem instance (say in the min-error formulation), we introduce a Budgeted Interdiction instance (with budget arbitrarily large) as follows. Each of the bridges is identified with a node on the path graph. For each traveler p we define an evader p on the interval I_p, where I_p are all bridges available to p. This produces $|N| + |D| \leq n(n-1)$ distinct intervals. The weight of evader p is set to negation of the traveler's cost: $w_p = -\hat{w}_p$.

The formulations are now equivalent: in the Bridges Problem, a traveler succeeds iff one or more of her bridges is open; in BI, an evader is interdicted iff one or more of the nodes in her interval is interdicted by a sensor.

Then we pass the instance to an adaptation of Algorithm 1: we remove the budget dimension from the dynamic programming table and also remove the outer loop iterating over budget values, saving a factor of $O(b)$ in running time. The resulting algorithm computes an optimal interdiction solution. (Recall that Algorithm 1 supports intervals with weights both positive and negative.) Given this solution, we then solve the Bridges problem by openning a bridge iff the corresponding node has a sensor placed at it. □

4.2   The Min-error $FP + FN$ Setting

NP-hardness of optimally solving the min-error setting follows from the hardness of the net-flow setting: maximizing $TN - FN$ is the same as minimizing $FN - TN = FN - (|N| - FP) = FP + FN - |N|$. The hardness of approximation properties, however, are not the same. In fact, the min-error problem is precisely the Positive-Negative Partial Set Cover Problem [18], which, as a generalization of Red-Blue Set Cover, is strongly inapproximable (hard to approximate with factor $\Omega(2^{\log^{1-\epsilon} m}))$ (where m is the number of sets) unless $NP \subseteq DTIME(m^{\mathrm{polylog}(m)})$ though approximable with factor $2\sqrt{(m + \pi)\log \pi}$, where π is the number of goods.

Glazer & Rubinstein define what we will call a *claw* as an object c consisting of a good g_c and minimal set of bads B_c such that for each bridge $s \in \sigma(g_c)$, s is also in $\sigma(b_i)$ for some bad $b_i \in B_c$, which means that in any consistent solution, either g_c must fail or at least one b_i must succeed. They show that this is also a sufficient condition for being a valid solution, and hence obtain a Set Cover problem: for each claw, choose a person to err on, with minimum total error cost over all claws. Unfortunately, this instance in general has exponentially many constraints (since for each good g with bridge set $\sigma(g)$, each of whose bridges admit some number $bads(s)$ of bads, there will be $|C| = \Pi_{s \in \sigma g} bads(s)$ many claws), and so the $O(\log |C|)$ approximability of set cover becomes trivially weak. We therefore modify the definition of claw slightly as follows.

Definition 5. *A* claw *is an object c consisting of a good g_c and, for each bridge $s_i \in \sigma(g_c)$ the set $b \in \sigma^{-1}(s_i)$ of all the bads who can use bridge s_i.*

Each claw c therefore imposes the following constraint: in any valid solution, either g_c must fail or all the bads in $\sigma^{-1}(s_i)$ for some $s_i \in \sigma(g_c)$ must succeed. Given c, let a *kill move* be the action of killing g_c; let an *open bridge move* be the action of opening some bridge s_i. Now we can interpret this problem as an instance of Submodular Cost Set Cover [15, 12] in which the elements are claws and there are two kinds of sets. For each possible kill move m_g, introduce a set $M_g = \{g\}$; for each possible open bridge move m_i, introduce a set M_i consisting of all the claws that opening bridge i would satisfy. There are N elements (claws) and $N + m$ sets (moves).

Theorem 8. *The general $FP + FN$ Bridges problem is $(1 + \max_{g \in N} |\sigma(g)|)$-approximable.*

Acknowledgments. We thank Amotz Bar-Noy and Rohit Parikh for useful discussions. This work was funded by the Department of Energy at the Los Alamos National Laboratory through the LDRD program, and by the Defense Threat Reduction Agency. Indexed as Los Alamos Unclassified Report LA-UR-11-10123.

References

1. Bar-Noy, A., Khuller, S., Schieber, B.: The complexity of finding most vital arcs and nodes. Technical report, University of Maryland, College Park, MD, USA (1995)
2. Corley, H.W., Sha, D.Y.: Most vital links and nodes in weighted networks. Operations Research Letters 1(4), 157–160 (1982)
3. Even, G., Levi, R., Rawitz, D., Schieber, B., Shahar, S., Sviridenko, M.: Algorithms for capacitated rectangle stabbing and lot sizing with joint set-up costs. ACM Transactions on Algorithms 4(3) (2008)
4. Even, S.: Graph Algorithms. Computer Science Press (1979)
5. Feige, U.: A threshold of ln for approximating set cover. J. ACM 45(4), 634–652 (1998)
6. Gavril, F.: Algorithms for minimum coloring, maximum clique, minimum covering by cliques, and maximum independent set of a chordal graph. SIAM J. Computing 1(2), 180–187 (1972)
7. Glazer, K., Rubinstein, A.: A study in the pragmatics of persuasion: A game theoretical approach. Theoretical Economics 1, 395–410 (2006)
8. Gutfraind, A., Ahmadizadeh, K.: Markovian Network Interdiction and the Four Color Theorem. Review with SIAM J. Discrete Math. (2009), http://arxiv.org/abs/0911.4322
9. Gutfraind, A., Hagberg, A., Izraelevitz, D., Pan, F.: Interdiction of a Markovian Evader. In: Dell, R., Wood, K. (eds.) Proc. INFORMS Computing Society Conference (January 2011)
10. Gutfraind, A., Hagberg, A., Pan, F.: Optimal Interdiction of Unreactive Markovian Evaders. In: van Hoeve, W.-J., Hooker, J.N. (eds.) CPAIOR 2009. LNCS, vol. 5547, pp. 102–116. Springer, Heidelberg (2009)
11. Corley, J.H.W., Chang, H.: Finding the n most vital nodes in a flow network. Management Science 21(3), 362–364 (1974)
12. Iwata, S., Nagano, K.: Submodular function minimization under covering constraints. In: FOCS, pp. 671–680 (2009)

13. Johnson, D.B.: Finding all the elementary circuits of a directed graph. SIAM Journal on Computing 4(1), 77–84 (1975)
14. Khot, S., Regev, O.: Vertex cover might be hard to approximate to within $2 - \epsilon$. J. Comput. Syst. Sci. 74(3), 335–349 (2008)
15. Koufogiannakis, C., Young, N.E.: Greedy Δ-Approximation Algorithm for Covering with Arbitrary Constraints and Submodular Cost. In: Albers, S., Marchetti-Spaccamela, A., Matias, Y., Nikoletseas, S., Thomas, W. (eds.) ICALP 2009. LNCS, vol. 5555, pp. 634–652. Springer, Heidelberg (2009)
16. McMasters, A.W., Mustin, T.M.: Optimal interdiction of a supply network. Naval Research Logistics Quarterly 17(3), 261–268 (1970)
17. Megiddo, N., Zemel, E., Hakimi, S.L.: The maximum coverage location problem. SIAM Journal on Algebraic and Discrete Methods 4(2), 253–261 (1983)
18. Miettinen, P.: On the positive-negative partial set cover problem. Inf. Process. Lett. 108(4), 219–221 (2008)
19. Pan, F., Charlton, W.S., Morton, D.P.: Interdicting smuggled nuclear material. In: Woodruff, D. (ed.) Network Interdiction and Stochastic Integer Programming, pp. 1–19. Kluwer Academic Publishers, Boston (2003)
20. Peleg, D.: Approximation algorithms for the label-cover$_{max}$ and red-blue set cover problems. J. Discrete Algorithms 5(1), 55–64 (2007)
21. Ratliff, H.D., Sicilia, G.T., Lubore, S.H.: Finding the n most vital links in flow networks. Management Science 21(5), 531–539 (1975)
22. Zuckerman, D.: Linear degree extractors and the inapproximability of max clique and chromatic number. Theory of Computing 3(1), 103–128 (2007)

A   Proofs

Proof (of Theorem 1). Consider an evader e_i with start nodes S_i and a target node t_i. We must capture evader e_i in the case of each starting point $s \in S_i$ before she reaches node t_i. Node s lies either to the left or right of t_i, assume to the left, i.e., $s < t_i$ (e.g., node 3 in Fig. 2). Evader e_i may (probabilistically) move to the left before returning right, and so a sensor placed to the left of s may capture the evader with positive probability. For capturing e_i with probability 1, however, it is necessary and sufficient to place a sensor somewhere in the interval $[s, t_i)$ ($[3, 6)$ for the first evader e_1 in Fig. 2).

Each starting point s of evader e_i will correspond to an interval $[s, t_i)$ or interval $(t_i, s]$, depending on the relative location of s to t_i. Each such interval must be pierced. Intervals of the former kind (with the evader approaching the target from the left) will form a sequences of suffix intervals; intervals of the latter kind (with the evader is approaching from the right) will form a sequence of prefix intervals. In the worst case, it could be necessary to consider $m = O(n^2)$ intervals because each interval may be traversed with positive probability by some evader. It suffices to consider each evader's smallest left interval and smallest right interval ($[3, 6)$ and $(6, 8]$ for e_1 in Fig. 2)), since each such interval is contained within all others in the sequence. We build an *interval graph H* by associating a node with each smallest interval (each of which can be found in time $O(\log n)$ by binary search) and placing an undirected edge for any two smallest intervals that intersect. Because the cost of piercing any interval is

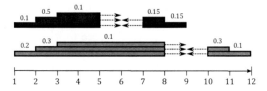

Fig. 2. An instance with two evaders in the graph P_{12}, one traveling from nodes 3 and 8 to 6, and one traveling from nodes 3 and 11 to 9

$c_v = 1$, and because each intersection of intervals corresponds to a clique of H, Full Interdiction is equivalent to Minimum Clique Cover on H. The latter is solvable in linear time on the interval graph (plus time for sorting) [3]. □

Proof (of Theorem 6). We reduce from Vertex Cover (VC) to the decision problem of determining whether the interdiction probability J can be raised to a certain threshold using at most B sensors. Given a VC problem instance, i.e., a graph G on n nodes and an integer B, we construct a network interdiction (NI) instance with a Markovian evader on a graph G'. The graph G' extends graph G by adding a target node t, which is made adjacent to all other nodes. We define the evader e thus. Each node corresponds to a state of its Markov chain. All non-target nodes are equally likely to be chosen as e's start node. When at a given node v, e moves to the target t with probability 50%; otherwise, e moves to one of v's other neighbors, chosen uniformly at random.

For a particular solution, let the *profit* for a node be the probability of interdiction if the evader starts at that node. We will now show that the VC instance admits a vertex cover of size B iff the NI instance admits a size-B solution of profit at least $B + (n - B)/2$. Note that an overall interdiction probability of $\frac{(n+B)}{2n}$ is the same as a total profit of $(n + B)/2 = B + (n - B)/2$ over all nodes.

First assume there is a size-B vertex cover C of G. Then an NI solution with sensors placed at all the nodes in C will have profit $B + \frac{(n-B)}{2}$: 1 for each of the B nodes in C plus $1/2$ for each of the remaining $n - B$ nodes, since for any node v not in C, all v's neighbors in G must be in C.

Now assume there is no size-B vertex cover, and consider a set S of B nodes, a set which must fail to cover some edge. Again for each of the B nodes in S we have profit 1. Every other node v will have profit at most $1/2$, since without its own sensor, an evader starting at v goes directly to t with probability $1/2$. But now consider an edge (u, v) that is left uncovered by S. The evasion probability when starting at u is greater than $1/2$—at least $1/2 + 1/(4 \deg(G))$—since if e reaches node v, it now has a second chance to move to t, and so the profit of u is less than $1/2$. Therefore the total profit is strictly less than $B + (n - B)/2$. □

Proof (of Theorem 7). We solve the problem by reducing to a Min Cut problem. Given a set of routes specifying the evader's behavior, we introduce a source node s pointing to all start nodes of its Markov chain. All edges that the evader has zero probability of reaching and crossing are removed from the graph G. Any unreachable nodes are also removed. Now, in order to interdict the evader before they reach t, we must delete vertices in order to separate s from t in G. It is well known that this Min Vertex Cut problem can be solved in polynomial time, by reduction to Directed Min Cut, as follows [4]. First replace any undirected edge with a pair of directed edges. Then replace each node v (other than s or t) with a pair of nodes and directed edge (v_a, v_b), where each edge directed to v is now directed to v_a and each edge directed from v is now directed from v_b. We compute a Min Cut on the resulting graph G'. If any edge is chosen that does not correspond to a node in G, we can substitute one of the edges corresponding to its two vertices (if one of these is the target, then the non-target node is chosen). The resulting modified Min Cut solution to G' will correspond to a Min Vertex Cut solution to G, and moreover to a Full Interdiction solution.   □

Proof (of Theorem 8). First we claim that the cost of a set of moves is submodular. Indeed, the cost of each kill move is simply the additive cost of the specified good failing; the marginal cost of an open bridge move is monotonically decreasing since it is based on the number of *additional* bads that opening the bridge then allows to succeed. Second we claim that the value of the total error of the Bridge solution returned is at most the cost of the moves chosen. Indeed, first, the only time bridges are opened is during bridge moves, and so the total cost of bads succeeding is at most the cost of the open bridge moves; second, when bridges are closed at the end, all constraints have been handled, and so the failures of all goods have already been "paid for", in the cost of the kill moves. Therefore the algorithms of [15, 12] apply, which provide a solution with approximation factor f, which is the maximum number of sets that any element appears in. In the constructed set cover instance, f translates into 1 plus $\max_{g \in N} |\sigma(g)|$.   □

B   Other Hardness Results

The following two results are approximation-preserving reductions from the Maximum Independent Set (MIS) problem, which is hard to approximate with factor $n^{1-\epsilon}$ (where $|V| = n$) for any $\epsilon > 0$ [22]. A MIS instance consists of a graph $G = (V, E)$ and a positive integer k.

Proposition 2. *The Bridges problem variant in which the goal is to maximize TN subject to a bound on FN is NP-hard to approximate with factor $n^{1-\epsilon}$.*

Proof. In our reduction, each vertex v becomes a bridge s_v and a bad b_v who can cross only s_v. Each edge (u, v) becomes $k + 1$ goods who can cross bridges s_u and s_v. The bound on FN is set to k, which prevents any two goods connected by an edge from both failing.   □

Proposition 3. *The net-flow $TN - FN$ setting of the Bridges problem is NP-hard to approximate with factor $n^{1-\epsilon}$.*

Proof. Omitted due to lack of space.   □

Proposition 4. *The Budgeted Interdiction problem in NP-hard to approximate within factor $1 - 1/e - \epsilon$ for any $\epsilon > 0$.*

Proof. We reduce from Maximum Coverage, which has the stated hardness property [5].

Given is a family of subsets S_i of a ground set $U = \{e_1, ..., e_n\}$. The task is to choose k subsets whose union is of maximum cardinality. For each set S_i we introduce a corresponding node v_i. For each element e_j we introduce a corresponding evader whose Markov chain takes it deterministically (in some arbitrary order) through all the nodes corresponding to sets containing e_j and thence to a special target node. Then a selection of sets covering evader paths is equivalent to a selection of sets covering elements, with exactly the same solution value.   □

Efficient Algorithms for Network Localization Using Cores of Underlying Graphs

Meng Li, Yota Otachi, and Takeshi Tokuyama

Graduate School of Information Sciences, Tohoku University, Sendai 980-8579, Japan
{limeng,otachi,tokuyama}@dais.is.tohoku.ac.jp

Abstract. Network localization is important for networks with no prefixed positions of network nodes such as sensor networks. We are given a subset of the set of $\binom{n}{2}$ pairwise distances among n sensors in some Euclidean space. We want to determine the positions of each sensors from the (partial) distance information. The input can be seen as an edge weighted graph. In this paper, we present some efficient algorithms that solve this problem using the structures of input graphs, which we call the *cores* of them. For instance, we present a polynomial-time algorithm solving the network localization problem for graphs with connected dominating sets of bounded size. This algorithm allows us to have an FPT algorithm for some restricted instances such as graphs with connected vertex covers of bounded size.

Keywords: Network localization, Point set reconstruction, Weighted graph embedding, Graph turnpike problem, Chordal graph, Connected dominating set.

1 Introduction

Nowadays sensor networks are used for many important practical applications such as monitoring environmental data (see e.g. [9,26]). Since the nodes in a sensor network do not have physical access to each other, sometimes we should construct it without prefixed positions of the nodes even if it is not a dynamic ad-hoc network; that is, the nodes are not moving. For example, assume that we want to monitor some contaminated environment. It is not possible to put a sensor node manually at a prefixed position since the area is contaminated. Thus we use some flying devices like unmanned helicopters to drop sensor nodes from high altitude. After that we can collect data by crawling the area by the same flying device. Using unmanned aerial vehicles has become a common technique in practical sensor networking [6]. To analyze the contaminated area in detail, it is useful to have spatial data of the nodes. With spatial information, we can decide which area is contaminated and which area is not. The problem to determine the positions of each node in network is the *network localization problem* [2]. Equipping each node with a GPS (Global Positioning System) device might be an answer. However, it would be too expensive and impractical if the number of nodes is large. Instead of equipping GPS devices, we consider the following setting:

- each node can communicate with *some* other nodes;
- if two nodes communicate, then they can measure the distance between them;
- the central device (e.g. a helicopter) collects the distance information with IDs.

T. Erlebach et al. (Eds.): ALGOSENSORS 2011, LNCS 7111, pp. 101–114, 2012.

The localization problem of this setting is formalized by using graphs as follows.

Problem: WEIGHTED GRAPH EMBEDDABILITY IN d-SPACE (WGEd)
Instance: A graph G with nonnegative weights $w_e \geq 0$ on each edge $e \in E(G)$.
Question: Is there a mapping $f: V(G) \rightarrow \mathbb{R}^d$ such that $w_{uv} = \mathrm{dist}(f(u), f(v))$ for each $uv \in E(G)$, where $\mathrm{dist}(f(u), f(v))$ is the Euclidean distance between $f(u)$ and $f(v)$? (We call such a mapping f a d-embedding of G.)

Unfortunately, WGEd is known to be strongly NP-hard in general and weakly NP-hard for cycles.

Theorem 1.1 (Saxe [24], Feder and Motwani [12]). *For every positive integer d, WGEd is NP-hard even if every edge has weight one or two. Furthermore, WGE1 is weakly NP-complete even for cycles.*

Theorem 1.1 implies that a partial distance matrix corresponding to a graph is not always helpful to decide the embeddability. Therefore, it is an interesting problem to ask which graphs (and which d) provide a sufficient condition for designing an efficient algorithm for deciding embeddability. This paper gives an initial work for this direction of research. Considering Theorem 1.1, we have the following natural questions: (1) If there is no long cycle without a chord, does the problem remain hard? (2) Is the complexity of the problem monotone with respect to the dimension d of the embedded space? (3) If there is a dominating set S for which the embedding can be uniquely determined or the number of possible embeddings is small enough, can we design an efficient algorithm for the reconstruction (this corresponds to the problem in surveying engineering)? We answer each of these questions. Namely, we give polynomial-time algorithms to solve WGEd for chordal graphs ($d \geq 1$), for cycles ($d \geq 2$), and for graphs with small connected dominating sets ($d = 1$). Our results with Theorem 1.1 give an evidence of that the complexities of the problem in lower- and higher-dimensions are incomparable in general. We also consider a variant of the problem defined by Feder and Motwani [12], in which two distinct points cannot have the same position.

We assume a computational model used by Saxe [25] in which real numbers are primitive data objects on which exact arithmetic operations (including comparisons and extraction of square roots) can be performed in constant time.

2   Preliminaries

All graphs in this paper are finite, undirected, edge-weighted, and without self-loops and parallel edges. We denote the vertex set and the edge set of a graph G by $V(G)$ and $E(G)$, respectively. A graph is *connected* if it has a path between each pair of vertices.

A graph H is a *subgraph* of G, if $V(H) \subseteq V(G)$ and $E(H) \subseteq E(G)$. A subgraph H of G is *induced* with $V(H)$ if $E(H) = E(G) \cap \binom{V(H)}{2}$. A graph G is *chordal* if every induced cycle of G is of length three [15].

A vertex set $S \subseteq V(G)$ is a *dominating set* of G, if each vertex in $V(G) \setminus S$ has a neighbor in S. A vertex set $S \subseteq V(G)$ is a *p-dominating set* if every vertex in $V(G) \setminus S$ has at least p neighbors in S. For example, in K_3 any two vertices form a 2-dominating set. A vertex set $S \subseteq V(G)$ is a *vertex cover* of G, if every edge of G has an end in

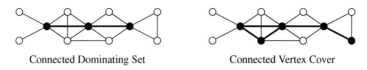

Connected Dominating Set   Connected Vertex Cover

Fig. 1. A connected dominating set and a connected vertex cover

S. From the definitions, it is easy to see that if a graph G has no isolated vertex, then any vertex cover of a graph G is a dominating set of G. A dominating set (a vertex cover) S is a *connected dominating set* (a *connected vertex cover*, respectively) if $G[S]$ is connected (see Fig. 1).

Feder and Motwani [12] studied th problem GRAPH TURNPIKE (GT), which is equivalent to the problem WGE1. They also studied the following variant of GT in which two distinct points are not allowed to have the same position.

Problem: GRAPH TURNPIKE WITH DISTINCTNESS (GTwD)
Instance: A graph G with nonnegative weights $w_e \geq 0$ on each edge $e \in E(G)$.
Question: Is there a mapping $f : V(G) \rightarrow \mathbb{R}$ such that $f(u) \neq f(v)$ for $u \neq v$, and $w_{uv} = |f(u) - f(v)|$ for each $uv \in E(G)$?

They showed that this variant is also weakly NP-hard for cycles [12]. Obviously, GTwD can be generalized to higher-dimensions. We call a variant of WGEd, in which two distinct points must have different positions, WGEd WITH DISTINCTNESS (WGEdwD).

3   The Length of Longest Induced Cycles and the Dimension of Spaces

In this section, we present answers to the following questions in Introduction.

1. If there is no long cycle without a chord, does the problem remains hard?
2. Is the complexity of the problem monotone with respect to the dimension d of the embedded space?

The first question is natural since no NP-hardness is known for the graphs of bounded length of induced cycles (this can be seen by carefully reading the proofs in [24,12]). We shall prove that if the length of every induced cycle is no more than three, then the problems WGEd and WGEdwD can be solved in polynomial time for any d. To answer the second question, we consider the problem for cycles in d-space with $d \geq 2$. It turns out that the problem is hard for cycles only if $d = 1$. Thus the case $d = 1$ is somewhat exceptional for them. We first show the easier result on cycles and then prove the tractability for chordal graphs.

3.1   Cycles in Higher-Dimensional Spaces

As we mentioned, it is known that WGE1 is NP-complete on cycles. Here, we shall show that for $d \geq 2$, WGEd can be solved in linear time for cycles.

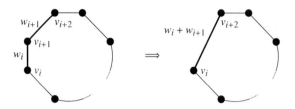

Fig. 2. Reducing a cycle

Theorem 3.1. *If $d \geq 2$, then WGEd is solvable in linear time for cycles*

Proof. Let C be a cycle with n vertices $v_1, v_2, \ldots, v_n$ and edges $v_1v_2, \ldots, v_{n-1}v_n, v_nv_1$. For the sake of simplicity, we denote $w_{v_iv_{i+1}}$ by w_i for $1 \leq i \leq n$ (with $w_n = w_{v_nv_1}$). Let $W = \sum_{1 \leq i \leq n} w_i$. If there exists an index i such that $w_i > W/2$, then C has no d-embedding for any positive integer d. We shall prove that C is 2-embeddable (and thus d-embeddable for $d \geq 2$) if $w_i \leq W/2$ for $1 \leq i \leq n$.

We proceed by an induction on n. If $n \leq 3$, then it is trivially true. Assume that $n \geq 4$ and the statement is true for any cycle with less than n vertices. Now there exists an index i such that $w_i + w_{i+1} \leq W/2$, since otherwise $2W = \sum_{i=1}^{n}(w_i + w_{i+1}) > nW/2$ which implies $n < 4$. Let i be an index such that $w_i + w_{i+1} \leq W/2$. By the following steps, we derive the new cycle C' (see Fig. 2):

1. remove the edges v_iv_{i+1} and $v_{i+1}v_{i+2}$;
2. remove the vertex v_{i+1};
3. add the edge v_iv_{i+2} with the weight $w_i + w_{i+1}$.

Then C' has a 2-embedding from the induction hypothesis. From a 2-embedding f of C', we can derive a 2-embedding of C by mapping v_{i+1} on a suitable point on the segment between $f(v_i)$ and $f(v_{i+2})$.

From the above observations, it follows that for $d \geq 2$, C is d-embeddable if and only if $w_i \leq W/2$ for $1 \leq i \leq n$. This characterization can be verified in linear time, and thus the theorem holds. $\square$

3.2   Polynomial-Time Algorithm for WGEd on Chordal Graphs

Next we prove that WGEd on chordal graphs can be solved in polynomial time for every fixed positive integer d. To this end, we need some definitions.

A *separator* of a graph G is a vertex set $S \subseteq V(G)$ such that there exist two vertices of G that are connected in G but not in $G - S$. A separator of a graph G is a *clique separator* if it induces a complete graph in G. A vertex v of G is *simplicial* if $N_G(v)$ induces a complete graph. Let G be an n-vertex graph and $v_1, v_2, \ldots, v_n$ be an ordering of $V(G)$. For $1 \leq i \leq n$, we define G_i to be the subgraph of G induced by $\{v_i, v_{i+1}, \ldots, v_n\}$. Then the ordering $v_1, v_2, \ldots, v_n$ is a *perfect elimination ordering* if for $1 \leq i \leq n$, the vertex v_i is simplicial in the graph G_i. Note that $N_{G_i}(v_i)$ is a clique separator of G_i.

It is well known that chordal graphs are characterized by perfect elimination ordering, and a perfect elimination ordering of a chordal graph can be found in linear time.

Theorem 3.2 (Fulkerson and Gross [13]). *A graph G is chordal if and only if G has a perfect elimination ordering.*

Theorem 3.3 (Rose, Tarjan, and Lueker [23] and Tarjan and Yannakakis [27]). *A perfect elimination ordering of a chordal graph can be found in linear time.*

Saxe [25] showed that if a graph is a complete graph, then WGEd on it is easy and its d-embedding, if any, is unique.

Theorem 3.4 (Saxe [25, Appendix II]). *For any fixed d, WGEd can be solved in $O(m)$ time for an edge-weighted complete graph G of m edges. Furthermore, if G has a d-embedding f, then it is unique up to rotation and translation and f can be found in $O(m)$ time.*

Using Theorems 3.2, 3.3, and 3.4, we shall prove the polynomial-time solvability of WGEd on chordal graphs. We first prove the following lemma, which is of independent interest.

Lemma 3.5. *Let G be a connected edge-weighted graph, d be a fixed positive integer, and $S \subseteq V(G)$ be a clique separator of G. Let G_1 and G_2 be two induced subgraphs of G such that $V(G_1) \cap V(G_2) = S$ and $V(G_1) \cup V(G_2) = V(G)$. Then, G has a d-embedding if and only if both G_1 and G_2 have d-embeddings.*

Proof. For the only-if part, assume that G has a d-embedding f. Then, it is not difficult to see that $f|_{V(G_i)}$ is a d-embedding of G_i for each i, where $f|_{V(G_i)}$ is the subfunction of f induced by $V(G_i) \subseteq V(G)$.

For the if part, assume that each G_i has a d-embedding f_i. By Theorem 3.4, d-embeddings of S is unique. Therefore, by appropriate rotation and translation of points in $f_2(V(G_2))$, we can obtain a d-embedding f_2' of G_2 such that $f_1|_S = f_2'|_S$. Then it is not difficult to see that the mapping $f : V(G) \to \mathbb{R}^d$ such that

$$f(v) = \begin{cases} f_1(v) & \text{if } v \in V(G_1), \\ f_2'(v) & \text{otherwise}, \end{cases}$$

is a d-embedding of G. This completes the proof. □

Now we are ready to prove the theorem.

Theorem 3.6. *For edge-weighted chordal graphs, WGEd can be solved in polynomial time for any fixed positive integer d.*

Proof. Let G be a given chordal graph with n vertices. We may assume without loss of generality that G is connected, since otherwise we can compute G's connected components in linear time by a standard DFS algorithm, and apply the following argument for each connected component.

We first compute a perfect elimination ordering $v_1, v_2, \ldots, v_n$ of G in linear time. Since v_i is simplicial in G_i for $1 \leq i \leq n$, each $N_{G_i}(v_i)$ is a clique of G_i. Thus, by Lemma 3.5, G_i has a d-embedding if and only if both $G_i[N_{G_i}[v_i]]$ and $G_i - v_i = G_{i+1}$ have d-embeddings. This implies that G_i has a d-embedding if and only if each complete graph $G_i[N_{G_i}[v_i]]$ has a d-embedding for $1 \leq i \leq n$. There are $O(n)$ complete graphs, and the number of edges of each complete graph is $O(n^2)$. Therefore, by Theorem 3.4, we can check in $O(n^3)$ time whether $G_i[N_{G_i}[v_i]]$ has a d-embedding for all $1 \leq i \leq n$. Thus the theorem holds.   □

Note that the result in this subsection can be seen as a variant of a result by Laurent [22] who showed that the problem to decide whether a chordal graph can be embedded in d-space, for some d (not given), is solvable in polynomial time.

4   Algorithms for Graphs with Dominating Cores

In geometry and surveying engineering, it is well known that if we have a position of a simplex T and one knows all distances from p to the set of $d + 1$ vertices of T, the position of p is uniquely determined. Thus, we can consider $d(d + 1)$ variables corresponding to the positions of vertices of T to have a system of equations that seems to be numerically soluble if d is a constant. However, we need to consider a degenerate case. For example, suppose that $d = 3$ and we have m points on a line in space, and the rest of $n - m$ points are located on a plane perpendicular to the line. Then, there remains exponential number of possible locations even if we have the set of all distances corresponding to the bipartite graph, and we currently have no polynomial-time solution for the general case. However, for $d \in \{1, 2\}$, we can solve the problem with some assumption.

4.1   General Frameworks for $d \in \{1, 2\}$

For $d \in \{1, 2\}$, we can solve the problem if a graph has a dominating set for which the possible embeddings are efficiently enumerated. Such a dominating set can be seen as a *core* of the sensor network. We first present the following general frameworks.

Theorem 4.1. *Let G and S be a given n-vertex graph and its dominating set which is also given. If the number of all possible candidates of 1-embeddings of $G[S]$ is $g(|S|)$, and all these candidates can be enumerated in $\mathrm{poly}(n)$ time for each, then we can solve WGE1 and WGE1wD in $O(g(|S|) \cdot (\mathrm{poly}(n) + n^2))$ time.*

Proof. First we fix a 1-embedding f_S of $G[S]$. We can check in $O(n^2)$ time whether f_S can be extended to a 1-embedding f of G such that $f|_S = f_S$ by reducing the problem to 2-SAT as follows.

   Let $V(G) \setminus S = \{v_1, \ldots, v_{n-|S|}\}$. For each $v_i \in V(G) \setminus S$, choose arbitrarily its neighbor in S and denote it by u_i. (Note that $u_i = u_j$ may hold for some $i \neq j$.) Then, it is easy to see that

$$f(v_i) \in \{f_S(u_i) + w_{u_i v_i}, f_S(u_i) - w_{u_i v_i}\}.$$

We put a variable x_i for each $v_i \in V(G) \setminus S$. We think that $x_i = 1$ means $f(v_i) = f_S(u_i) + w_{u_i v_i}$ and $x_i = 0$ means $f(v_i) = f_S(u_i) - w_{u_i v_i}$.

   Now it is easy to see that for each $v_i \in V(G) \setminus S$,

$$f(v_i) \in \bigcap_{u \in N_G(v_i)} \{f_S(u) + w_{uv_i}, f_S(u) - w_{uv_i}\}.$$

If the right-hand side has two elements, then we do nothing here. If the right-hand side is empty, then we can conclude that this f_S can not be extended to a 1-embedding of G, and introduce two clauses x_i and $\bar{x}_i$ which make the SAT instance unsatisfiable. If the right-hand side has exactly one elements, then we can fix the position of v_i by introducing a clause with only one literal x_i or $\bar{x}_i$; if $f(v_i)$ must be $f_S(u) + w_{uv_i}$, then the clause has the literal x_i, otherwise the clause has the literal $\bar{x}_i$. The set C of clauses introduced in this phase is as follows:

$$C = \left\{ \bar{x}_i \mid f_S(u_i) + w_{u_iv_i} \notin \bigcap_{u \in N_G(v_i)} \{f_S(u) + w_{uv_i}, f_S(u) - w_{uv_i}\} \right\}$$

$$\cup \left\{ x_i \mid f_S(u_i) - w_{u_iv_i} \notin \bigcap_{u \in N_G(v_i)} \{f_S(u) + w_{uv_i}, f_S(u) - w_{uv_i}\} \right\}.$$

Next, for each edge in $E(G - S)$, we put at most four clauses with two literals. Let $v_i, v_j \in V(G) \setminus S$ be adjacent vertices. For each combination of the positions of v_i and v_j, we check whether the combination contradicts the weight of the edge v_iv_j. If it does, then we put a clause that forbids the combination. For example, if $w_{v_iv_j} \neq |(f_S(u_i) + w_{u_iv_i}) - (f_S(u_j) + w_{u_jv_j})|$, then we put the clause $\bar{x}_i \vee \bar{x}_j$. More precisely, the set C' of clauses is defined as follows:

$$C' = \{\bar{x}_i \vee \bar{x}_j \mid v_iv_j \in E(G),\ w_{v_iv_j} \neq |(f_S(u_i) + w_{u_iv_i}) - (f_S(u_j) + w_{u_jv_j})|\}$$
$$\cup \{\bar{x}_i \vee x_j \mid v_iv_j \in E(G),\ w_{v_iv_j} \neq |(f_S(u_i) + w_{u_iv_i}) - (f_S(u_j) - w_{u_jv_j})|\}$$
$$\cup \{x_i \vee \bar{x}_j \mid v_iv_j \in E(G),\ w_{v_iv_j} \neq |(f_S(u_i) - w_{u_iv_i}) - (f_S(u_j) + w_{u_jv_j})|\}$$
$$\cup \{x_i \vee x_j \mid v_iv_j \in E(G),\ w_{v_iv_j} \neq |(f_S(u_i) - w_{u_iv_i}) - (f_S(u_j) - w_{u_jv_j})|\}.$$

Clearly, $C \cup C'$ is satisfiable if and only if f_S is a 1-embedding of S and f_S can be extended to a 1-embedding f of G such that $f|_S = f_S$. If the problem is WGE1wD, then we need the following set C'' of additional clauses that forbid any coincidence of points:

$$C'' = \{\bar{x}_i \mid \exists u \in S,\ f_S(u_i) + w_{u_iv_i} = f_S(u)\}$$
$$\cup \{x_i \mid \exists u \in S,\ f_S(u_i) - w_{u_iv_i} = f_S(u)\}$$
$$\cup \{\bar{x}_i \vee \bar{x}_j \mid |(f_S(u_i) + w_{u_iv_i}) - (f_S(u_j) + w_{u_jv_j})| = 0\}$$
$$\cup \{\bar{x}_i \vee x_j \mid |(f_S(u_i) + w_{u_iv_i}) - (f_S(u_j) - w_{u_jv_j})| = 0\}$$
$$\cup \{x_i \vee \bar{x}_j \mid |(f_S(u_i) - w_{u_iv_i}) - (f_S(u_j) + w_{u_jv_j})| = 0\}$$
$$\cup \{x_i \vee x_j \mid |(f_S(u_i) - w_{u_iv_i}) - (f_S(u_j) - w_{u_jv_j})| = 0\}.$$

It is not difficult to verify that $C \cup C' \cup C''$ is satisfiable if and only if f_S is a 1-embedding of S with distinctness and f_S can be extended to a 1-embedding f of G with distinctness such that $f|_S = f_S$. In both cases, the number of variables is $O(n)$ and the number of clauses is $O(n^2)$. Since 2-SAT is solvable in linear time in the number of variables and clauses [3], we can check whether f_S can be extended to f in $O(n^2)$ time for both cases.

From the above observation, we can solve the problem by checking all the candidates of embeddings of $G[S]$, the number of which is $g(|S|)$, whether it is a 1-embedding of

$G[S]$ (with or without distinctness) in $O(m)$ time and whether it can be extended to a 1-embedding of G (with or without distinctness, respectively) in $O(n^2)$ time. Therefore, we have the theorem.   □

Theorem 4.2. *Let G and S be a given n-vertex graph and its 2-dominating set which is also given. If the number of all possible candidates of 2-embeddings of $G[S]$ is $g(|S|)$, and all these candidates can be enumerated in* poly(n) *time for each, then we can solve WGE2wD in $O(g(|S|) \cdot (\text{poly}(n) + n^2))$ time.*

Proof. Since the problem has the distinctness constraint, we can assume that each edge in G has positive weight. Here we use an almost the same argument as in the proof of Theorem 4.1. We first guess a 2-embedding f_S of S. Next we construct an instance of 2-SAT from G and f_S such that the instance is a yes-instance if and only if f_S can be extended to a 2-embedding of whole G. The construction of the 2-SAT instance is almost the same as in the proof of Theorem 4.4. There are only two differences: the first one is the distance function; the second one is that for each vertex $v_i \in V(G) \setminus S$, we select its two neighbors u_i and w_i arbitrarily from S (these two vertices in S restrict the position of v_i to only two points). The instance has $O(n)$ variables and $O(n^2)$ clauses. Thus for each guessed embedding of S, we can check its extendability in $O(n^2)$ time. This completes the proof.   □

Note that our proof technique used in the proofs of Theorems 4.1 and 4.2 can not be used directly for the case $d \geq 3$. This is because instead of assuming distinctness, we have to assume the *general position* constraint for $d \geq 3$. However, if we use SAT as in the proofs to check the general position constraint, then we have some clauses with more than two literals. This make the SAT instance intractable since the k-SAT problem is NP-hard for any fixed $k \geq 3$ [14].

4.2   Applications of General Frameworks

In this subsection, we present several practical applications of our frameworks; that is Theorems 4.1 and 4.2. The simplest application is for graphs with dominating cliques. Combining Theorems 3.4, 4.1, and 4.1, we have the following corollary.

Corollary 4.3. *For graphs with dominating cliques, WGE1 and WGE1wD can be solved in $O(n^2)$ time. For graphs with 2-dominating cliques, WGE2wD can be solved in $O(n^2)$ time, where n is the number of vertices.*

From the corollary above, one may think that if a graph has a dominating core with a unique embedding, then the localization problem can be solved in polynomial time. In practice, if sensors of a two-dimensional sensor network are densely enough distributed, then it is likely that the sensor network has a large subgraph G that has 2-dominating set S such that $G[S]$ has a unique embedding. If the localization problem can be solved for $G[S]$, then the problem is also solvable for G by Theorems 4.2. If G covers a large part of the sensor network, then we can just ignore the remaining part or may locate the remaining part using the embedding of G. Aspnes et al. [2] studied the localization problem for graphs with unique embeddings using *rigidity theory* (see e.g. [16,20,21]), and show that the localization problem for these graphs is NP-hard, unfortunately. However, it is not known whether the problem is NP-hard for rigid graphs with additional conditions; for example, rigid *unit disk graphs* (see [5] for the definition of unit disk graphs).

The next application shows that although its embedding is not unique, a small connected dominating set makes the problem easy.

Theorem 4.4. *Given an edge-weighted graph G with n vertices and its connected dominating set S of size k, WGE1 and WGE1wD can be solved in $O(2^k n^2)$ time.*

Proof. Let T be a spanning tree of $G[S]$. From a 1-embedding of T, we can obtain an orientation of the edges $E(T)$. If f_S is a 1-embedding of $G[S]$, then it is also a 1-embedding of T. Since the number of possible orientations of T is 2^{k-1}, we can conclude that the number of all non-congruent 1-embeddings of $G[S]$ is at most 2^{k-1}. Now we can apply Theorem 4.1. This completes the proof. □

Note that the above theorem is a generalization of Theorem 3 in [12], which states that WGE1 and WGE1wD can be solved in polynomial time if the input graph has a vertex adjacent to all other vertices.

An example of graphs that have small connected dominating sets is a graph G with a spanning complete bipartite graph K_{n_1, n_2}. Let $v_1, v_2 \in V(G)$ be vertices that have different colors in a proper coloring of its spanning complete bipartite graph. Clearly, $S = \{v_1, v_2\}$ is a connected dominating set of G. Thus we have the following corollary.

Corollary 4.5. *Let G be an edge-weighted n-vertex graph with a spanning complete bipartite graph. Then WGE1 and WGE1wD can be solved in $O(n^2)$ time.*

Graphs with spanning complete bipartite graphs are called *join graphs*, since they are constructed by the *join* operation [18]. The class of join graphs includes very important graphs such as complete graphs, complete bipartite graphs, and complete k-partite graphs. More generally, any connected *cograph* [7] is a join graph. Cographs play important roles in algorithmic graph theory, since they are precisely the graphs of *clique-width* at most two [8,19].

In Theorem 4.4, we assumed that a small connected dominating set is given. Therefore, if it is not given, then we should find a small connected dominating set. A naive way is to enumerate all vertex subset of size at most k in $O(n^k)$ time. For each subset, we can check whether it is a connected dominating set in $O(m)$ time. Therefore, we have the following corollary.

Corollary 4.6. *Given a graph with n vertices and m edges, we can solve WGE1 and WGE1wD in $O(n^k m + 2^k n^2)$ time if the graph has a connected dominating set of size at most k.*

Note that since the problem of finding a connected dominating set is W[2]-hard when parameterized by the solution size (see e.g. [11]), it is impossible to improve upon the $O(n^k)$ time complexity for finding a connected dominating set to $O(c^k \text{poly}(n))$ time for any constant c unless W[2] = FPT.[1] Since every vertex cover of a connected graph is

---

[1] If W[2] = FPT, then *Exponential Time Hypothesis* fails [10].

its dominating set an FTP algorithm for connected vertex covers immediately yields an FPT time algorithm for WGE1 and WGE1wD parameterized by the size of the minimum connected vertex cover. It is known that a connected vertex cover of size k can be found, if any, in $O(6^k n + 4^k n^2 + n^2 \log n + mn)$ time [17]. However, we use an $O(mn)$-time 2-approximation algorithm presented by Arkin, Halldórsson, and Hassin [1] to obtain a better running time.

Corollary 4.7. *Given a graph with n vertices and m edges, we can solve WGE1 and WGE1wD in $O(4^k n^2 + mn)$ time if the graph has a connected vertex cover of size at most k.*

Proof. We first find a connected vertex cover C of size at most $2k$ by using the $O(mn)$-time 2-approximation algorithm of Arkin et al. [1]. By Theorem 4.4, we can solve WGE1 and WGE1wD in $O(4^k n^2)$ time since C is also a connected dominating set of size at most $2k$. The combined time complexity is $O(4^k n^2 + mn)$. □

In the rest of this section, we shall discuss the two-dimensional case. We need the notion of *k-trees* which is defined as follows:

- the complete graph of k vertices is a k-tree;
- if G is a k-tree, then the graph obtained from G by adding a simplicial vertex of degree k is also a k-tree.

It is easy to see that a k-tree is a chordal graph. With these terminologies, we can have a two-dimensional generalization of Theorem 4.4 as follows.

Theorem 4.8. *Given an edge-weighted graph G with n vertices and its 2-dominating set S of size k such that $G[S]$ have a spanning 2-tree, WGE2wD can be solved in $O(2^k n^2)$ time.*

Proof. By Theorem 4.2, it suffices to show that all 2-embeddings of $G[S]$ can be enumerated in $O(2^k)$ time. Since the problem has the distinctness constraint, we can assume that each edge in G has positive weight. Let R be a spanning 2-tree of $G[S]$, and let $r_1, \ldots, r_k$ be a perfect elimination ordering of R. We shall construct a 2-embedding by embedding vertices in the reverse ordering $r_k, r_{k-1}, \ldots, r_1$. We can first embed r_k and r_{k-1} uniquely. Then, when embedding each r_i, $1 \le i \le k - 2$, r_i has two neighbors that are already embedded and have different positions. Thus, we have only two possibilities for each r_i. This implies that the number of possible 2-embeddings (up to motion) of S is 2^{k-2}. The enumeration of the candidates can be easily done in $O(2^k)$ time. Thus the theorem holds. □

An example of graphs that have small 2-dominating sets with 2-tree spanning trees is a graph G with a spanning complete tripartite graph K_{n_1, n_2, n_3}. Let $v_1, v_2, v_3 \in V(G)$ be vertices that have different colors in a proper coloring of its spanning complete tripartite graph. Then, it is not difficult to see that the set $S = \{v_1, v_2, v_3\}$ is a 2-dominating set of G, and the triangle $G[S]$ itself is a spanning 2-tree of $G[S]$. It is easy to see that such a set S can be found in $O(n^4)$ time by naively examine all $\binom{n}{3}$ vertex triples in $O(n)$ time. Therefore, we have the following corollary.

Corollary 4.9. *Let G be an edge-weighted n-vertex graph with a spanning complete tripartite graph. Then WGE2wD can be solved in $O(n^4)$ time.*

5   Concluding Remarks

We approached the localization problem from a graph embedding perspective. Since it is hard to embed cycles into a line, we analyzed difficulty of the problem according to the dimension of the space and structures of graphs. We have shown that WGEd can be solved in polynomial time for chordal graphs ($d \geq 1$) and for cycles ($d \geq 2$). We have also studied the problems on graphs with small connected dominating set, and have shown that for such graphs WGE1 and WGE1wD can be solved in polynomial time and WGE2wD can be solved in polynomial time if we add a condition. Our results on graphs with small connected dominating set may be considered as that if a sensor network has a small *core*, then the localization problem can be solved efficiently.

To obtain a practical localization method, there are still many issues to resolve. Our general framework is hard to be extended into higher dimension case due to the general position assumption. The running time is also highly depend on the rigidity of cores. For instance, it will be quite fast when the core is a clique as we can compute its unique embedding efficiently. In contrast, the running time will be exponential to the size of the core in the case that the core is a tree. In the latter case, it requires the network to have cores of logarithmic size if we are eager to achieve an efficient computing time and this requirement is difficult to be fulfilled in practice. These remain our future work to do.

In addition, the rigidity of graphs is still not studied thoroughly yet now. This property is important because that not only it relates to computing time but also it is a basic requirement for the network localization. The localization problem is NP-hard even for the graph with a unique embedding [2]. It is not known whether the problem is NP-hard for rigid graphs with additional conditions; for example, rigid *unit disk graphs*. If the sensor network is dense enough, it is likely that there exist a core such that it has a unique embedding. However, we still lack of a theoretical guarantee by now. How to obtain a rigid and easily localizable graph structure remains a challenge for us.

Furthermore, we only consider exact graph embedding in this paper. However, there are many errors with the input data in actual engineering. It is likely that there is no solution for the input instance. Instead, an approximation one is necessary in this case. In the 2-SAT part of our general framework, it is possible to allow some forbidden cases happen to receive an approximate solution. A naive idea is to obtain an approximation such that it satisfies the forbidden clauses as much as possible and this is MAX 2-SAT problem. How to adjust the graph to obtain a high quality approximation, further study is necessary.

Finally, there is a problem left for theoretical interest. Feder and Motwani [12] studied a variant of WGE1, denoted by GTwD, in which two distinct points cannot have the same position. This variant is very natural, and should be investigated more extensively. There is an interesting problem on GTwD.

Problem 5.1. Can GTwD be solved in polynomial time for trees?

We think it might be NP-hard. It is not difficult to see that any tree can be embedded in the line (if we do not care about distinctness) by putting the roof r of a tree at the origin and putting the other points v at the point ℓ, where ℓ is the sum of the weights of edges in a unique r–v path in the tree. Also, by slightly modifying this embedding, we can derive an 2-embedding of the tree in which any two distinct vertices have different positions. Note that embedding trees in $\mathbb{Z}^2$ with distinctness is NP-hard even if every edge has the same weight [4].

References

1. Arkin, E.M., Halldórsson, M.M., Hassin, R.: Approximating the tree and tour covers of a graph. Inform. Process. Lett. 47, 275–282 (1993)
2. Aspnes, J., Eren, T., Goldenberg, D.K., Morse, A.S., Whiteley, W., Yang, Y.R., Anderson, B.D.O., Belhumeur, P.N.: A theory of network localization. IEEE Trans. Mobile Comput. 5, 1663–1678 (2006)
3. Aspvall, B., Plass, M.F., Tarjan, R.E.: A linear-time algorithm for testing the truth of certain quantified boolean formulas. Inform. Process. Lett. 8, 121–123 (1979)
4. Bhatt, S.N., Cosmadakis, S.S.: The complexity of minimizing wire lengths in VLSI layouts. Inform. Process. Lett. 25, 263–267 (1987)
5. Clark, B.N., Colbourn, C.J., Johnson, D.S.: Unit disk graphs. Discrete Math. 86, 165–177 (1990)
6. Corke, P., Hrabar, S., Peterson, R., Rus, D., Saripalli, S., Sukhatme, G.: Autonomous deployment and repair of a sensor network using an unmanned aerial vehicle. In: IEEE International Conference on Robotics and Automation (2004)
7. Corneil, D.G., Lerchs, H., Burlingham, L.S.: Complement reducible graphs. Discrete Appl. Math. 3, 163–174 (1981)
8. Courcelle, B., Olariu, S.: Upper bounds to the clique width of graphs. Discrete Appl. Math. 101, 77–114 (2000)
9. Dargie, W., Poellabauer, C.: Fundamentals of Wireless Sensor Networks: Theory and Practice. Wiley (2010)
10. Downey, R.G., Estivill-Castro, V., Fellows, M.R., Prieto, E., Rosamond, F.A.: Cutting up is hard to do: the parameterized complexity of k-cut and related problems. Electron. Notes Theor. Comput. Sci. 78, 209–222 (2003)
11. Downey, R.G., Fellows, M.R.: Parameterized Complexity. Springer, Heidelberg (1998)
12. Feder, T., Motwani, R.: On the graph turnpike problem. Inform. Process. Lett. 109, 774–776 (2009)
13. Fulkerson, D.R., Gross, O.A.: Incidence matrices and interval graphs. Pacific J. Math. 15, 835–855 (1965)
14. Garey, M.R., Johnson, D.S.: Computers and Intractability: A Guide to the Theory of NP-Completeness. Freeman (1979)
15. Golumbic, M.C.: Algorithmic Graph Theory and Perfect Graphs, 2nd edn. Annals of Discrete Mathematics, vol. 57. North Holland (2004)
16. Graver, J., Servatius, B., Servatius, H.: Combinatorial Rigidity. AMS (1993)
17. Guo, J., Niedermeier, R., Wernicke, S.: Parameterized complexity of vertex cover variants. Theory Comput. Syst. 41, 501–520 (2007)
18. Harary, F.: Graph Theory. Addison-Wesley, Reading (1969)
19. Hliněný, P., Oum, S., Seese, D., Gottlob, G.: Width parameters beyond tree-width and their applications. Comput. J. 51, 326–362 (2008)
20. Jackson, B., Jordán, T.: Connected rigidity matroids and unique realizations of graphs. J. Combin. Theory Ser. B 94, 1–29 (2005)
21. Laman, G.: On graphs and rigidity of plane skeletal structures. J. Eng. Math. 4, 331–340 (2002)

22. Laurent, M.: Polynomial instances of the positive semidefinite and euclidean distance matrix completion problems. SIAM J. Matrix Anal. Appl. 22, 874–894 (2000)
23. Rose, D.J., Tarjan, R.E., Lueker, G.S.: Algorithmic aspects of vertex elimination on graphs. SIAM J. Comput. 5, 266–283 (1976)
24. Saxe, J.B.: Embeddability of weighted graphs in k-space is strongly NP-hard. In: 17th Allerton Conf. Commun. Control Comput., pp. 480–489 (1979)
25. Saxe, J.B.: Two papers on graph embedding problems. Technical Report CMU-CS-80-102, Department of Computer Science, Carnegie-Mellon University (1980)
26. Sohraby, K., Minoli, D., Znati, T.: Wireless Sensor Networks: Technology, Protocols, and Applications. Wiley-Interscience (2007)
27. Tarjan, R.E., Yannakakis, M.: Simple linear-time algorithms to test chordality of graphs, test acyclicity of hypergraphs, and selectively reduce acyclic hypergraphs. SIAM J. Comput. 13, 566–579 (1984)

A   Proof of Theorem 3.4

For readers' convenience, we provide a proof of Theorem 3.4 due to Saxe [25] (the technical report is not available online).

Theorem A.1 (Saxe [25, Appendix II]). *For any fixed k, WGEk can be solved in $O(m)$ time for an edge-weighted complete graph G of m edges. Furthermore, if G has a k-embedding f, then it is unique up to rotation and translation and f can be found in $O(m)$ time.*

Proof. Let $G = (V, E)$ be a complete weighted graph with n vertices $x_1, \ldots, x_n$, where each edge $x_i x_j \in E$ has weight $w_{i,j}$. To test the embeddability of G, we will attempt to position the vertices of G successively in a $(k + 1)$-dimensional coordinate space. Without loss of generality, we may send x_1 to the origin and x_2 to $(w_{i,j}, 0, \ldots, 0)$. For each m, $1 \leq m \leq n$, we define

$$d(m) = \min\{j \mid G[\{x_i \mid 1 \leq i \leq m\}] \text{ is } j\text{-embeddable}\}.$$

If $G[\{x_i \mid 1 \leq i \leq m\}]$ is not j-embeddable for any j, then $d(m)$ is undefined. For each j, $0 \leq j \leq k$, we define

$$p(j) = \min\{m \mid d(m) = j\}.$$

If there is no m such that $d(m) = j$, then $p(j)$ is undefined. Note that if $p(j)$ is well-defined, then $p(0), \ldots, p(j)$ are all well defined. As we locate each vertex, we enforce the restriction that at most the first $d(m)$ coordinates of x_m may be non-zero. By following this rule, we guarantee that after the x_m has been located (if this is possible), we will know the value of $d(m)$ and of $p(0), \ldots, p(d(m))$. The procedure for locating x_{m+1} (for $1 \leq m \leq n$) is as follows:

1. Note that there is at most one possible location for x_{m+1} which will satisfy the following criteria:
   - The correct weights are induced for the $d(m) + 1$ edges $x_{p(j)} x_{m+1}, 0 \leq j \leq d(m)$.
   - At most the first $d(m) + 1$ coordinates of the location are non-zero.
   - The $(d(m) + 1)$st coordinate of the location is non-negative.

2. If there are no such locations, or if the $(k + 1)$st coordinate of the unique location satisfying the criteria is non-zero, halt asserting that G is not k-embeddable. Otherwise, without loss of generality, assign x_{m+1} to the unique location satisfying the criteria.

3. Check that the weights induced for the remaining $x_i x_{m+1}$ (where $1 \leq i \leq m$ and $i \neq p(j)$ for any j) are correct. If any are not, the halt asserting that G is not k-embeddable. Note that the time for this step is $O(n)$, since we always have $m < n$.

If we manage to place all the vertices without discovering that G is not k-embeddable, then we will have found a k-embedding for G (and this embedding is unique up to congruence). In any case, the time required is linear in the number of edges and the space will be linear in the number of vertices.   □

Minimizing Average Interference through Topology Control

Tiancheng Lou[1], Haisheng Tan[1,*], Yuexuan Wang[1], and Francis C.M. Lau[2]

[1] Institute for Interdisciplinary Information Sciences,
Tsinghua University, Beijing, 100084, China
[2] Department of Computer Science, The University of Hong Kong,
Pokfulam Road, Hong Kong, China

Abstract. Reducing interference is one of the main challenges in wireless communication. To minimize interference through topology control in wireless sensor networks is a well-known open algorithmic problem. In this paper, we answer the question of how to minimize the average interference when a node is receiving a message. We assume the receiver-centric interference model where the interference on a node is equal to the number of the other nodes whose transmission ranges cover the node. For one-dimensional (1D) networks, we propose a fast polynomial exact algorithm that can minimize the average interference. For two-dimensional (2D) networks, we give a proof that the maximum interference can be bounded while minimizing the average interference. The bound is only related to the distances between nodes but not the network size. Based on the bound, we propose the first exact algorithm to compute the minimum average interference in 2D networks. Optimal topologies with the minimum average interference can be constructed through traceback in both 1D and 2D networks.

Keywords: Wireless Sensor Networks, Interference Minimization, Topology Control, Combinatorial Optimization.

1 Introduction

A wireless sensor network (WSN) consists of a set of nodes deployed across a region of interest. The nodes can adjust their transmission powers to achieve their desired transmission ranges with which a multi-hop network is then formed. WSNs have many applications in real life such as environmental monitoring, intrusion detection, and health care.

Energy is a precious resource in wireless sensor networks. One way to conserve energy, and to simultaneously improve communication efficiency, is to reduce *interference* due to concurrent transmissions of two or more nearby nodes. There exist numerous models for capturing the essence of interferences in a wireless network at various abstraction levels of interest. Two types of models that have been

---

* Contact him at tan@tsinghua.edu.cn. Part of the work was done when the author was studying at the Department of Computer Science, The University of Hong Kong.

T. Erlebach et al. (Eds.): ALGOSENSORS 2011, LNCS 7111, pp. 115–129, 2012.
© Springer-Verlag Berlin Heidelberg 2012

frequently studied in recent algorithmic research on wireless sensor networks are graph-based *protocol models* and SINR-based *physical models* [1]. Each type has its own merits. SINR-based protocols capture more accurately certain important wireless signal propagation characteristics([2]). The graph-based protocol models, although simplistic, are a good estimation of interference, which have been particularly popular with high-layer protocol designers.

One of the graph-based protocol models is the *sender-centric model*, where interference is computed for each edge [3–8]. The interference of an edge (u, v) is the number of other nodes that are covered by the disk centered at u or v with radius $|uv|$—that is, interference is considered at the sender but not the receiver. However, interference actually prevents correct data reception in the real networks. Thus, the authors in [9, 10] proposed *the receiver-centric model*, where the interference on a node is the number of other nodes whose transmission ranges cover the node. In Figure 1, the interference on the node v is 3 as all the other nodes can interfere with it. In this work, we consider ways to minimize the number of the other nodes that can interfere with a node when it is receiving a message. Therefore, the receiver-centric model is adopted.

Fig. 1. The receiver-centric interference: the disk centered at a node is the node's transmission range; the number beside a node is interference on it

Generally, *topology control* refers to selecting a subset of the available communication links for data transmission, which helps save energy and reduce interference. The problem of minimizing (receiver-centric) interference through topology control is one of the most well-known open algorithmic problems in wireless communication. Researchers study the problem in two directions: minimizing the maximum interference and minimizing the average interference. Interference minimization is hard because it entails an unusually complicated combinatorial structure, and some intuitive ideas, such as low node degree, spare topology and Nearest Neighbor Forest (connecting each node to its nearest neighbor) can not guarantee low interference [4, 9].

In the literature, interference minimization is studied in both 1D and 2D networks. Despite their simplicity, 1D networks, i.e. the nodes are arbitrarily distributed along a line, have revealed many interesting challenges and features of the problem in general. Studying 1D networks is justified also from a practical point of view as some real networks are one-dimensional, such as the sensors deployed along a railway, a corridor, or inside a tunnel. For 1D networks, paper [9] bounded *the minimum maximum interference* (MMI) by $O(\sqrt{\Delta})$ and presented an approximation with ratio $O(\sqrt[4]{\Delta})$. Here Δ is the maximum node degree when each node is connected to all the other nodes within the maximum transmission range r_{max}. The only sub-exponential-time (but super-polynomial) exact algorithm to minimize the maximum interference was given in [11]. For 2D networks, the problem of computing the MMI was shown to be NP-complete in [12]. The algorithm in [13] could bound the maximum interference by $O(\sqrt{\Delta})$. For the problem of computing *the minimum average interference* (MAI), better results are known. In [11], a polynomial-time, $O(n^3 \Delta^3)$ algorithm is proposed to minimize the average interference in a 1D network, where n is the network size. For 2D networks, the authors of [14] gave an asymptotically optimal approximation algorithm with an approximation ratio $O(\log n)$.

Our Contribution: In this paper, we answer the question of how to minimize the average interference when a node is receiving a message.

1. To minimize the average interference in 1D networks, we propose an exact algorithm that substantially improves the time complexity from $O(n^3 \Delta^3)$ [11] to $O(n\Delta^2)$.
2. In previous work, the MAI and the MMI were studied separately. We give a proof that the maximum interference can be bounded by $O(\log \lambda)$ while minimizing the average interference. Here $\lambda = \frac{min(d_{max}, r_{max})}{d_{min}}$, where d_{max} and d_{min} are the longest and shortest distance between two nodes respectively. The upper bound is only determined by the distances between nodes but not the network size.
3. Based on the upper bound, we propose an exact algorithm to compute the MAI in 2D networks exactly in time $n^{O(m \log \lambda)}$, where m is the minimum number of parallel lines so that all the nodes are located on the lines. Optimal topologies with the MAI can be constructed trough traceback. To the best of our knowledge, it is the first exact algorithm that computes the MAI in 2D networks.

The rest of the paper is organized as follows. We give some formal definitions in Section 2. In Section 3, we propose a fast exact algorithm to compute the MAI in 1D networks. The upper bound of the MMI while minimizing the average interference is proved in Section 4. Section 5 presents the exact algorithm to compute the minimum average interference in 2D networks. Section 6 concludes the paper and suggests some future work.

2   Problem Definitions

We model a wireless sensor network as an undirected graph $G = (V, E)$, where V is the set of nodes and E is the set of communication links. The nodes have the same maximum transmission radius, r_{max}. Each node can self-adjust its transmission radius from 0 to r_{max} in a continuous manner. An edge $(u, v) \in E$ exists only if both transmission radii, r_u and r_v, are not shorter than the

Euclidean distance $|uv|$. Therefore, in G, the transmission radius of a node is set to the distance to its farthest neighbor. (Two nodes are neighbors means there is an edge incident on them.) We assume the unit disk graph $UDG(V)$, in which each node connects to all the other nodes within a distance of r_{max}, is connected.

We adopt the receiver-centric interference model. The interference of a node v, denoted as $RI(v)$, is defined as the number of other nodes whose transmission ranges can cover v:

$$RI(v) = |\{u|u \in V \setminus \{v\}, |uv| \le r_u\}|. \tag{1}$$

The average node interference in G, $RI_{avg}(G)$, can be defined as:

$$RI_{avg}(G) = \frac{\sum_{v \in V} RI(v)}{|V|}. \tag{2}$$

For a node v with transmission radius r_v, the interference created by v is defined as the number of the other nodes covered by the transmission range of v:

$$CI(v, r_v) = |\{u|u \in V \setminus \{v\}, |uv| \le r_v\}|. \tag{3}$$

Therefore, we can have

$$RI_{avg}(G) = \frac{\sum_{v \in V} RI(v)}{|V|} = \frac{\sum_{v \in V} CI(v, r_v)}{|V|}. \tag{4}$$

It will not increase any interference by deleting an edge. Therefore, the optimal connected topology with minimum interference should be a spanning tree. Therefore, our problem can be defined as:

Problem 1. Given n nodes arbitrarily distributed in a 1D or 2D region, construct a spanning tree, $G = (V, E)$, to connect all the nodes with edges no longer than r_{max}, that induces the minimum average interference.

3   Minimizing Average Interference in 1D Networks

3.1   Independent Subproblems

For a 1D network, the n nodes in $V = \{v_0, v_1, ..., v_{n-1}\}$ are arbitrarily deployed along a line from left to right. We can view the line as an x-axis, and set $v_0 = 0$. For a segment $\overline{v_s v_t}$ on the line, where $s \le t$, the nodes *located on* $\overline{v_s v_t}$ are $\{v_s, v_{s+1}, ..., v_{t-1}, v_t\}$; the nodes outside $\overline{v_s v_t}$ are the other nodes not including the ones that are on the line; the nodes *inside* $\overline{v_s v_t}$ are $\{v_{s+1,}, ..., v_{t-1}\}$.

We draw all the edges on one side of the line. A *cross* is defined as two edges that share at least a common point excluding their endpoints. Paper [11] presents the *no-cross property* as described in Theorem 1.

Theorem 1 (No-cross Property). *For any spanning tree connecting the nodes on a line with crosses, there is always another spanning tree to remove the crosses without increasing interference on any node.*

Based on the no-cross property, if there is an edge $(v_s v_t)$, $s < t$, the nodes inside the segment $\overline{v_s v_t}$ can not be adjacent to the nodes outside. Further, according to Equation 4, we compute the average interference by dividing the sum of the interference created by all the nodes by the network size. The interference created by a node is only related to its transmission radius and the positions of the other nodes. Recall that the node transmission radius is set to be the distance to its farthest neighbor, and the nodes are stationary after deployment. Therefore, for an edge (v_s, v_t), $s < t$, the total interference created by the nodes inside $\overline{v_s v_t}$ is independent of the topology of the nodes outside, and vice versa. Thus, we can now compute the MAI in 1D networks through dynamic programming.

3.2   Algorithms

For $s < t$, we define a topology $A(s,t)$, called an *arch*, for the nodes from v_s to v_t, such that 1) there is an edge (v_s, v_t); 2) $A(s,t)$ is a connected subgraph; and 3) there is no cross. In addition, several auxiliary functions are defined in Table 1.

Table 1. Definition of the functions $(s < t)$

Function	Definition
$f(s,t)$	In $A(s,t)$, returns the minimum total interference created by the nodes inside $\overline{v_s v_t}$
$f_1(s,p,m)$	In $A(s,t)$ and $s \le p < m < t$, returns the minimum total interference created by nodes inside $\overline{v_s v_m}$ when v_p is the leftmost node adjacent to v_m.
$f_2(m,p,t)$	In $A(s,t)$ and $s < m < p \le t$, returns the minimum total interference created by nodes inside $\overline{v_m v_t}$ when v_p is the rightmost node adjacent to v_m.
$f_1'(s,m)$	In $A(s,t)$ and $s \le m < t$, returns the minimum total interference created by nodes $v_{s+1}, v_{s+2}, ..., v_m$.
$f_2'(m,t)$	In $A(s,t)$ and $s < m \le t$, returns the minimum total interference created by nodes $v_m, v_{m+1}, ..., v_{t-1}$.
$g(p,m)$	When v_p is the leftmost node adjacent to v_m, returns the minimum total interference created by nodes $v_0, v_1, ..., v_{m-1}$.

As there is no cycle, in $A(s,t)$, there must be a node v_m $(s \le m < t)$ such that no other links cross the line $x = \frac{v_m + v_{m+1}}{2}$ except (v_s, v_t) (Figure 2). So, we calculate

$$f(s,t) = \begin{cases} 0 & t \le s+1 \\ min\{f_1'(s,m) + f_2'(m+1,t)|s \le m < t\} & \text{otherwise.} \end{cases} \quad (5)$$

Here, we have

$$f_1'(s,m) = min\{f_1(s,p,m) + CI(v_m, |v_p v_m|)|s \le p < m\}, \quad (6)$$

$$f_2'(m+1,t) = min\{f_2(m+1,p,t) + CI(v_{m+1}, |v_{m+1} v_p|)|m+1 < p \le t\}. \quad (7)$$

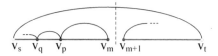

Fig. 2. The structure of $A(s,t)$: $f_1'(s,m)$ is the minimum total interference created by the nodes on the red segment, and $f_2'(m+1,t)$ that on the blue segment.

Specifically, we show how to compute $f_1(s,p,m)$ efficiently (Figure 2). When $p = s$, $f_1(s,p,m) = f(s,m)$. For $p > s$,

$$f_1(s,p,m) = min\{f_1(s,q,p) + f(p,m) + CI(v_p, max(|v_p v_q|, |v_p v_m|)) \, |s \le q < p\}.$$

By setting

$$Case_1 = min\{f_1(s,q,p) + CI(v_p, |v_p v_q|) \, |s \le q < p \, \& \, |v_p v_q| \ge |v_p v_m|\} + f(p,m), \tag{8}$$

$$Case_2 = min\{f_1(s,q,p) \, |s \le q < p \, \& \, |v_p v_q| < |v_p v_m|\} + CI(v_p, |v_p v_m|) + f(p,m), \tag{9}$$

we have when $p > s$,

$$f_1(s,p,m) = min\{Case_1, Case_2\}. \tag{10}$$

In Equations 8 and 9, the values of q are continuous numbers. Therefore, we can use RMQ (Range Minimum Query) [15] to compute them. $f_2(m+1,p,t)$ can be computed similarly.

With $f(s,t)$, the function $g(p,m)$ can be computed as:

$$g(p,m) = \begin{cases} f(0,m) + CI(v_0, |v_0 v_m|) & p = 0, \\ min\{g(q,p) + CI(v_p, max(|v_p v_q|, |v_p v_m|)) + f(p,m)|0 \le q < p\} \\ \quad 0 < p < m \le n-1. \end{cases} \tag{11}$$

Finally, the minimum average interference, AVG_{min}, can be calculated as:

$$AVG_{min} = \frac{min\{g(p,n-1) + CI(v_{n-1}, |v_{n-1} v_p|)|0 \le p < n-1\}}{n}. \tag{12}$$

3.3   Analysis

Our algorithm actually compares the average interference on all the spanning trees without a cross, which guarantees the output is optimal with the MAI. Further, our methods have also been verified by comparing the results with the outputs generated by the brute-force search, which runs slowly in time $O(n^4)$.

According to the process of dynamic programming, the computation of the different functions $f_1(s,p,m)$ and $f_2(m,p,t)$ (as defined in Table 1) contributes the main part of the time complexity. Δ is the maximum number of neighbors for a node constrained by the maximum transmission radius r_{max}. v_t is a neighbor of v_s. For a given s, there are at most Δ different choices of t and at most $t - s$ choices of m. Since all the nodes are deployed along a line, $t - s \leq \Delta$. Also, for a given m, there are at most Δ choices of p as v_p is a neighbor of v_m. Therefore, the total amount of different functions $f_1(s, p, m)$ is $O(n\Delta^2)$. A similar result can be achieved for $f_2(m, p, t)$. Thus, the time complexity to compute the MAI in 1D networks is $O(n\Delta^2)$. The optimal spanning tree can be computed through traceback efficiently. Because of limited space, we omit the details of the traceback here.

4   Bound on MMI while Minimizing Average Interference

In this section, we derive an upper bound on the MMI while minimizing the average interference.

4.1   Preliminaries

Firstly, we define the following property, dubbed the EX property which stands for 'mutual EXclusion of the long edges'.

Definition 1 (EX property). *For four nodes a, b, c, and d, if* $\min(|ab|, |cd|) > \max(|ad|, |bc|)$, *the edges (a, b) and (c, d) are not in a spanning tree simultaneously. It also holds when $a = d$.*

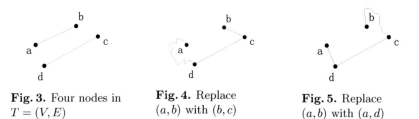

Fig. 3. Four nodes in $T = (V, E)$

Fig. 4. Replace (a, b) with (b, c)

Fig. 5. Replace (a, b) with (a, d)

Next, we show that we can always find an optimal spanning tree with the MAI that satisfies the EX property.

Theorem 2. *For a set of nodes V deployed in a 2D plane, there is always a spanning tree, $T_{ex} = (V, E_{ex})$, with the MAI that satisfies the EX property.*

Proof. For a spanning tree $T = (V, E)$ with the MAI, if it satisfies the EX property, we set $T_{ex} = T$ and we have the proof. If not, we can construct T_{ex} as follows. For each set of four nodes a, b, c and d such that $\min(|ab|, |cd|) > \max(|ad|, |bc|)$ and $(a, b) \in E, (c, d) \in E$ (Note that here a and d can be the same node.) (Figure 3),

1. if a has a path to d in the graph $T_1(V, E - \{(a, b), (c, d)\})$, we set $E' = E - (a, b) + (b, c)$ (Figure 4);
2. if a does not have a path to d in the graph $T_1(V, E - \{(a, b), (c, d)\})$, we set $E' = E - (a, b) + (a, d)$ (Figure 5).

Firstly, we show that T_{ex} is a spanning tree. According to the construction of T_{ex}, in case 1, as a and d have a path, the four nodes are still connected and $|E_{ex}| = |E| = n - 1$; therefore, T_{ex} is a spanning tree. The same result can be obtained similarly for case 2. Secondly, we show that T_{ex} also has the MAI. In case 1, we delete (a,b) and add (b,c). As $|bc| < |ab|$ and $|bc| < |cd|$, the modification does not increase the transmission radii of any node, which means that the total interference created by the nodes is not increased. The same conclusion applies to case 2. Thus, T_{ex} is a spanning tree with the MAI that satisfies the EX property. The theorem is proved.

$\square$

As T_{ex} satisfies the EX property, we have

Corollary 1. *For two regions S_1 and S_2 of diameters d_1 and d_2 respectively, there is at most one edge $(u, v) \in E_{ex}$ such that $|u, v| > max(d_1, d_2)$ with $u \in S_1$ and $v \in S_2$. (Figure 6).*

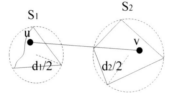

Fig. 6. There is at most one edge $(u, v) \in E_{ex}$ where $u \in S_1$, $v \in S_2$ and $|u, v| > max(d_1, d_2)$

4.2   The Upper Bound

According to Corollary 1, we can bound the maximum interference in T_{ex} as described in Theorem 3.

Theorem 3. *In the spanning tree T_{ex}, the maximum interference is bounded by $O(log\lambda)$, where $\lambda = \frac{min(d_{max}, r_{max})}{d_{min}}$. d_{max} and d_{min} are the longest and shortest distance between any two nodes respectively.*

Proof. For any node $v \in E_{ex}$, the set H contains the other nodes that can interfere with v. We separate the elements in H into subsets according to their transmission radii as follows:

$$h_i = \{u|u \in H \quad and \quad (1+\epsilon)^{i-1}d_{min} \leq r_u < (1+\epsilon)^i d_{min}\}, \quad i = 1, 2, 3... \quad (13)$$

where ϵ is a positive constant. The subsets have the following properties:

$$H = \sum_i h_i \quad and \quad \{h_i \cap h_j = \varnothing \quad if \quad i \neq j\}. \quad (14)$$

Since the possible longest transmission radius in T_{ex} is $\lambda \times d_{min}$, we have the maximal i, denoted as i_{max} as

$$(1+\epsilon)^i \leq \lambda \Rightarrow i_{max} = O(\log \lambda). \tag{15}$$

As the transmission radii of the nodes in h_i are smaller than $(1+\epsilon)^i d_{min}$, the nodes and their neighbors are all inside the circle[1] $c(v, 2(1+\epsilon)^i d_{min})$. We use a set of squares, the length of whose edges is $\frac{\sqrt{2}}{4}(1+\epsilon)^{i-1}d_{min}$, to fully cover the area inside the circle $c(v, 2(1+\epsilon)^i d_{min})$. So, the number of the squares needed is

$$c_0 = (\lceil \frac{2 \times 2(1+\epsilon)^i d_{min}}{\frac{\sqrt{2}}{4}(1+\epsilon)^{i-1}d_{min}} \rceil)^2 = (\lceil 8\sqrt{2}(1+\epsilon) \rceil)^2. \tag{16}$$

For each node $u \in h_i$, since $r_u \geq (1+\epsilon)^{i-1}d_{min}$, u must have an edge $(uu') \in E_{ex}$ which lies inside the circle $c(v, 2(1+\epsilon)^i d_{min})$ such that $|uu'| \geq (1+\epsilon)^{i-1}d_{min}$.

The diameter of each square is $\frac{(1+\epsilon)^{i-1}d_{min}}{2}$. According to Corollary 1, for each pair of the squares, s_1 and s_2, there is at most one edge $(v_1 v_2)$ such that $|v_1 v_2| \geq (1+\epsilon)^{i-1}d_{min}$ and $v_1 \in s_1$, $v_2 \in s_2$. Therefore, the number of nodes in h_i is:

$$|h_i| \leq 2 \times \binom{c_0}{2} = c_1 \tag{17}$$

where c_1 is a constant. Based on Equation 15, the interference on the node v is

$$RI(v) = |H| = \sum_i |h_i| \leq c_1 \times i_{max}. \tag{18}$$

According to Equations 15 and 18, we have

$$RI(v) = O(\log \lambda). \tag{19}$$

Therefore, the maximum interference in T_{ex} is bounded by $O(\log \lambda)$. The theorem is proved.

□

Based on the above theorem, we have the following corollary:

Corollary 2. *In 2D networks, it is possible to bound the MMI by $O(\log \lambda)$ while minimizing the average interference.*

5   Minimizing Average Interference in 2D Networks

5.1   Basic Ideas

Given n nodes arbitrarily deployed in a 2D region, we can simply find the minimum number, denoted as m, of parallel lines so that all the nodes are located

---

[1] $c(v, r)$ stands for a circle centering at point v with radius of r.

on the lines (Figure 7). We set a parallel line as the x-axis, and list the n nodes from left to right as $V = \{v_0, v_1, ..., v_{n-1}\}$, where for two nodes $v_i = (x_i, y_i)$ and $v_j = (x_j, y_j)$,

$$i < j \quad iff \quad x_i < x_j \text{ or } \{x_i = x_j \text{ and } y_i < y_j\}. \tag{20}$$

According to Equation 18, we can construct the topology with the MAI while the maximum interference does not exceed $k = \min(c_1 \times i_{max}, n-1)$. Here, we restrict the maximum interference because it is a critical parameter to determine the time complexity of our algorithm which will be analyzed in Section 5.3.

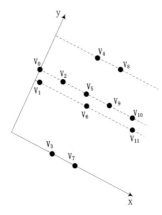

Fig. 7. 12 nodes deployed in a 2D region with the minimum number of parallel lines covering them.

We assume a virtual line $clin$ that separates the nodes into the left and the right parts. Initially, there is only v_0 that is on the left of $clin$. We move rightward (and rotate if necessary) the line to include one more node on its left each time until all the nodes are on the left of $clin$. When moving $clin$ to include v_p ($0 \leq p < n$) in the left part, we compute the minimum total interference created by the nodes inside $[0, p]$.[2] while the maximum interference does not exceed k and the total topology for the n nodes is connected. Here, the nodes left of $clin$ may connect to and interfere with the nodes on the right, and vice versa. When computing the topology for the nodes left of $clin$, we need to assume a topology on the right and take the mutual interference into account. Thus, for an interval $[s, t]$ ($0 \leq s \leq t \leq n-1$), we define the following items:

- $c[s,t]$: record how the nodes inside $[s, t]$ interfere with the nodes outside. $c[s, t]$ contains the nodes and their transmission radii that can interfere with the nodes outside $[s, t]$.
- $s[s,t]$: record all the connected components of the nodes in $c[s, t]$.

---

[2] For an interval $[s, t]$, $s \leq t$, the nodes inside $[s, t]$ are the ones from v_s to v_t. The nodes outside $[s, t]$ are the ones left of $[s, t]$ (the nodes from v_0 to v_{s-1}) and right of $[s, t]$ (the nodes from v_{t+1} to v_{n-1}).

As the maximum interference does not exceed k, we call $c[s,t]$ *valid* if and only if there are no more than k nodes inside $[s,t]$ that interfere with the same node outside $[s,t]$. With the above definitions, we now introduce the algorithms to compute the MAI while the maximum interference does not exceed k.

5.2   Algorithms to Compute MAI

We define a function $F(p, c[0,p], c[p+1, n-1], s[0,p]), 0 \le p < n-1$, to construct a topology minimizing the interference created by the nodes inside $[0,p]$ while satisfying the following conditions:

1. the interference from nodes inside $[0,p]$ to the nodes inside $[p+1, n-1]$ is the same as that recorded in $c[0,p]$;
2. the interference from nodes inside $[p+1, n-1]$ to the nodes inside $[0,p]$ is the same as that recorded in $c[p+1, n-1]$;
3. the connectivity of the nodes in $c[0,p]$ is the same as that recorded in $s[0,p]$;
4. all the nodes inside $[0,p]$ but not in $c[0,p]$ have a path to at least one node in $c[0,p]$;
5. the interference on each node inside $[0,p]$ does not exceed k.

If F returns $+\infty$, it means there is no such topology that satisfies all the conditions. Here, conditions 1, 2 and 5 are to guarantee that the maximum interference in the final topology does not exceed k. Conditions 3 and 4 are for the requirement of connectivity. Specifically, condition 4 is to guarantee that the nodes in $[0,p]$ but not in $c[0,p]$ can connect to the nodes in $[p+1, n-1]$ through the nodes in $c[0,p]$. The function F can be calculated in Algorithm 1. In Algorithm 1, $R(v) = \{|uv| | u \in V \text{ and } |uv| \le r_{max}\}$, which is the set of potential transmission radii of u. Lines 1–5 are the boundary condition. Lines 7–10 are to enumerate the possible situations. Line 11 is to connect v_p to nodes in $[0, p-1]$ to maintain connectivity. In Line 12, $c'[0,p]$ and $s'[0,p]$, which are defined as the same as $c[0,p]$ and $s[0,p]$ respectively, are computed based on $c[0, p-1]$, $s[0, p-1]$ and the newly added edges in Line 11. Line 13–16 are to check all the conditions and compute the minimum total interference.

The MAI of all the nodes can be computed in the algorithm MAI-GRID (Algorithm 2). MAI-GRID checks the interference on v_{n-1} and makes sure that all the nodes in $s[0, n-2]$ have a path to v_{n-1} such that the network connectivity is maintained. MAI-GRID computes the minimum total interference by the sum of interference created by nodes in $[0, n-2]$ and the interference created by v_{n-1}. After computing MAI-GRID, we can also construct the optimal spanning tree with the MAI through traceback. Figure 8 is an example of the optimal topology.

5.3   Analysis

Based on the definition of the function F, Condition 4 and the operation of connecting v_{n-1} to all the nodes within its transmission range (Line 5 in Algorithm 2) guarantee the connectivity of our output; Condition 5 and the check of

---

Algorithm 1. Compute $F(p, c[0, p], c[p+1, n-1], s[0, p])$

---

1   **if** $p = 0$ **then**   /* the boundary condition */

2   **if** there are more the k nodes in $c[p+1, n-1]$ that can interference with v_0 **then**

3   **return** $+\infty$;

4   **else**

5   **return** $CI(v_0, r_{v_0})$;

6   $total \leftarrow +\infty$;

7   **foreach** valid $c[0, p-1]$ **do**

8   **foreach** valid $c[p, n-1]$ **do**

9   **foreach** $s[0, p-1]$ **do**

10   **foreach** $r_{v_p} \in R(v_p)$ **do**

11   Connect v_p to the nodes in $\{v | v$ is inside $[0, p-1]$ **and** $|vv_p| \leq \min(r_v, r_{v_p})\}$;

12   Compute $c'[0, p]$ and $s'[0, p]$;

13   **if** $c[0, p] = c'[0, p]$ **and** $s[0, p] = s'[0, p]$ **and** all the nodes in $[0, p]$ but not in $c[0, p]$ have a path to at least one node in $c[0, p]$ **and** the interference on v_p does not exceed k **then**

14                      $tmp \leftarrow F(p-1, c[0, p-1], c[p, n-1], s[0, p-1]) + CI(v_p, r_{v_p})$;

15   **if** $tmp < total$ **then**

16                          $Total \leftarrow tmp$;

17 **return** Total;

Algorithm 2. MAI-GRID: compute the MAI in a grid network

---

1   $k \leftarrow \min(c_1 \times i_{max}, n-1)$, $total \leftarrow +\infty$;

2   **foreach** valid $c[0, n-2]$ **do**

3   **foreach** $s[0, n-2]$ **do**

4   **foreach** $r_{v_{n-1}} \in R(v_{n-1})$ **do**

5   Connect v_{n-1} to the nodes in $\{v | v$ is inside $[0, n-2]$ **and** $|vv_{n-1}| \leq \min(r_v, r_{v_{n-1}})\}$;

6              $c[n-1, n-1] = \{v_{n-1}, r_{v_{n-1}}\}$;

7   **if** the interference on v_{n-1} does not exceed k **and** all the nodes in $s[0, n-2]$ has a path to v_{n-1} **then**

8                  $t \leftarrow F(n-2, c[0, n-2], c[n-1, n-1], s[0, n-2]) + CI(v_{n-1}, r_{v_{n-1}})$;

9   **if** $t < total$ **then**

10                    $Total \leftarrow t$;

11 **return** $\frac{total}{n}$;

---

the interference on v_{n-1} (Line 7 in Algorithm 2) guarantee the maximum interference of our output does not exceed k. Further, our algorithm actually compares all the possible connected topology with the maximal interference equal or smaller than k. Therefore, our method output the optimal topology with the MAI while the maximum interference does not exceed k. The correctness of the algorithms has been established through comparing our results with the outputs of the brute-force search which runs in time $O(n^{\Delta})$.

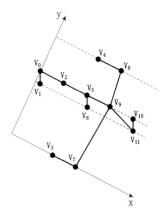

Fig. 8. The optimal topology with the MAI, which is $\frac{29}{12}$

The main complexity to construct the optimal spanning tree is to compute the F functions. In our optimal topologies, the maximum interference does not exceed k. If there are more than mk nodes in $c[s, t]$ that interfere with the nodes on the left of $[s, t]$, there must be a parallel line, and the rightmost node left of $[s, t]$ on the line will experience interference larger than k. Therefore, in a valid $c[s, t]$, there are at most $\min(mk, n)$ nodes that can interfere with one node left of $[s, t]$. Similarly, there are at most mk nodes interfering with one node right of $[s, t]$. The number of different transmission radii of a node v is at most Δ. Therefore, the number of valid $c[0, p]$ is $O((n\Delta)^{mk})$. A similar result can be achieved for $c[p + 1, n - 1]$. The number of variations of $s[0, p]$ is $O((mk)^{mk})$. As $\Delta \leq n - 1$ and $k = O(log\lambda)$, the time complexity to construct the optimal spanning tree with the MAI is $n^{mO(\log \lambda)}$.

As the minimum number of parallel lines to cover all the nodes can be linear to n, $m = O(n)$. Therefore, the time complexity is still exponential in the worst cases. However, in some cases when the nodes are deployed along a few parallel lines, e.g. m is a small constant, our algorithm runs fast.

6   Conclusion

In this paper, we study how to minimize the average interference while preserving connectivity through topology control in wireless sensor networks. In 1D networks, based on the no-cross property and dynamic programming, we propose a fast exact algorithm to compute the minimum average interference. In 2D networks, using computational geometry, we prove that the minimum maximum interference can still be bounded while minimizing the average interference. Moreover, we propose exact algorithms to compute the minimum average interference in 2D networks. In this work, we assume that the interference range is the same as the transmission range. It is meaningful in the future to study interference minimization in networks where the interference range is larger than the transmission range. Other future work directions include interference minimization in 3D networks, and how to reduce interference for network properties besides connectivity, such as planarity, low node degree and small spanner.

Acknowledgements. The research was supported in part by the National Basic Research Program of China grants 2007CB807900 and 2007CB807901, the National Natural Science Foundation of China grants 61073174, 61033001, and 61061130540, the Hi-Tech research and Development Program of China grant 2006AA10Z216, and Hong Kong RGC-GRF grants 714009E and 714311.

References

1. Gupta, P., Kumar, P.R.: The Capacity of Wireless Networks. IEEE Transactions on Information Theory 46(2), 388–404 (2000)
2. Moscibroda, T., Wattenhofer, R., Weber, Y.: Protocol Design Beyond Graph-Based Models. In: Proc. of the 5th Workshop on Hot Topics in Networks, HotNets (2006)
3. Benkert, M., Gudmundsson, J., Haverkort, H., Wolff, A.: Constructing minimum-interference networks. Computational Geometry 40(3), 179–194 (2008)
4. Burkhart, M., von Rickenbach, P., Wattenhofer, R., Zollinger, A.: Does Topology Control Reduce Interference? In: Proc. of the 5th ACM International Symposium on Mobile Ad Hoc Networking and Computing (MobiHoc), pp. 9–19 (2004)
5. Johansson, T., Carr-Motyčková, L.: Reducing Interference in Ad Hoc Networks Through Topology Control. In: Proc. of the 2nd ACM SIGACT/SIGMOBILE International Workshop on Foundations of Mobile Computing (DIALM-POMC), pp. 17–23 (2005)
6. Moaveni-Nejad, K., Li, X.-Y.: Low-interference topology control for wireless ad hoc networks. International Journal of Ad Hoc & Sensor Wireless Networks 1, 41–64 (2005)
7. Nguyen, T., Lam, N., Huynh, D., Bolla, J.: Minimum Edge Interference in Wireless Sensor Networks. In: Pandurangan, G., Anil Kumar, V.S., Ming, G., Liu, Y., Li, Y. (eds.) WASA 2010. LNCS, vol. 6221, pp. 57–67. Springer, Heidelberg (2010)
8. Wu, K.-D., Liao, W.: On Constructing Low Interference Topology in Multihop Wireless Networks. International Journal of Sensor Networks 2, 321–330 (2007)
9. von Rickenbach, P., Schmid, S., Wattenhofer, R., Zollinger, A.: A robust interference model for wireless ad hoc networks. In: Proc. of the 5th International Workshop on Algorithms for Wireless, Mobile, Ad Hoc and Sensor Networks, WMAN (2005)
10. von Rickenbach, P., Wattenhofer, R., Zollinger, A.: Algorithmic Models of Interference in Wireless Ad Hoc and Sensor Networks. IEEE/ACM Transation on Networking (TON) 17(1), 172–185 (2009)

11. Tan, H., Lou, T., Lau, F.C.M., Wang, Y., Chen, S.: Minimizing Interference for the Highway Model in Wireless Ad-hoc and Sensor Networks. In: Černá, I., Gyimóthy, T., Hromkovič, J., Jefferey, K., Králović, R., Vukolić, M., Wolf, S. (eds.) SOFSEM 2011. LNCS, vol. 6543, pp. 520–532. Springer, Heidelberg (2011)
12. Buchin, K.: Minimizing the Maximum Interference is Hard. arXiv: 0802.2134v1 (2008)
13. Halldórsson, M.M., Tokuyama, T.: Minimizing Interference of a Wireless Ad-Hoc Network in a Plane. In: Nikoletseas, S.E., Rolim, J.D.P. (eds.) ALGOSENSORS 2006. LNCS, vol. 4240, pp. 71–82. Springer, Heidelberg (2006)
14. Moscibroda, T., Wattenhofer, R.: Minimizing interference in ad hoc and sensor networks. In: Proc. of the 2nd ACM SIGACT/SIGMOBILE International Workshop on Foundations of Mobile Computing (DIALM-POMC), pp. 24–33 (2005)
15. Yuan, H., Atallah, M.J.: Data Structures for Range Minimum Queries in Multidimensional Arrays. In: Proc. of the 21st Annual ACM-SIAM Symposium on Discrete Algorithms, SODA (2010)

On Barrier Resilience of Sensor Networks

Kuan-Chieh Robert Tseng and David Kirkpatrick

Department of Computer Science,
University of British Columbia, Canada

Abstract. Various notions of coverage have been introduced as basic quality-of-service measures for wireless sensor networks. One natural measure of coverage is referred to as *resilience*: given a starting region S and a target region T, the resilience a sensor configuration with respect to S and T is the minimum number of sensors that need to be deactivated before an $S - T$ path can exist that does not cross any active sensor region. We demonstrate that determining resilience of a network of unit-line-segment sensors is NP-hard. Furthermore, we can extend our proof to show that the resilience problem remains NP-hard for other types of non-symmetric sensor coverage regions.

Keywords: resilience, barrier coverage, wireless sensor network.

1 Introduction

The specification and evaluation of domain coverage continue to be fundamental issues in analysing the effectiveness of wireless sensor networks. A comprehensive overview of research on coverage problems, including the identification of different notions of coverage, can be found in the survey papers of Meguerdichian *et al.* [11], Cardei and Wu [3] as well as the Ph.D. thesis of Kumar [8]. In general, coverage problems can be expressed geometrically. Individual sensors are represented by their *coverage region*, which specifies the set of points, within some underlying surveillance domain, that are *covered* by the sensor. For brevity, we specify the type of a sensor by the shape of its coverage region (e.g. disk sensors denote sensors with a disk shape coverage region).

Coverage problems arise in many different applications, for example border control [9], multi-robot mine sweeping and sentry duty [4], oceanographic analysis using satellite data [6], and habitat monitoring [8]. Different applications motivate different notions of coverage. In this paper, we focus on the notion of *barrier coverage*, introduced in [4,9]. The goal here is to ensure that all paths joining a specified start region S to a specified target region T must intersect the coverage regions associated with one or more distinct sensors.

Barrier coverage is attractive because it guarantees that there are no undetected transitions from S to T, without requiring that every point in the surveillance domain be covered. However, in its simplest formulation, barrier coverage is not robust in the face of sensor change or failure: if even one sensor has its coverage region slightly reduced, the sensor configuration may no longer form

T. Erlebach et al. (Eds.): ALGOSENSORS 2011, LNCS 7111, pp. 130–144, 2012.

a barrier. Several methods have been suggested to capture more robust notions of barrier coverage. For example, Meguerdichian *et al* [11] proposed measuring the coverage of a sensor network using a *maximal breach path* - a path that maximizes the distance to the closest sensor. A closely related idea is a *minimum exposure path* [12] - a path that minimize the total degree of "exposure" to sensors. Other models of barrier coverage introduce probabilistic assumptions [10].

Perhaps the most natural way to address the robustness of barrier coverage is the notion of *k-barrier coverage*, introduced by Kumar *et al.* [9]: a sensor network is said to provide *k*-barrier coverage if every path from the start region S to target region T intersects the coverage regions of at least k distinct sensors. Kumar *et al.* showed that in one restricted setting, where unit disk sensors are deployed in a rectangular strip, one can efficiently determine the maximum k for which the sensor configuration forms a k-barrier to paths crossing the strip of the sensor network by a straightforward reduction to network flow. Furthermore, by a direct application of Menger's theorem, it follows that in this setting any k-barrier can be realized as the disjoint union of 1-barriers. Unfortunately, these results do not seem to generalize.

In an attempt to address k-barrier coverage in a more general setting, Bereg and Kirkpatrick [2] specified two measures of barrier impermeability, with respect to a given pair of regions S and T: *thickness*, defined as the minimum number of sensors regions crossed–*including* duplicate crossings–by any $S - T$ path, and *resilience*, defined as the minimum number of distinct sensors regions crossed, i.e. *ignoring* duplicate crossings. They used barrier thickness, which can be efficiently computed using shortest path algorithms, as the basis of an efficient algorithm that approximates the resilience of an arrangement of unit-disk sensors to within a factor of 3 (or 5/3 with mild assumptions on the separation of S and T). The computational complexity of the exact resilience problem for unit disks, or other basic sensor types, as well as the problem of constructing efficient algorithms with tighter guaranteed approximation factors, were left as an open problems.

In this paper we return to the general resilience problem, with sensors deployed at at arbitrary locations and S and T located at arbitrary points in the corresponding arrangement. A sensor network is described by a pair $(U, \mathcal{A})$, where U is a set of sensors described by the shape of their coverage regions and $\mathcal{A} : U \to \mathbb{R}^2$ is an arrangement of the sensors in U on the plane. We only consider the case where the coverage regions of all sensors in U are congruent.

We focus our attention on unit-line-segment sensors. As shown in [2] for the case of unit disk sensors, the thickness of a configuration of unit-line-segment sensors with respect to a given pair of points S and T can be computed efficiently. Unfortunately the ratio of thickness to resilience can be arbitrarily large for unit-line-segment sensors, so even finding a constant approximation of resilience seems to be challenging in this case. In fact, we will show that determining (or even finding a fully polynomial-time approximation scheme for) the resilience of a configuration of unit-line-segment sensors is NP-hard.

The decision problem for the resilience of unit-line-segment sensors is defined as follows:

Resilience of Unit-Line-Segment Sensor Network (ULS-RES)
Instance: $(\mathcal{A}, S, T, m)$, where $\mathcal{A}$ is an arrangement of unit-line-segment sensors in the plane, S and T are two points in the plane, and m is a positive integer.
Question: Is $\rho(\mathcal{A}, S, T)$, the resilience of $\mathcal{A}$ with respect to S and T, at most m?

We will establish the NP-hardness of ULS-RES by reduction from the following problem that is well known to be be NP-complete [5] (and, in fact, APX-hard [7]):

Maximum 2-Satisfiability (MAX-2-SAT)
Instance: $\{X, C, k\}$, where $X = \{x_1, x_2, \ldots, x_n\}$ is a set of Boolean variables, $C = \{c_1, c_2, \ldots, c_m\}$ is a set of 2-literal clauses over X and k is a positive integer.
Question: Is $\sigma(X, C)$, the maximum number of clauses in C satisfiable by some truth assignment to the variables of X, at least k?

We present our reduction in two stages. First, in Section 2, we reduce the MAX-2-SAT problem to an edge-colouring problem in a special family of graphs. Then, through a careful embedding, we reduce this edge-colouring problem to ULS-RES , in Section 3. Due to space constraints, it is not possible to present all of the details. (See [13] for an expanded version of this paper.) An extension of the proof to sensors with other shapes is discussed in Section 4.

It should be noted that the NP-hardness of the problem of determining the resilience of a collection of sensors whose coverage regions form line segments of *arbitrary* length (and orientation) was recently established by Alt *et al.* [1]. In fact, their proof also uses a reduction from MAX-2-SAT . In this sense, although our stronger result involves a fundamentally different construction for *unit* line segments, the result of Alt *et al.* should be recognized as an important precursor of our work.

2   Reduction to Edge Colouring of $(\mathbf{Bi})^3$-graphs

2.1   Problem Statement

A *bi-vertex* $^-v|v^+$ is a special type of node that consists of two halves: the negative half (^-v) and the positive half (v^+). A *k-chain* is an alternating sequence $(e_1, {}^-v_1|v_1^+, \ldots e_{k-1}, {}^-v_{k-1}|v_{k-1}^+, e_k)$, where $^-v_i|v_i^+$, $1 \le i < k$, is a bi-vertex and e_j, $1 \le j \le k$, is an edge, with e_j incident on ^-v_j, for $1 \le j < k$, and v_{j-1}^+, for $1 < j \le k$. Edges e_1 and e_k are referred to as the *end-edges* of the chain. Any k-chain with *even* k is referred to as a *bi-chain*.

A *bipartite, bi-vertex, bi-chain graph* (a *(bi)^3-graph* for short) is a triple $(^-V_1^+, ^-V_2^+, B)$, where $^-V_1^+$ and $^-V_2^+$ are disjoint sets of bi-vertices, and B is a set of bi-chains each of which has one end-edge incident with one half of a bi-vertex in $^-V_1^+$ and the other end-edge incident with one half of a bi-vertex in $^-V_2^+$. For each bi-vertex we refer to the edges incident with its positive (resp., negative) half as the *positively* (resp., *negatively*)-*incident edges*.

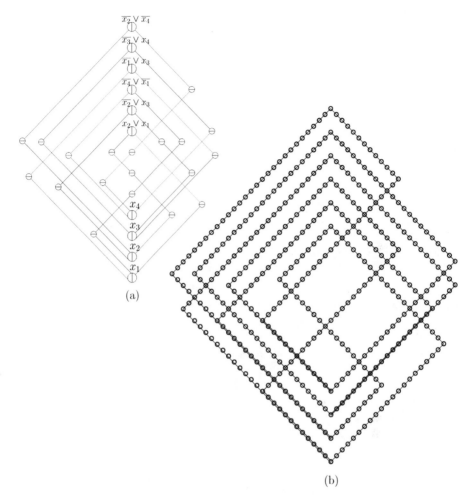

Fig. 1. (a) an example of a (bi)^3-graph arising from our transformation of a 2-SAT instance; and (b) an embedding of the same graph using unit line-segment sensors

An *edge bi-colouring* of a (bi)^3-graph is an assignment of the colour *red* or *blue* to each of the edges making up its bi-chains. Such a colouring is said to *saturate* a bi-vertex if either all of its positively-incident edges or all of its negatively-incident edges are coloured red; it is said to *saturate the entire graph* if it saturates all of its bi-vertices (including those in the interior of bi-chains).

Saturating Edge Bi-Colouring of (Bi)^3-graphs (SEB-C)
Instance: (G, r), where $G = (^-V_1^+, ^-V_2^+, B)$ is a (bi)^3-graph and r is a positive integer.
Question: Does there exists an edge bi-colouring saturating G, that colours at most r edges red?

Note that in any saturating bi-colouring, every k-chain has the property that at least one of every pair of consecutive edges must to be coloured red. Consequently, at least half of the edges of every bi-chain must be coloured red. Furthermore, any colouring that assigns red to exactly half of the edges of a bi-chain must, like its complementary colouring, assign red to exactly one of its two end-edges.

2.2   Reduction

Let $P = (X, C, k)$ be an instance of MAX-2-SAT . We begin by describing how to construct a corresponding $(\text{bi})^3$-graph $G = (^-V_1^+, {}^-V_2^+, B)$. The first step is to represent each variable x_i in X by a bi-vertex $^-v_{1,i}|v_{1,i}^+$ in $^-V_1^+$ and each clause c_j in C by a bi-vertex $^-v_{2,j}|v_{2,j}^+$ in $^-V_2^+$. We will refer to the bi-vertices in $^-V_1^+$ and $^-V_2^+$ as *variable bi-vertices* and *clause bi-vertices*, respectively. For each clause $c_j = l_1 \vee l_2$ in C, we add two bi-chains to B:

(a) The first bi-chain has one of its end-edges incident on $^-v_{2,j}$. Its other end-edge is incident to $^-v_{1,i}$ (resp., $v_{1,i}^+$) if $l_1 = x_i$ (resp., $l_1 = \overline{x_i}$).

(b) The second bi-chain has one of its end-edges incident on $v_{2,j}^+$. Its other end-edge is incident to $^-v_{1,i}$ (resp., $v_{1,i}^+$) if $l_1 = x_i$ (resp., $l_1 = \overline{x_i}$).

To complete the reduction, we set $r = |E|/2 + |C| - k$, where E denotes the set of edges appearing in bi-chains of C. Fig. 1a depicts the $(\text{bi})^3$-graph obtained from the instance of MAX-2-SAT with $X = \{x_1, x_2, x_3, x_4\}$ and $C = \{(x_1 \vee x_2), (x_3 \vee \overline{x_2}), (\overline{x_1} \vee \overline{x_4}), (x_3 \vee \overline{x_1}), (x_4 \vee \overline{x_3}), (\overline{x_4} \vee \overline{x_2})\}$. The positive and negative half of each of the variable and clause bi-vertices are the right and left half, respectively.

2.3   Proof of Correctness

We will show that $P = (X, C, k)$ is a yes-instance of MAX-2-SAT if and only if $P' = (G, r)$ is a yes-instance of SEB-C .

Suppose we are given a truth assignment $\mathcal{T}$ to X that satisfies exactly k of the $|C|$ clauses in P. If $\mathcal{T}$ assigns true to the variable x_i then we alternately colour the edges of every bi-chain incident with $v_{1,i}^+$ (resp., $^-v_{1,i}$), starting with blue (resp., red). Similarly, if $\mathcal{T}$ assigns false to the variable x_i then we alternately colour the edges of every bi-chain incident with $^-v_{1,i}$ (resp., $v_{1,i}^+$), starting with blue (resp., red). It follows, by the even length of bi-chains, that if clause c_j is satisfied by the truth assignment $\mathcal{T}$ then at least one of the two bi-chains incident on the vertex $^-v_{2,j}|v_{2,j}^+$ must have its incident end-edge coloured red. Thus the only bi-vertices of G left unsaturated by the specified chain colourings are those corresponding to the clauses that are *not* satisfied by $\mathcal{T}$. Hence, if we change the colour (from blue to red) of either one of the end edges incident on each of the $|C| - k$ such bi-vertices, we produce an edge bi-colouring of G that saturates all of its bi-vertices. The total number of red edges used is r ($|E|/2$ from the alternate colouring of the bi-chains, plus $|C| - k$ to complete the saturation of the bi-vertices corresponding to unsatisfied clauses).

On the other hand, suppose we are given an edge bi-colouring that saturates G and uses $r = |E|/2 + |C| - k$ red edges. Since all of the blue edges incident on a variable bi-vertex $^{-}v_{1,i}|v_{1,i}^{+}$ are incident with just one side, we can interpret this as a truth assignment to the variable x_i: if all of the blue edges are incident with $v_{1,i}^{+}$ then x_i is assigned `true`, otherwise `false`. (If $^{-}v_{1,i}|v_{1,i}^{+}$ has no incident blue edges the assignment can be made arbitrarily.) Since (i) every bi-chain must have at least half of its edges coloured red, and (ii) a colouring with exactly half, including exactly one of the end-edges, coloured red is always possible, we can assume, without loss of generality, that at least one of the end edges of each bi-chain is coloured red, and at most $|C| - k$ bi-chains have both end-edges coloured red. But, if clause c_j is not satisfied by the this truth assignment it must have an incident bi-chain both of whose end-edges are coloured red. Thus, the truth assignment must satisfy at least k of the clauses in C.

It follows from the discussion above that the SEB-C problem is NP-hard. Thus, to establish the NP-hardness of ULS-RES it will suffice to describe a polynomial-time reduction from SEB-C . We turn to this in the next section.

3   Reduction to ULS-RES

3.1   Relationship to Resilience of a Sensor Network

Consider the (bi)^3-graph shown in Fig. 1a. We have purposely drawn all the clause and variable bi-vertices on one vertical line, with the clause bi-vertices above the variable bi-vertices to accentuate the bipartite nature of the graph. Furthermore the bi-chains depicted are of two types: 2-chains joining bi-vertices on the same (either positive or negative) side and 4-chains joining bi-vertices on opposite sides. The fact that all edges are drawn as straight lines in one of the two diagonal directions foreshadows the representation of this graph in our next construction where it appears embedded in the plane with edges realized by unit-line-segment sensors in restricted orientations. (For the latter, we will exploit the fact that our first reduction did not need to specify the actual length of the bi-chains.)

To understand the reduction to the sensor resilience problem, first pretend that the line segments in Fig. 1a are line segment sensors placed in the plane at the illustrated locations (ignoring for now the constraint that all line segments sensors need to have the same length). Bi-vertices represent points in the plane where the end points of multiple sensors happen to coincide. We partition the sensors (segments) whose end points are incident to a common point into positively and negatively incident sensors based on a line through the point: those segments above (or to the right of) the line are positive; those below (or to the left of) the line are negative. Consequently, these points still retain the "two-halves" property: any sensor whose end points coincide with a bi-vertex attaches either to its positive half or its negative half.

In addition to sensors that correspond to the edges of the underlying (bi)^3-graph G, we will introduce additional sensors to create an environment of obstacles that must be avoided by any path that minimizes the total number of sensor crossings. Suppose now that we have identified two points S and T in the plane, and that we have embedded the entire configuration of sensors in an environment of obstacles. We say that an obstacle-avoiding $S - T$ path *skirts* bi-vertex $^-v|v^+$ *positively* (resp., *negatively*) if it crosses all of the sensors that are positively-incident (resp., negatively-incident) at $^-v|v^+$. Our objective is to construct the obstacle environment such that the following property holds:

> **Environment Property:** *For every obstacle-avoiding $S-T$ path π and every bi-vertex $^-v|v^+$ (including clause, variable and chain bi-vertices):*
> *(i) π must skirt $^-v|v^+$, either positively or negatively, and*
> *(ii) if π skirts $^-v|v^+$ positively (resp., negatively) then there is another obstacle-avoiding $S - T$ path π' that skirts $^-v|v^+$ negatively (resp., positively) and skirts all other bi-vertices on the same side as π.*

The first part of this property is very similar to the condition of a colouring scheme that saturates bi-vertex $^-v|v^+$ – we have simply replaced the notion of colouring an edge red by crossing the corresponding sensor with an $S - T$ path, and saturating a bi-vertex by skirting its associated point. The second condition ensures that all possible colourings that saturate G can be represented.

With this interpretation, a colouring scheme that saturates G using exactly r red edges corresponds to an obstacle-avoiding $S - T$ path that intersects exactly r distinct sensors (and vice versa). The latter, of course, is a demonstration that the resilience of the full sensor network (including the environment) is at most r. This is the core idea that we will use to reduce SEB-C to ULS-RES . The full reduction involves a number of details that have been necessarily brushed over above. Specifically, two main issues need to be dealt with: (i) we need to ensure that in our reduction, all sensors used are the same length (this is clearly not the case for the example illustrated in Fig. 1a); and (ii) we need to show how to construct an environment of obstacles that imposes the Environment Property.

The first of these issues is handled by exploiting the fact that we are free to replace the bi-chains of G by bi-chains of any (polynomially bounded) length. Fig. 1b demonstrates the desired embedding of the SEB-C instance shown in Fig. 1a. The second issue, constructing a suitable obstacle environment, is where most of the subtlety of our reduction resides; we describe the overall form of the construction in the next section. While our running example serves to illustrate many of the general features of the reduction (for example, it is easy to see from their general form that all of the edges of our bi-chains are paired by their common projection on the x-axis, making it trivial to confirm that these chains do, in fact, have even length), other issues (for example the apparent overlap of some of the embedded bi-chains in Fig. 1b) requires some additional treatment to ensure that it is possible for an $S - T$ path to only cross some of the sensors but not others even if they reside at the same location in this embedding of bi-chains. The reader is invited to consult [13] for the full details of the embedding of both the sensors and the environment.

3.2 Building the Obstacle Environment

We now deal with the second issue of the reduction - how to configure "sensor obstacles" in such a way that the Environment Property is enforced. The key idea is to arrange barriers into one long corridor that straddles every bi-vertex in the underlying graph with one side of the corridor intersecting all of the positively-incident edges and the other side intersecting all of the negatively incident edges. It is not obvious *a priori* that such an arrangement is always possible. What we describe is a rather generic maze-like construction using horizontal and vertical corridor segments that makes it easy to visualize the interactions with the diagonally-aligned segments that describe the underlying $(\text{bi})^3$-graph.

Walls and Corridors. A *wall* is a collection of unit-line-segment sensors superimposed to form an unbroken unit. The key property is that the number of coincident sensors at any point on a wall must be large enough so that any path which crosses the wall can not possibly realize the minimum number of sensor crossings. This allows us to restrict our attention to $S - T$ paths that avoid walls. Walls in turn are the basic building blocks for creating the environment of obstacles. By using several walls, we can create "obstacle" corridors to steer the minimal resilience path. For example, Fig. 2a illustrates how a corridor can be used to implement a bi-vertex with two incident edges. Any $S - T$ path that follows the corridor must intersect either the right (positively-incident) sensors or the left (negatively incident) sensors. This enforces the first part of the Environment Property. Furthermore if all bi-vertices interact with the corridor independently, in this same fashion, then the second part of the Environment Property is also ensured.

Some coordinated bi-vertex/corridor interactions are straightforward. For example, Fig. 2b shows how a corridor that sweeps back and forth horizontally can be used to enforce the Environment Property for a bi-chain. Establishing the independence of other bi-vertex/corridor interactions requires some care.

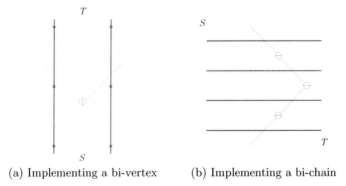

(a) Implementing a bi-vertex   (b) Implementing a bi-chain

Fig. 2. Constructing parts of the environment. Bold lines represent walls.

Constructing the Maze Environment. Given an realization of a $(bi)^3$-graph as a configuration of unit-line-segment sensors, as described above, we now show how to construct the full environment of corridors so that all of the bi-vertex constraints are obeyed. We illustrate how this can be done by continuing our example. Fig. 3 shows how the $(bi)^3$-graph realization illustrated in Fig. 1b can be embedded in a generic (i.e. graph-independent) maze-like obstacle environment. For clarification, the points S and T lie at the ends of the right-most and leftmost columns (shown highlighted). By design any obstacle-free $S - T$ path must traverse all of the corridors on the right half, from top to bottom, then all of the corridors on the left side, from bottom to top, before traversing the full central column.

For the most part the interactions between elements of the embedded $(bi)^3$-graph and the obstacle environment are exactly as illustrated in Fig. 3. Where two embedded bi-chains intersect some local adjustments are needed to keep the bi-vertex/corridor interactions independent. The local adjustments are illustrated in the uppermost blow-up shown to the right in Fig. 3. The idea is to use an additional wall segment as an *island* in the middle of the corridor, making it possible to slightly offset one of the chains so that the intersection between the two bi-chains does not occur exactly at a bi-vertex. In a sense such islands play the role of extended bi-vertices.

Fig. 3 illustrates two additional subtleties–shifts to ensure a proper bi-vertex/corridor interaction at corridor turn points, and shifts to avoid coincident bi-chains–both of which are also addressed by the use of island barriers.

3.3   Correctness of the Reduction

To establish the correctness for the reduction let $P = (G, r)$ be an instance of SEB-C problem, where $G = (^-V_1^+, ^-V_2^+, B)$ is a $(bi)^3$-graphand et $P' = (\mathcal{A}, S, T, r)$ be the ULS-RES instance constructed from P as described above.

Lemma 1. *If there exists a saturating edge colouring scheme for G with r red edges, then the resilience of the sensor network described in P' is at most r.*

Proof. It suffices to show that there exists a $S - T$ path for P' which intersects at most r distinct sensors. Since the path does not intersect any walls, it will only intersect the sensors used to construct the bi-chains. Thus, by the Environment Property, we can treat such a path as a series of independent decisions where for each bi-vertex, the path chooses whether to intersect all positively or all negatively incident sensors (or both).

We now construct an $S - T$ path based on the colouring scheme. First, the path considers the bottom and top bi-vertices. For each bi-vertex, the path will choose intersect all positively incident sensors if and only if for the corresponding bi-vertex in G, the edge colouring scheme coloured all positively incident edges red. Otherwise, the path will choose to intersect all negatively incident sensors (this means that the colouring scheme must have coloured all negatively incident edges red).

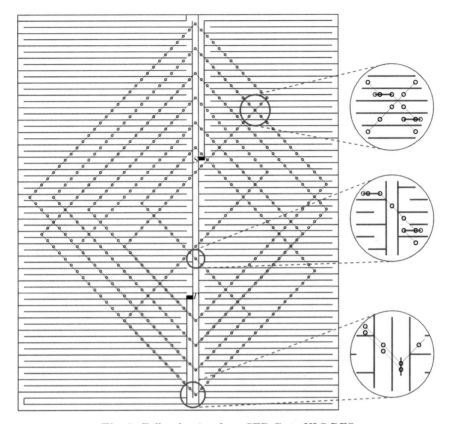

Fig. 3. Full reduction from SEB-C to ULS-RES

At this point, it must be the case that that for every embedded bi-chain, the $S - T$ path has already decided whether to intersect the two end sensors or not (since the end sensors of the bi-chains are exactly the sensors incident on the top and bottom bi-vertices). These bi-chains are no longer correlated and we can analyze each chain independently. There are three cases to consider: when neither end sensor is intersected by the path, when exactly one end sensor is intersected by the path, and when both end sensors are intersected by the path.

We can skirt every bi-vertex in the bi-chain by intersecting exactly p sensors (if one or fewer of the end sensors are intersected) or $p + 1$ sensors (if both end sensors are intersected). Thus, by following the above scheme for every bi-chain, the total number of sensors crossed is r. □

Lemma 2. *If the resilience of the sensor network described in P' is at most r, then there exists a saturating edge colouring scheme for G with r red edges.*

Proof. If the resilience of the sensor network is at most r, then there must exists a $S - T$ path π which intersects at most r distinct sensors. By construction, this path will not cross any walls and will satisfy the Environment Property. Therefore, for every embedded bi-chain, at least half of the sensor must be intersected by the path.

We now construct a saturating colouring scheme for G. We begin by colouring the edges incident on the bi-vertices in $^-V_1^+$ and $^-V_2^+$ (whose corresponding bi-vertices in P' are the bottom and top bi-vertices, respectively). For each bi-vertex, we colour all positively incident edges red if and only if the path π intersected all positively incident sensors for the corresponding bi-vertex in P'. Otherwise, we colour all negatively incident edges red (this means that that path must have intersected all negatively incident sensors). Similarly, we colour the internal edges of a bi-chain red if the corresponding sensor was crossed by π.

Since the resulting colouring scheme saturates all of the bi-vertices in G and uses no more than r red edges, the result follows.   □

With all of the details of the reduction in hand (cf. [13]) it is straightforward to establish the following:

Lemma 3. *Let $P = (G, r)$ be an instance of SEB-C , where $G = (^-V_1^+, {}^-V_2^+, B)$ is a $(bi)^3$-graph. The reduction to an instance P' of ULS-RES is constructible in time that is bounded by some polynomial in $|^-V_1^+|$ and $|^-V_2^+|$.*

The following theorem is an immediate consequence of the preceding three lemmas:

Theorem 1. *ULS-RES is NP-hard.*

4   Extension to Other Sensor Shapes

The core idea of our reduction is to first construct a sensor network consisting of bi-chains connecting appropriate bi-vertices. Then, the network is embedded within a maze of sensor obstacles in order to implement the constraint on each bi-vertex (expressed as the Environment Property). The realization of bi-chains or the environment maze are individually independent on the shape of the sensors. However once the embedding occurs, we need to ensure that the Environment Property is imposed. Thus, there are two things we need to handle when extending the reduction to other sensors shapes. First, we need to be able to implement the basic components: bi-vertices, bi-chains, walls and corridors. Second, we need to be able to handle bi-chains as they intersect with each other (ie. a cross-over gadget) and with the environment.

We believe that for any sensor shapes except for disks, the above two requirements can be satisfied. We sketch below the modifications necessary to extend our hardness result for unit square sensors; in [13], we demonstrate the corresponding result for (proper) elliptical sensors . The reason that the reduction does not extend for disk sensors is due to the inability to construct a cross-over gadget. Consider the cross-over gadget for the examples given (Fig. 3 and 5). For both squares and ellipses, we exploited the fact that the associated sensor regions do not intersect as pseudo-disks (i.e. they can be made to cross).

Fig. 4 demonstrates how to implement a biparite chain with square sensors. Note that consecutive sensors in the chain are not physically connected. This is because corridors of the maze are too wide. Instead, we add additional walls to connect the two consecutive sensors. Since a $S - T$ path will not intersect the wall, the result is that one of the two consecutive sensors must still be intersected. We remark that adding walls between consecutive sensors of a bi-chain is not necessary. The alternative is to make the corridor width more narrow. We have opted for the former approach here simply because it makes the picture clearer.

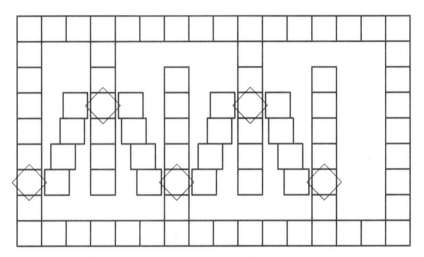

Fig. 4. Realizing a bi-chain with square sensors

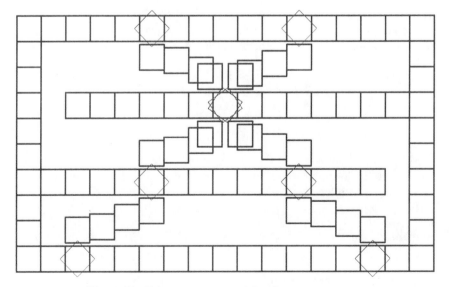

Fig. 5. Realizing cross-overs with other square sensors

Fig. 5 demonstrates how to construct a cross-over gadget using square sensors. Note that we needed to slightly rotate the square sensors at the cross-over point. The result is that one square sensor "pokes" out of the square sensor from the other chain.

Of course, we have only sketched how one may approach extending the reduction for other sensor shapes. The problem of designing a a precise construction for every non-symmetric shape contains many subleties and, although we believe that a general proof is possible, establishing this is certainly beyond the scope of this paper.

5   Hardness of Approximation

Recall that if (X, C) is an instance of 2-SAT, we defined $\sigma(X, C)$, to be the maximum number of clauses in C satisfiable by some truth assignment to the variables of X. Furthermore, if $\mathcal{A}$ is an arrangement of sensors then we defined $\rho(\mathcal{A}, S, T)$ to be the resilience of $\mathcal{A}$, with respect to faces S and T of $\mathcal{A}$.

Our reductions described in Sections 2 and 3 can be composed to show that any 2-SAT instance (X, C) can be transformed, in time bounded by some polynomial in its size, to an arrangement $\mathcal{A}$, with distinguished faces S and T, such that

$$\sigma(X, C) = \rho(\mathcal{A}, S, T) - |\mathcal{A}|/2 - |C|$$

where $|\mathcal{A}|$ denotes the number of sensors in $\mathcal{A}$. Thus, the reduction can be used to convert an approximation algorithm Ξ' for $\rho(\mathcal{A}, S, T)$ into an approximation algorithm Ξ for $\sigma(X, C)$.

Specifically, suppose that $\mathcal{A}$, S and T are formed by our reduction from a 2-SAT instance (X, C). We know that $\rho(\mathcal{A}, S, T)$ is bounded by some polynomial $\lambda(|X|, |C|)$. Suppose that ϵ' is chosen to be $\epsilon/\lambda(|X|, |C|)$. Now if Ξ' guarantees a $(1 + \epsilon')$-approximation $\rho'(\mathcal{A}, S, T)$ of $\rho(\mathcal{A}, S, T)$, then the value $\rho'(\mathcal{A}, S, T) - |\mathcal{A}|/2 - |C|$ provides a $(1 - \epsilon)$-approximation of $\sigma(X, C)$, since

$$\begin{aligned}
\rho'(\mathcal{A}, S, T) &\le (1 + \epsilon')\rho(\mathcal{A}, S, T) \\
&\le \rho(\mathcal{A}, S, T) + \epsilon\sigma(X, C) \\
&\le |\mathcal{A}|/2 + |C| - (1 - \epsilon)\sigma(X, C)
\end{aligned}$$

The MAX-2-SAT problem is known to be APX-hard [7]. This implies that, unless P=NP, it does not admit a polynomial-time approximation scheme. Our results imply a similar (but weaker) hardness-of-approximation result for the ULS-RES problem.

Theorem 2. *Unless P=NP, there does not exists a fully polynomial-time approximation scheme for the ULS-RES problem.*

Proof. Suppose the contrary and let Ξ' be a fully polynomial-time approximation scheme (FPTAS) for the ULS-RES problem. By the discussion above, this implies the existence of an FPTAS for the MAX-2-SAT problem, contradicting the fact that, being APX-hard, MAX-2-SAT does not admit a polynomial-time approximation scheme, unless P=NP [7]. (Note that our reduction is not guaranteed to produce a polynomial-time approximation scheme (PTAS) if Ξ' is a PTAS but not a FPTAS, since ϵ' depends on the size of the problem instance, as well as ϵ.)   □

6   Conclusion

Resilience is a natural measure of the robustness of a sensor network. What we have shown is that computing robustness is hard if the network is formed by unit-line-segment sensors. In fact, our reduction shows that this is true even if the segments-sensors are oriented horizontally, vertically, and diagonally. It is natural to ask if this remains true even if sensors are restricted to two orientations, say horizontal and vertical. In fact our constructions can be modified (replacing diagonal chains by "staircases") to establish this slightly stronger result, at the cost of considerable additional complexity.

We also argued that the reduction can be extended to sensors with non-symmetric shape. Unfortunately, our techniques do not allow us to show whether the problem is hard for circular sensors. This is because circles are perfectly symmetrical and we could not construct a cross-over gadget (even if the circles can be different sizes). Thus, the complexity of computing resilience for networks of disk sensors remains an open problem. It should be noted that the three-dimensional version of the problem (computing resilience for a network unit sphere sensors) has been shown to be NP-hard [13].

For practical applications, we often turn to approximation algorithms for NP-hard problems. In Section 5, we showed that, unless P=NP, there does not exists a fully polynomial-time approximation scheme for the ULS-RES problem. However, it remains open whether there exists a less demanding PTAS. We note that it has been shown that for 2D unit disk sensors, the thickness of the sensor network (which is computable using a shortest path algorithm) provides a 2-approximation for resilience [2] . Unfortunately, this does not extend for other type of sensor shapes. Thus, finding constant approximation algorithm for the resilience of line-segment sensor networks is another problem worth exploring.

References

1. Alt, H., Cabello, S., Giannopoulous, P., Knauer, C.: On some connection problems in straight-line segment arrangements. In: 27th European Workshop on Computational Geometry, pp. 27–30 (2011)
2. Bereg, S., Kirkpatrick, D.: Approximating Barrier Resilience in Wireless Sensor Networks. In: Dolev, S. (ed.) ALGOSENSORS 2009. LNCS, vol. 5804, pp. 29–40. Springer, Heidelberg (2009)
3. Cardei, M., Wu, J.: Coverage in wireless sensor networks. In: Handbook of Sensor Networks: Compact Wireless and Wired Sensing Systems, pp. 432–446. CRC Press (2005)

4. Gage, D.W.: Command control for many-robot systems. In: Proceedings of the 19th Annual AUVS Technical Symposium, AUVS 1992, pp. 28–34 (1992)
5. Garey, M.R., Johnson, D.S., Stockmeyer, L.: Some simplified NP-complete graph problems. Theoretical Computer Science pp. 237 – 267 (1976)
6. Gregg, W., Esaias, W., Feldman, G., Frouin, R., Hooker, S., McClain, C., Woodward, R.: Coverage opportunities for global ocean color in a multimission era. IEEE Transactions on Geoscience and Remote Sensing, 1620–1627 (1998)
7. Håstad, J.: Some optimal inapproximability results. In: Proceedings of the 29th Annual ACM Symposium on Theory of Computing, pp. 1–10 (1997)
8. Kumar, S.: Foundations of coverage in wireless sensor networks. Ph.D. thesis, Ohio State University (2006)
9. Kumar, S., Lai, T.H., Arora, A.: Barrier coverage with wireless sensors. In: Proceedings of the 11th Annual International Conference on Mobile Computing and Networking, pp. 284–298 (2005)
10. Liu, B., Dousse, O., Wang, J., Saipulla, A.: Strong barrier coverage of wireless sensor networks. In: Proceedings of the 9th ACM International Symposium on Mobile Ad Hoc Networking and Computing, pp. 411–420 (2008)
11. Meguerdichian, S., Koushanfar, F., Potkonjak, M., Srivastava, M.: Coverage problems in wireless ad-hoc sensor networks. In: INFOCOM 2001. Twentieth Annual Joint Conference of the IEEE Computer and Communications Societies. Proceedings. IEEE, pp. 1380–1387 (2001)
12. Meguerdichian, S., Koushanfar, F., Qu, G., Potkonjak, M.: Exposure in wireless ad-hoc sensor networks. In: Proceedings of the 7th Annual International Conference on Mobile Computing and Networking, pp. 139–150 (2001)
13. Tseng, K.C.R.: Resilience of Wireless Sensor Networks. Master's thesis, University of British Columbia (2011)

Distributed (Δ + 1)-Coloring
in the Physical Model

Dongxiao Yu[1], Yuexuan Wang[2], Qiang-Sheng Hua[2,1], and Francis C.M. Lau[1]

[1] Department of Computer Science, The University of Hong Kong,
Pokfulam, Hong Kong, P.R. China
[2] Institute for Interdisciplinary Information Sciences,
Tsinghua University, Beijing, 100084, P.R. China

Abstract. In multi-hop radio networks, such as wireless ad-hoc and sensor networks, nodes employ a MAC (Medium Access Control) protocol such as TDMA to coordinate accesses to the shared medium and to avoid interference of close-by transmissions. These protocols can be implemented using standard node coloring. The (Δ + 1)-coloring problem is to color all nodes in as few timeslots as possible using at most $\Delta + 1$ colors such that any two nodes within distance R are assigned different colors, where R is a given parameter and Δ is the maximum degree of the modeled unit disk graph using the scaling factor R. Being one of the most fundamental problems in distributed computing, this problem is well studied and there are a long chain of algorithms for it. However, all previous work are based on models that are highly abstract, such as message passing models and graph based interference models, which limit the utility of these algorithms in practice.

In this paper, for the first time, we consider the distributed Δ + 1-coloring problem under the more practical SINR interference model. In particular, without requiring any knowledge about the neighborhood, we propose a novel randomized (Δ + 1)-coloring algorithm with time complexity $O(\Delta \log n + \log^2 n)$. For the case where nodes can not adjust their transmission power, we give an $O(\Delta \log^2 n)$ randomized algorithm, which only incurs a logarithmic multiplicative factor overhead.

1 Introduction

The node coloring problem underpins the design of interference avoidance mechanisms in many multi-hop radio networks including wireless ad-hoc and sensor networks. In these networks, radio communications are subject to interference, and messages may be lost due to interference. Without any interference avoidance mechanism, coordinating the nodes to achieve efficient and reliable communication is a time consuming task. Traditionally, nodes employ MAC (Medium Access Control) protocols to coordinate their accesses to the shared medium and to avoid interference of close-by transmissions, such as TDMA (Time Division Multiple-Access). These MAC protocols can all be reduced to the classical node coloring problem. For example, by assigning different colors to different time

T. Erlebach et al. (Eds.): ALGOSENSORS 2011, LNCS 7111, pp. 145–160, 2012.

slots in a TDMA scheme, a proper coloring with parameter d corresponds to a MAC layer without "close-by" interference, i.e., no two nodes within distance d of each other transmit at the same time. In [3], it is shown that even under the complicated (but more realistic) SINR model, we can still implement an interference free TDMA-like MAC protocol by computing a proper coloring for a well defined d if we adopt a uniform power assignment. Conventionally, the node coloring problem is one of the most fundamental problems related to symmetry breaking, and therefore has attracted a great deal of attention in the distributed computing community.

Almost all previous work to derive distributed node coloring algorithms assume the graph based model in which interference is represented by a localized function—a message can be correctly received only if there are no other simultaneously transmitting senders in the receiver's neighborhood. However, in multi-hop radio networks, interference is cumulative and is caused by all simultaneously transmitting nodes, near by and far away. The physically based Signal-to-Interference-plus-Noise-Ratio (SINR) model [7] captures this reality in wireless networks more closely. Under the SINR model, the signal strength fades with distance to the power of some path-loss exponent α and a message can be successfully received if the ratio of the received signal strength and the sum of the interference caused by simultaneously transmitting nodes plus noise is above a certain hardware-defined threshold β.

1.1   Related Work

In the absence of global knowledge, to derive a $(\Delta + 1)$-coloring in a distributed manner is challenging and has attracted much attention in the distributed computing community for more than two decades. The traditional message passing model was first considered. Since Cole and Vishkin presented the first distributed $(\Delta + 1)$-coloring for rings in [2], a long line of papers were devoted to this problem. The state-of-the-art results are the $O(\Delta) + \frac{1}{2} \log^* n$ algorithm for arbitrary graphs in [1] and the optimal $O(\log^* n)$ algorithm for bounded-independence graphs in [14]. However, the message passing model abstracts away some crucial elements of wireless networks, such as interference, collision and asynchrony. Taking interference into account and assuming a locally synchronous circumstance, Schneider and Wattenhofer [15] proposed a distributed $(\Delta + 1)$-coloring algorithm with running time $O(\Delta + \log \Delta \log n)$ and $O(\Delta + \log^2 n)$ with and without knowledge of Δ respectively. When further considering asynchrony, assuming prior knowledge of n and Δ, Moscibroda and Wattenhofer [10] gave an $O(\Delta \log n)$ distributed coloring algorithm for the simple unit disk graph model which only considers direct interferences from neighbors. In an extended version [11], the result was generalized for the bounded-independence graph. In a recent paper [3], Derbel and Talbi showed that the algorithm in [11] also works under the SINR model within the same time bound. However, all the above three algorithms need $O(\Delta)$ colors instead of at most $\Delta + 1$ colors.

In the SINR model, the interference is modeled as a global function, which makes the design of efficient distributed algorithms with global performance guarantee difficult. In spite of this, there have been many attempts in recent years. In [13], assuming that all nodes can perform physical carrier sensing, Scheideler et al. derived an $O(\log n)$ distributed algorithm for computing a constant approximate dominating set. The first distributed local broadcasting algorithm was presented by Goussevskaia et al. in [4] and the result is improved in a recent paper [17]. Kesselheim and Vöcking [8] considered the contention resolution problem and showed that their distributed algorithm is asymptotically optimal up to a $\log^2 n$ factor.

1.2   Our Contribution

To the best of our knowledge, this work is the first one considering the distributed $(\Delta + 1)$-coloring problem under the physical model. Without any knowledge on neighborhood, we give an $O(\Delta \log n + \log^2 n)$ time randomized distributed $(\Delta + 1)$-coloring algorithm for asynchronous wake-up multi-hop radio networks under the physical model. Our result even matches the coloring algorithm in [3] for large Δ, e.g., $\Delta \geq \log n$, which needs a linear estimate of Δ and uses $O(\Delta)$ colors. In our algorithm, we adopt a clustering coloring strategy, i.e., a Maximal Independent Set (MIS) is first computed, and then the nodes in the MIS assign colors for their neighbors. To make the strategy available, we first show that the MIS algorithm in [12] still works under the SINR model by carefully tuning the parameters. This algorithm is of independent interest, since it is the first MIS algorithm in the physical model.

Furthermore, if nodes can not adjust their transmission powers, we also give a distributed $(\Delta+1)$-coloring algorithm with time complexity $O(\Delta \log^2 n)$ by iteratively carrying out the MIS algorithm, which also does not need any knowledge on neighborhood.

2   Problem Definitions and Model

For two nodes u and v, we use $d(u, v)$ to denote the Euclidian distance between u and v. Given a distance parameter R, we say two nodes u and v are neighbors if $d(u, v) \leq R$. The neighborhood of a node v is the set of all its neighbors, denoted by $N(v)$. Additionally, we use $N[v]$ to denote the set $N(v) \cup \{v\}$. For a node v, we denote by Δ_v the number of nodes in v's neighborhood. We write $\Delta = \max_{v \in V} \Delta_v$. A set of nodes S is called an independent set if any two nodes of S are not in each other's neighborhood. A node coloring is proper if each set of nodes with the same color is an independent set, i.e., the distance between any two nodes with the same color is larger than R. Then the $(\Delta + 1)$-*coloring problem* is to color all nodes properly in as few timeslots as possible using at most $\Delta + 1$ colors.

In this work, we deal with unstructured radio networks [9]. In particular, nodes may wake up asynchronously or be woken up by incoming messages without access to a global clock. After waking up, nodes may start executing the algorithm at any time and nodes can not perform physical carrier sensing. The only prior knowledge given to nodes is a polynomial estimate of the number n of nodes in the network and nodes are clueless about the number of nodes in its close proximity. We also assume that every node v has a unique ID_v. Additionally, we assume that nodes are placed arbitrarily on the plane. We define a node v's running time as the length of the interval from the timeslot when v starts executing the algorithm to the timeslot when v quits the algorithm. The time complexity of the algorithm is the maximum of all the nodes' running times.

We adopt the practical physical model (or the SINR model) [7] in this paper. In particular, a message sent by node u to node v can be correctly received at v iff

$$\frac{\frac{P_u}{d(u,v)^\alpha}}{N + \sum_{w \in V \setminus \{u,v\}} \frac{P_w}{d(w,v)^\alpha}} \geq \beta, \tag{1}$$

where P_u (P_w) is the transmission power for node u (w), α is the path-loss exponent whose value is normally between 2 and 6, β is a hardware determined threshold value which is greater than 1, N is the ambient noise, and $\sum_{w \in V \setminus \{u,v\}} \frac{P_w}{d(w,v)^\alpha}$ is the interference experienced by the receiver v caused by all simultaneously transmitting nodes in the network.

The transmission range R_T of a node v can be defined as the maximum distance at which a node u can receive a clear transmission from v ($SINR \geq \beta$) when there are no other simultaneous transmissions in the network. From the SINR condition (1), $R_T \leq R_{max} = (\frac{P}{\beta \cdot N})^{1/\alpha}$ for the given power level P. We further assume that $R_T < R_{max}$ and define $R_T = (P/cN\beta)^{1/\alpha}$, where $c > 1$ is a constant determined by the environment.

In subsequent sections, when we say "an event occurs with high probability" we mean that the event occurs with probability $1 - n^{-c}$ for a constant $c > 0$, and "a node correctly get a color" means that the resulting coloring of the network is proper. Greek letters represent constants. The following Definition 1 and Lemma 1 will be used in the analysis of algorithms.

Definition 1. *For a node $v \in V$, the probabilistic interference at v, Ψ_v, is defined as the expected interference experienced by v in a certain timeslot t.*

$$\Psi_v = \sum_{u \in V \setminus \{v\}} \frac{P_u p_u}{d(u,v)^\alpha}, \tag{2}$$

where P_u is the transmission power and p_u is the sending probability of node u in timeslot t.

Lemma 1 ([4]). *Consider two disks D_1 and D_2 of radii R_1 and R_2, $R_1 > R_2$, we define $\chi(R_1, R_2)$ to be the smallest number of disks D_2 needed to cover the larger disk D_1. It holds that: $\chi(R_1, R_2) \leq \frac{2\pi}{3\sqrt{3}} \cdot \frac{(R_1 + 2R_2)^2}{R_2^2}$.*

3   An $O(\Delta \log n + \log^2 n)$ $(\Delta + 1)$-Coloring Algorithm

In this section, we give a distributed randomized coloring algorithm as described in Algorithm 1. It is assumed that every node v possesses a color list from which it chooses a color. Without loss of generality, we assume that all nodes' color lists are $\{0, 1, \ldots, n-1\}$, where n is the estimate of the number of nodes. Algorithm 1 has two main steps. A Maximal Independent Set (MIS) in terms of $3R$, i.e., every pair of nodes in the MIS has distance larger than $3R$, is first computed; the nodes in this MIS are the leaders of their neighbors. Then by communicating with their neighbors within distance R, each leader decides when their neighbors can choose an available color. Without confusion, we will just call Algorithm 1 excluding the MIS algorithm as the coloring algorithm. In order to compute a maximal independent set, we first show that the distributed MIS algorithm in [12] still works under the SINR model by carefully tuning the parameters. Due to asynchrony, when some nodes execute the MIS algorithm, other nodes may be carrying out the coloring algorithm. Here we show that under such an asynchronous circumstance, the MIS algorithm can still correctly output an independent set in any timeslot with high probability. Due to the space limit, we put the description and the analysis of the MIS algorithm in the full version [16]. In addition, nodes adopt different transmission powers when executing different operations in Algorithm 1. Generally speaking, nodes adopt the transmission power of $P_M = c \cdot 3^\alpha N \beta R^\alpha$ when they execute the MIS algorithm and transmit a *StartTransmit* message in state $\mathcal{G}$, while nodes adopt the transmission power of $P_C = cN\beta R^\alpha$ when they perform other operations. By the definition in Section 2, the transmission ranges of nodes are $3R$ and R for P_M and P_C, respectively.

There are four states in the coloring algorithm. After executing the MIS algorithm, all leaders in the computed independent set join state $\mathcal{G}$, while all nodes within distance $3R$ from these leaders join state $\mathcal{S}$. Then each node in $\mathcal{G}$ makes its neighbors within distance R join state $\mathcal{C}_1$. By continuously transmitting an *AskColor* message, each node in state $\mathcal{C}_1$ endeavors to acquire a *Grant* message from its leader. After receiving the *Grant* message from the leader, a node in state $\mathcal{C}_1$ joins state $\mathcal{C}_2$, in which it chooses a color that has not been chosen by its neighbors, and transmits its choice to all neighbors. Nodes still in state $\mathcal{S}$ keep silence so that they do not interfere with the coloring process of their neighbors. Next we describe Algorithm 1 in more details.

After waking up, a node v will first wait for at most $2\mu \log n$ timeslots. During the process, if v received a message $DoNotTransmit_u$, it enters state $\mathcal{S}$ and adds u into its forbidden set F_v. Otherwise, it starts executing the MIS algorithm after waiting for $2\mu \log n$ timeslots. After executing the MIS algorithm, each node will either join state $\mathcal{M}$ meaning that it is a member of the computed independent set, or join state $\mathcal{S}$. Here we must point out a difference of our MIS algorithm from that in [12] in state $\mathcal{M}$. In our algorithm, when a node v joins state $\mathcal{M}$, it first uses $\mu \log n$ timeslots to wake up all nodes within distance $3R$ by transmitting a message with constant probability. Then v transmits a $DoNotTransmit_v$ message forcing all nodes within distance $3R$ to join state $\mathcal{S}$. After doing this, v will join state $\mathcal{G}$ and start executing the coloring algorithm.

In the coloring algorithm, the leaders in state $\mathcal{G}$ first choose color 0 as its own color. Then they transmit a *StartColoring* message making their neighbors within distance R join state $\mathcal{C}_1$. While in state $\mathcal{G}$, a node v adds each of its neighbors that send an *AskColor* message to v into a set Q_v. If Q_v is not empty, it deletes the first node u from Q_v and transmits a *Grant$_u$* message with constant probability for $2\mu \log n$ timeslots. We assign two counters c_v and b_v to each node v in state $\mathcal{G}$. In particular, c_v is used to count the number of timeslots that v has not received any *AskColor* message since the last one, while b_v is for counting the number of *Grant* messages that have been transmitted by v. These two counters are set for guaranteing that with high probability, v will not quit the algorithm until all neighbors have been colored. Then if Q_v is empty and $c_v > b_v \cdot 5\mu \log n + 3\mu \log^2 n + \mu \log n$, v quits the algorithm after transmitting a *StartTransmit$_v$* message for $\mu \log n$ timeslots adopting power P_M. By doing so, v removes its restriction on nodes within distance $3R$ caused by the message *DoNotTransmit$_v$*.

For each node u in state $\mathcal{S}$, it will do nothing except listening. When u stays in state $\mathcal{S}$, it adds the nodes that send *DoNotTransmit* messages to u into its forbidden set F_u, and it removes a node v from F_u if it receives a message *StartTransmit$_v$*. Node u will not leave state $\mathcal{S}$ until F_u is empty or it receives a *StartColoring* message from a leader node v. For the first case, u starts executing the MIS algorithm. For the second case, it joins state $\mathcal{C}_1$ and starts competing for the right of choosing a color. After joining state $\mathcal{C}_1$, node u starts transmitting an *AskColor$_u$* message with a small initial transmission probability. Then if u did not receive any *Grant* message and did not change its transmission probability for $3\mu \log n$ timeslots, it doubles the transmission probability. While in state $\mathcal{C}_1$, if u receives a *Grant* message and the *Grant* message is not for u, it halves the transmission probability. By doing this, it is guaranteed that the sum of transmission probabilities in any local region of the network can be bounded with high probability, which helps bound the interference caused by simultaneously transmitting nodes. If the received *Grant* message is for u, it joins state $\mathcal{C}_2$. After joining $\mathcal{C}_2$, u chooses the first color remaining in its color list except color 0 and transmits a *Color$_u$* message with constant probability for $\mu \log n$ timeslots to inform its neighbors of its choice. After waking up, each node will delete the color in the received *Color* message from its color list; hence it will not choose a color that has been chosen by its neighbors. In order to make sure that Algorithm 1 is correct with high probability, we assign $\mu = \dfrac{2^{\omega+8} \cdot 4^{3 \cdot 2^{1-\omega}} \cdot \chi (3^{1+2/(\alpha-2)} R_I + 3R, 0.5R)}{1 - 1/\rho}$, where ρ and R_I (Equation (3) below) are constants defined in the following analysis.

3.1 Analysis

In this section, we will show that with high probability, each node can correctly get a color after executing Algorithm 1 for $O(\Delta \log n + \log^2 n)$ timeslots, and the

---

Algorithm 1. $(\Delta + 1)$-Coloring

Initially, $p_v = \frac{2^{-\omega-1}}{n}; c_v = 0; b_v = 0; t_v = 0; Q_v = \emptyset; T_v = \emptyset; \omega = 6.4;$

Upon node v wakes up
1: wait for $2\mu \log n$ timeslots
2: **if** Received $DoNotTransmit_u$ from node u **then** add u into F_v; $state = \mathcal{S}$;
3: **Else** execute the MIS algorithm adopting transmission power P_M **end if**

Message Received
1: **if** Received $Color_w$ **then** delete the color in $Color_w$ from its color list **end if**

Node v in state $\mathcal{G}$
1: choose color 0;
2: **for** $\mu \log n$ timeslots **do** transmit $StartColoring_v$ adopting power P_C with probability $2^{-\omega}$ **end for**
3: **if** Q_v is not empty **then**
4:     $b_v = b_v + 1$;
5:     **for** $2\mu \log n$ timeslots **do** delete the first node u from Q_v and transmit $Grant_u$ adopting power P_C with probability $2^{-\omega}$; $c_v = c_v + 1$ **end for**
6: **else** $c_v = c_v + 1$ **end if**
7: **if** Q_v is empty and $c_v > b_v \cdot 5\mu \log n + 3\mu \log^2 n + \mu \log n$ **then**
8:     **for** $\mu \log n$ timeslots **do** transmit $StartTransmit_v$ adopting power P_M with probability $2^{-\omega}$ **end for**
9: quit
10: **end if**

Message Received
1: **if** Received $AskColor_u$ **then** add u into Q_v; $c_v = 0$ **end if**

Node v in state $\mathcal{S}$
1: **if** F_v is empty **then** execute the MIS algorithm with power P_M **else** listen **end if**

Message Received
1: **if** Received $DoNotTransmit_w$ from node w **then** add w into F_v **end if**
2: **if** Received $Color_w$ **then** delete the color in $Color_w$ from its color list **end if**
3: **if** Received $StartTransmit_w$ from node w **then** delete w from F_v **end if**
4: **if** Received $StartColoring_w$ from node w **then** $state = \mathcal{C}_1$ **end if**

Node v in state $\mathcal{C}_1$
1: $t_v = t_v + 1$
2: **if** $t_v > 3\mu \log n$ **then** $p_v = 2P_v$; $t_v = 0$ **end if**
3: transmit $AskColor_v$ adopting power P_C with probability p_v;

Message Received
1: **if** received $Grant_v$ **then** $state = \mathcal{C}_2$ **end if**
2: **if** received $Grant_w$ for some node w that has not been received before **then** $p_v = p_v/2$; $t_v = 0$ **end if**
3: **if** Received $Color_w$ **then** delete the color in $Color_w$ from its color list **end if**

Node v in state $\mathcal{C}_2$
1: choose the first available color from its color list;
2: **for** $\mu \log n$ timeslots **do** transmit a message $Color_v$ containing its color adopting power P_C with probability $2^{-\omega}$ **end for**
3: quit;

---

total number of colors used is at most $\Delta + 1$. We first give some definitions and notations that will be used in the subsequent analysis. A new parameter R_I is defined as follows, for bounding the interference.

$$R_I = R \left(2^{7-\omega} 3^{\alpha+1} \sqrt{3} \pi \rho \beta \cdot \frac{1}{1 - 1/c} \cdot \frac{\alpha - 1}{\alpha - 2} \right)^{1/(\alpha-2)}, \tag{3}$$

where ρ is a constant larger than 1. We choose ρ such that $R_I > 2R$. Furthermore, we denote T_i, D_i and I_i as the disks centered at node i with radius R, $\frac{R}{2}$ and R_I, respectively. By E_i^r we denote the disk centered at node i with radius r. Without confusion, we also use T_i, D_i, I_i and E_i^r to denote the set of nodes in T_i, D_i, I_i and E_i^r, respectively.

Before analyzing Algorithm 1, we first give a lemma on the time complexity and the correctness of the MIS Algorithm, which is proved in the full version [16].

Lemma 2. *With probability $1 - O(n^{-3})$, every node $v \in V$ decides whether it joins the computed independent set or state $\mathcal{S}$ after executing the MIS algorithm for at most $O(\log^2 n)$ timeslots. Furthermore, with probability at least $1 - O(n^{-3})$, in any timeslot t, the independent set computed by the MIS algorithm is correct.*

The following property is also proved to be correct with probability at least $1 - O(n^{-3})$ in the analysis of the MIS algorithm which is put in the full version [16].

Property 1. For any disk D_i and in any timeslot t throughout the execution of the algorithm, the sum of transmission probabilities of nodes that are executing the MIS algorithm is at most $3 \cdot 2^{-\omega}$.

In order to bound the interference, we present Property 2 which can be proved to be correct with probability at least $1 - O(n^{-1})$ in Lemma 9.

Property 2. For any disk D_i and in any timeslot t throughout the execution of the algorithm,
  (i) There is at most one node in state $\mathcal{C}_2$;
  (ii) The sum of transmission probabilities of nodes in state $\mathcal{C}_1$ is at most $\sum_{u \in \mathcal{C}_1} \leq 2^{-\omega}$;
  (iii) There is at most one node in state $\mathcal{G}$.

Based on Property 1, Property 2 and the transmission probability in each state, we can bound the sum of transmission probabilities as follows.

Lemma 3. *Assume that Property 1 and Property 2 hold. For any disk D_i and in any timeslot t throughout the execution of the algorithm, the sum of transmission probabilities can be bounded as $\sum_{v \in D_i} p_v \leq 3 \cdot 2^{1-\omega}$.*

In the subsequent lemma 4, we show that the interference by far-away nodes can be bounded by a constant, and then in Lemma 5, we give a sufficient condition for a successful transmission. The proofs of Lemma 4 and Lemma 5 are put in the full version [16].

Lemma 4. *Assume that Property 1 and Property 2 hold. Then for every node u, the probabilistic interference caused by nodes outside I_u can be bounded as:* $\Psi_u^{v\notin I_u} \le \frac{(1-1/c)P_C}{\rho\beta R^\alpha}$.

Lemma 5. *Assume that Property 1 and Property 2 hold. If node v is the only sending node in $E_v^{R_I+R}$, with probability $1 - \frac{1}{\rho}$, the message sent by v will be received successfully by all nodes in T_v.*

Based on the sufficient condition for a successful transmission in Lemma 5, in the following Lemma 6, we show the successful transmissions of messages used in the algorithm in given timeslots with high probability. Then in Lemma 7, we state that with high probability, a leader will not quit the algorithm until all its neighbors have been colored.

Lemma 6. *Assume that Property 1 and Property 2 hold. Then with probability at least $1 - \frac{1}{n^4}$, the following results are correct:*

(i) After entering state $\mathcal{G}$, a node v can successfully send a message StartColoring to all its neighbors in $\mu\log n$ timeslots.

(ii) A node v in state $\mathcal{G}$ can successfully send a message Grant to all its neighbors in $\mu\log n$ timeslots.

(iii) A node v in state $\mathcal{G}$ can successfully send a message StartTransmit to all nodes within distance $3R$ in $\mu\log n$ timeslots.

(iv) A node v in state $\mathcal{C}_2$, after choosing a color, can successfully send a message $Color_v$ to all neighbors in $\mu\log n$ timeslots.

Proof. We only prove (i) here. $(ii), (iii), (iv)$ can be proved similar to (i).

Proof of (i): As shown in Lemma 5, if v is the only sending node in $E_v^{R_I+R}$, with probability $1 - \frac{1}{\rho}$, the message *StartColoring* sent by v can be received successfully by all nodes in T_v. Let P_1 denote the event that v is the only sending node in $E_v^{R_I+R}$, then

$$P_1 = 2^{-\omega} \prod_{u\in E_v^{R_I+R}\setminus\{v\}} (1-p_u) \ge 2^{-\omega} \prod_{u\in E_v^{R_I+R}} (1-p_u)$$

$$\ge 2^{-\omega} \cdot \left(\frac{1}{4}\right)^{\sum_{u\in E_v^{R_I+R}} p_u} \ge 2^{-\omega} \cdot \left(\frac{1}{4}\right)^{3\cdot 2^{1-\omega}\cdot\chi(R_I+R,0.5R)} \tag{4}$$

The last inequality is by Lemma 1 and Lemma 3. Then the probability P_{no} that v fails to transmit the message *StartColoring* to all nodes in T_v is at most

$$P_{no} \le \left(1 - (1-1/\rho)2^{-\omega} \cdot \left(\frac{1}{4}\right)^{3\cdot 2^{1-\omega}\cdot\chi(R_I+R,0.5R)}\right)^{\mu\log n} \tag{5}$$

$$\le e^{-(1-1/\rho)2^{-\omega}\mu\log n\cdot\left(\frac{1}{4}\right)^{3\cdot 2^{1-\omega}\cdot\chi(R_I+R,0.5R)}} \in n^{-4}.$$

Lemma 7. *Assume that Property 1 and Property 2 hold. Then with probability at least $1 - \frac{1}{n^4}$, a node v in state $\mathcal{G}$ will not quit the algorithm until all its neighbors have been colored.*

Proof. Assume that v quits the algorithm in timeslot t when there are $d > 0$ neighbors staying in state $\mathcal{C}_1$. Denote the set of these d nodes as T. We further assume that v forces d_v neighbors joining state $\mathcal{C}_1$ after transmitting the *StartColoring$_v$* message. Thus before time t, v has transmitted $(d_v - d)$ *Grant* messages. Then by Algorithm 1, v has not receive an *AskColor* message since the timeslot $t - ((d_v - d) \cdot 5\mu \log n + 3\mu \log^2 n + \mu \log n)$. Next we show that during the interval $[t - ((d_v - d) \cdot 5\mu \log n + 3\mu \log^2 n + \mu \log n), t)$, there is at least one node that can successfully transmit an *AskColor* message to v with high probability. Then v will not quit the algorithm in timeslot t. This contradiction completes the proof.

By Algorithm 1, the initial transmission probability of each node in T is assigned as $\frac{2^{-\omega - 1}}{n}$, and each node in T will either doubles its transmission probability every $3\mu \log n$ timeslots, or received a *Grant* message from v and halves the transmission probability. Because v received the last *AskColor* message before the timeslot $t - ((d_v - d) \cdot 5\mu \log n + 3\mu \log^2 n + \mu \log n)$ and v transmits each *Grant* message for $2\mu \log n$ timeslots, v have completed the transmission of $(d_v - d)$ *Grant* messages by the timeslot $t - ((d_v - d) \cdot 5\mu \log n + 3\mu \log^2 n + \mu \log n) + 2(d_v - d)\mu \log n - 1$. So in timeslot $t^* = t - ((d_v - d) \cdot 3\mu \log n + 3\mu \log^2 n + \mu \log n)$, each node in T has transmission probability at least $\frac{2^{-\omega - 1 - d_v + d}}{n}$. From t^*, each node in T doubles its transmission probability every $3\mu \log n$ timeslots. In timeslot $t - \mu \log n$, each node in T has a constant transmission probability of $2^{-\omega - 1}$. Then using a similar argument as in the proof of Lemma 6, we can get that with probability at least $1 - n^{-4}$, there is at least one node in T that can successfully transmit an *AskColor* message to v by the timeslot $t - 1$.   □

Lemma 8. *Assume Property 1 and Property 2 hold. A node v will correctly get a color after waking up for $O(\Delta \log n + \log^2 n)$ timeslots with probability $1 - O(n^{-2})$.*

Proof. After waking up for at most $2\mu \log n$ timeslots, v enters state $\mathcal{S}$ or starts executing the MIS algorithm. If v takes part in the MIS algorithm, by Lemma 2, with probability $1 - O(n^{-3})$, it will correctly enter state $\mathcal{S}$ or state $\mathcal{G}$ after $O(\log^2 n)$ timeslots. Next we bound the time v stays in state $\mathcal{C}_1$, $\mathcal{C}_2$ and $\mathcal{G}$.

We first bound the time that node v would stay in state $\mathcal{C}_1$. Assume that u is the leader of v. By Algorithm 1, during every $3\mu \log n$ timeslots, either v receives at least one new *Grant* messages from u, or it doubles its transmission probability. If the received *Grant* message is not for v, it means that a node in $N(u)$ will join state $\mathcal{C}_2$. By Lemma 2, with probability $1 - O(n^{-3})$, when u stays in state $\mathcal{M}$, there is not another node in E_u^{3R} staying in state $\mathcal{M}$. By the MIS algorithm and the analysis for the MIS algorithm in the full version [16], with probability $1 - O(n^{-4})$, u can force all other nodes in E_u^{3R} to join state $\mathcal{S}$ and not to restart competing for joining state $\mathcal{M}$ until receiving a *StartTransmit$_u$* message from u. Thus, with probability $1 - O(n^{-3})$, there are no other nodes in E_u^{3R} joining state $\mathcal{G}$ when u stays in state $\mathcal{G}$. Additionally, only nodes in $N(u)$ and $E_u^{3R} \setminus E_u^{2R}$ may join state $\mathcal{C}_1$ by receiving a *StartColoring* message before u quits. Thus all nodes in $E_u^{2R} \setminus N(u)$ will stay in state $\mathcal{S}$ while u stays in state $\mathcal{G}$.

Then after at most $(\Delta - 1 + \log n)3\mu \log n$ timeslots, either v receives a $Grant_v$ message and joins state $\mathcal{C}_2$, or v has transmission probability of $2^{-1-\omega}$, since v can receive at most $\Delta - 1$ $Grant$ messages not for v and each of which would halve v's transmission probability. Then by a similar argument as in Lemma 6, v will successfully transmit an $AskColor$ message to u in $2\mu \log n$ timeslots with probability $1 - n^{-4}$. Furthermore, by Lemma 7, with probability $1 - n^{-4}$, u did not quit the algorithm before receiving the $AskColor$ message from v. After successfully transmitting message $AskColor_v$ to u, by Algorithm 1 and Lemma 6 (ii), with probability $1 - n^{-4}$, v will receive a $Grant_v$ message from u in at most $2\mu\Delta \log n$ timeslots. So each node will stay in state $\mathcal{C}_1$ for at most $5\mu\Delta \log n + 3\mu \log^2 n$ timeslots with probability at least $1 - O(n^{-3})$. By Algorithm 1, it is easy to see that each node stays in state $\mathcal{C}_2$ for $\mu \log n$ timeslots.

Next we bound the time that a node v stays in state $\mathcal{G}$. By Lemma 6 (i), after entering state $\mathcal{G}$ for $\mu \log n$ timeslots, v will successfully send a $StartColoring$ message to all its neighbors with probability $1 - n^{-4}$. Then all nodes in $N(v)$ without choosing their colors will enter state $\mathcal{C}_1$. As shown above, with probability at least $(1 - O(n^{-3}))^{\Delta} \in 1 - O(n^{-2})$, each node in $N(v)$ will join state $\mathcal{C}_2$ after joining state $\mathcal{C}_1$ for at most $O(\Delta \log n + \log^2 n)$ timeslots. Then by the algorithm, v will quit from the algorithm after waiting for additional $O(\Delta \log n + \log^2 n)$ timeslots by noticing that b_v is at most Δ. So with probability at least $1 - O(n^{-2})$, the total time that v stays in state $\mathcal{G}$ is at most $O(\Delta \log n + \log^2 n)$.

Next we bound the time from v waking up to it next entering state $\mathcal{C}_1$ or $\mathcal{G}$. By the algorithm, after waking up for at most $2\mu \log n$ timeslots, either v starts executing the MIS algorithm or there comes a node in E_v^{3R} joining state $\mathcal{G}$. If v starts executing the MIS algorithm, by Lemma 2, with probability at least $1 - O(n^{-3})$, there will be a node in E_v^{3R} joining state $\mathcal{G}$. So after waking up for at most $O(\log^2 n)$ timeslots, a node in E_v^{3R} will join state $\mathcal{G}$. From then on, by Algorithm 1 and the analysis above, with probability at least $1 - O(n^{-2})$, after every $O(\Delta \log n + \log^2 n)$ timeslots, there will be at least one node u in E_v^{3R} joining state $\mathcal{G}$ and all nodes in $N[u]$ quit from the algorithm. We can see that all nodes joining state $\mathcal{G}$ are independent in terms of R. So there are only a constant number of nodes in E_v^{3R} being able to join state $\mathcal{G}$, denoted by c'. Then after at most $c'O(\Delta \log n + \log^2 n)$ timeslots, there will be a node in $N[v]$ joining state $\mathcal{G}$. Thus, with probability at least $1 - O(n^{-2})$, the total time that v spends before entering state $\mathcal{C}_1$ or $\mathcal{G}$ after waking up is at most $O(\Delta \log n + \log^2 n)$.

Combining all the above, with probability $1 - O(n^{-2})$, every node stays in the algorithm for at most $O(\Delta \log n + \log^2 n)$ timeslots. Finally, we prove that each node can correctly get a color with probability at least $1 - O(n^{-2})$. As shown before, with probability $1 - O(n^{-3})$, when a node v is in state $\mathcal{G}$, there is not another node in E_v^{3R} staying in state $\mathcal{G}$ as well. By Lemma 7, with probability $1 - O(n^{-4})$, v will not leave state $\mathcal{G}$ until all its neighbors get colored. Thus, with probability $1 - O(n^{-2})$, all nodes with color 0, i.e., all nodes used to join state $\mathcal{G}$, are independent in terms of R. If v chooses another color, by the algorithm, it will choose an available color and broadcast the chosen color to its neighbors as soon as it receives the $Grant$ message from its leader. By Property 2 (i), there is not a node in $N(v)$ staying in state C_2 when v is in state C_2. By Lemma 6 (iv), when staying in state C_2, v can successfully send its color to its neighbors with probability $1 - n^{-4}$. Note also that in Algorithm 1, v has been woken up before the first node in its neighborhood starts choosing a color with probability $1 - n^{-4}$. Thus when v chooses a color in state C_2, with probability $1 - n^{-3}$, v has received all the colors chosen by its neighbors and there are no other nodes in $N(v)$ choosing a color at the same time. So v will correctly select a color with probability $1 - O(n^{-2})$.   □

Lemma 9. *Property 2 holds with probability $1 - O(n^{-1})$.*

Proof (Sketch proof). We prove Property 2 by showing that with high probability, none of (i) (ii) and (iii) is the first property to be violated.

Claim. With probability at least $1 - O(n^{-1})$, Property 2 (i) is not the first property to be violated.

Proof. Otherwise, assume that D_i is the disk violating Property 2 (i) in timeslot t. We further assume that node $v \in D_i$ joins state C_2 in timeslot t and another node u also stays in state C_2 in timeslot t. Assume that w is u's leader. We can still assume that all properties are correct before t. Then it can be shown that w must also be v's leader with probability $1 - O(n^{-4})$. Furthermore, w must have started transmitting $Grant_v$ before the timeslot t. Hence, by Algorithm 1, w must have started transmit $Grant_u$ by the timeslot $t - 2\mu \log n$. Then by Lemma 6 (ii), u have received $Grant_u$ from w by $t - \mu \log n - 1$ with probability $1 - n^{-4}$. Noting that u stays in state C_2 for $\mu \log n$ timeslots, u have quit from the algorithm before t with probability $1 - n^{-4}$. This contradiction shows that Property 2 (i) is not the first violated property when u stays in state C_2 with probability $1 - O(n^{-3})$. Then for D_i, the Claim is true with probability $1 - O(n^{-2})$. And the Claim is correct for every disk with probability $1 - O(n^{-1})$.   □

Claim. With probability at least $1 - n^{-1}$, Property 2 (ii) is not the first property to be violated.

Proof. Otherwise, assume that D_i is the first disk violating Property 2 (ii) in timeslot t^*. Before timeslot t^*, we can still assume that all properties hold. Assume that v is the leader of some nodes of D_i that stays in C_1. Denote $C_{v1}(t)$ as the set of node in $N(v)$ that are in state C_1 in timeslot t. Then it can be shown that in timeslot t^*, with probability at least $1 - O(n^{-4})$, all nodes in D_i that are in state C_1 have the same leader v. Next we prove a little stronger result: with probability at least $1 - O(n^{-2})$, in any timeslot t, the sum of transmission probability of all nodes in $C_{v1}(t)$ is at most $2^{-\omega}$. Otherwise, assume that in timeslot t, $\sum_{u \in C_{v1}(t)} p_u > 2^{-\omega}$. Denote $I = [t - 3\mu \log n, t)$. By Algorithm 1, every node in C_{v1} doubles its transmission probability at most once during the interval. Furthermore, the sum of transmission probabilities of newly joined nodes is at most $\frac{2^{-\omega-1}}{n} \cdot n = 2^{-\omega-1}$. Hence, it holds that in timeslot $t - 3\mu \log n$, the sum of transmission probabilities is at least $2^{-2-\omega}$. Consequently, during the interval I, $2^{-2-\omega} \leq \sum_{u \in C_{v1}} p_u < 2^{-\omega}$. Furthermore, during the interval I, for any disk D_j,

$j \neq i$, $\sum_{v \in D_j} p_v \leq 3 \cdot 2^{1-\omega}$. Then using these transmission probability bounds, it can be shown that at least one node in C_{v1} can send a message $AskColor$ to v during the interval $I_1 = [t - 3\mu \log n, t - 2\mu \log n - 1]$ with probability $1 - n^{-4}$. Then in the interval $(t - 3\mu \log n, t - 1]$, with probability $1 - n^{-4}$, all nodes in C_{v1} receives a new $Grant_w$ message and halve their transmission probability except w which enters state C_2. Thus with probability $1 - O(n^{-4})$, D_i will not violate Property 2 (ii) in timeslot t. By Lemma 8, v stays in state $\mathcal{G}$ for at most $O(\Delta \log n + \log^2 n)$ timeslots with probability $1 - O(n^{-2})$. Thus when v stays in state $\mathcal{G}$, there is not a violation timeslot for D_i with probability $1 - O(n^{-2})$. Additionally, when there are nodes in D_i which are in state C_1, it means that there is a node staying in state $\mathcal{G}$ in $E_i^{\frac{3R}{4}}$. From Algorithm 1, we know that all nodes that joined state $\mathcal{G}$ during executing the algorithm are independent in terms of R. Hence, there are at most constant nodes in $E_i^{\frac{3R}{4}}$ which can join state $\mathcal{G}$. Thus D_i is not the first disk violating Property 2 (ii) with probability $1 - O(n^{-2})$. Then the Claim is true for all disks with probability $1 - O(n^{-1})$. $\quad\square$

Claim. With probability at least $1 - O(n^{-2})$, Property 2 (iii) is not the first property to be violated.

Proof. Otherwise, assume that D_i violates it in timeslot t for the first time. Then there is a new node u in D_i joining state $\mathcal{G}$ in timeslot t, while there has been another node v in D_i staying in state $\mathcal{G}$ in timeslot t. Before t, we can still assume that all properties are correct. By Algorithm 1, each node in E_v^{3R} will not try to join state $\mathcal{G}$ until it receives the $StartTransmit_v$ from v. By Algorithm 1, v has not started transmitting $StartTransmit_v$ by the timeslot $t - \mu \log n$, since v still stays in state $\mathcal{G}$ in timeslot t. Also noticing that each node need $\Omega(\log^2 n)$ timeslots to join state $\mathcal{G}$ by executing the MIS algorithm. So there will not come up another node in E_v^{3R} joining state $\mathcal{G}$ by the timeslot $t + \Omega(\log^2 n)$ with probability $1 - O(n^{-4})$. This contradicts with the fact that u joins state $\mathcal{G}$ in timeslot t. Thus when v stays in state $\mathcal{G}$, there is not such a violation timeslot t with probability $1 - O(n^{-4})$. Then with probability $1 - O(n^{-3})$, there is not a timeslot such that Property 2 (iii) is first violated in D_i. This is true for every disk with probability $1 - O(n^{-2})$. $\quad\square$

Theorem 1. *After waking up for $O(\Delta \log n + \log^2 n)$ timeslots, every node v will correctly get a color from $\{0, 1, \ldots, \Delta_v\}$ with probability at least $1 - O(n^{-1})$.*

Proof. Since Properties 1 and 2 have been shown to be correct with probability $1 - O(n^{-1})$, by Lemma 8, with probability at least $1 - O(n^{-1})$, every node v will correctly choose a color after executing Algorithm 1 for at most $O(\Delta \log n + \log^2 n)$ timeslots. Furthermore, when v chooses a color, either v chooses color 0, or it chooses the first available color in its color list by Algorithm 1. Because v receives at most $\Delta_v - 1$ colors from its neighbors (one of its neighbors is a leader), v can still choose a color from $\{0, 1, \ldots, \Delta_v\}$. $\quad\square$

4 Distributed ($\Delta + 1$)-Coloring for Uniform Power Assignment

In some multi-hop radio networks, nodes may not be able to adjust their transmission powers. In such a case, assuming that nodes adopt uniform power assignment, i.e., all nodes transmit with the same power level, we can obtain a distributed ($\Delta + 1$)-coloring algorithm by iteratively carrying out the MIS algorithm. We only need to change the operations in the last state $\mathcal{M}$ in the MIS algorithm. Each node in state $\mathcal{M}$ first chooses an available color that has not been chosen by its neighbors, and then transmits a message m_C containing its choice to its neighbors for $\mu \log n$ timeslots with constant probability after waking up all its neighbors. Then all the nodes having received the message m_C delete the received color from their color list and restart executing the algorithm. By Lemma 2, we know that with high probability, in any timeslot, all nodes in state $\mathcal{M}$ form an independent set. Furthermore, similar to the proof of Lemma 6, we can show that with high probability, each node can successfully transmit its choice to its neighbors before any neighbor starts choosing a color. These two points ensure the correctness of the computed coloring. We assume that all nodes transmit with power $P = cN\beta R^\alpha$. Then we can get the following lemma, based on which the theorem on the correctness and the time complexity of the proposed coloring algorithm can be proved.

Lemma 10. *With probability at least $1 - O(n^{-2})$, a node v will correctly get a color in $O(\Delta_v^{2R} \log^2 n)$ timeslots after starting executing the algorithm, where Δ_v^{2R} is the number of nodes in E_v^{2R}. Furthermore, v will choose a color from $\{0, 1, \cdots, \Delta_v\}$.*

Proof. Using a similar argument as in the analysis of the MIS algorithm (in the full version[16]), we can get that after a node v starts or restarts the algorithm for $O(\log^2 n)$ timeslots, there will be a node in E_v^{2R} joining state $\mathcal{M}$ with probability $1 - O(n^{-3})$. Thus after at most $O(\Delta_v^{2R} \log^2 n)$ timeslots, v will join state $\mathcal{M}$ with probability at least $1 - O(n^{-2})$. Furthermore, using a similar manner for proving Lemma 6, we can show that all neighbors of v which have chosen colors before v have informed v their choices with probability $1 - O(n^{-3})$. And by Lemma 2, when v is in state $\mathcal{M}$, with probability $1 - O(n^{-3})$, none of v's neighbors stay in state $\mathcal{M}$ simultaneously. Thus v will correctly choose a color different from all its neighbors with probability at least $1 - O(n^{-3})$. Putting all together, we know that with probability at least $1 - O(n^{-2})$, v will correctly get a color in $O(\Delta_v^{2R} \log^2 n)$ timeslots after starting executing the algorithm. Finally, since there are Δ_v nodes in v's neighborhood, v have deleted at most Δ_v different colors from its color list when v chooses a color. Thus v can choose a color from $\{0, 1, \cdots, \Delta_v\}$. □

Theorem 2. *If the nodes adopt the uniform power assignment, there exists a distributed algorithm such that with probability at least $1 - O(n^{-1})$, each node will correctly get a color after executing the algorithm for $O(\Delta \log^2 n)$ timeslots. Furthermore, the total number of colors used is at most $\Delta + 1$.*

Proof. By Lemma 10, for a node v, with probability at least $1 - O(n^{-2})$, it will correctly get a color in $O(\Delta_v^{2R} \log^2 n)$ timeslots after starting executing the algorithm, where Δ_v^{2R} is the number of nodes in E_v^{2R}. Furthermore, v will choose a color from $\{0, 1, \cdots, \Delta_v\}$. Thus the theorem is correct for all nodes with probability $1 - O(n^{-1})$ by noting that $\Delta_v^{2R} \le \chi(2R, R)\Delta \in O(\Delta)$.

5   Conclusion

In this paper, we study the distributed $\Delta + 1$-coloring problem in unstructured multi-hop radio networks under the SINR interference model. Without any knowledge of the neighborhood, our proposed new distributed $(\Delta + 1)$-coloring algorithm has time complexity $O(\Delta \log n + \log^2 n)$. Our result even matches the $O(\Delta)$-coloring algorithm in [3] for large Δ; their algorithm needs a prior estimate of Δ. For networks in which the nodes can not adjust their transmission powers, we give a $(\Delta + 1)$-coloring algorithm with time complexity $O(\Delta \log^2 n)$. Furthermore, by carefully tuning the parameters, we show that the maximal independent set algorithm in [12] still works under the SINR constraint, which is of independent interest.

Acknowledgement. The authors would like to thank Dr. Thomas Moscibroda for his valuable comments on a preliminary version of this paper. This work was supported in part by Hong Kong RGC-GRF grants 714009E and 714311, the National Basic Research Program of China grants 2007CB807900 and 2007CB807901, the National Natural Science Foundation of China grants 61073174, 61033001, 61103186 and 61061130540, and the Hi-Tech research and Development Program of China grant 2006AA10Z216.

References

1. Barenboim, L., Elkin, M.: Distributed $(\Delta + 1)$-coloring in linear (in Δ) time. In: STOC (2009)
2. Cole, R., Vishkin, U.: Deterministic coin tossing with applications to optimal parallel list ranking. Inf. Control 70(1), 32–53 (1986)
3. Derbel, B., Talbi, E.-G.: Distributed node coloring in the SINR model. In: ICDCS (2010)
4. Goussevskaia, O., Moscibroda, T., Wattenhofer, R.: Local broadcasting in the physical interference model. In: DialM-POMC (2008)
5. Goussevskaia, O., Oswald, Y.A., Wattenhofer, R.: Complexity in geometric SINR. In: Mobihoc (2007)
6. Goussevskaia, O., Pignolet, Y.A., Wattenhofer, R.: Efficiency of wireless networks: approximation algorithms for the physical interference model. Foundations and Trends in Networking 4(3), 313–420 (2010)
7. Gupta, P., Kumar, P.R.: The capacity of wireless networks. IEEE Transaction on Infromation Theorey 46(2), 388–404 (2000)
8. Kesselheim, T., Vöcking, B.: Distributed Contention Resolution in Wireless Networks. In: Lynch, N.A., Shvartsman, A.A. (eds.) DISC 2010. LNCS, vol. 6343, pp. 163–178. Springer, Heidelberg (2010)

 9. Kuhn, F., Moscibroda, T., Wattenhofer, R.: Initializing newly deployed Ad Hoc and sensor networks. In: MOBICOM (2004)
10. Moscibroda, T., Wattenhofer, R.: Coloring unstructured radio networks. In: SPAA (2005)
11. Moscibroda, T., Wattenhofer, R.: Coloring unstructured radio networks. Distributed Computing 21(4), 271–284 (2008)
12. Moscibroda, T., Wattenhofer, R.: Maximal independent sets in radio networks. In: PODC (2005)
13. Scheideler, C., Richa, A., Santi, P.: An O(logn) dominating set protocol for wireless ad-hoc networks under the physical interference model. In: Mobihoc (2008)
14. Schneider, J., Wattenhofer, R.: A log-star distributed maximal independent set algorithm for growth-bounded graphs. In: PODC (2008)
15. Schneider, J., Wattenhofer, R.: Coloring unstructured wireless multi-hop networks. In: PODC (2009)
16. Yu, D., Hua, Q.-S., Wang, Y., Lau, F.C.M.: Distributed $(\Delta + 1)$-Coloring in the Physical Model, http://i.cs.hku.hk/~qshua/algosensorsfullversion.pdf
17. Yu, D., Wang, Y., Hua, Q.-S., Lau, F.C.M.: Distributed local broadcasting algorithms in the physical interference model. In: DCOSS (2011)

Continuous Monitoring in the Dynamic Sensor Field Model[*]

Carme Àlvarez[1], Josep Díaz[1], Dieter Mitsche[2], and Maria Serna[1]

[1] LSI Dept. Universitat Politècnica de Catalunya, Barcelona
{alvarez,diaz,mjserna}@lsi.upc.edu
[2] Dept. of Mathematics, Ryerson University, Toronto
dmitsche@ryerson.ca

Abstract. In this work we consider the problem of continuously monitoring a collection of data sets produced by sensors placed on mobile or static targets. Our computational model, the *dynamic sensor field* model, is an extension of the static sensor field model [3] allowing computation in the presence of mobility. The dynamicity comes from both the mobile communication devices and the data sensors. The mobility of devices is modeled by a dynamic communication graph depending on the position of the devices. Data mobility is due to measurements performed by sensing units that are not placed on fixed positions but attached to mobile agents or targets. Accordingly, we introduce two additional performance measures: the total traveled distance in a computational step and the gathering period.

We study the *Continuous Monitoring* problem providing bounds on performance for several protocols that differ in the use of mobility and the placement of the devices. Our objective is to analyze formally the computational resources needed to solve the Continuous Monitoring in a dynamic context. For doing so, we consider a particular scenario in which communication devices and data sensors move on top of a squared terrain discretized by a mobility grid. We also consider two scenarios, the *static data setting* in which sensors are placed at fixed but unknown positions and the *dynamic data setting* in which sensors are placed on dynamic targets and follow a passive mobility pattern.

Keywords: Tiny artifacts, sensor networks, continuous monitoring problem, sensor field model, computational complexity.

1 Introduction

The use of networks of heterogeneous tiny artifacts is becoming a key ingredient in the technological development of our society. The study of such systems involves several and very different areas of computing. The computational system

[*] Partially supported by the ICT Program of the European Union under contract number 215270 (FRONTS). The first, second and, fourth authors were also supported by the Spanish project TIN-2007-66523 (FORMALISM).

T. Erlebach et al. (Eds.): ALGOSENSORS 2011, LNCS 7111, pp. 161–172, 2012.

arising from the ad-hoc computation network point of view has been modeled by combining the notion of distributed data streams [8] with classic distributed approaches to solve problems on particular topologies [10] such as the *sensor field model* (SSSF) [3]. The sensor field model captures some characteristic differences of networks with sensors: it is composed by *actuator devices*, which communicate among them, measure and signal the environment. The SSSF model assumes that those devices synchronize at barriers, marking rounds, in a similar way to the BSP model [12]. During a computational round, a device accesses the received messages and the data provided by the environment, performs some computation, and finally sends messages to its neighbors and to the environment. The data measured from the environment is modeled by a data stream.

In this paper we continue the study of computational issues for networks of tiny artifacts in the presence of mobility. We analyze two potential sources of mobility: The *passive mobility of the targeted data* and the *active mobility of the network devices*. For the first source of mobility we assume that the set of sensors is attached to mobile agents, so the data in an input data stream is not originated in a fixed location. For the second source we assume that the devices are able to move in order to obtain readings from far away sensors or signal the environment at different positions. The present work introduces an extension of the SSSF model, the *Dynamic Sensor Field* model (DSSF), with the following fundamental features: Devices are able to receive readings from any sensor in the sensing range of the device. Moreover, devices can move at the same time that they perform local computations. These features mainly, among others, distinguish this model from the ad-hoc mobility models surveyed in [4]. Besides considering the worst case performance on parameters such as *latency*, *message number*, or *message length*, (the ones considered for the analysis of the SSSF model in [3]), this work also introduces and examines two additional parameters that have relevance due to mobility. The *traveled distance* per step, which measures the maximum distance traveled by a device in a computational step, and the *gathering period*, which measures the number of computational steps needed to obtain a reading from each sensor (data stream).

We analyze the *Continuous Monitoring* problem in which in every period there should be a report on the aggregate measure obtained of the reading from each sensor. In fact, this problem is a reformulation of the *Average Monitoring* problem in which a set of sensors were located at fixed and known positions [3], to the dynamic scenario in which sensors and devices might move.

We propose several protocols in the dynamic sensor field model for solving the continuous monitoring problem on different scenarios, according to the mobility patterns of the data and the devices. In particular, we consider two scenarios: The case in which the *data is static* but originated at unknown position, *the static data setting*, and the case in which the *data is mobile* and follows a passive mobility model, *the dynamic data setting*. Moreover, the devices in the network are either *static* or perform some *random walk* in the monitored terrain. Our mobility model is similar to the *walkers model* introduced in [5], however they differ on the random walk performed in the grid and the hypothesis on communication.

Our objective is to perform a theoretical analysis of the complexity measures as it was done in the SSSF model for data originated at a known position. In this initial work we restrict ourselves to analyze the case in which data and devices are restricted to move on top of a grid.

The paper is organized as follows. In Section 2 we introduce the model an the main hypothesis on mobility. In Section 3 we propose and analyze protocols for the static data setting. Sections 4 and 5 are devoted to the dynamic data setting. In Section 4 the devices in the sensor field do not move but the ones in Section 5 move. We conclude with some open questions in Section 6. Due to lack of space the proofs are not given. We refer the interested reader to the long version of the paper.

2   The Dynamic Sensor Field Model

In the following, the notation is taken from [3] (see also [2]). A *data stream* d is a possible infinite sequence of data items $d = d^1 d^2 \ldots d^i \ldots$. For any $i \geq 1$, $d[i]$ denotes the i-th element of d. For any $n \geq 1$, an *n-data stream* $\mathbf{d}$ is an n-tuple of data streams; $\mathbf{d} = (d_1, \ldots, d_n)$. For any $i \geq 1$, $\mathbf{d}[i]$ denotes the n-tuple composed by all the i-th elements of each data stream, let $\mathbf{d}[i] = (d_1[i], \ldots, d_n[i])$. Each data stream is associated to a sensor with one reading per time step. In a SSSF the data items in a data stream were assumed to be produced by a sensor placed in a fixed location and attached to a communication device in the same position. In the Dynamic Sensor Field model we consider a set W of g data streams obtained by the sensors. The sensors either do not move or each of them moves following an independent random walk. Therefore the data items in a data stream can be obtained at different locations at different time steps. The sensors interact with a collection of N mobile devices that can access the measurements of nearby sensors. This fact can be modeled with the *data stream accessibility relation* at time step t, $D_t \subseteq N \times W$. We denote by $(k, \alpha) \in D_t$ the event that sensor α can be detected by device k at time step t. Observe that, additional information, like location of the target at the moment of the reading, could be attached to the data items, however we will not use this feature in our results.

A *communication graph* is a directed graph $G = (N, E)$, where each node $k \in N$ is associated to a device and each edge $(i, j) \in E$ specifies that device i can send messages to device j. In a Dynamic Sensor Field the communication graph might also change during the computation due to device mobility. Hence, we consider a sequence of graphs $\{G_t\}_{t \geq 0}$, where $G_t = (N, E_t)$ denotes the communication graph at computational step t. In the SSSF it is assumed that the communication graph is the same at all time steps.

We assume that at each step t, all devices might receive data from their neighbors (according to the graph G_t) and from the environment (nearby sensors), apply their own process changing in this way their actual configuration, possibly make a move, and send data to their neighbors (according to the graph G_{t+1}) and to the environment (output data stream). We assume that the devices can move only while they perform their local computation. Synchronization takes place after the local computation and the movement are performed.

The *stream behavior* of a computation on a Dynamic Sensor Field is defined in terms of the tuple of output data streams obtained by processing the tuple of input data streams, as defined in [3] for the static case. We also use the term *the sensor field $\mathcal{F}$ computes the tuple of output data streams* $\mathbf{v} = (v_k)_{k \in N}$, *given the tuple of input data streams* $\mathbf{u} = (u_k)_{k \in N}$, meaning that $\mathbf{v}[1, t]$ is determined by $\mathbf{u}[1, t]$ for any $t \geq 1$. Note that $\mathbf{u}$ and $\mathbf{v}$ have in general infinite length, but the behavior of a DSSF is defined in terms of all the finite prefixes of the stream.

We consider the following worst case complexity measures on the computation of a DSSF: *Size* (N): the number of devices that take part in the computation. *Time* $(\mathcal{T}(n))$: the maximum number of operations. *Space* $(\mathcal{S}(N))$: the maximum memory space used by any device. *MessageLength* $(\mathcal{L}(n))$: the maximum number of data items sent in a message. *MessageNumber* $(\mathcal{M}(n))$: the maximum number of sent messages. *Distance* $(\mathcal{D}(n))$: the maximum distance traversed by a device. Here the maximum is taken over all devices and steps.

An important difference between the study of computational sensing problems in the DSSF model with respect to the SSSF model of [3] is the following: In the dynamic setting, the data is originated in mobile targets or the devices that have to collect the data can also move. In those situations, the precondition that the network has access to all the sensors (input data) at any time step might not be possible. Therefore, to monitor continuously a wide area where the g targets move, we require only to get a reading from any sensor inside a reporting period. For instance, the equivalent to the Average monitoring in [3], is defined as follows:

Continuous Monitoring: Given a set of g mobile data streams $(u_\alpha)_{1 \leq \alpha \leq g}$ for some $g \geq 1$, compute m data streams $(v_k)_{1 \leq k \leq m}$ such that, for some period $p > 0$, any $1 \leq k \leq m$, and $t > 0$, $v_k[tp] = (u_1[t_1] + \cdots + u_g[t_g])/g$ for some $(t-1)p \leq t_1, \ldots, t_g < tp$. We call parameter p the *gathering period*.

In this paper, we analyze the complexity of several protocols to solve the continuous monitoring problem, when devices and sensors act according to the following scenario: We assume that the data of interest is accessible in a predetermined square shaped area discretized as a grid. The devices have two associated ranges, a *sensing range* s and a *communication range* r. A device can read data from any sensor within grid distance s and can communicate (in a bidirectional way) to any device within grid distance r. In order to simplify the analysis, we assume that three squared grids (mobility, sensing and communicating) are embedded in the terrain. The *mobility grid* Λ_m is formed by $m \times m$ nodes that serve as reference positions for the movement of the targets with attached sensors and for the movement of the computing devices.

We assume that sensors and devices stop at grid nodes labeled by coordinates (i, j), $1 \leq i, j \leq m$, and they move following paths on the grid. That is, at the beginning/end of a step all devices and sensors are at a grid point. We assume the distance among two neighboring nodes in Λ_m is of unit length. As a subgrid of Λ_m, we have the *sensing grid* Δ_σ of size $\sigma \times \sigma$, where $2s$ is the distance between nodes in Δ_σ. Observe that by placing devices in all the nodes in Δ_σ, any sensor signal originated in a node in Λ_m will be detected by at least one device. As a subgrid of Δ_σ we have the *communicating grid* Γ_n, with $n \times n$ nodes, where r is the distance among nodes in Γ_n. The subgrid Γ_n is selected in order to guarantee that two devices in neighboring positions can communicate, that is to guarentee that neighboring vertices are at distance at most r. Note that σ is obtained as a function of m and s and n as function of m and r. For simplicity we also assume that r is a multiple of $2s$. In the case that $r \leq 2s$ we have that Γ_n is also a sensing grid. In this case we take $\sigma = n$. Therefore, we can assume that $n \leq \sigma \leq m$. We use $\mathcal{T}(n, \sigma, m)$ to denote the terrain in such scenario.

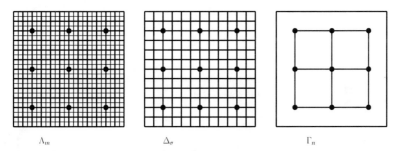

$$\Lambda_m \qquad\qquad \Delta_\sigma \qquad\qquad \Gamma_n$$

Fig. 1. The three fundamental grids for mobility, sensing and communicating, embedded in a terrain $\mathcal{T}$ with $m = 25$, $\sigma = 13$ and $n = 3$.

By placing σ^2 devices, one at each node of Δ_σ, we can detect in one step any signal originated in a sensor placed at any position of Λ_m. Therefore, the continuous monitoring problem can be solved in gathering period 1, using an algorithm for the average monitoring for the bidirectional grid from [3].

Lemma 1. *There is a sensor field that solves the continuous monitoring problem on terrain $\mathcal{T}(n, \sigma, m)$ and g sensors with $N = \sigma^2$ devices , latency σ, gathering period 1, $\mathcal{T}(N) = \mathcal{L}(N) = \mathcal{S}(N) = \mathcal{O}(g)$, $\mathcal{M}(N) = 2$ and, $\mathcal{D}(N) = 0$.*

In the following sections, we analyze formally several protocols solving the Continuous Monitoring problem in the DSSF model. All these proposals contain two distinguished algorithmic parts: The *gathering* part that solves the problem of obtaining a reading from any sensors and will determine the gathering period. And the *averaging* part that computes the average of the measures taken during a gathering period. As we will see, the gathering part requires in general more steps than the averaging part. Therefore the devices, just after the first gathering period finishes, run in parallel both algorithms. When both algorithms finalize, the process is repeated with the new gathered data. The computing devices are arranged either as a line or as a grid.

In the *static data setting* we assume that input data streams are originated at some positions in the grid Λ_m, and that devices move on top of Γ_n. In the *dynamic data setting* we consider a set of g walkers $\mathcal{W}$ moving on the mobility grid Λ_m, under the following random mobility model.

Initially g walkers, $w_1, \ldots, w_g$, are sprinkled uniformly at random on the m^2 vertices of the grid. At each step, every w_i, not on the boundary, chooses with probability $\frac{1}{4}$ one of the four possible directions and makes a step in the chosen direction. If w_i is in the corner, it chooses with probability $\frac{1}{2}$ any of the two possible directions, and if it is touching the boundary in one dimension only, w_i chooses with probability $\frac{1}{2}$ the only available direction in the dimension touching the boundary, and with probability $\frac{1}{4}$ the other two directions in the perpendicular dimension.

Finally, we assume that the devices have sense of direction (up-down, left-right) and are able to detect whether they are positioned on a border/corner of the grid. They know the number g of sensors but do not know the number of devices nor the size of the mobility grid.

3   Continuous Monitoring of Static Data

Our first protocol for the static data setting is designed to solve the particular case $n = \sigma$. The protocol is Line sweeping.

> Line sweeping for a terrain $\mathcal{T}(n, n, m)$ and g sensors at unknown but fixed locations.
> - Initially, we place n devices in the bottom row of Γ_n. This guarantees that any sensor placed in the m/n bottom rows of Λ_m can be detected. We assume that the devices are able to detect when they are positioned on a border or on a corner of the grid. Furthermore, they have sense of direction, so that they can change the direction of their movement when arriving to a border. Devices know that they are initially positioned on the bottom line of the grid. They also are aware of the number of sensors g but not of the number of devices n.
> - *Gathering phase.* Devices move from one border of the mesh to the other border. During the sweep they collect all the obtained readings in a table of size g.
> - *Averaging phase.* Devices positioned in the corners initiate a sending to the center protocol with the data gathered in the previous sweep. Each device, after receiving a message, merges the received data with its own table. The merged table is sent to the other neighbor. The *central node* is the device that receives messages from both neighbors. Notice that there might be two central nodes when n is even. The central node computes the average (or the aggregate measure) and broadcasts it to the corners.

Observe that in the Line sweeping sensor field we only require that the devices have some knowledge of their position (inside/border/corner) and have sense of direction (up/down). In particular, the number of devices in the network is not assumed to be known by themselves (although they could perform a count at the expense of increasing the memory usage up to $\mathcal{O}(\log n)$). Furthermore, every time that the sweeping line of sensors reaches the top or the bottom row of Γ_n the network has collected at least one reading from each sensor. Thus we have that the gathering period $p = n$. The averaging phase requires also n steps, each device sends at most two messages with g data. Both phases can be run

together after the first gathering period finishes. Putting all together we have
the following:

Theorem 1. *The sensor field Line sweeping solves the continuous monitoring
problem on a terrain* $\mathcal{T}(n, n, m)$ *and* g *static sensors, with* n *devices, latency* n,
gathering period n, $\mathcal{T}(n) = \mathcal{L}(n) = \mathcal{S}(n) = \mathcal{O}(g)$, $\mathcal{M}(n) = 2$ *and* $\mathcal{D}(n) = r$.

For the case in which $n < \sigma$, devices have to move closer to the sensors to
obtain readings. We use the sensing grid Γ_n as a mobility grid for the devices.
Finally, we assign to a node in Γ_n a part of the sensing grid surrounding it,
its *surveillance area*. This assignment is done in such a way that pieces have
the same size and with the property that if we place the devices in the bottom
left corner of their surveillance area they form a communicating grid. For the
gathering phase the devices follow a *snake* walk, following the rows, covering all
the nodes in the assigned subgrid synchronously.

Our second algorithm, the Surveillance strip, is similar to the Line sweeping. The
Surveillance strip sensor field arranges the devices in the form of a sensing line,
initially in the bottom-left corners of the surveillance strip. Each device receives
as surveillance area a vertical strip of the sensing grid formed by $r/2s$ columns.
Each device follows the same snake-like walk covering the assigned strip. Once
the devices reach the final point in the walk they walk backwards towards the
initial position. The averaging part is the same as in the Line sweeping. Observe
that the devices have to know at least the dimensions of the surveillance area in
addition to the requirements for the Line sweeping protocol.

Theorem 2. *The sensor field Surveillance strip solves the continuous monitoring
problem on a terrain* $\mathcal{T}(n, \sigma, m)$ *and* g *static sensors, with* n *devices, latency* n,
gathering period $nr/2s$, $\mathcal{T}(n) = \mathcal{L}(n) = \mathcal{S}(n) = \mathcal{O}(g)$, $\mathcal{M}(n) = 2$ *and* $\mathcal{D}(n) = 2s$.

Our third algorithm, the Surveillance grid, reduces the gathering phase and uses
a higher number of devices. The Surveillance grid sensor field places n^2 devices
initially in the bottom-left corners of the surveillance area, now a squared por-
tion of the sensing grid with dimensions $r/2s \times r/2s$. For the gathering phase
the devices follow again a snake walk. The averaging part is an extension of
the averaging for the Line sweeping sensor field. Data is collected by the central
node in each row and in a second phase the central node in the central column
gathers all the data and computes the average. Finally the average is broad-
casted to the devices. In the case that $(r/2s)^2 < n$ the second gathering phase
finalizes before the first averaging phase. However, the data flow of the protocol
allows the pipelining of the averaging phases without conflicts. In such a case
the devices have to increase its memory size in order to keep the data required
for the following averaging phases. The required memory additional memory is
$O(2n(2s/r)^2 g)$.

The following proposition presents the results obtained for the algorithm in
the previous discussion.

Theorem 3. *The sensor field* **Surveillance grid** *solves the continuous monitoring problem on a terrain* $\mathcal{T}(n, \sigma, m)$ *and* g *static sensors, with* n^2 *devices, latency* $2n$, *gathering period* $(r/2s)^2$, $\mathcal{T}(n) = \mathcal{L}(n) = \mathcal{O}(g)$, $\mathcal{S}(n) = O(2n(2s/r)^2 g)$, $\mathcal{M}(n) = 2$ *and* $\mathcal{D}(n) = 2s$.

4   Continuous Monitoring of Dynamic Data Using Static Devices

We propose three different sensor fields for solving the continuous monitoring problem when the input data streams follow the walker mobility model presented before.

For the case in which $n = \sigma$, we consider the **Central line** sensor field in which n devices are placed onto the central line of Γ_n (the $m/2$-th row) and remain there. Devices collect data until the gathering period finalizes and combine this protocol with an averaging protocol identical as the one for the **Line sweeping** sensor field. The crucial part of the analysis requires an analysis of the number of steps needed to finalize the gathering period. For doing so we consider the weakest detection model; the case when a sensor is detected by a device if it passes through the position $(i, \frac{m}{2})$, for some i.

For a fixed $w \in \mathcal{W}$, let T_w be the random variable counting the number of steps it takes to detect walker w and denote by T the random variable counting the number of steps to detect all walkers. We prove an upper bound on $\mathbf{E}[T]$, $\mathbf{E}[T] \leq g(m^2/2 - 2m + 2)$. The proof is done by analyzing a coupling of the random walk with a walk on the line. Taking into account that the bound for the gathering period is bigger than the duration of the averaging phase, we get the following result.

Theorem 4. *The sensor field* **Central line** *solves the continuous monitoring problem on a terrain* $\mathcal{T}(n, n, m)$ *and* g *mobile sensors, with* n *devices, latency* n, *expected gathering period at most* $gm^2/2$, $\mathcal{T}(n) = \mathcal{L}(n) = \mathcal{S}(n) = \mathcal{O}(g)$, $\mathcal{M}(n) = 2$ *and* $\mathcal{D}(n) = 0$.

Next, we analyze a **Central line with holes** sensor field in which n fixed devices are placed onto the central line of Γ_n such that the distance between any two consecutive devices is exactly r, and the distance between the leftmost device and the boundary of Γ_n as well as the distance between the rightmost device and the boundary of Γ_n is exactly $\frac{r}{2}$ (we assume w.l.o.g. that n and m are chosen in such a way that such a splitting is possible, and all numbers are integer. Assume furthermore that $m/2$ is an integer multiple of $r/2$). Defining as before T to be the random variable counting the number of steps to detect all $w \in \mathcal{W}$, by applying directly Threorem 1 [7], we get $\mathbf{E}[T] \leq gm^6$, and therefore we have:

Theorem 5. *The sensor field* **Central line with holes** *solves the continuous monitoring problem on a terrain* $\mathcal{T}(n, \sigma, m)$ *and* g *mobile sensors, with* n *devices, latency* n, *expected gathering period at most* gm^6, $\mathcal{T}(n) = \mathcal{L}(n) = \mathcal{S}(n) = \mathcal{O}(g)$, $\mathcal{M}(n) = 2$ *and* $\mathcal{D}(n) = 0$.

For the general case $n < \sigma$ we first consider the Communicating grid sensor field that places a device at any node of Γ_n. Again devices gather data until the gathering period finalizes and combine this protocol with the averaging protocol used in the Surveillance grid protocol. Assuming w.l.o.g. that $2n$ divides $m-1$, the sensors are placed on positions $(\frac{m-1}{2n} + 1 + i\frac{m-1}{n}, \frac{m-1}{2n} + 1 + j\frac{m-1}{n})$, for $0 \le i \le n-1, 0 \le j \le n-1$. Denote by $M := \frac{m-1}{n}$ the maximum (grid) distance between a sensor and its closest device $\mathcal{S}$. Again we assume the weakest detection model: a sensor w is detected by a device, if w passes through the position of that device. Define T_w as the random variable variable counting the number of steps until w is detected and denote by T the random variable counting the number of steps until all $w \in \mathcal{W}$ are detected. We provide upper and lower bounds on $\mathbf{E}\left[T\right]$, which are polynomial in M. First we show that the random walk takes in expectation at most a time polynomial in M, $2gM^{20}$ (without caring about optimality of the exponent). Note that the simple approach applied in the case of all sensors on the central line gives an exponential upper bound, since on all the points, which are on the same horizontal or vertical line as its closest sensor and at distance at most $M/2$ of this sensor, the probability that the distance decreases is only $\frac{1}{4}$. The proof uses again a coupling argument. The difference is that now the movements of the walker are coupled with two random walks on a line, corresponding to the horizontal and vertical movements. Using similar ideas as in the case of the Central line sensor field, we give an easy lower bound which is quadratic in M for the expected gathering period of the Communicating grid sensor field.

By Theorem 1 of [7], for any connected graph on n vertices, the cover time is at most $O(n^3)$. Thus, applying a union bound, we obtain $\mathbf{E}\left[T\right] \le \min\{2gM^{20}, gm^6\}$.

Theorem 6. *The sensor field Communicating grid solves the continuous monitoring problem for g mobile sensors on a terrain $\mathcal{T}(n, \sigma, m)$, with $N = n^2$ devices, latency $2n$, expected gathering period at most $\min\{2g\left(\dfrac{m-1}{n}\right)^{20}, gm^6\}$, $\mathcal{T}(N) = \mathcal{L}(N) = \mathcal{S}(N) = \mathcal{O}(g)$, $\mathcal{M}(n) = 2$ and $\mathcal{D}(n) = 0$.*

5 Continuous Monitoring of Dynamic Data Using Dynamic Devices

Our first protocol is a variation of the Line sweeping sensor field in which the per step traveled distance is halved, called Slow line sweeping. In our model we assume that a device is unable to get readings from a sensor while moving. Therefore, by advancing r positions, some of the sensors can cross the sweeping line without being detected. However if we reduce the distance traveled to $r/2$ all the sensors are detected in a sweep of the terrain.

Theorem 7. *The sensor field Slow line sweeping solves the continuous monitoring problem with g mobile sensors on a terrain $\mathcal{T}(n, n, m)$ with n devices, latency $2n$, gathering period $4n$, $\mathcal{T}(n) = \mathcal{L}(n) = \mathcal{S}(n) = \mathcal{O}(g)$, $\mathcal{M}(n) = 2$ and $\mathcal{D}(n) = r/2$.*

Now we consider protocols in which the network is reduced to a single device placed initially at any node of Γ_n. This device is allowed to move, and we consider two protocols: the Random device sensor field, in which the device follows a random walk, and the Snake sweep sensor field, in which the device follows a snake path covering Λ_m.

In the Random device protocol the device performs a random walk on the same grid as the sensors, independent of all sensors, but having the same transition probabilities at any point. We suppose also that the device performs jumps to one neighbor at discrete time steps which are 1 unit apart from each other, but which do not coincide with the sensors' moves (who also perform their jumps at different time instants). As before, the device collects data until the gathering period finalizes, and the analysis requires an upper bound on the number of steps to finalize the gathering period. Also, we assume that a sensor is detected by a device if there exists some time t where the position of the sensor is exactly equal to the position of the device.

Theorem 8. *The sensor field Random device solves the continuous monitoring problem with g mobile sensors on a terrain $\mathcal{T}(n, \sigma, m)$ with 1 device, latency 1, gathering period gm^{20}, $\mathcal{T}(n) = \mathcal{L}(n) = \mathcal{S}(n) = \mathcal{O}(g)$, $\mathcal{M}(n) = 0$ and $\mathcal{D}(n) = 1$.*

In the Snake sweep protocol the device performs a snake walk on Λ_m. Once arrived at the last point of the grid, the device performs the same sweep backwards, and so on. As in the random case, the device performs jumps (at time instants which do not coincide with any of the sensors' jumping times and are at time distance 1 apart), and whenever at some point a sensor and the device are at the same position, the sensor is detected by the device.

Theorem 9. *The sensor field Snake sweep solves the continuous monitoring problem with g mobile sensors on a terrain $\mathcal{T}(n, \sigma, m)$ with 1 device, latency 1, gathering period $O(gm^5)$, $\mathcal{T}(n) = \mathcal{L}(n) = \mathcal{S}(n) = \mathcal{O}(g)$, $\mathcal{M}(n) = 0$ and $\mathcal{D}(n) = 1$.*

6 Conclusion and Open Problems

We have introduced the dynamic sensor field model and we have shown that the model allows a theoretical analysis of the complexity of different protocols for the continuous monitoring problem. An overview of the bounds of the fundamental complexity measures for the protocols analyzed in this paper is given in Table 1.

The *gathering period* is an important parameter in the analysis of protocols that solve the continuous monitoring problem and the key difficulty in our analysis. In the protocols that use a randomized mobility pattern we analyze another relevant parameter: *the number of steps for a device to detect a target*. This parameter is relevant for obtaining upper bounds on the gathering period. Although bounds for the covering time of networks could be used to obtain bounds for hitting times of mobile agents to fixed positions in a graph [1,11], in some cases the proofs in the present work, that use a coupling argument of random walks on the truncated integer line, yield better bounds for our specific problems.

Table 1. A summary of our results for the continuous monitoring of g sensors in a terrain $\mathcal{T}(n, \sigma, m)$. In all the cases $\mathcal{T}(n) = \mathcal{L}(n) = \mathcal{S}(n) = O(g)$ except for the Communicating grid sensor field for which $\mathcal{S}(n) = O(n(s/r)^2 g)$.

Algorithm	N	latency	gathering period	$\mathcal{M}(N)$	$\mathcal{D}(N)$
static data setting					
Line sweeping ($n = \sigma$)	n	n	n	2	r
Surveillance strip	n	n	$nr/2s$	2	$2s$
Surveillance grid	n^2	n	$(r/2s)^2$	2	$2s$
dynamic data setting with static devices					
Central line ($n = \sigma$)	n	n	$gm^2/2$	2	0
Central line with holes	n	n	gm^6	2	0
Communicating grid	n^2	$2n$	$\min\{2g(\frac{m-1}{n})^{20}, gm^6\}$	2	0
dynamic data setting with dynamic devices					
Slow line sweeping ($n = \sigma$)	n	$2n$	$4n$	2	$r/2$
Random device	1	1	gm^2	0	1
Snake sweep	1	1	gm^5	0	1

Nevertheless, in some cases, there is a huge gap between the lower and upper bounds, and closing this gap would be interesting. In particular, we believe that the exponent 20 in the bound for the gathering period of the Communicating grid sensor field is far from being optimal.

There remain a bunch of open questions on the performance of protocols for the continuous monitoring problem. Our results hold only for mobility graphs with a highly regular pattern. It would be interesting to analyze protocols for general mobility graphs, even for the particular case in which the mobility graph is a grid with holes.

The protocols proposed in this paper have been inspired by classical algorithms for synchronous network topologies [10]. It would be nice to show whether other algorithmic approaches can also be adapted and analyzed theoretically in the dynamic sensor field model. In particular, we would like to consider protocols in which there are no additional devices and the meetings among targets are used to exchange the collected data and compute the average measures. This approach has been used in the ZebraNet project[1] [9], but no theoretical complexity analysis is provided in the paper.

Another line of research is to determine whether the Sensor Field model can be extended to a limited asynchronous setting. One idea would be to follow the assumptions of the model considered in [6] or a similar model with some other limited level of asynchronicity that still would allow a complexity analysis.

---

[1] http://www.princeton.edu/~mrm/zebranet.html

References

1. Aldous, D., Fill, J.: Reversible Markov Chains and Random Walks on Graphs. Electronic Draft (2002), at `http://stat-www.berkeley.edu/users/aldous/RWG/book.html`
2. Àlvarez, C., Duch, A., Gabarro, J., Michail, O., Serna, M., Spirakis, P.: Computational models for networks of tiny artifacts: a survey. Computer Science Review 5(1), 7–25 (2011)
3. Àlvarez, C., Duch, A., Gabarro, J., Serna, M.: Sensor Field: A Computational Model. In: Dolev, S. (ed.) ALGOSENSORS 2009. LNCS, vol. 5804, pp. 3–14. Springer, Heidelberg (2009)
4. Díaz, J., Mitsche, D., Santi, P.: Theoretical aspects of graph models for MANETs. In: Nikoetseas, S., Rolim, J. (eds.) Theoretical Aspects of Distributed Computing in Sensor Networks. Monographs in Theoretical Computer Science, pp. 161–190. Springer, Heidelberg (2011)
5. Díaz, J., Pérez, X., Serna, M., Wormald, N.: Walkers on the cycle and the grid. SIAM Journal on Discrete Mathematics 22(2), 747–775 (2008)
6. Eyal, I., Keidar, I., Rom, R.: LiMoSense – Live Monitoring in Dynamic Sensor Networks. In: Erlebach, T., Nikoletseas, S., Orponen, P. (eds.) ALGOSENSORS 2011. LNCS, vol. 7111, pp. 72–85. Springer, Heidelberg (2012)
7. Feige, U.: A tight upper bound on the cover time for random walks on graphs. Random Struct. Algorithms 6(1), 51–54 (1995)
8. Gibbons, P., Tirthapura, S.: Estimating simple functions on the union of data streams. In: Proceedings of the 13th Annual ACM Symposium on Parallel Algorithms and Architectures, SPAA 2001, pp. 281–291 (2001)
9. Juang, P., Oki, H., Wang, Y., Martonosi, M., Henzinger, L.-S.P., Rubenstein, D.: Energy-efficient computing for wildlife tracking: Design tradeoffs and early experiences with ZebraNet. In: ASPLOS 2002, pp. 96–107 (2002)
10. Leighton, F.T.: Introduction to Parallel Algorithms and Architectures: Arrays, Trees, Hypercubes. Morgan Kaufmann, San Mateo (1993)
11. Spitzer, F.: Principles of Random Walk, 2nd edn. Springer, New York (2001)
12. Valiant, L.: A bridging model for parallel computation. Communications of the ACM 33(8), 103–111 (1990)

Minimum-Cost Broadcast through Varying-Size Neighborcast[*]

Amotz Bar-Noy[1], Prithwish Basu[2], Matthew P. Johnson[3],
and Ram Ramanathan[2]

[1] City University of New York Graduate Center and Brooklyn College
[2] Raytheon BBN Technologies
[3] Pennsylvania State University

Abstract. In traditional multihop network broadcast problems, in which a message beginning at one node is efficiently relayed to all others, cost models typically used involve a charge for each *unicast* or each *broadcast*. These settings lead to a minimum spanning tree (MST) problem or the Connected Dominating Set (CDS) problem, respectively. Neglected, however, is the study of intermediate models in which a node can choose to transmit to an arbitrary subset of its neighbors, at a cost based on the number of recipients (due e.g. to acknowledgements or repeat transmissions). We focus in this paper on a transmission cost model of the form $1 + Ak^b$, where k is the number of recipients, $b \geq 0$, and $A \geq 0$, which subsumes MST, CDS, and other problems.

We give a systematic analysis of this problem as parameterized by b (relative to A), including positive and negative results. In particular, we show the problem is approximable with a factor varying from $2 + 2H_\Delta$ down to 2 as b varies from 0 to 1 (via a modified CDS algorithm), and thence with a factor varying from 2 to 1 (i.e., optimal) as b varies from 1 to $\log_2(\frac{1}{A} + 2)$, and optimal thereafter (both via spanning tree).

For arbitrary cost functions of the form $1 + Af(k)$, these algorithms provide a $2 + 2H_\Delta$-approximation whenever $f(k)$ is sublinear and a $(1 + A)/A$-approximation whenever $f(k)$ is superlinear, respectively. We also show that the problem is optimally solvable for any b when the network is a clique or a tree.

1 Introduction

A key problem in multihop wireless networks and in networking more generally is that of *network-wide broadcast*, in which a message sourced at one node

[*] Research was sponsored by the Army Research Laboratory and was accomplished under Cooperative Agreement Number W911NF-09-2-0053. The views and conclusions contained in this document are those of the authors and should not be interpreted as representing the official policies, either expressed or implied, of the Army Research Laboratory or the U.S. Government. The U.S. Government is authorized to reproduce and distribute reprints for Government purposes notwithstanding any copyright notation here on.

T. Erlebach et al. (Eds.): ALGOSENSORS 2011, LNCS 7111, pp. 173–187, 2012.
© Springer-Verlag Berlin Heidelberg 2012

(the root) must be disseminated to all nodes efficiently. Network-wide broadcast is applicable to dissemination of routing control messages such as link-state updates and route requests, as well as global awareness data (e.g. situation reports). Central to the problem is the notion of cost incurred at each hop in the dissemination process. Cost models have typically been based on charges for one of two sorts of transmissions: *unicast*, in which a node sends a message to one of its neighbors, or *broadcast*, in which a node sends a message to all its neighbors, for a fixed cost, regardless of the number of neighbors receiving. The first method means finding a spanning tree; the second means solving a Connected Dominating Set (CDS) problem. Since individual unicasts are prohibitively expensive for all but very sparse networks, the de facto approach for the network-wide broadcast problem today is to use variants of CDS.

Most work to date has focused on the reliable version of CDS (each broadcast transmission is assumed to perfectly reach all its recipients). In real-world networks, however, this is seldom guaranteed; when the network-wide broadcast is of control packets, the effects of unreliability can be particularly onerous. In this paper, we consider the network-wide broadcast problem with reliable multicasting at the link layer, which leads to a non-trivial cost model for each transmission. That is, unlike the CDS problem where the cost of each broadcast is the same, the cost in a reliable multicast model depends on the number of receivers due to the need for acknowledgements and retransmissions.

More generally, the sender at each hop must ensure that all intended recipients, namely the downstream nodes in the constructed broadcast tree, receive the packet. This typically involves sending the packet, waiting for feedback from the intended receivers, and resending to those who did not receive, iterating until obtaining confirmation that all receivers have the packet. This motivates a cost model with a constant term for the transmission itself plus a cost that is a function of the number of recipients k (i.e., $1 + f(k)$).

To find candidates for the function $f(k)$, we consider a range of protocols from the reliable multicast literature, e.g. [13,9,6,14]. These various solutions incur varying costs in the overhead and delay at each hop, ranging from *sublinear* to *linear* to *superlinear* in the number of receivers, as we now outline.

In [13,9], the feedback takes the form of a *busy tone*, which is a narrow-band signal transmitted in a channel orthogonal to the one used for packets. Since tones are impervious to collisions (if two nodes place a busy tone on a channel, a busy tone is received), the feedback cost is independent of number of receivers, and so depends only on the expected number of retransmissions. As shown in an appendix omitted due to lack of space, the expected number of repetitive transmissions to deliver reliably (without any feedback) to k receivers, via a channel with packet error probability p, is concave in k, and hence the cost function is *sublinear* in k.

Although busy tones reduce the cost of feedback, they require special hardware. A simpler approach is to use acknowledgment (ACK) packets from each receiver. Several techniques may be employed to prevent ACK collisions. In [6], the ACKs are sent sequentially from the receivers and are subject to loss and collisions (in presence of hidden terminals and in very dense scenarios). Under this approach data packets retransmission is caused not just by the loss of data packets but also by the loss of ACKs, which can occur repeatedly, yielding a cost *superlinear* in k. This is also likely when receivers contend for access using ALOHA or CSMA/CA. On the other hand, if TDMA is employed giving "perfect" access to the ACKs, the cost is clearly linear in number of receivers. Roughly linear cost in k models the protocol in [14] as well. In that, a Request ACK (RAK) and ACK handshake is performed for each receiver that protects ACKs from colliding with hidden terminals and therefore avoids superlinearity while increasing (perhaps significantly) the linear coefficient.

These are but a few reliable MAC protocols. Since a network-wide broadcast application may be serviced by any of these or others, depending on the system, we are interested in a general cost framework that approximately captures a wide range of protocols. In this paper we focus on a stylized family of k-neighborcast cost functions of the form $1 + Ak^b$, where $A > 0$ and $0 \leq b < \infty$, which varies from sublinear to linear to superlinear, depending on the value of b, and subsumes the broadcast and unicast models mentioned above. We find that parameter A in isolation is of relatively little consequence, but the character of the problem depends dramatically on the value of b (relative to A). This leads to approximation guarantees that are parameterized by the value A but, more significantly, to different algorithms for different ranges of b values.

Contributions. Modeling the cost of transmitting to k neighbors as $1 + Ak^b$, we give a systematic analysis of the problem of minimizing the total cost of network-wide broadcast. We give positive and negative results for our problem in a variety of special cases parameterized by b, summarized (for the special case of $A = 1$) in Table 1. In particular, we show the problem is approximable with a factor smoothly varying from $2 + 2H_\Delta$[1] down to 2 as b varies from 0 to 1 (via a modified CDS algorithm; see Fig. 1), and thence with a factor smoothly varying from 2 to 1 (i.e., optimal) as b varies from 1 to $\log_2(\frac{1}{A} + 2)$, and optimal thereafter (both via any spanning tree; see Fig. 2).

For arbitrary cost functions of the form $1 + Af(k)$, these algorithms provide a $2 + 2H_\Delta$-approximation whenever $f(k)$ is sublinear and a $(1 + A)/A$-approximation whenever $f(k)$ is superlinear, respectively. We also show that the problem is optimally solvable for any b when the network is a clique or a tree.

Our algorithms assume for simplicity that there is a specified root v_0; the algorithms and guarantees extend straightforwardly to the setting in which any node can be chosen as root.

Related Work. Dominating Set is a classical optimization problem equivalent to Set Cover approximable with factor $H_{\Delta+1}$ which is essentially the best possible [15]. Connected Dominating Set was studied by [7], which gave an approximation algorithms with factors $2H_\Delta + 2$ and $H_\Delta + 2$ for the unweighted setting, as well as results for the weighted setting which were later improved by [8], using the techniques of [10]. Dominating Set has long been known to be APX-hard for

---

[1] Δ is the maximum degree, and H_n is the nth harmonic number $\sum_{i=1}^{n} 1/i$.

Table 1. Special cases of the problem when $A = 1$, parameterized by cost exponent b

b value	$b = 0$	$0 < b < 1$	$b = 1$	$1 < b < \log_2 3$	$\log_2 3 \leq b$
solution	CDS	Algorithm 1	pruned CDS; ST	ST	ST
approx	$H_\Delta + 2$	$2^{1-b} + (2H_\Delta)^{1-b} + o(1)$	$\frac{2}{1+1/(H_\Delta+2)}$; 2	$c(b)$	1
approx LB	$(1 - \epsilon) \ln n$	$\frac{(1-\epsilon)\ln n + n^b}{1+n^b}$	$\frac{2}{1+1/((1-\epsilon)\ln n)}$	NP-hard	1

bounded-degree and cubic graphs [12,1], but hardness results for cubic CDS were given more recently [2,11]. The network-wide broadcasting problem—an application of CDS—has received much attention in the networking community [17]. In [4,3], a PTAS for the CDS problem is give when the input is restricted to unit disk graphs. Power considerations are taken into account in [18]. In [5], the minimum latency broadcast problem is studied. Distributed algorithms for connected dominating set are given in [16,5].

Organization. The rest of the paper is organized as follows. In Section 2 we formally define the problem, present an IP formulation, discuss some special graph topologies that are optimally solvable, and in an omitted appendix we discuss a sublinear setting modeling the cost of acknowledgements. In Section 3, we analyze a number of special cases of the problem parameterized by the value b. Section 4 concludes the paper.

2   Preliminaries

Given is an undirected graph G on n nodes and with maximum degree Δ in which the presence of an edge (u, v) indicates the possibility of directional communication between u and v. A message originating at the root must be relayed to all other nodes. The goal is to minimize the total cost of the transmissions. A node can send the message targeted to a specific subset of neighbors, an action we sometimes call *neighborcasting*. While the message may be heard by other nodes in the vicinity, the chosen receivers are guaranteed to receive the message, at a cost which depends on their number. We do not address the problem of scheduling of broadcasts, ACKs, downstream rebroadcasts etc. in a collision-free manner. We concentrate purely on the total cost incurred during broadcast obeying the idealized cost model defined as follows. The cost of multicasting a message from a node to k neighbors (which we call a *k-cast*) is:

$$m(k) = 1 + Ak^b$$

for some constants $A > 0$ and $b \geq 0$. (We use $a = 1/A$ rather than A when convenient; when $A = 0$, the problem becomes equivalent to Connected Dominating Set.) The problem solution is specified by the neighborcast(s) performed by each node. We emphasize that a node can perform multiple neighborcasts, which can be preferable when $b > 1$. The optimal cost of a send node with $d \leq \Delta$ receivers is the total cost $M(d)$ of the best partition of d into p neighborcast sets (with p possibly 1) of sizes $k_1 + k_2 + \cdots + k_p = d$. In discussing a particular multicast solution, we refer to non-leaf nodes, i.e. nodes performing transmissions (of which there are some number s), as *send nodes* or *senders*; we refer to all nodes other than the root as *receivers* (of which there are $m = n - 1$). We use *multicast*, *neighborcast*, and *transmission* interchangeably.

Assuming $M(d)$ is precomputed for each $1 \leq d \leq \Delta$ (see below), the problem can be defined by integer programming formulation (1-7), which requires that all the transmissions of node v be "paid for" by a single y_{vi}, which is then done with the optimal cost $M_i = M(i)$ for one node transmitting (possibly using multiple transmissions) to i neighbors.

$$\min \sum_{v,i} M_i y_{vi} \tag{1}$$

$$\text{s.t.} \sum_v x_{vu} = 1 \qquad\qquad \forall u \neq v_0 \tag{2}$$

$$i \cdot y_{vi} \geq \sum_{u \in N(v)} x_{vu} - n \cdot (1 - y_{vi}) \qquad\qquad \forall v, i \tag{3}$$

$$\sum_i y_{vi} = 1 \qquad\qquad \forall v \tag{4}$$

$$z_{uv} \geq x_{uv} \qquad\qquad \forall u \neq v \tag{5}$$

$$z_{uv} + z_{vu} \leq 1 \qquad\qquad \forall u \neq v \tag{6}$$

$$z_{uw} \geq z_{uv} + z_{vw} - 1 \qquad\qquad \forall \text{ distinct } u, v, w \tag{7}$$

$$x_{vu}, y_{vi}, z_{uv} \in \{0, 1\}$$

Constraint set 2 ensures that every non-root node receives a transmission from some other node. Constraint set 3 ensures that if $y_{vi} = 1$ (in which case $1 - y_{vi} = 0$) then v transmits to at most i other nodes (where $N(v)$ is the set of v's neighbors); if $y_{vi} = 0$ then the constraint is satisfied trivially. Constraint set 4 ensures that every node $v$has recorded some number, possibly 0, of children. Finally, constraint sets 5,6,7 define a partial order on nodes corresponding to children receiving from parents, which prevents cycles in message-passing.

A straightforward way to compute the $M(d)$ values in quadratic total time is by dynamic programming as follows: $M(0) = 0$ and for any $1 \leq e \leq d$,

$$M(e) = \min_{1 \leq h \leq e} \{m(h) + M(e - h)\} \tag{8}$$

In fact, though, we can compute it more quickly.

Proposition 1. *Each $M(d)$ can be computed in constant time.*

Proof. When $b \leq 1$ a single transmission to all neighbors will be optimal, so consider $b > 1$. Ideally all nodes that transmit will have the same number k of receivers, yielding total cost

$$\frac{n-1}{k}(1 + Ak^b)$$

Allowing k to be fractional, this value is minimized when

$$\frac{d}{dk}\left(\frac{n-1}{k}(1 + Ak^b)\right) = 0$$

which occurs when $A(b-1)k^b = 1$ or

$$k = \left(A(b-1)\right)^{-1/b}$$

This value k in general will be fractional, but numbers of recipients must be integral. Since k^b is convex when $b > 1$, the optimal set of receiver set cardinalities will be $\lfloor k \rfloor$ and $\lceil k \rceil$, so that $x \cdot \lfloor k \rfloor + y \cdot \lceil k \rceil = m$ for some integers x, y. If

$$\frac{m(\lfloor k \rfloor)}{\lfloor k \rfloor} < \frac{m(\lceil k \rceil)}{\lceil k \rceil}$$

then the optimal solution will perform $\lfloor k \rfloor$-casts as aggressively as possible. Then $m = x \cdot \lfloor k \rfloor + y \cdot \lceil k \rceil = (x + y) \cdot \lfloor k \rfloor + y$ implies $x + y = (m \div \lfloor k \rfloor)$, and thus there will be $y = (m \% \lfloor k \rfloor)$ $\lceil k \rceil$-casts and $x = (m \div \lfloor k \rfloor - y)$ $\lfloor k \rfloor$-casts (where $\div$ indicates integer division and $\%$ remainder). Otherwise, performing $\lceil k \rceil$-casts as aggressively as possible will be optimal. In this case, $m = x \cdot \lfloor k \rfloor + y \cdot \lceil k \rceil = (x+y) \cdot \lceil k \rceil - x$ implies $x+y = \lceil m/ \lceil k \rceil \rceil$, and thus there will be $y = (\lceil m/ \lceil k \rceil \rceil - x)$ $\lceil k \rceil$-casts and $x = -(m \tilde{\%} \lceil k \rceil)$ $\lfloor k \rfloor$-casts (where *negative remainder* $r = Z \tilde{\%} d$ is the unique integer r satisfying $-d < r \le 0$ and $Z = qd + r$ for some nonnegative integer q). $\qquad\square$

From this and the fact that the transmission tree in a clique will be a star graph, we have the following:

Corollary 1. *The optimal multicast strategy can be computed in constant time in a clique and in linear time in a (rooted) tree.*

3   Problem Settings Parameterized by b

We now turn to general graphs, analyzing the problem for different values of b.

3.1 $b = 0$ and $b = 1$

When $b = 0$, any transmission costs $1 + Ak^0 = 1 + A$, and so the problem is equivalent to Connected Dominating Set and thus admits the following:

Proposition 2. *When $b = 0$ the problem is approximable with factor $H_\Delta + 2$ [7] but is not approximable with factor $(1 - \epsilon) \ln n$ for any $\epsilon > 0$ (unless $NP \subseteq DTIME(n^{O(\log \log n)}))$ [15].*

When $b = 1$, the receiving costs sum to exactly $A(n - 1)$, and so the objective is simply to minimize the number of senders (and hence maximize the number of leaves).

Proposition 3. *When* $b = 1$ *the problem is approximable with factor* $\frac{A+1}{A+1/(H_\Delta+2))}$ *but not approximable with factor* $\frac{A+1}{A+1/((1-\epsilon)\ln n)}$ *(unless* $NP \subseteq DTIME(n^{O(\log\log n)})$*).*

Proof. When $b = 1$, each transmission to k recipients has cost exactly $1 + Ak$. In a solution with exactly t transmitters that transmit exactly once to each node other than the root, the sum of the transmission costs will be $t + A(n - 1)$. That is, the total cost of receiving is invariant (assuming that we take care never to transmit to a node that has already received), and so the objective again becomes minimizing the number of transmitters.

The cost of transmissions can be approximated within factor $f = H_\Delta + 2$ using the unweighted CDS algorithm of [7], which we then prune, i.e. remove redundant edges from the implied multicasts. For the overall approximation ratio we then have:

$$\frac{ALG_{CDS} + A \cdot (n-1)}{OPT_{CDS} + A \cdot (n-1)} \leq \frac{f \cdot OPT_{CDS} + A \cdot (n-1)}{OPT_{CDS} + A \cdot (n-1)}$$
$$\leq \frac{f \cdot (n-1)/f + A \cdot (n-1)}{(n-1)/f + A \cdot (n-1)}$$
$$\leq \frac{1 + A}{1/f + A}$$

The second inequality follows because the preceding expression is maximized when OPT_{CDS} is as large as possible.

For hardness of approximation, an approximation of factor $\frac{A+1}{A+1/((1-\epsilon)\ln n)}$ would yield an approximation of factor $(1 - \epsilon)\ln n$ for CDS. $\square$

As n goes to infinity, the approximation guarantee of the subroutine also goes to infinity, and so becomes weaker and weaker, converging to 2. In fact, this factor can be obtained more easily.

Corollary 2. *Using any algorithm to compute a CDS or ST as a subroutine would yield an approximation with factor* $(1 + A)/A$ *(or 2 in the case of* $A = 1$*) when* $b = 1$.

Moreover, for similar reasons, we have:

Corollary 3. *Using any algorithm to compute a CDS or ST as a subroutine would yield an approximation with factor* $(1 + A)/A$ *(or 2 in the case of* $A = 1$*) when the cost function is of the form* $1 + m(k)$ *for superlinear* $m(k)$.

3.2 $b \geq \log_2 3$

We find a threshold for b for which unicasting performs within a factor $c \geq 1$ of any multicasting solution:

$$cm(k) \geq km(1) \qquad \text{iff}$$
$$1 + Ak^b \geq k/c + kA/c \quad \text{iff}$$
$$b \geq \frac{\log\left(\frac{k/c-1}{A} + k/c\right)}{\log k}$$
$$= \log_k\left((a+1)\,k/c - a\right) \tag{9}$$

The meaning of the Ineq. 9 is that whenever it holds then for these choices of k, a, b unicasting necessarily performs within a factor c of multicasting. We first consider $c = 1$.

Lemma 1. $f(k,a) = \log_k\left((a+1)k - a\right)$ *is a decreasing function in* $k, \forall a > 0$.

Proof. Differentiating $f(k,a)$ with respect to k, we get:

$$f'(k,a) = \frac{(a+1)\,k \log k - ((a+1)k - a)\,\log\left((a+1)k - a\right)}{k\,((a+1)k - a)\,\log^2 k} \tag{10}$$

We can prove the lemma by showing that $f'(k,a) < 0$, for $k > 1, a > 0$. Let us denote the numerator of Eq. 10 by:

$$h(k,a) = (a+1)\,k \log k - ((a+1)k - a)\,\log\left((a+1)k - a\right)$$

It is easy to verify that $h(1,a) = 0$. Differentiating $h(k,a)$ with respect to k, we get:

$$h'(k,a) = (a+1)k\frac{1}{k} + (a+1)\log k - ((a+1)k - a)\cdot$$
$$\frac{a+1}{(a+1)k - a} - (a+1)\log\left((a+1)k - a\right)$$
$$= (a+1)\log\frac{k}{(a+1)k - a}$$
$$< 0 \quad \text{(since } (a+1)k - a > k \text{ for } a > 0, k > 1) \tag{11}$$

From Ineq. 11 and the fact that $h(1,a) = 0$, we conclude that $h(k,a) < 0$ for $k > 1, a > 0$; since the denominator of Eq. 10 is positive, it immediately follows that $f'(k,a) < 0$ for $k > 1, a > 0$, and therefore $f(k,a)$ is a decreasing function in k for $a > 0$. □

Proposition 4. *Let* $b \geq \log_2(a+2)$. *Then unicasting always (i.e., by any spanning tree (ST)) performs at least as well as any multicasting solution.*

Proof. From Lemma 1, $f(k,a)$ is a decreasing function in k for $a = 1/A > 0$. Therefore its maximum for an integer $k > 1$ is obtained for $k = 2$. Hence, by Ineq. 9 the condition that

$$b \geq \log_2\left(a+2\right)$$

suffices for unicasting to performs at least as well as multicasting for any value of k. □

Remark 1. Of course k^b is superlinear for any $b > 1$. What this shows is that for $b > \log_2(a+2)$, k receivers should never be divided into multiple transmissions.

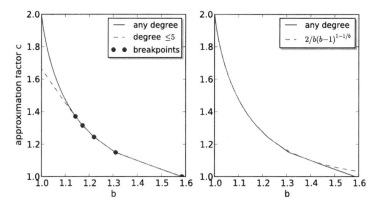

Fig. 1. Approximation factor provided by a spanning tree for each value b (with $A = 1$)

3.3 $1 \leq b \leq \log_2 3$

Now we consider the intermediate setting of $1 \leq b \leq \log_2(a + 2)$. We know that at the extremes of 1 and $\log_2(a + 2)$, the approximation ratios provided by any spanning tree (ST) are 2 and 1, respectively. Let $b_{a,c}(k) = \log_k((a + 1)k/c - a)$, and let $b_a(c) = \max_{k=2}^{\infty} b_{a,c}(k)$, which by Ineq. 9 is the minimum value of b for which any spanning tree provides a c-approximation. We now invert this function to find the approximation factor c as a function of b.

Theorem 1. *Any spanning tree will provide approximation factor*
$c_a(b) = \max_{k=2}^{\Delta} 2k/(a + k^b)$.

Proof. The value of $b_a(c)$ for each input c will be equal to $b_{a,c}(k)$ for some input k. Fix k, and consider the function (of c) $b_{a,k}(c) = b_{a,c}(k)$ and its inverted form $c_{a,k}(b) = 2k/(a + k^b)$. For each value k, unicasting to k receivers will have cost at most $c_{a,k}(b)$ times the cost of multicasting to k receivers. The value k can vary from 2 to Δ. Therefore the approximation factor based on b will be $c_a(b) = \max_{k=2}^{\Delta} c_{a,b}(k)$. That is, the function $c_a(b)$ will be composed piecewise of segments of the functions $c_{a,k}(b)$ (see Fig. 1), with *knees* (or breakpoints) at the values b for which $\frac{k}{k+1} = \frac{k^b + a}{(k+1)^b + a}$. ☐

We now give a simpler though more conservative approximation guarantee.

Proposition 5. *The approximation factor of spanning tree is upper-bounded as a function of b by the function $\hat{c}_a(b) = \frac{2(b-1)}{a+b-1}(\frac{a}{b-1})^{1/b}$ (or $\hat{c}_a(b) = \frac{2}{b}(b - 1)^{1-1/b}$ when $a = 1$).*

Proof. Since the goal is to find an envelope of the function $c_a(b)$, we attempt to find the maximum of the function $c_{a,b}(k)$. Differentiating with respect to k and equating the result to 0, we get:

$$c'_{a,b}(k) = \frac{2a - 2(b-1)k^b}{(a + k^b)^2} = 0$$

Solving for the optimal k we get $k = (\frac{a}{b-1})^{1/b}$; and plugging this into $c_{a,b}(k)$ we have:

$$c_{a,b}(k) \leq c_{a,b}\left(\left(\frac{a}{b-1}\right)^{1/b}\right) = \frac{2(b-1)}{a+b-1}\left(\frac{a}{b-1}\right)^{1/b}$$

which simplifies to $\frac{2}{b}(b-1)^{1-1/b}$ when $a = 1$. □

3.4 $0 < b < 1$

We now give an algorithm for the $0 < b < 1$ setting which is an adaptation of the Algorithm I of [7]. The algorithm takes the root node v_0 as a parameter; if any root can be chosen, the algorithm can be run using every possible starting node.

Algorithm 1. $0 < b < 1$ Greedy (given root v_0)

1: color v_0 gray and color all other nodes white
2: **while** there remain nonblack nodes **do**
3:     make a most cost-effective move, using a gray node v_1 and possibly a nonblack neighbor v_2 of v_1
4:     color v_1 (and v_2 if used) black and color all white neighbors of v_1 (and v_2) gray
5: **end while**

The algorithm grows a multicast tree by repeatedly making one of two kinds of moves: 1) a one-node move, choosing a leaf of the current tree to transmit to all its nontree neighbors (i.e., those not yet in the tree); or 2) or a two-node move, choosing a leaf v_1 plus a nontree neighbor v_2 of v_1 and transmitting to all nontree neighbors of v_1 and v_2.

The *cost-effectiveness* of a move is the ratio of its total cost to the number of new nodes added to the tree. Because the cost of each transmission is sublinear in number of receivers, the best move will transmit to all the neighbors of the move's one or two transmitting nodes; the best two-node move will have one of the nodes transmit to all its nontree neighbors and then the other transmit to all its remaining nontree neighbors. Therefore at each step there are only a linear number of moves to consider.

We now prove the approximation guarantee, adapting the arguments of [7].

Theorem 2. *For $0 < b < 1$, Algorithm 1 provides an approximation of factor $2^{1-b} + (2H_\Delta)^{1-b} + o(1)$ for any $A > 0$.*

Proof. Let OPT be the set of transmissions defining some minimum-cost multicast tree. Let S_i be the set of nodes that are children of some transmitting node v_i in OPT. Since the cost function is sublinear, all the nodes of S_i will receive from a single transmission of v_i. The sets S_i are disjoint. In each move, we add one or two senders to the multicast tree; the cost the move will be charged (divided equally) to the new nodes added to the tree. In the optimal solution, the total cost of transmitting to S_i is exactly $a + |S_i|^b$. We now bound the total cost

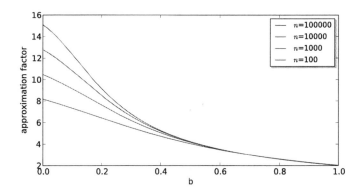

Fig. 2. Approximation factor provided (see the LHS of Ineq. 13) by Algorithm 1 for each value b and several values n (with $A = 1$)

charged to the members of S_i. Let u_j be the number of nodes in S_i remaining uncovered just after move j so that $u = u_0 = |S_i|$ and $u_k = 0$ after some move k. (We restrict our attention to those moves covering nodes in S_i.)

In the first move exactly $u - u_1$ nodes are marked, at a total cost of at most $\max\{a + (u - u_1)^b, 2a + 2((u - u_1)/2)^b\} \le 2a + 2^{1-b}(u - u_1)^b \le 2a + 2^{1-b}u^b$.

After the first move (after at least one node in S_i is added to the tree) it becomes possible to choose node v_i in a two-node move. Therefore in any subsequent move $j > 1$, we could cover all u_j remaining nodes of S_i with cost $2a + 2^{1-b}u_j^b$, and so the cost-effectiveness of move j is at worst $(2a + 2^{1-b}u_j^b)/u_j$. These costs sum to:

$$2a + 2^{1-b}u^b + \sum_{j=1}^{k-1} \frac{2a + 2^{1-b}u_j^b}{u_j}(u_j - u_{j+1})$$

$$= (2a + 2^{1-b}u^b) + 2a\sum_{j=1}^{k-1} \frac{u_j - u_{j+1}}{u_j} + 2^{1-b}\sum_{j=1}^{k-1} \frac{u_j^b(u_j - u_{j+1})}{u_j}$$

$$\le (2a + 2^{1-b}u^b) + 2a\sum_{j=1}^{k-1} \frac{u_j - u_{j+1}}{u_j} + 2^{1-b}\sum_{j=1}^{k-1} \frac{u_j - u_{j+1}}{u_j^{1-b}} \qquad (12)$$

$$\le (2a + 2^{1-b}u^b) + 2aH_u + 2^{1-b}H_u^{(1-b)}$$

Here $H_n^{(x)}$ indicates the generalized harmonic number $\sum_{i=1}^{n} 1/i^x$. The last inequality follows from the observation that for monotonically decreasing integers u_j, $u_k = 0$, and $0 \le b \le 1$, we have $\sum_{j=1}^{k-1} \frac{u_j - u_{j+1}}{u_j^{1-b}} \le H_u^{(1-b)}$. That is, the sum is maximized when $u_{j+1} - u_j = 1$ for each j. Otherwise, if there were some u_j such that $u_j - u_{j+1} = d > 1$, then the sum could be increased by replacing d/u_j with $\sum_{\ell=0}^{d-1} 1/(u_j - \ell)$.

When $b = 0$, an approximation guarantee of $2H_\Delta + 2$ obtains, since the algorithm's behavior collapses to that of [7]. Now let $b > 0$. The cost of sending to S_i in OPT is exactly $a + u^b$, which yields the following approximation factor:

$$\frac{(2a + 2^{1-b}u^b) + 2aH_u + 2^{1-b}H_u^{(1-b)}}{a + u^b} \le 2^{1-b} + o(1) + \frac{2^{1-b}H_u^{(1-b)}}{u^b} \qquad (13)$$

$$\le 2^{1-b} + o(1) + (2H_\Delta)^{1-b}$$

The last inequality follows by application of the "counting measure" special case of Hölder's inequality, substituting $a_i = 1$, $c_i = 1/i^{1-b}$, $p = 1/b$, $q = 1/(1-b)$ (note that $1/p + 1/q = 1$ as required):

$$\sum_{i=1}^u a_i c_i \le \left(\sum_{i=1}^u a_i^p \right)^{1/p} \cdot \left(\sum_{i=1}^u c_i^q \right)^{1/q}$$

$$H_u^{(1-b)} = \sum_{i=1}^u 1/i^{1-b} \le \left(\sum_{i=1}^u 1 \right)^b \cdot \left(\sum_{i=1}^u (1/i^{1-b})^{1/(1-b)} \right)^{1-b} = u^b (H_u)^{1-b}$$

□

More generally, we have:

Corollary 4. *For $m(k) = a + f(k)$ where $f(k)$ is an arbitrary sublinear monotonic increasing cost function, Algorithm 1 provides a $2 + 2H_\Delta$ approximation.*

Proof. We upper-bound the cost of the first move by $2a + 2f(u)$ and the second sum in Ineq. 12 by $2f(u)H_u$ rather than $2^{1-b}H_u^{1-b}$. Substituting this into the LHS of Ineq. 13 yields:

$$\frac{(2a + 2f(u)) + 2aH_u + 2f(u)H_u}{a + f(u)} \le 2 + 2H_\Delta$$

□

In an omitted appendix we observe that Corollary 4 applies to the repeated broadcast transmission model. In Appendix A we prove a two-part NP-hardness result for each *particular* value of $b \in [0, \log_2(3))$, combining the ranges $b < 1.395...$ and $b \ge 1.395...$, the value of b at which $m(3) = m(1) + m(2)$ (when $A = 1$), i.e. $3^b = 2 + 2^b$. We also show a hardness of approximation result for $b \in (0, 1)$.

4   Conclusion

In this paper we presented positive and negative results for a multicast problem with cost function $1 + Ak^b$ and for $1 + m(k)$ with $m(k)$ sublinear or superlinear. As stated in the introduction, part of our motivation is that such cost functions can (approximately) model the cost of a transmission to k neighbors in various sorts of realistic systems. In ongoing experimental research, we are pursuing two directions:

- learning the parameters b and A that are (approximately) satisfied by certain network models and systems
- evaluating our algorithms performance based on not just the idealized cost model $1 + Ak^b$ but also on the *systems' actual transmission costs*

References

1. Alimonti, P., Kann, V.: Some apx-completeness results for cubic graphs. Theor. Comput. Sci. 237(1-2), 123–134 (2000)
2. Bonsma, P.S.: Max-leaves spanning tree is apx-hard for cubic graphs. CoRR, abs/0912.0226 (2009)
3. Cheng, X., Huang, X., Li, D., Wu, W., Du, D.-Z.: A polynomial-time approximation scheme for the minimum-connected dominating set in ad hoc wireless networks. NETWORKS 42(4), 202–208 (2003)
4. Das, B., Bharghavan, V.: Routing in ad hoc networks using minimum connected dominating sets. In: Proceedings of the International Conference on Communications, ICC (1997)
5. Gandhi, R., Mishra, A., Parthasarathy, S.: Minimizing broadcast latency and redundancy in ad hoc networks. IEEE/ACM Transactions on Networking 16(4), 840–851 (2008)
6. Gossain, H., Nandiraju, N., Anand, K., Agrawal, D.P.: Supporting mac layer multicast in ieee 802.11 based manets: Issues and solutions. In: LCN, pp. 172–179 (2004)
7. Guha, S., Khuller, S.: Approximation algorithms for connected dominating sets. Algorithmica 20(4), 374–387 (1998)
8. Guha, S., Khuller, S.: Improved methods for approximating node weighted steiner trees and connected dominating sets. Inf. Comput. 150(1), 57–74 (1999)
9. Gupta, S., Shankar, V., Lalwani, S.: Reliable multicast mac protocol for wireless lans. In: IEEE International Conference on Communications, ICC 2003, vol. 1, pp. 93–97 (May 2003)
10. Klein, P.N., Ravi, R.: A nearly best-possible approximation algorithm for node-weighted steiner trees. J. Algorithms 19(1), 104–115 (1995)
11. Lemke, P.: The maximum-leaf spanning tree problem in cubic graphs is np-complete. Technical report, University of Minnesota, Mineapolis (1988)
12. Papadimitriou, C.H., Yannakakis, M.: Optimization, approximation, and complexity classes. J. Comput. Syst. Sci. 43(3), 425–440 (1991)
13. Si, W., Li, C.: Rmac: a reliable multicast mac protocol for wireless ad hoc networks. In: International Conference on Parallel Processing, ICPP 2004, vol. 1, pp. 494–501 (August 2004)
14. Sun, M.-T., Huang, L., Wang, S., Arora, A., Lai, T.-H.: Reliable mac layer multicast in ieee 802.11 wireless networks. Wireless Communications and Mobile Computing 3(4), 439–453 (2003)
15. Vazirani, V.V.: Approximation algorithms. Springer, Heidelberg (2001)
16. Wan, P.-J., Alzoubi, K.M., Frieder, O.: Distributed construction of connected dominating set in wireless ad hoc networks. MONET 9(2), 141–149 (2004)
17. Wu, J., Li, H.: A dominating-set-based routing scheme in ad hoc wireless networks. Telecommunication Systems 18(1-3), 13–36 (2001)
18. Wu, J., Wu, B., Stojmenovic, I.: Power-aware broadcasting and activity scheduling in ad hoc wireless networks using connected dominating sets. Wireless Communications and Mobile Computing 3(4), 425–438 (2003)

A Hardness Results

When $b \approx 1.395$, we have $m(3) = m(1) + m(2)$ (when $A = 1$), because this b is the root of $3^b = 2 + 2^b$. This is the point at which a 3-transmission goes cheaper than a 1-transmission plus a 2-transmission to more expensive. We prove hardness for $0 \leq b \leq \log_2 3$ by considering values of b both less than and greater than 1.395.

Lemma 2. *For each particular $b \in [0, 1.395...)$ the problem (with $A = 1$) is NP-hard, even on cubic graphs.*

Proof. We reduce from Connected Dominating Set restricted to cubic graphs (i.e., every vertex of degree 3), which is known to be APX-hard [2].

Given the CDS instance I_{CDS}, the multicast problem instance I consists of the same graph, combined with the specified b value and $A = 1$. Now, consider an optimal solution OPT to I with s send nodes. Since the graph is cubic, there can be at most one node that performs a transmission to three receivers—the root. Since for $b < 1.395...$ we have these inequalities:

$$m(3) < m(1) + m(2) \tag{14}$$

$$m(2) < m(1) + m(1) \tag{15}$$

Then in any optimal solution the root transmits to three receivers (due to Ineq. 14) and no send node will perform two separate transmissions (due to Ineqs. 14 and 15). Therefore $s_1 + s_2 = s - 1$, where s_i is the number of send nodes transmitting to exactly i receivers.

Now suppose there were a solution to I_{CDS} with $s' < s$ (set $j = s - s'$) send nodes. We will show this implies the existence of a multicast solution of cost less than OPT. Let s'_i be the number of nodes transmitting to exactly i receivers in a minimum-cost assignment of receivers to the s' nodes in the I_{CDS} solution. Note that we may assume that also in *this* solution the root transmits to three receivers (with one transmission); if not, we can reverse the edges between it and any of its neighbors it does not send to, which again by Ineq. 14 will only lower the cost (and perhaps shrink s'). Thus we have $s'_1 + s'_2 = s' - 1 = s_1 - j + s_2$. Observe that we then have $s'_1 = s_1 - 2j$ and $s'_2 = s_2 + j$, and so the net change in the receiver cost is the removal of $2j$ nodes transmitting to 1 receiver each and the addition of j nodes transmitting to two nodes. The net effect of these changes on cost is $j \cdot (1 + 2^b - 2 \cdot (1 + 1^b))$, which is negative for any $b \leq 1$. Thus we obtain a contradiction, and so the s senders constitute an optimal CDS solution.   □

Lemma 3. *For each particular $b \in [1.395..., \log_2(3))$ the problem (with $A = 1$) is NP-hard, even on cubic graphs.*

Proof. For b in the specified range, Ineq. 14 no longer holds, and so an optimal solution will never send to 3 receivers in a single transmission, but only to groups of 1 or 2. Since Ineq. 15 continues to hold, an optimal solution will try to perform as many 2-casts as possible. A node performing only 2-casts will have an even number of children and, unless it is the root, therefore have odd degree in the tree induced by the transmissions. In the case of a graph with n even, therefore, the ideal situation will be for every node but one (the root) to have an even number of children and hence for every node in the induced tree to have odd degree. Determining whether a cubic graph with even n admits a spanning tree with all node degrees odd, however, is known to be NP-hard [11].

Combining Lemmas 2 and 3 we obtain:

Theorem 3. *For each particular* $b \in [0, \log_2(3))$ *(with* $A = 1$*) the problem is NP-hard, even on cubic graphs.*

We now give a hardness of approximation result for $0 < b < 1$ (which, note, does not cover the same range as Lemma 2).

Theorem 4. *For each particular* $b \in (0, 1)$*, the problem not approximable with factor* $\frac{(1-\epsilon)\ln n + n^b}{1+n^b}$ *for any* $\epsilon > 0$ *(unless* $NP \subseteq DTIME(n^{O(\log \log n)})$*).*

Proof. Let OPT be the optimal solution value. Let $OPT' = OPT'_s + OPT'_r$ be the best possible solution value for a solution whose set of senders constitutes an optimal solution to the corresponding unweighted CDS problem. Note that $OPT \leq OPT'$. Let $ALG = ALG_s + ALG_r$ be the cost of a solution returned by some algorithm. (In the sublinear setting we can assume each sender transmits only once.) Let $m = n - 1$ be the number of receivers, and let f upper-bound the ratio ALG_s/OPT_s, which cannot be as good as $(1 - \epsilon) \ln n$ for any $\epsilon > 0$ (absent the hardness assumption invoked the theorem statement). Then the most optimistic case for the approximation ratio of ALG compared to OPT' is for ALG to do $ALG_s - 1$ unicasts and for OPT' to do OPT'_s equal-sized transmissions, i.e.:

$$
\begin{aligned}
\frac{ALG_s + ALG_r}{OPT'_s + OPT'_r} &= \frac{fOPT'_s + fOPT'_s + (m - fOPT'_s)^b}{OPT'_s + OPT'_s(n/OPT_s)^b} \\
&\geq \frac{fOPT'_s + m^b}{OPT'_s + (OPT'_s)^{1-b}m^b} \\
&\geq \frac{(1 - \epsilon)\ln n \cdot OPT'_s + m^b}{OPT'_s + (OPT'_s)^{1-b}m^b} \\
&\geq \frac{(1 - \epsilon)\ln n \cdot OPT'_s + n^b}{OPT'_s(1 + n^b)} \\
&\geq \frac{(1 - \epsilon)\ln n + n^b}{1 + n^b} \quad \text{(for } n \text{ large enough)}
\end{aligned}
$$

Therefore since ALG cannot approximate OPT' within the stated factor, neither can it do so for the only smaller OPT. $\square$

Real-Time Video Streaming
in Multi-hop Wireless Static Ad Hoc Networks*

Guy Even, Yaniv Fais, Moti Medina, Shimon (Moni) Shahar,
and Alexander Zadorojniy

School of Electrical Engineering, Tel-Aviv Univ., Tel-Aviv 69978, Israel
{guy,yanivfai,medinamo,moni,sasha}@eng.tau.ac.il

Abstract. We deal with the problem of streaming multiple video streams between pairs of nodes in a multi-hop wireless ad hoc network. The nodes are static,
know their locations, and are synchronized (via GPS). We introduce a new interference model that uses variable interference radiuses. We present an algorithm
for computing a frequency assignment and a schedule whose goal is to maximize throughput over all the video streams. In addition, we developed a localized
flow-control mechanism to stabilize the queue lengths.

We simulated traffic scheduled by the algorithm using OMNET++/MixiM
(i.e., physical SINR interference model with 802.11g) to test whether the computed throughput is achieved. The results of the simulation show that the computed solution is SINR-feasible and achieves predictable stable throughputs.

1 Introduction

We address the problem of routing real-time video streams (VS's) in static ad hoc wireless networks. Our goal is to develop and implement an efficient algorithm and test it in
a realistic physical model. Many works have been published on the topic of multi-hop
routing in wireless networks including real-time video streaming (see [19,13,20,21]). In
these works it is acknowledged that cross layer algorithms are required to utilize the capacity of the network. These papers evaluate specific algorithms and scenarios using approximate models for wireless network, and thus the question of developing integrated
realistic solutions remains open. In particular, a solution must address a combination
of specifications including: maximize throughput, fairness, minimize delay, stability of
throughput, stability of queue lengths in intermediate nodes, bounded number of lost
packets, and predictability.

One of the main issues in wireless networks is how to model interferences. In the
communication community, one uses the signal-to-interference-plus-noise ratio (SINR)
to determine if a received signal is decoded without an error [9]. On the other hand, the
algorithms community has used the graph model (or protocol model) to model feasible
communication patterns [12,1]. For the graph model, multi-hop routing algorithms with
a constant approximation ratio have been developed [15,1,4,22]. In fact, Wan [22] even
presents a (theoretical) PTAS for the problem. On the other hand, to date approximation algorithms for throughput maximization in the SINR model do not have a constant
approximation ratio. For example, in [5], the approximation ratio is logarithmic in the

---

* The full version of this paper can be found in http://arxiv.org/abs/1104.0779.

T. Erlebach et al. (Eds.): ALGOSENSORS 2011, LNCS 7111, pp. 188–201, 2012.
© Springer-Verlag Berlin Heidelberg 2012

ratio between the longest link and the shortest link (for uniform transmission powers), and in [8] the approximation ratio is logarithmic in the number of nodes (for the linear power model).

The study of wireless algorithms in the SINR model has been motivated by its realistic appeal. In fact, it has been argued that the performance of graph based algorithms is inferior to algorithms in the SINR model [10]. In [17,18] a logarithmic ratio between the throughput in the SINR model and the throughput in the graph model is presented. A closer look at studies that compare the interference models and algorithms for these models shows only a constant gap if the ratios of the max-to-min power and max-to-min distance are constant. In [11] the same asymptotic throughput is obtained in both models with respect to random instances. In [17], the example only gives a constant ratio if the the power ratio and the distance ratio are constant. In [5], an example with a constant gap is presented for constant uniform power. In [3], the theorems do not utilize the ability to increase the interference radius or to apply collision avoidance methods used in the 802.11 MAC.

The questions we study in this paper are as follows. (i) How much of the traffic computed by a graph model based routing algorithm can be routed in realistic scenarios with constant max-to-min powers and constant max-to-min distances? Namely, does the approximate nature of the graph model lead to useful solutions? (ii) How to integrate a graph-model based routing-algorithm in a system that supports real-time video streaming? Such a system must combine goals such as: fairness, predictable throughput, few lost packets, bounded intermediate queues, reasonable and steady end-to-end delay.

Previous Work. The necessity of cross layer designs has been recognized for satisfying the special characteristics of real-time video streaming over wireless networks [20,19,13]. We continue this line of work.

The multi-hop routing problem for ad hoc networks was investigated thoroughly. One of the commonly used heuristics for routing is based on finding paths with maximum bottlenecks, namely, paths for which the edge with the lowest capacity is maximum [7]. We used this algorithm in our benchmarks (we call it SHORTP). A different approach for the routing problem is based on solving a linear program. In [15,12,1], routing algorithms in the graph model are designed, analyzed, and simulated. One drawback in [15,12,1] is that the simulations were run also in the graph model and not in the physical model. Wan [22] pointed out various errors in previous algorithms and presented a new linear program that corrects the problem. He proved that: (i) there is a 23-approximation algorithm based on the linear program, and (ii) there is a polynomial time scheme (PTAS) for the problem. However, this PTAS is not practical. Namely, the PTAS requires solving a linear program that might not be solved by LP-solvers even for moderate sized networks.

Chafekar et al. [5,6] considered routing algorithms in the SINR model. The approximation ratio of their algorithm with uniform power assignments is logarithmic in the ratio between the longest link and the shortest link. Their communication model does not include ACK packets. Hence, interference is caused only by the sender and not by the receiver. In [6], simulations are described in the physical model, but these simulations do not use the 802.11 MAC (i.e., no RTS, CTS, ACK packets are used). A discussion on the scenarios that are simulated in [6] can be found in the full version.

Due to space limitations, some of the formulations, algorithms' listings, and experimental results were omitted and can be found in the full version.

Our Contributions. (I) We do not modify the 802.11g MAC. This approach has two advantages. First, we do not bypass the wireless NIC and its collision avoidance features. Hence, even if the algorithm suggests a schedule with interferences, these interferences are resolved by the MAC. Second, the network can support limited additional traffic that is not routed or scheduled by the algorithm (i.e. messages for controlling the network). We choose the 802.11g because of its popularity in laptops and mobile devices. (II) Simulation in the physical model. The simulation is in a standard 802.11g setting using OMNET++/MixiM (see the full version for more details). In this setting, all WiFi frames are transmitted (i.e., RTS,CTS, packet, ACK), and interferences between frames are analyzed using the SINR-model, and taking into account the Modulation Coding Schemes (MCS). (III) We introduce new interference constraints that constitute an intermediate model between the physical SINR-model and the graph based protocol model (see Sec. 3.1). The interference set of a link is a function of the signal-to-noise ratio of the link and the MCS of the link. As the signal-to-noise ratio (without interferences) of a link is closer to the SINR-threshold, the interference set grows, so that SINR is not in the "waterfall" region of the PER function.[1] One advantage of this new interference model is that it is easy to formulate interference constraints in the linear program formulation (see the full version). (IV) We formulate the problem of minimizing end-to-end delay incurred by a schedule that supports a given multi-flow. We developed and implemented a scheduling algorithm that addresses this problem of reducing end-to-end delays while supporting a similar throughput (see Sec 4.3). In [15,1,4] the effect of the schedule on the delay is not mentioned. (V) We developed and implemented a flow control algorithm that stabilizes the queue lengths and controls the data-rate along the links. This flow control algorithm is executed locally by the nodes. (VI) We evaluated the performance of the proposed algorithm with respect to video streaming. In particular, we measured the throughput, end-to-end delay, fraction of dropped packets, queue lengths, and the stability of these parameters.

Techniques. Following [15,1,4,5,8], we formulate an LP, and apply greedy coloring to obtain a schedule. Interestingly, the greedy coloring incurs high end-to-end-delays, so we developed a path-peeling scheduler that trades delay for throughput. Stability is maintained by a flow control algorithm that monitors flow through incoming and outgoing links, and continuously balances the two. This method utilizes the ability of video encoders to adjust the compressed bit-rate.

2   Problem Definition

Setting. We consider a WiFi 802.11g static ad hoc network with 3 non-interfering radio channels with the assumptions: (i) Single radio: each node has a single wireless network interface controller (WNIC). (ii) Each node is equipped with a GPS so that

---

[1] The packet-error-rate (PER) is a function of the SINR. This function increases very steeply in the neighborhood of the critical threshold β. This phenomenon is referred to as the "waterfall" region of the PER function.

it knows its location and the nodes are synchronized. (iii) The WNICs support quick synchronized hops between frequency channels. (iv) Isotropic antennas. (v) We also assume that the nodes have already joined the network and that there is at least one node (i.e., center node) that holds full information about the network (i.e., nodes and locations). Accumulating this information can be done in a distributed low-bandwidth fashion after building a spanning tree [2].

Problem Definition. The input to the algorithm consists of: (I) A set V of n nodes in the plane. A transceiver is located in each node. (II) A set of k VS requests $\{r_i\}_{i=1}^k$. Each stream request is a triple $r_i \triangleq (a_i, b_i, d_i^*)$, where a_i is the source (e.g., camera) of the stream, b_i is the destination, and d_i^* is the required data-rate. Ideally, we would like to satisfy all the requests, namely, for each VS r_i, route packets using multi-hops from a_i to b_i. We assume that there is a path in the network between each source-destination pair (otherwise, the request is rejected).

Let d_i denote the data-rate achieved for the ith stream. The service ratio ρ_i of the ith demand is defined by $\rho_i \triangleq d_i/d_i^*$. Our goal is to maximize the minimum service ratio, namely, $\max \min_i \rho_i$.

Additional performance measures are: (i) End-to-end delay - this is the time it takes a packet to reach its destination. We are interested in reducing the maximum delay (among the packets that are delivered) since the video is real-time. In addition, the maximum delay determines the size of the jitter buffer in the receiving side. (ii) Number of dropped packets. Queue management may drop packets. A dropped packet never reaches its destination. (iii) Queue lengths in intermediate nodes tell us how much memory should be allocated and also give an indication of the delay per hop.

3 Preliminaries

3.1 Interference Models

Bidirectional Interference. The delivery of a message in the WiFi MAC requires transmission of frames by both sides (e.g., RTS and packet are transmitted by the sender, CTS and ACK are transmitted by the receiver). Hence, interferences can be caused also by frames transmitted by a the receiving side.

The SINR Model. The SINR model, also called the physical interference model, defines successful communication as follows. Let $d_{u,v}$ denote the distance between nodes u and v. Suppose a subset $S_t \subseteq V$ of the nodes are transmitting simultaneously in the same frequency channel as u. The signal-to-interference-plus-noise ratio (SINR) for the reception by $v \in V \setminus S_t$ of the signal transmitted by $u \in S_t$ in the presence of the transmitters S_t is defined by $\text{SINR}(u, v, S_t) \triangleq \frac{P/d_{u,v}^\alpha}{N + \sum_{x \in S_t \setminus \{u\}} P/d_{x,v}^\alpha}$. Each transmitter can use one of several modulation coding schemes (MCS). The message transmitted by u in an MCS m is successfully received by v if $\text{SINR}(u, v, S_t) \geq \beta_m$, where β_m is the minimum SINR-threshold for the MCS m.

Protocol Model. The protocol model, also called the graph model, is specified by two radii: (i) A communication distance r. (ii) An interference distance R. The rule for successful communication between two nodes u and v is that v receives the message from u if $d_{u,v} < r$ and every other node x that transmits at the same time satisfies $d_{x,v} > R$. In this model, a communication graph is defined over the nodes. Two nodes are linked by an edge if their distance is less than the communication distance r.

Since the WiFi MAC requires transmission by both sides, an *interference* is defined between two links (u, v) and (u', v') if $\min\{d_{u,u'}, d_{u,v'}, d_{v,u'}, d_{v,v'}\} < R$. We say that a subset L of links is *non-interfering* if no two links in L interfere. In the protocol model, a *schedule* is a sequence $\{L_i\}_i$ of subsets of non-interfering links.

Our New Model. The new model is an intermediate model between the SINR model and the protocol model. The idea is that, as the SNR of a link grows, the link can tolerate more interference. Hence, the interference distance is not fixed.

Consider a pair (u, v) of nodes and an MCS m. The triple (u, v, m) is a *link* in the new model if $\text{SINR}(u, v, \emptyset) \geq \beta_m$.

Since both sides of a link transmit and receive, the interference set of a link must take into account interferences caused by other transmissions both in the receiver and the sender. However, the frames sent by the receiving side are in MCS 0, therefore, reception of these frames depends on the SINR-threshold β_0.

The interference set $V_{u,v,m}$ of the link $e = (u, v, m)$ is defined by $V_{u,v,m} \triangleq \{x \in V \setminus \{u\} \mid \text{SINR}(u, v, \{x\}) < \mu \cdot \beta_m \text{ or } \text{SINR}(v, u, \{x\}) < \mu \cdot \beta_0\}$.

Geometrically, the set $V_{u,v,m}$ consists of the set of nodes that belong to the union of two disks. One disk is centered at u and its radius is a function of $\text{SINR}(u, v, \emptyset)$ and β_m. The second is centered at v and its radius is a function of $\text{SINR}(v, u, \emptyset)$ and β_0. Unlike the standard graph, the radiuses of these disks vary from link to link.

The motivation for this definition is that transmissions of nodes in $V_{u,v,m}$ interfere with the reception of v by u, or vice versa. The choice of $\mu = 1.585$ gives us a margin of 2dB above the SINR-threshold. This margin keeps the SINR above the threshold due to interferences caused by transmitters not in $S_{u,v,m}$.

We also define the interfering set of edges with respect to the link $e = (u, v, m)$, $I_{u,v,m} \triangleq \{e' = (u', v', m') \mid \{u', v'\} \cap (V_{u,v,m} \cup V_{v,u,m}) \neq \emptyset\} \setminus \{(u, v, m)\}$. The interference set $I_{u,v,m}$ contains a link e' if either endpoint of e' interferes with reception at the endpoints u or v.

Notation. Let u and v denote nodes and m denote an MCS. A link is a triple (u, v, m) such that $\text{SINR}(u, v, \emptyset) \geq \beta_m$. This definition implies that there can be multiple parallel links between u and v, each with a different MCS. We denote the set of links by E. The set $E_{out}(v)$ (resp. $E_{in}(v)$) denotes the set of links that emanate from (resp. enter) v. Let $E(v)$ denote the set of links $E_{in}(v) \cup E_{out}(v)$. For a link $e = (u, v, m)$, let $\text{MCS}(e) = m$, i.e., the MCS m of the link e.

4   Algorithm MF-I-S

4.1   Networks Governed by Time-Slotted Frequency Tables

Two tables govern the communication in the network. The first table A is a time-slotted frequency table. The dimensions of A are $F \times T$, where F denotes the number of frequency channels and T denotes the number of time slots. There is one row for each frequency channel and one column for each time slot. (In our implementation we used

$F = 3$ and $T = 200$). The table A determines a periodic schedule. The second table is a multi-flow table mf. The dimensions of mf are $|E| \times k$ (recall that k equals the number of VS's). The entry $mf(e, s)$ specifies the number of packets-per-period that should be delivered along link e for stream s.

Each table entry $A[j, t]$ is a subset of links, i.e., $A[j, t] \subseteq E$. The table governs communication in the sense that, in slot t', the links in $A[j, t' \pmod T)]$ try to deliver packets using frequency channel j.

We use $A[\cdot, t]$ to denote the set of links $\cup_{j \in F} A[j, t]$. Since we assume that each node is equipped with a single radio, it follows that two links that share an endpoint cannot be active in the same time slot. Hence, for every node v, $E(v) \cap A[\cdot, t]$ may contain at most one link.

A time-slotted frequency table schedules active links (see Algorithm TX-RX in the full version). Each node v executes Algorithm TX-RX(v) locally. Since $E(v) \cap A[\cdot, t]$ may contain at most one link, a node v is either a receiver, a sender, or inactive in each time slot.

4.2 Algorithm Specification

The input to the routing algorithm is specified in Sec. 2. The output consists of two parts: (i) a time-slotted frequency table A, and (ii) a multi-flow $mf(e, s)$, for every link e and stream $1 \le s \le k$. We note that the units of flow are packets-per-period. The period equals $T \cdot \sigma$, where σ is the duration of a time slot, and T equals the number of time-slots in a period.

The multi-flow $mf(e, s)$ determines the routing and the throughout of each stream. The role of the frequency/time-slot table A and the multi-flow tables is to specify a periodic schedule that determines which links are active in which time slots (see Sec. 4.1).

Although we use fixed length packets (e.g., 2KB), the MCS of a link determines the amount of time required for completing the delivery of a packet. This means, that within one time slot, multiple packets may be delivered along a single link. Let $pps(e)$ denote the number of packets-per-slot that can be delivered along e. Namely, node u can transmit at most $pps(e)$ packets to node v along link $e = (u, v, m)$ in one time-slot. Note that the value of $pps(e)$ is a function of the MCS of the link e.

We say that table A *supports* the flow mf if the following properties hold:

1. Every entry $A[j, t]$ in the table is a set of non-interfering links. Thus, the links in $A[j, t]$ may be active simultaneously.
2. The data-rates $mf(e, s)$ are supported by the table. Namely,

$$\sum_{s=1}^{k} mf(e, s) \le |\{A[j, t] : e \in A[j, t]\}| \cdot pps(e) . \tag{1}$$

4.3 Algorithm Description

Algorithm MF-I-S consists of two parts: (i) computation of a multi-commodity flow with conflict constraints, and (ii) scheduling of the multi-commodity flow in a time-slotted frequency table. We elaborate on each of these parts.

Multi-commodity Flow with Conflict Constraints. We formulate the problem of routing and scheduling the VS's by a linear program (LP). A similar LP is used in [15,1,4] with respect to the graph model. We use our new interference model for the interference constraints.

The variables $f_i^j(e)$ of the LP signify the amount of flow along link e in frequency channel j for stream i. The full LP appears in the full version. Let $f^j(e) \triangleq \sum_{i=1}^k f_i^j(e)$, namely, $f^j(e)$ is the flow in frequency j along link e. Let $c(e) \triangleq T \cdot pps(e)$ denote the number of packets-per-period that can be delivered along the link e.
We elaborate on two main features of the LP:

1. The conflict constraints. The ratio $f^j(e)/c(e)$ equals the fraction of the time that the link e is active in transmission in frequency j. Since each node is equipped with a single WNIC, transmissions emanating or entering the same node may not occur simultaneously (in any frequency). In addition, the links in I_e may not transmit in frequency j whenever e is transmitting in frequency j. Thus, the conflict constraint is formulated as follows. For every link $e = (u, v, m) \in E$, and for each frequency $j \in [1..3]$:

$$\frac{f^j(e)}{c(e)} + \sum_{j' \neq j} \sum_{e' \in E(u) \cup E(v)} \frac{f^{j'}(e')}{c(e')} + \sum_{e' \in I_e} \frac{f^j(e')}{c(e')} \leq 1. \tag{2}$$

2. Max-Min throughput. For each requested stream r_i, we define the supply ratio ρ_i to be the ratio between the flow allocated to the i'th stream and the demand d_i^* of the stream. The objective of the LP is to maximize $\min_i \rho_i$. A secondary objective is to maximize the total throughput.

Scheduling of the Multi-commodity Flow in a Time-Slotted Frequency Table. In the scheduling step we are given the multi-commodity flows $f_i^j(e)$. The task is to allocate entries in a time-slotted frequency table A that supports these flows.

We first determine how many time-slots should be allocated for $f^j(e)$, for each link e and each frequency channel j. Similarly to Eq. 1, $|\{t \in [1..T] : e \in A[j,t]\}| \cdot pps(e) \geq f^j(e)$. Hence,

$$|\{t \in [1..T] : e \in A[j,t]\}| \geq \left\lceil \frac{f^j(e)}{pps(e)} \right\rceil. \tag{3}$$

The Greedy Scheduler. The simplest way to assign flows to the table A is by applying a greedy algorithm (similar to greedy coloring). The greedy algorithm scans the links and frequency channels, one by one, and assigns $\ell(e, j)$ slots to each link e and frequency channel j. Based on [1,14,4], the interference constraints in Eq. 2 imply that the greedy algorithm succeeds in this assignment provided that

$$\ell(e, j) = \left\lfloor \frac{f^j(e)}{pps(e)} \right\rfloor. \tag{4}$$

The issue of dealing with this rounding problem (i.e., the difference between the round-down and the round-up in Eqs. 3 and 4) is discussed in [22], where it is pointed out that routing all the flow requires a super exponential period T. Such a period is obviously not practical; the computation of the table takes too long, the table is too long to be broadcast to all nodes, and the schedule will incur huge delays.

We show that the rounding problem is not an important issue both theoretically and in practice. We define $f_i(e)$ to be the combined flow along e for stream i over all frequency channels. Since each flow f_i can be decomposed into at most $|E|$ flow paths, it follows that the values of $\{f_i^j(e)\}_{e \in E, j \in F}$ can be "rounded" so that at most $|E| \cdot \max_e\{pps(e)\}$ packets are lost per period. Note that this lost flow can be made negligible by increasing the period T. As T increases, the amount of flow per period tends to infinity, and hence, the lost flow is negligible. In our experiments, we used a period of $T = 200$ time slots, with a duration of $5ms$ per slot. The greedy scheduler was able to schedule almost all the flow in all the instances we considered. The multi-flow table is set so that $mf(e, s)$ equals the amount of flow from $f_s(e)$ that the scheduler successfully assigned.

The greedy scheduler incurred a delay roughly of one period per hop. The reason is that it schedules all the receptions to a node before the transmissions from the node. To avoid this delay, we designed a new scheduler, described below.

The Path-Peeling Scheduler. The path peeling scheduler tries to reduce the time that an incoming packet waits till it is forwarded to the next node. This is achieved as follows.

1. Decomposes each flow f_i into flow paths such that the flow along each path equals the bottleneck, i.e., the minimum $pps(e)$ along the path. Let $\{f_i(p)\}_{p \in \mathcal{P}(i)}$ denote this decomposition.
2. While not all the flow is scheduled,
   (a) For $i = 1$ to k do:
   (b) If $\mathcal{P}(i) \neq \emptyset$, then schedule a path $p \in \mathcal{P}(i)$ and remove p from $\mathcal{P}(i)$.

The scheduling of a flow path $p \in \mathcal{P}(i)$ tries to schedule the links in p one after the other (cyclically) to reduce the time a packet needs to wait in each node along p. The scheduling simply scans the links in p in the order along p, and finds the first feasible time slot (in cyclic order) for each link $e \in p$.

We point out that in Line 2a, we schedule one path from each stream to maintain fairness in allocation and delays. On the average, each stream suffers from the same "fragmentation" problems in the table A.

In our experiments, the path-peeling scheduler succeeded in scheduling 70% of the flow. The advantage, compare to the greedy scheduler, is that delays are significantly reduced.

5   Flow Control

The multi-flow table computed by the algorithm determines the number of packets $mf(e, s)$ that should be sent along each link e for stream s during each period. Each node v monitors the following information for each link $e \in E_{out}(v)$. (1) $P(e, s, t)$ - the number of packets belonging to stream s sent along the link e during the period t. (2) $P^+(e, s, t)$ - the maximum number of packets belonging to stream s that can be sent along the link e during the period t. Note that $P^+(e, s, t) \geq P(e, s, t)$; inequality may happen if the queue $Q(e, s)$ is empty when a packet is scheduled to be transmitted along the link e. Note that if e is not planned to deliver packets of stream s, then $P^+(e, s, t) = 0$. We remark that a node v can also monitor $P(e, s, t)$ for a link $e \in E_{in}(v)$. However, the value $P^+(e, s, t)$ for a link $e \in E_{in}(v)$ must be sent to v (e.g., by appending it to one of the delivered packets).

The Flow-Control algorithm is executed locally by all the nodes in the network. Let $e = (u, v, m)$ denote a link from u to v, and let s denote a stream. Each node executes a separate instance per stream. In the end of each period t, each node u "forwards" the value of $P^+(e, s, t)$ to node v. In addition, in the end of each period t, node v sends "backwards" the value $R(e, s)$ to u. The value $R(e, s)$ specifies the number of packets from stream s that v is willing to receive along the link e in the next period $t + 1$.

Algorithm 1. Flow-Control(v, s) - a local algorithm for managing the local queue and requested incoming rate at node v for stream s.

---

1. Initialize: for all $e \in E_{in}(v)$, $R(e, s) \leftarrow mf(e, s)$.
2. For $t = 1$ to ∞ do
   (a) Measure $P(e, s, t)$ for every $e \in E(v)$, and $P^+(e, s, t)$ for every $e \in E_{out}(v)$.
   (b) Receive $P^+(e, s, t)$ for every $e \in E_{in}(v)$, and $R(e, s)$ for every $e \in E_{out}(v)$.
   (c) $R_{in} \leftarrow \min\{\sum_{e \in E_{out}(v)} R(e, s),$
        $\sum_{e \in E_{out}(v)} P^+(e, s, t), \sum_{e \in E_{in}(v)} P^+(e, s, t), \}$.
   (d) For every $e \in E_{in}(v)$: $R(e, s) \leftarrow R_{in} \cdot \frac{P^+(e, s, t)}{\sum_{e' \in E_{in}(v)} P^+(e', s, t)}$.
   (e) Drop oldest packets from $Q(v, s)$, if needed, so that $|Q(v, s)| \leq R_{in}$.

The Flow-Control algorithm is listed as Algorithm 1. It equalizes the incoming and outgoing packet-rates in intermediate nodes as follows. The requested packet-rate $R(e, s)$ is initialized to be the value $mf(e, s)$ derived from the table. The Flow-Control algorithm is activated in the end of each period. It uses the values $P(e, s, t)$ and $P^+(e, s, t)$ for every link e incident to v. Some of these values are computed locally and some sent by the neighbors. The incoming packet-rate R_{in} is computed in line 2c, and is divided among the incoming links in line 2d. Excess packets in the queue $Q(v, s)$ are dropped so that the number of packets in $Q(v, s)$ is at most R_{in}. The rational is that, in the next period, at most R_{in} packets will be delivered, and hence, excess packets might as well be dropped.

We now elaborate on the boundary cases of the flow-control for a source a_s and a destination b_s of stream s. The destination b_s simply sends a fixed request for each incoming link $e \in E_{in}(b_s)$, i.e., $R(e, s) \leftarrow mf(e, s)$. The source a_s, does not execute line 2d; instead, it sets the packet-rate of the video encoder to R_{in}.

6   Experimental Results

In this section we summarize the main experimental results. An elaborated discussion of the experimental results appears in the full version.

6.1 Scenarios

We ran the experiments on two main types of arrangements of the nodes in the plane, a circle and a grid: (1) In the grid arrangement, we positioned 49 nodes in a $1km \times 1km$ square. The nodes are positioned in a 7×7 lattice, so that the horizontal and vertical distance between adjacent nodes is $1000/7 = 142$ meters. The source and destination of the streams in the grid arrangement are chosen randomly. (2) In the circle arrangement, we positioned 24 nodes on a circle of radius 500 meters. The nodes were positioned every $360/24$ degrees. The source and destination of the streams in the circle arrangement are chosen deterministically as follows: $a_1 = \lceil 24/k \rceil$, $b_i = (a_i + \lfloor 24/k \rfloor) \bmod 24$, $a_{i+1} = b_i$, where k denotes the number of streams.

We point out that random locations of 50 nodes in a square kilometer induces a communication graph with a high degree and a diameter of 2 or 3 [16]. In addition, the interference set of each link contains almost all the other links. Hence, this setting has a low capacity and is not an interesting setting for the problem we study.

The requests demand d_i^* is set to 10Mbps. Such a demand with $k \geq 6$ streams is above the capacity of the network. This enables us to study the performance in a congested setting.

6.2 Benchmarks

We ran the experiments using six algorithms. (1) MF-I-S. In the MF-I-S benchmark all three parts of our algorithm are used: computation of a multicommodity flow with interference constraints, the path-peeling scheduler, and the Flow-Control algorithm.

(2) SHORTP-S. A shortest path maximum bottleneck routing algorithm with the path-peeling scheduler. Let $pps(e)$ denote the number of packets-per-slot in the MCS used by the link e. Let $hops(p)$ denote the number of hops along a path p. We define a (lexicographic) order over paths from a_s to b_s as follows: $p \leq q$ if (1) $\min_{e \in p} pps(e) \geq \min_{e \in q} pps(e)$ or (2) $\min_{e \in p} pps(e) = \min_{e \in q} pps(e)$ and $hops(p) \leq hops(q)$. Formally, in SHORTP-S, the stream s is routed along a path p that is minimal in the lexicographic order.

In SHORTP-S, the paths are computed in an oblivious manner, namely, congestion does not play a role. This means that we must execute a flow control algorithm to adjust the data-rate.

Each stream in the SHORTP-S benchmark is assigned a random frequency channel. (3) The remaining algorithms are MF (only multi-commodity flow without interference constraints without a scheduler), MF-I (only multicommodity flow with interference constraints without a scheduler), MF-S (multi-commodity flow without interference constraints with a scheduler), SHORTP (shortest paths but without a scheduler). A detailed description appears in the full version. We point out that whenever the scheduler is not invoked, each node must have 3 WNICS. The reason is that a node does not know the frequencies of incoming packets.

We made the following change in the WiFi WNICs when there is a scheduler. The noise threshold for allowing a transmission of an RTS frame is reduced to match the interference distance. The reduced threshold relaxes the conservative collision avoidance to allow for simultaneous transmissions by links approved by the scheduler.

6.3 Results

Comparison between MF-I-S and SHORTP-S. We focus on two properties: min-throughput (i.e., the lowest throughput over all the streams) and the end-to-end delay.

Table 1. Comparison of steady state min-throughput between MF-I-S and SHORTP-S in the grid scenario. The number of requests is denoted by k.

k	MF-I-S's min Throughput Mbps	SHORTP-S's min Throughput Mbps	Ratio
8	0.576	0.45	1.28
12	0.448	0.325	1.3785
16	0.368	0.22	1.6727

Table 1 lists the effect of the number of requests k on the minimum throughputs of MF-I-S and SHORTP-S in the grid scenario. MF-I-S outperforms SHORTP-S by 28-67%.

Comparison with Greedy Scheduler. In Figure 1 we compare MF-I-S with the greedy scheduler and the path-peeling scheduler. The path peeling scheduler significantly reduces the end-to-end delay while slightly reducing the throughput. Note that the min-throughput is bigger with the path peeling scheduler (i.e., stream #8), hence, fairness is improved.

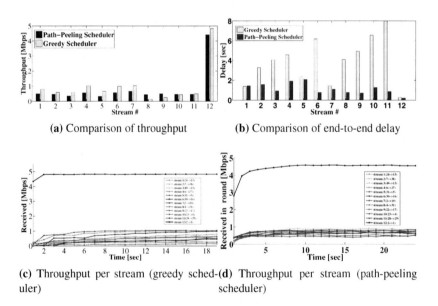

(a) Comparison of throughput

(b) Comparison of end-to-end delay

(c) Throughput per stream (greedy scheduler)

(d) Throughput per stream (path-peeling scheduler)

Fig. 1. Comparison of MF-I-S with the greedy scheduler and the path-peeling scheduler in the grid arrangement with $k = 12$ and $d_i^* = 10$Mbps. The experiment's duration is 25 seconds.

7   Conclusions

The algorithm consists of two parts: a multi-commodity flow computation and a scheduler. Our simulations demonstrate the robustness of the scheduler. Namely, the flows *mf* that are supported by the time-slotted frequency table A are successfully routed in the SINR-model. Thus, in our simulations the modified graph model results with SINR-feasible schedules.

The role of the multi-commodity flow computation with interference constraints is to maximize the minimum throughput. Indeed, in the grid scenario, routing along shortest paths resulted with smaller throughputs.

The flow control algorithm succeeds in stabilizing the queue lengths for all benchmarks that used the scheduler. Without the scheduler, stability was not obtained, and many packets were dropped.

Our results show that one can compute a routing and scheduling that succeeds in the SINR-model while using a simpler interference model. In addition, we successfully combined the various goals required to support video streaming.

8   Discussion

We propose a centralized algorithm for computing a routing, scheduling, and frequency assignment for real-time VS's in static ad-hoc wireless networks. The algorithm consists of two parts: a linear program and a scheduler. In addition, each node locally runs a flow-control algorithm to control the queues and stabilize data-rate along the links. Although the algorithm is centralized, it can be executed by multiple nodes in the network provided that they hold full information of the network (i.e., locations, requests). The output of the algorithm consists two tables that can be easily broadcast to all the nodes.

We implemented the algorithm and experimented using a setting that uses the physical model (with a 802.11g MAC) to verify the validity of the algorithm. Our experiments show that the traffic routed and scheduled by the algorithm is successfully delivered in two congested scenarios in the SINR-model.

We propose a scheduling algorithm, called the path peeling scheduler, that is designed to reduce the end-to-end delay incurred by the greedy scheduler. The path peeling scheduler succeeded in reducing the delay in streams with many hops. Even in a congested scenario, the path peeling scheduler successfully scheduled at least 70% of the flow.

Acknowledgments. We thank Nissim Halabi and Magnus M. Halldorsson for useful discussions. This work was supported in part by the Israeli Ministry of Industry and Trade under project MAGNET by the RESCUE Consortium.

References

1. Alicherry, M., Bhatia, R., Li, L.E.: Joint channel assignment and routing for throughput optimization in multi-radio wireless mesh networks. In: Proceedings of the 11th Annual International Conference on Mobile Computing and Networking, pp. 58–72. ACM (2005)

2. Awerbuch, B.: Optimal distributed algorithms for minimum weight spanning tree, counting, leader election, and related problems. In: Proceedings of the Nineteenth Annual ACM Symposium on Theory of Computing, pp. 230–240. ACM (1987)

3. Behzad, A., Rubin, I.: On the performance of graph-based scheduling algorithms for packet radio networks. In: IEEE Global Telecommunications Conference, GLOBECOM 2003, vol. 6, pp. 3432–3436. IEEE (2003)

4. Buragohain, C., Suri, S., Tóth, C.D., Zhou, Y.: Improved Throughput Bounds for Interference-Aware Routing in Wireless Networks. In: Lin, G. (ed.) COCOON 2007. LNCS, vol. 4598, pp. 210–221. Springer, Heidelberg (2007)

5. Chafekar, D., Kumart, V.S.A., Marathe, M.V., Parthasarathy, S., Srinivasan, A.: Approximation algorithms for computing capacity of wireless networks with SINR constraints. In: INFOCOM 2008. The 27th Conference on Computer Communications, IEEE, pp. 1166–1174. IEEE (2008)

6. Chafekar, D.R.: Capacity Characterization of Multi-Hop Wireless Networks-A Cross Layer Approach. PhD thesis, Virginia Polytechnic Institute and State University (2009)

7. Draves, R., Padhye, J., Zill, B.: Routing in multi-radio, multi-hop wireless mesh networks. In: Proceedings of the 10th Annual International Conference on Mobile Computing and Networking, pp. 114–128. ACM (2004)

8. Even, G., Matsri, Y., Medina, M.: Multi-hop Routing and Scheduling in Wireless Networks in the SINR Model. In: Erlebach, T., Nikoletseas, S., Orponen, P. (eds.) ALGOSENSORS 2011. LNCS, vol. 7111, pp. 202–214. Springer, Heidelberg (2012), http://arxiv.org/abs/1104.1330

9. Gallager, R.G.: Information theory and reliable communication. John Wiley & Sons, Inc., New York (1968)

10. Goussevskaia, O., Oswald, Y.A., Wattenhofer, R.: Complexity in geometric SINR. In: Proceedings of the 8th ACM International Symposium on Mobile Ad Hoc Networking and Computing, pp. 100–109. ACM (2007)

11. Gupta, P., Kumar, P.R.: The capacity of wireless networks. IEEE Transactions on Information Theory 46(2), 388–404 (2000)

12. Jain, K., Padhye, J., Padmanabhan, V.N., Qiu, L.: Impact of interference on multi-hop wireless network performance. Wireless Networks 11(4), 471–487 (2005)

13. Khan, S., Peng, Y., Steinbach, E., Sgroi, M., Kellerer, W.: Application-driven cross-layer optimization for video streaming over wireless networks. IEEE Communications Magazine 44(1), 122–130 (2006)

14. Kumar, V.S., Marathe, M.V., Parthasarathy, S., Srinivasan, A.: End-to-end packet-scheduling in wireless ad-hoc networks. In: Proceedings of the Fifteenth Annual ACM-SIAM Symposium on Discrete Algorithms, pp. 1021–1030. Society for Industrial and Applied Mathematics (2004)

15. Kumar, V.S., Marathe, M.V., Parthasarathy, S., Srinivasan, A.: Algorithmic aspects of capacity in wireless networks. In: Proceedings of the 2005 ACM SIGMETRICS International Conference on Measurement and Modeling of Computer Systems, pp. 133–144. ACM (2005)

16. Marina, M.K., Das, S.R., Subramanian, A.P.: A topology control approach for utilizing multiple channels in multi-radio wireless mesh networks. Computer Networks 54(2), 241–256 (2010)

17. Moscibroda, T., Wattenhofer, R., Weber, Y.: Protocol design beyond graph-based models. In: Hotnets (2006)

18. Moscibroda, T., Wattenhofer, R., Zollinger, A.: Topology control meets sinr: the scheduling complexity of arbitrary topologies. In: Proceedings of the 7th ACM International Symposium on Mobile Ad Hoc Networking and Computing, pp. 310–321. ACM (2006)

19. Setton, E., Yoo, T., Zhu, X., Goldsmith, A., Girod, B.: Cross-layer design of ad hoc networks for real-time video streaming. IEEE Wireless Communications 12(4), 59–65 (2005)
20. Shan, Y.: Cross-layer techniques for adaptive video streaming over wireless networks. EURASIP Journal on Applied Signal Processing 2005, 220–228 (2005)
21. van Der Schaar, M.: Cross-layer wireless multimedia transmission: challenges, principles, and new paradigms. IEEE Wireless Communications 12(4), 50–58 (2005)
22. Wan, P.J.: Multiflows in multihop wireless networks. In: Proceedings of the Tenth ACM International Symposium on Mobile Ad Hoc Networking and Computing, pp. 85–94. ACM (2009)

Multi-hop Routing and Scheduling in Wireless Networks in the SINR Model*

Guy Even, Yakov Matsri, and Moti Medina

School of Electrical Engineering, Tel-Aviv Univ., Tel-Aviv 69978, Israel
{eveng,yakovmat,medinamo}@post.tau.ac.il

Abstract. We present an algorithm for multi-hop routing and scheduling of requests in wireless networks in the SINR model. The goal of our algorithm is to maximize the throughput or maximize the minimum ratio between the flow and the demand.

Our algorithm partitions the links into buckets. Every bucket consists of a set of links that have nearly equivalent reception powers. We denote the number of nonempty buckets by σ. Our algorithm obtains an approximation ratio of $O(\sigma \cdot \log n)$, where n denotes the number of nodes. For the case of linear powers $\sigma = 1$, hence the approximation ratio of the algorithm is $O(\log n)$. This is the first practical approximation algorithm for linear powers with an approximation ratio that depends only on n (and not on the max-to-min distance ratio).

If the transmission power of each link is part of the input (and arbitrary), then $\sigma \leq \log \Gamma + \log \Delta$, where Γ denotes the ratio of the max-to-min power, and Δ denotes the ratio of the max-to-min distance. Hence, the approximation ratio is $O(\log n \cdot (\log \Gamma + \log \Delta))$.

Finally, we consider the case that the algorithm needs to assign powers to each link in a range $[P_{\min}, P_{\max}]$. An extension of the algorithm to this case achieves an approximation ratio of $O[(\log n + \log \log \Gamma) \cdot (\log \Gamma + \log \Delta)]$.

1 Introduction

In this paper we deal with the problem of maximizing throughput in a wireless network. Throughput is a major performance criterion in many applications, including: file transfer and video streaming. It has been acknowledged that efficient utilization of network resources require so called cross layered algorithms [LSS06]. This means that the algorithm deals with tasks that customarily belong to different layers of the network. These tasks include: routing, scheduling, management of queues in the nodes, congestion control, and flow control.

The problem we consider is formulated as follows. We are given a set V of n nodes in the plane. A link e is a pair (s_e, r_e) of nodes with a power assignment P_e. The node s_e is the transmitter and the node r_e is the receiver. In the SINR model, r_e receives a signal from s_e with power $S_e = P_e/d_e^\alpha$, where d_e is the distance between s_e, and r_e and α is the path loss exponent. The network is given a set of requests $\{R_i\}_{i=1}^k$. Each request is a 3-tuple $R_i = (\hat{s}_i, \hat{t}_i, b_i)$, where $\hat{s}_i \in V$ is the source, $\hat{t}_i \in V$ is

---

* The full version of this paper can be found in http://arxiv.org/abs/1104.1330

T. Erlebach et al. (Eds.): ALGOSENSORS 2011, LNCS 7111, pp. 202–214, 2012.

the destination, and b_i is the requested packet rate. The output is a multi-commodity flow $f = (f_1, \ldots, f_k)$ and an SINR-schedule $S = \{L_t\}_{t=0}^{T-1}$ that supports f. Each L_t is a subset of links that can transmit simultaneously (SINR-feasible). The goal is to maximize the total flow $|f| = \sum_{i=1}^{k} |f_i|$. We also consider a version that maximizes $\min_{i=1}^{k} |f_i|/b_i$. Let $\Delta \triangleq d_{\max}/d_{\min}$ is the ratio between the maximum and minimum length of a link, and $\Gamma \triangleq P_{\max}/P_{\min}$ the ratio between the maximum and minimum transmission power. For the case in which $\max_{e \neq e'} \frac{S_e}{S_{e'}} = O(1)$, the approximation ratio achieved by the algorithm is $O(\log n)$. For arbitrary powers and link lengths, the approximation ratio achieved by the algorithm is $O(\log n \cdot (\log \Gamma + \log \Delta))$.

Previous Work. Gupta and Kumar [GK00] studied the capacity of wireless networks in the SINR-model and the graph model for random instances in a square. The SINR-model for wireless networks was popularized in the algorithmic community by Moscibroda and Wattenhofer [MW06]. NP-Completeness for scheduling a set of links was proven by Goussevskaia [GOW07].

Algorithms for routing and scheduling in the SINR-model can be categorized by four main criteria: maximum capacity with one round vs. scheduling, multi-hop vs. single-hop, throughput maximization vs. latency minimization, and the choice of transmitter powers. In the single-hop setting, routing is not an issue, and the focus is on scheduling. If the objective is latency minimization, then each request is treated as a task, and the goal is to minimize the makespan.

The following problems are considered. (1) CAP-1SLOT: find a subset of maximum cardinality that is SINR-feasible. (2) LAT-1HOP: find a shortest SINR-schedule for a set of links. (3) LAT-PATHS: find a shortest SINR-schedule for a set of paths. (4) LAT-ROUTE: find a routing and a shortest SINR-schedule for a set of multi-hop requests. (5) THROUGHPUT-ROUTE: find a routing and maximum throughput SINR-schedule for a set of multi-hop requests. We briefly review some of the algorithmic results in this area published in the last three years.

Chafekar et al. [CKM+07] present an approximation algorithm for LAT-ROUTE. The approximation ratio is $O(\log n \cdot \log \Delta \cdot \log^2 \Gamma)$. Fanghänel et al. [FKV10] improved this result to $O(\log \Delta \cdot \log^2 n)$. Goussevskaia et al. [GWHW09] pointed out that $\log \Delta$ can be $\Omega(n)$, and presented the first approximation algorithm whose approximation ratio is always nontrivial. In fact, the approximation ratio obtained by Goussevskaia et al. [GWHW09] is $O(\log n)$ for the case LAT-1HOP with uniform power transmissions.

Halldorsson [Hal09] presented algorithms for LAT-1HOP with mean power assignments. He presented an $O(\log n \log \log \Delta)$-approximation and an $O(\log \Delta)$-online algorithm that uses mean power assignments with respect to OPT that can choose arbitrary power assignments (see also [Ton10]).

Halldorsson and Mitra [HM11a] presented an constant approximation algorithm for CAP-1SLOT problem with uniform, linear and mean power assignments. In addition, by using the mean power assignment, the algorithm obtains a $O(\log n + \log \log \Delta)$-approximation with respect to arbitrary power assignments

Kesselheim and Vöcking [KV10] give a distributed randomized algorithm for LAT-1HOP that obtains an $O(\log^2 n)$-approximation using uniform and linear powers. Halldorson and Mitra [HM11b] improve the analysis to achieve an $O(\log n)$-approximation.

Kesselheim [Kes11] presents approximation results in the SINR-model: an $O(1)$-approximation for CAP-1SLOT, an $O(\log n)$-approximation for LAT-1HOP, an $O(\log^2 n)$-approximation for LAT-PATHS and LAT-ROUTE. In [Kes11] there is no limitation on power assignment imposed neither on the solution nor on the optimal solution. In practice, power assignments are limited, especially for mobile users with limited power supply.

The most relevant work to our result is by Chafekar et al. [CKM$^+$08] who presented approximation algorithms for THROUGHPUT-ROUTE. They present the following results, an $O(\log \Delta)$-approximation for uniform power assignment and linear power assignment, and an $O(\log \Gamma \cdot \log \Delta)$ for arbitrary power assignments.

For linear powers, Wan et al. [WFJ$^+$11] obtain a $O(\log n)$-approximation for THROUGHPUT-ROUTE. The algorithm is based on a reduction to the single-slot problem using the ellipsoid method. In [Wan09], Wan writes that "this algorithm is of theoretical interest only, but practically quite infeasible." For the case that the algorithm assigns powers from a limited range, Wan et al. [WFJ$^+$11] achieve an $O(\log n \cdot \log \Gamma)$-approximation ratio.

Our Result. We present an algorithm for THROUGHPUT-ROUTE. Our algorithm partitions the links into buckets. Every bucket consists of a set of links that have nearly equivalent reception powers. We denote the number of nonempty buckets (also called the signal diversity of the links) by σ. Our algorithm obtains an approximation ratio of $O(\sigma \cdot \log n)$, where n denotes the number of nodes.

For the case of linear power assignment the signal diversity is $\sigma = 1$, hence the approximation ratio of the algorithm is $O(\log n)$. This is the first practical approximation algorithm for linear powers that obtains an approximation ratio that depends only on n (and not on ratio of the max-to-min distance). This improves the $O(\log \Delta)$-approximation of Chafekar et al. [CKM$^+$08] for linear power assignment. As pointed out in [GWHW09], $\log \Delta$ can be $\Omega(n)$. The linear power assignment model makes a lot of sense since it implies that, in absence of interferences, transmission powers are adjusted so that the reception powers are uniform.

In the case of arbitrary given powers, the signal diversity is $\sigma \leq \log \Gamma + \log \Delta$. Hence, the approximation ratio is $O(\log n \cdot (\log \Gamma + \log \Delta))$. For arbitrary power assignments Chafekar et al. [CKM$^+$08] presented approximation algorithm that achieves approximation ratio of $O(\log \Gamma \cdot \log \Delta)$. In this case, the approximation ratio of our algorithm is not comparable with the algorithm presented by Chafekar et al. [CKM$^+$08] (i.e., in some cases it is smaller, in other cases it is larger).

For the case of limited powers where the algorithm needs to assign powers between $P_{\min}$ and $P_{\max}$, we give a $O[(\log n + \log \log \Gamma) \cdot (\log \Gamma + \log \Delta)]$-approximation algorithm.

Our results apply both for maximizing the total throughput and for maximizing the minimum fraction of supplied demand. Other fairness criteria apply as well (see also [Cha09]).

Techniques. Similarly to [CKM$^+$08] our algorithm is based on linear programming relaxation and greedy coloring. The linear programming relaxation determines the routing and the flow along each route. Greedy coloring induces a schedule in which, in every slot, every link is SINR-feasible with respect to longer links in the same slot.

We propose a new method of classifying the links. In [CKM+08, Hal09] the links are classified by lengths and by transmitted powers. On the other hand, we classify the links by their *received power*.

We present a new linear programming formulation for throughput maximization in the SINR-model. This formulation uses novel symmetric interference constraints, for every link e, that bound the interference incurred by other links in the same bucket as well as the interference that e incurs to other links. We show that this formulation is a relaxation due to our link classification method.

We then apply a greedy coloring procedure for rounding the LP solution. This method follows [ABL05, CKM+08, Wan09] and others (the greedy coloring is described in Section 6.3).

The schedule induced by the greedy coloring is not SINR-feasible. Hence, we propose a refinement technique that produces an SINR-feasible schedule. We refine each color class using a bin packing procedure that is based on the symmetry of the interference coefficients in the LP. We believe this method is of independent interest since it mitigates the problem of bounding the interference created by shorter links.

Organization. In Sec. 2 we present the definitions and notation. The throughput maximization problem is defined in Sec. 3. In Sec. 4, we present necessary conditions for SINR-feasibility for links that are in the same bucket. The results in Sec. 4 are used for proving that the linear programming formulation presented in Sec. 5 is indeed a relaxation of the throughput maximization problem. The algorithm for linear powers is presented in Sec. 6 and analyzed in Sec. 7. In Sections 8-9 we extend the algorithm so that it handles arbitrary powers.

2   Preliminaries

We briefly review definitions used in the literature for algorithms in the SINR model (see [HW09, CKM+08]).

We consider a wireless network that consists of a set V of n nodes in the plane. Each node is equipped with a transmitter and a receiver. We denote the distance between nodes u and v by d_{uv}.

A *link* is a 3-tuple $e = (s_e, r_e, P_e)$, where $s_e \in V$ is the transmitter, $r_e \in V$ is the receiver, and P_e is the transmission power. In the general setting we allow parallel links with different powers. The set of links is denoted by $\mathcal{L}$ and $m \triangleq |\mathcal{L}|$. We abbreviate and denote the distance $d_{s_e r_e}$ by d_e. Similarly, we denote the distance $d_{s_e r_{e'}}$ by $d_{ee'}$. Note that according to this notation, $d_{ee'} \neq d_{e'e}$.

We use the following radio propagation model. A transmission from point s with power P is received at point r with power P/d_{sr}^{α}. The exponent α is called the *path loss exponent* and is a constant. In most practical situations, $2 \leq \alpha \leq 6$; our algorithm works for any constant $\alpha \geq 0$. For links e, e', we use the following notation: $S_e \triangleq P_e/d_e^{\alpha}$ and $S_{e'e} \triangleq P_{e'}/d_{e'e}^{\alpha}$.

A subset of links $L \subseteq \mathcal{L}$ is SINR-feasible if $S_e/(N + \sum_{e' \in L - \{e\}} S_{e'e}) \geq \beta$, for every $e \in L$. This ratio is called the *signal-to-noise-interference ratio* (SINR), where the constant N is positive and models the noise in the system. The threshold β is a positive constant. The ratio S_e/N is called the *signal-to-noise ratio* (SNR).

A link e can tolerate an accumulated interference $\sum_{e'} S_{e'e}$ that is at most $(S_e - \beta N)/\beta$. This amount can be considered to be the "interference budget" of e. Let $\gamma_e \triangleq (\beta S_e)/(S_e - \beta N)$. We define three measures of how much of the interference budget is "consumed" by a link e'. $\hat{a}_{e'}(e) \triangleq \frac{S_{e'e}}{S_e}$, $a_{e'}(e) \triangleq \gamma_e \cdot \hat{a}_{e'}(e)$, and $\bar{a}_{e'}(e) \triangleq \min\{1, a_{e'}(e)\}$. The value of $a_{e'}(e)$ is called the *affectance* [HW09] of the link e' on the link e. The affectance is additive, so for a set $L \subseteq \mathcal{L}$, let $a_L(e) \triangleq \sum_{\{e' \in L : e' \neq e\}} a_{e'}(e)$.

Proposition 1 ([HW09]). *A set $L \subseteq \mathcal{L}$ is SINR-feasible iff $a_L(e) \leq 1$, for every $e \in L$.*

Following [HW09], we define a set $L \subseteq \mathcal{L}$ to be a p-signal, if $a_L(e) \leq 1/p$, for every $e \in L$. Note that L is SINR-feasible iff L is a 1-signal. We also define a set $L \subseteq \mathcal{L}$ to be a $\bar{p}$-signal, if $\bar{a}_L(e) \leq 1/p$, for every $e \in L$. Note that L is SINR-feasible iff L is a $(1 + \varepsilon)$-signal for some $\varepsilon > 0$.

By Shannon's theorem on the capacity of a link in an additive white Gaussian noise channel [Gal68], it follows that the capacity is a function of the SINR. Since we use the same threshold β for all the links, it follows that the Shannon capacity of a link is either zero (if the SINR is less than β) or a value determined by β (if the SINR is at least β). We set the length of a time slot and a packet length so that, if interferences are not too large, each link can deliver one packet in one time slot. By setting a unit of flow to equal a packet-per-time-slot, all links have unit capacities. We do not assume that $\beta \geq 1$; in fact, in communications systems β may be smaller than one.

Multi-Commodity Flows. Recall that a function $g : \mathcal{L} \to \mathbb{R}^{\geq 0}$ is a flow from s to t, where $s, t \in V$, if it satisfies capacity constraints (i.e., $g(e) \leq 1$, for every $e \in \mathcal{L}$) and flow conservation constraints in every vertex $v \in V \setminus \{s, t\}$ (i.e., $\sum_{e \in \text{in}(v)} f(e) = \sum_{e \in \text{out}(v)} f(e)$).

We use multi-commodity flows to model multi-hop traffic in a network. The network consists of the nodes V and the arcs $\mathcal{L}$, where each arc has a unit capacity. There are k commodities $R_i = (\hat{s}_i, \hat{t}_i, b_i)$, where $\hat{s}_i$ and $\hat{t}_i$ are the *source* and *sink*, and b_i is the *demand* of the ith commodity. Consider a vector $f = (f_1, \ldots, f_k)$, where each f_i is a flow from $\hat{s}_i$ to $\hat{t}_i$. We use the following notation: (i) $f_i(e)$ denotes the flow of the ith flow along e, (ii) $|f_i|$ equals the amount of flow shipped from $\hat{s}_i$ to $\hat{t}_i$, (iii) $f(e) \triangleq \sum_{i=1}^{k} f_i(e)$, (iv) $|f| \triangleq \sum_{i=1}^{k} |f_i|$. A vector $f = (f_1, \ldots, f_k)$ is a multi-commodity flow if $f(e) \leq 1$, for every $e \in \mathcal{L}$.

We denote by $\mathcal{F}$ the polytope of all multi-commodity flows $f = (f_1, \ldots, f_k)$ such that $|f_i| \leq b_i$, for every i. For a $\rho > 0$, we denote by $\mathcal{F}_\rho \subseteq \mathcal{F}$ the polytope of all multi-commodity flows such that $|f_i|/b_i \geq \rho$.

Schedules and Multi-Commodity Flows. We use periodic schedules to support a multi-commodity flow using packet routing as follows. We refer to a sequence $\{L_t\}_{t=0}^{T-1}$, where $L_t \subseteq \mathcal{L}$ for each i, as a *schedule*. A schedule is used periodically to determine which links are active in each time slot. Namely, time is partitioned into disjoint equal time slots. In time slot t', the links in L_t, for $t = t' \pmod{T}$ are *active*, namely, they transmit. Each active link transmits one packet of fixed length in a time slot (recall that all links have the same unit capacity). The number of time slots T is called the *period* of the schedule. We sometimes represent a schedule $S = \{L_t\}_{t=0}^{T-1}$ by a multi-coloring $\pi : \mathcal{L} \to 2^{\{0, \ldots, T-1\}}$. The set L_t simply equals the preimage of t, namely, $L_t = \pi^{-1}(t)$, where $\pi^{-1}(t) \triangleq \{e : t \in \pi(e)\}$.

An SINR-*schedule* is a sequence $\{L_t\}_{t=0}^{T-1}$ such that L_t is SINR-feasible for every t. Consider a multi-commodity flow $f = (f_1, \ldots, f_k)$ and a schedule $S = \{L_t\}_{t=0}^{T-1}$. We say that the schedule S *supports* f if $\forall e \in \mathcal{L}$: $T \cdot f(e) \leq |\{t \in \{0, \ldots, T-1\} : e \in L_t\}|$.

The motivation for this definition is as follows. Consider a store-and-forward packet routing network that schedules links according to the schedule S. This network can deliver packets along each link e at an average rate of $f(e)$ packets-per-time-slot.

Buckets and Signal Diversity. We partition the links into buckets by their received power S_e. Let $S_{\min} \triangleq \min_{e \in \mathcal{L}} S_e$. The ith bucket B_i is defined by
$B_i \triangleq \{e \in \mathcal{L} \mid 2^i \cdot S_{\min} \leq S_e < 2^{i+1} \cdot S_{\min}\}$. For a link $e \in \mathcal{L}$, define $i(e) \triangleq \lfloor \log_2(S_e/S_{\min}) \rfloor$. Then, $e \in B_{i(e)}$. The *signal diversity* σ of $\mathcal{L}$ is the number of nonempty buckets.

Lemma 1. $\sigma \leq \log_2 \Delta + \log_2 \Gamma$.

Power Assignments. In the *uniform power assignment*, all links transmit with the same power, namely, $P_e = P_{e'}$ for every two links e and e'. In the *linear power assignment*, all links receive with the same power, namely, $S_e = S_{e'}$ for every two links e and e'.

Assumption on SNR. Our analysis requires that, for every link e, $S_e/N \geq (1 + \varepsilon) \cdot \beta$, for a constant $\varepsilon > 0$. Note that if $S_e/N = \beta$, then the link cannot tolerate any interference at all, and $\gamma_e = \infty$. Our assumption implies that $\gamma_e \leq (1 + \varepsilon) \cdot \beta/\varepsilon$. This assumption can be obtained by increasing the transmission power of links whose SNR almost equals β. Namely, if $S_e/N \approx \beta$, then $P_e \leftarrow (1 + \varepsilon) \cdot P_e$. A similar assumption is used in [CKM$^+$08], where it is stated in terms of a bi-criteria algorithm. Namely, the algorithm uses transmission powers that are greater by a factor of $(1 + \varepsilon)$ compared to the transmission power of the optimal solution.

Assumption 1. *For every link* $e \in \mathcal{L}$, $S_e/N \geq (1 + \varepsilon) \cdot \beta$.

Proposition 2. *Under Assumption 1,* $\beta < \gamma_e \leq (1 + \varepsilon) \cdot \beta/\varepsilon$.

3   Problem Definition

The problem MAX THROUGHPUT is formulated as follows. The input consists of: (i) A set of nodes V in $\mathbb{R}^2$ (ii) A set of links $\mathcal{L}$. The capacity of each link equals one packet per time-slot. (iii) A set of requests $\{R_i\}_{i=1}^k$. Each request is a 3-tuple $R_i = (\hat{s}_i, \hat{t}_i, b_i)$, where $\hat{s}_i \in V$ is the source, $\hat{t}_i \in V$ is the destination, and b_i is the requested packet rate. We assume that every request can be routed, namely, there is a path from $\hat{s}_i$ to $\hat{t}_i$, for every $i \in [1..k]$. Since the links have unit capacities, we assume that the requested packet rate satisfies $b_i \leq n$. The output is a multi-commodity flow $f = (f_1, \ldots, f_k) \in \mathcal{F}$ and an SINR-schedule $S = \{L_t\}_{t=0}^{T-1}$ that supports f. The goal is to maximize the total flow $|f|$.

The MAX-MIN THROUGHPUT problem has the same input and output. The goal, however, is to maximize ρ, such that $f \in \mathcal{F}_\rho$. Namely, maximize $\min_{i=1\ldots k} |f_i|/b_i$.

4   Necessary Conditions: SINR-Feasibility for Links in the Same Bucket

In this section we formalize necessary conditions so that a set of links in the same bucket is SINR-feasible. In Section 5 we use these conditions to build a LP-relaxation for the problem.

We begin by expressing $\hat{a}_{e_1}(e_2)$ in terms of the distances $d_{e_1}, d_{e_2}, d_{e_1 e_2}$. Note that $\hat{a}_{e_1}(e_2)$, with respect to links that are in the same bucket, depends solely on d_{e_1} and $d_{e_1 e_2}$. On the other hand, $\hat{a}_{e_1}(e_2)$, with respect to the uniform power model, depends solely on d_{e_2} and $d_{e_1 e_2}$.

Proposition 3.

$$\forall i \ \forall e_1, e_2 \in B_i : \ \frac{1}{2} \cdot \left(\frac{d_{e_1}}{d_{e_1 e_2}} \right)^\alpha < \hat{a}_{e_1}(e_2) < 2 \cdot \left(\frac{d_{e_1}}{d_{e_1 e_2}} \right)^\alpha ,$$

$$\forall e_1, e_2 \in \mathcal{L} : \ \hat{a}_{e_1}(e_2) = \left(\frac{d_{e_2}}{d_{e_1 e_2}} \right)^\alpha \ \text{in the uniform power model.}$$

Throughout this section we assume the following. Let $L \subseteq \mathcal{L}$ denote an SINR-feasible set of links such that all the links in L belong to same bucket B_i. Let $e \in B_i$ denote an arbitrary link (not necessarily in L).

Notation. Define: $L^\ell \triangleq \{e' \in L : d_{e'} \le d_{e'e}\}$, and $L^g \triangleq \{e' \in L : d_{e'} > d_{e'e}\}$.

4.1   A Geometric Lemma

The following lemma claims that for every $e \in B_i$ (not necessarily in L), there exits a set of at most six "guards" that "protect" e from interferences by transmitters in L^ℓ.

Lemma 2. *There exists a set G of at most six receivers of links in L^ℓ such that*

$$\forall e' \in L^\ell \ \exists g \in G : d_{e'g} \le 2 \cdot d_{e'e}.$$

4.2   Necessary Conditions

Recall that Let $L \subseteq \mathcal{L}$ is an SINR-feasible set of links that belong to same bucket B_i. Let $e \in B_i$ denote an arbitrary link (not necessarily in L).

Lemma 3. $\sum_{e' \in L^\ell} \bar{a}_{e'}(e) = O(1)$.

Lemma 4. $\sum_{e' \in L^g} \bar{a}_{e'}(e) = O(1)$.

Lemmas 3 and 4 imply the following theorem.

Theorem 1. *Let L denote an SINR-feasible set of links. If $L \subseteq B_i$, then $\forall e \in B_i$:* $\sum_{\{e' \in L : d_{e'} \ge d_e\}} \bar{a}_{e'}(e) \le \bar{a}_L(e) + \bar{a}_e(e) = O(1)$.

The following theorem follows from [Kes11, Thm 1].

Theorem 2. *Let L denote an SINR-feasible set of links. If $L \subseteq B_i$, then $\forall e \in B_i$:* $\sum_{\{e' \in L : d_{e'} \ge d_e\}} \bar{a}_e(e') = O(1)$.

5   LP Relaxation

In this section we formulate the linear program for the MAX THROUGHPUT and
MAX-MIN THROUGHPUT problems with arbitrary power assignments. The linear program formulation that we use for computing the multi-commodity flow f is as follows.

$\text{MAXTH}_{LP} : F^* = \text{maximize } |f| \text{ subject to}$

$$f \in \mathcal{F} \tag{1}$$

$$\forall i \ \forall e \in B_i \quad f(e) + \sum_{\{e' \in B_i : d_{e'} \geq d_e\}} (\bar{a}_{e'}(e) + \bar{a}_e(e')) \cdot f(e') \leq 1 \tag{2}$$

$\text{MAXMINTH}_{LP} : R^* = \text{maximize } \rho \text{ subject to}$

$$f \in \mathcal{F}_\rho \tag{3}$$

$$\forall i \ \forall e \in B_i \quad f(e) + \sum_{\{e' \in B_i : d_{e'} \geq d_e\}} (\bar{a}_{e'}(e) + \bar{a}_e(e')) \cdot f(e') \leq 1 \tag{4}$$

Recall that $\mathcal{F}$ denotes the polytope of all multi-commodity flows $f = (f_1, \ldots, f_k)$ such
that $|f_i| \leq b_i$, for every i. Also recall that $\mathcal{F}_\rho \subseteq \mathcal{F}$ for $\rho > 0$ denotes the polytope of
all multi-commodity flows such that $|f_i|/b_i \geq \rho$. Constraints 1, 3 in MAXTH$_{LP}$ and
MAXMINTH$_{LP}$ respectively require that the f is a feasible multi-commodity flow with
respect to $\mathcal{F}$ and $\mathcal{F}_\rho$.

Constraints 2, 4 in MAXTH$_{LP}$ and MAXMINTH$_{LP}$ respectively require that for
every bucket B_i and for every link $e \in B_i$ the amount of flow $f(e)$ plus the amount
of the weighted symmetric interferences is bounded by one. Note that this symmetric
interference constraint is with respect to links that are longer than e.

The objective function of MAXTH$_{LP}$ is to maximize the total flow $|f|$. The objective
function of MAXMINTH$_{LP}$ is to maximize ρ, such that $f \in \mathcal{F}_\rho$. Namely, maximize
$\min_{i=1\ldots k} |f_i|/b_i$.

We prove on Section 7 that the linear programs MAXTH$_{LP}$ and MAXMINTH$_{LP}$ are
relaxations of the MAX THROUGHPUT and MAX-MIN THROUGHPUT problems.

6   Algorithm

6.1   Algorithm Description

For simplicity, we assume in this section that all the links are in the same bucket, that is
$\mathcal{L} \subseteq B_i$ for some i. In Section 8 we show how to handle arbitrary power assignment.

Algorithm Overview. We overview the algorithm for the MAX THROUGHPUT problem.
Assume for simplicity that, $\mathcal{L} \subseteq B_i$ for some i. First, the optimal flow f^* is obtained
by solving the linear program MAXTH$_{LP}$. We need to find an SINR-feasible schedule
that supports a fraction of f^*. Second, we color the links using greedy multi-coloring.
This coloring induces a preliminary schedule, in which every color class is "almost"

SINR-feasible. This preliminary schedule is almost SINR-feasible since in every color class and every link e, the affectance of links that are longer than e on e is at most 1. However, the affectance of shorter links on e may be still unbounded. Finally, we refine this schedule in order to obtain an SINR-feasible schedule. Note that the returned SINR-feasible schedule supports a fraction of the flow f^*. We show in Section 7 that this fraction is at least $\Omega(1/\log n)$.

Algorithm Description. The algorithm for the MAX THROUGHPUT problem proceeds as follows.

1. Solve the linear program MAXTH$_{LP}$. Let f^* denote the optimal solution.
2. Remove flow paths that traverse edges with $f^*(e) < 1/(2nm)$. Let $\hat{f}$ denote the remaining flow.
3. Set $T = 2nm$. Apply the greedy multi-coloring algorithm *greedy-coloring* (see Section 6.3) on the input $((\mathcal{L}, \mathcal{L}^2), \hat{f}, d, w, T)$, where the pair $(\mathcal{L}, \mathcal{L}^2)$ is a complete graph whose set of vertices is $\mathcal{L}$, for every link in $e \in \mathcal{L}$, $d(e) = d_e$, and $w(e, e') \triangleq \bar{a}_e(e') + \bar{a}_{e'}(e)$ is a weight function over pair of links in $\mathcal{L}$. Let $\pi : \mathcal{L} \to 2^{\{0, \dots T-1\}}$ denote the computed multi-coloring.
4. Apply procedure *disperse* to each color class $(\pi^{-1}(t))$, where $t \in \{0, \dots T - 1\}$. Let $\{L_{t,i}\}_{i=1}^{\ell(t)}$ denote the dispersed subsets.
5. Return the schedule $\{L_{t,i}\}_{t=0..T-1, i=1..\ell(t)}$ and the flow $f = (f_1, \dots, f_k)$, where $f = f^*/(2 \cdot \ell(t))$.

Clearly steps 1 and 5 are polynomial. In Section 6.3 we show that step 3 is polynomial. In Section 6.4 we show that *disperse* is polynomial. Therefore, the running time of the algorithm is polynomial.

Remark 1. *The following changes are needed in order to obtain an algorithm for the* MAX-MIN THROUGHPUT *problem: (i) In Item 1 solve the linear program* MAXMINTH$_{LP}$, *(ii) In Item 3 set* $T = 2n^2 km$.

6.2 Removing Minuscule Flow Paths

The greedy multi-coloring algorithm cannot support flows $f^*(e) < 1/(2nm)$. We mitigate this problem simply by peeling off flow paths that traverse edges with a flow smaller than $1/(2nm)$. The formal description of this procedure is as follows. (1) Initialize $\hat{f} \leftarrow f$. (2) While there exists an edge e with $\hat{f}(e) < 1/(2nm)$, remove flow from $\hat{f}$ until $\hat{f}(e) = 0$. This is done by computing flow paths for the flow that traverses e, and zeroing the flow along these paths.

6.3 Greedy Multi-coloring

Let $G = (V, E)$ denote an undirected graph with edge weights $w : E \to [0, 1]$ and node demands $x : V \to [0, 1]$. Assume an ordering of the nodes induced by distinct node lengths $d(v)$. For a set $V' \subset V$, let $w(V', u) \triangleq \sum_{v \in V'} w(v, u)$. Assume that

$$\forall u \in V : x(u) + \sum_{\{v \in V : d(v) > d(u)\}} w(v, u) \cdot x(v) \le 1. \tag{5}$$

Indeed, Constraints 2, 4 in MAXTH$_{LP}$ and MAXMINTH$_{LP}$, respectively, imply that the input to the greedy coloring algorithm satisfies the assumption in Equation 5.

Lemma 5 (Greedy Coloring Lemma). *For every integer* T, *there is multi-coloring* $\pi : V \rightarrow 2^{\{0,\dots,T-1\}}$, *such that*

1. $\forall c \in \{0, \dots, T-1\} \forall u \in \pi^{-1}(c) : \sum_{\{v \in V : d(v) > d(u)\}} w(v, u) \leq 1$,
2. $\forall u \in V : |\pi(u)| \geq \lfloor x(u) \cdot T \rfloor$.

The required multi-coloring is found by applying a "first-fit" greedy multi-coloring described in the full version.

6.4   The Dispersion Procedure *disperse*

The input to the dispersion procedure *disperse* consists of a set $L \subseteq \mathcal{L}$ of links that are assigned the same color by the multi-coloring procedure (see Section 6.3). This implies that

$$\forall e \in L : \sum_{\{e' \in L \setminus \{e\} : d_{e'} \geq d_e\}} (\bar{a}_e(e') + \bar{a}_{e'}(e)) \leq 1. \tag{6}$$

The dispersion procedure works in two phases. In the first phase, called Algorithm $\frac{1}{3}$-*disperse*(L) (described in the full version), L is partitioned into $\overline{1/3}$-signal sets $\{L_i\}_i$. Algorithm $\frac{1}{3}$-*disperse*(L) disperses L into at most $\log_2 |L|$ subsets. In the second phase, each subset L_i is further partitioned into $\overline{7/6}$-signal sets $\{L_i\}_{i=1}^{\ell(t)}$. Recall that a set of links L_i is SINR-feasible iff L_i is a $\overline{(1+\varepsilon)}$-signal for some $\varepsilon > 0$. Since every set in $\{L_i\}_{i=1}^{\ell(t)}$ is $\overline{(7/6)}$-signal, it follows that every set in $\{L_i\}_{i=1}^{\ell(t)}$ is SINR-feasible.

The second phase follows [HW09, Thm 1]. This phase is implemented by two first-fit bin packing procedures. In the first procedure, open 7 bins, scan the links in some order and assign each link to the first bin in which its affectance is at most $3/7$. In the second procedure, partition each bin into 7 sub-bins. Scan the links in the reverse order, and again, assign each link to the first bin in which its affectance is at most $3/7$.

7   Algorithm Analysis

In this section we analyze the algorithm presented in Section 6. Recall that it is assumed that all the links are in the same bucket, that is $\mathcal{L} \subseteq B_i$ for some i. First, we prove that the LP is a fractional relaxation of problem. We then show that the greedy coloring computes a schedule that supports the flow given by the LP. Unfortunately, this schedule is not a SINR-feasible schedule. We then prove that the refinement procedure (Step 3 of the algorithm) generates an SINR-feasible schedule with an $O(\log n)$ increase in the approximation ratio.

Let f^* denote an optimal solution of the linear program MAXTH$_{LP}$, i.e., $F^* = |f^*|$. The following lemma shows that the linear program MAXTH$_{LP}$ is a relaxation of the MAX THROUGHPUT problem.

Lemma 6. *There exists a constant* $\lambda \geq 1$ *such that, if* $S = \{L_t\}_{t=0}^{T-1}$ *is an SINR-feasible schedule that supports a multi-commodity flow* f, *then* f/λ *is a feasible solution of the linear program* MAXTH$_{LP}$. *Hence,* $F^* \geq |f|/\lambda$.

Analogously, one could prove also that the linear program MAXMINTH$_{LP}$ is a relaxation of the MAX-MIN THROUGHPUT problem.

Lemma 7. *Suppose* $S = \{L_t\}_{t=0}^{T-1}$ *is an SINR-feasible schedule that supports a multi-commodity flow* f. *If* $\rho \triangleq \min_i |f_i|$, $R^* \geq \rho/\lambda$, *for the same constant* $\lambda \geq 1$ *in Lemma 6.*

The following proposition gives a lower bound on the optimal throughput.

Proposition 4. $F^* \geq \frac{1}{n}$ *and* $R^* \geq \frac{1}{n^2 k}$.

Proposition 5. $|\hat{f}| \geq |f^*/2|$

Proposition 6. *If* $T \geq 2nm$, *then the greedy multi-coloring algorithm computes a multi-coloring* π *that induces a schedule that supports* $\hat{f}/2$.

For the case of MAXMINTH$_{LP}$, one can show the same result if $T \geq 2n^2 km$.

Lemma 8. *If* $L \subseteq \mathcal{L}$ *satisfies Eq. 6, then there exists a subset* $J \subseteq L$ *such that: (i)* J *is a* $\overline{1/3}$-*signal, and (ii)* $|J| \geq |L|/2$.

Proposition 7. *The dispersion procedure partitions every color class* $\pi^{-1}(t)$ *into* $O(\log m)$ *SINR-feasible sets.*

Theorem 3. *If Assumption 1 holds, and all the links are in the same bucket, then there exists an* $O(\log n)$-*approximation algorithm for the* MAX THROUGHPUT *and the* MAX-MIN THROUGHPUT *problems.*

Since in the linear power assignment all links receive with same power, all the links are in the same bucket. We conclude with the following result for the linear power assignment.

Corollary 4. *If Assumption 1 holds, then there exists an* $O(\log n)$-*approximation algorithm for the* MAX THROUGHPUT *and the* MAX-MIN THROUGHPUT *problems in the linear power assignment.*

8   Given Arbitrary Transmission Powers

In this section we show how to apply the algorithm presented in Section 6 to the case in which transmission power P_e of each link e is part of the input. Note that P_e may be arbitrary.

Theorem 5. *If Assumption 1 holds, then there exists an* $O(\log n \cdot (\log \Delta + \log \Gamma))$-*approximation algorithm for the* MAX THROUGHPUT *and the* MAX-MIN THROUGHPUT *problems when the link transmission powers are part of the input.*

9 Limited Powers

In this section we consider the case in which the algorithm needs to assign a power P_e to each link. The assigned powers must satisfy $P_{\min} \leq P_e \leq P_{\max}$. To simplify the description, assume that $\log_2(P_{\max}/P_{\min})$ is an integer, denoted by k.

We reduce this problem to the case of given arbitrary powers as follows. For each pair of nodes (u, v), define $k + 1$ parallel links, where the transmission power of the ith copy equals $2^i \cdot P_{\min}$.

Theorem 6. *Assume that, for every link e, $(P_{\max}/d_e^{\alpha})/N \geq (1 + \varepsilon) \cdot \beta$. Then, there exists an $O((\log n + \log \log \Gamma) \cdot (\log \Delta + \log \Gamma))$-approximation algorithm for the* MAX THROUGHPUT *and the* MAX-MIN THROUGHPUT *problems when the link transmission powers are in the range $[P_{\min}, P_{\max}]$.*

Acknowledgments. We thank Nissim Halabi and Moni Shahar for useful conversations. This project was partially funded by the Israeli ministry of Science and Technology.

References

[ABL05]   Alicherry, M., Bhatia, R., Li, L.E.: Joint channel assignment and routing for throughput optimization in multi-radio wireless mesh networks. In: MobiCom, pp. 58–72. ACM (2005)

[Cha09]   Chafekar, D.R.: Capacity Characterization of Multi-Hop Wireless Networks-A Cross Layer Approach. PhD thesis, Virginia Polytechnic Institute and State University (2009)

[CKM+07]   Chafekar, D., Kumar, V.S., Marathe, M.V., Parthasarathy, S., Srinivasan, A.: Cross-layer latency minimization in wireless networks with SINR constraints. In: MobiHoc, pp. 110–119. ACM (2007)

[CKM+08]   Chafekar, D., Kumart, V.S.A., Marathe, M.V., Parthasarathy, S., Srinivasan, A.: Approximation algorithms for computing capacity of wireless networks with SINR constraints. In: INFOCOM 2008, pp. 1166–1174 (2008)

[FKV10]   Fanghänel, A., Kesselheim, T., Vöcking, B.: Improved algorithms for latency minimization in wireless networks. Theoretical Computer Science (2010)

[Gal68]   Gallager, R.G.: Information theory and reliable communication. John Wiley & Sons, Inc., New York (1968)

[GK00]   Gupta, P., Kumar, P.R.: The capacity of wireless networks. IEEE Transactions on Information Theory 46(2), 388–404 (2000)

[GOW07]   Goussevskaia, O., Oswald, Y.A., Wattenhofer, R.: Complexity in geometric SINR. In: MobiHoc, pp. 100–109. ACM (2007)

[GWHW09]   Goussevskaia, O., Wattenhofer, R., Halldórsson, M., Welzl, E.: Capacity of arbitrary wireless networks. In: INFOCOM 2009, pp. 1872–1880 (2009)

[Hal09]   Halldórsson, M.: Wireless Scheduling with Power Control. In: Fiat, A., Sanders, P. (eds.) ESA 2009. LNCS, vol. 5757, pp. 361–372. Springer, Heidelberg (2009)

[HM11a]   Halldórsson, M., Mitra, P.: Wireless Capacity with Oblivious Power in General Metrics. In: SODA (2011)

[HM11b]   Halldorsson, M.M., Mitra, P.: Nearly optimal bounds for distributed wireless scheduling in the sinr model. Arxiv preprint arXiv:1104.5200 (2011)

[HW09]   Halldórsson, M.M., Wattenhofer, R.: Wireless Communication is in APX. In: Albers, S., Marchetti-Spaccamela, A., Matias, Y., Nikoletseas, S., Thomas, W. (eds.) ICALP 2009. LNCS, vol. 5555, pp. 525–536. Springer, Heidelberg (2009)

[Kes11]   Kesselheim, T.: A constant-factor approximation for wireless capacity maximization with power control in the SINR model. In: Proceedings of the 22nd ACM-SIAM Symposium on Discrete Algorithms, SODA (2011)

[KV10]   Kesselheim, T., Vöcking, B.: Distributed contention resolution in wireless networks. Distributed Computing, 163–178 (2010)

[LSS06]   Lin, X., Shroff, N.B., Srikant, R.: A tutorial on cross-layer optimization in wireless networks. IEEE Journal on Selected Areas in Communications 24(8), 1452–1463 (2006)

[MW06]   Moscibroda, T., Wattenhofer, R.: The complexity of connectivity in wireless networks. In: Proc. of the 25th IEEE INFOCOM. Citeseer (2006)

[Ton10]   Tonoyan, T.: Algorithms for Scheduling with Power Control in Wireless Networks. Arxiv preprint arXiv:1010.5493 (2010)

[Wan09]   Wan, P.J.: Multiflows in multihop wireless networks. In: MobiHoc, pp. 85–94. ACM (2009)

[WFJ$^+$11] Wan, P.J., Frieder, O., Jia, X., Yao, F., Xu, X., Tang, S.: Wireless link scheduling under physical interference model (2011)

Wireless Capacity with Arbitrary Gain Matrix

Magnús M. Halldórsson and Pradipta Mitra

ICE-TCS, School of Computer Science
Reykjavik University
101 Reykjavik, Iceland
mmh@ru.is, ppmitra@gmail.com

Abstract. Given a set of wireless links, a fundamental problem is to find the largest subset that can transmit simultaneously, within the SINR model of interference. Significant progress on this problem has been made in recent years. In this note, we study the problem in the setting where we are given a fixed set of arbitrary powers each sender must use, and an arbitrary gain matrix defining how signals fade. This variation of the problem appears immune to most algorithmic approaches studied in the literature. Indeed it is very hard to approximate since it generalizes the max independent set problem. Here, we propose a simple semi-definite programming approach to the problem that yields constant factor approximation, if the optimal solution is strictly larger than half of the input size.

Keywords: Wireless Networks, Capacity, SINR Model, Semidefinite programming.

1 Introduction

We consider the fundamental problem of wireless network capacity. Given is a set $L = \{\ell_1, \ell_2, \ldots, \ell_n\}$ of links, where each link ℓ_v represents a communication request from a sender s_v to a receiver r_v. We are also given, for every $\ell_v \in L$, a transmission power $P_v > 0$. The powers received from senders to receivers are defined by an $n \times n$ dimensional gain matrix G with positive entries. Specifically, the signal received from s_v at r_w is $G_{wv} \cdot P_v$. Thus an instance in this model can be described by the tuple (L, P, G) where P is the vector of the power assignments P_v for all ℓ_v.

Simultaneously communicating links interfere with each other, following physical model or "SINR model" of interference. Due to its higher fidelity to reality [10,22,26], this model of interference has recently gained substantial attention in the analysis of wireless networks. In this model, a receiver r_v successfully receives a message from a sender s_v if and only if the following condition holds:

$$\frac{G_{vv} \cdot P_v}{\sum_{\ell_w \in S \setminus \{\ell_v\}} G_{vw} \cdot P_w + N} \geq \beta, \tag{1}$$

where N is a universal constant denoting the ambient noise, $\beta \geq 1$ denotes the minimum SINR (signal-to-interference-noise-ratio) required for a message to be

T. Erlebach et al. (Eds.): ALGOSENSORS 2011, LNCS 7111, pp. 215–224, 2012.

successfully received, and S is the set of concurrently scheduled links in the same *slot*. We say that a link ℓ_v is feasible in S if Eqn. 1 is satisfied for ℓ_v. A set S is feasible if each of its link is feasible.

Note that what we described above is the abstract SINR model. In the more commonly studied geometric SINR model, G_{vw} is a polynomial function of $d(s_w, r_v)$, where $d(x, y)$ is the distance between two points x and y. Our results naturally apply to that model as well. Given that the geometric SINR model does not capture obstacles, reflections and other real life distortions, it is interesting to see what can be proven in the abstract model.

Our setting where the powers are given as part of the input is often called the *fixed* power case, as opposed to the *power control* case where the algorithm can choose the power assignment. So far, research on fixed power has focused on *oblivious* power assignments, where the power of a link is a (usually simple) function of the length of the link [13,5,20,12]. Recently, a constant factor approximation algorithm to find the capacity in the power control case has also been achieved [19]. Unfortunately, none of these techniques appear to extend to the case of arbitrary fixed powers (for either arbitrary or geometric gain matrices). Yet, the problem of arbitrary fixed powers is not only natural, but has practical relevance, as commercial hardware often do not have the capacity of choosing precise powers to implement either an arbitrary assignment à la [19], or to implement many of the oblivious power assignments found in literature.

In this paper, we prove the following theorem.

Theorem 1. *Assume* (L, P, G) *is an instance of the capacity problem in the abstract SINR model, such that* $|OPT| > \frac{1}{2}(1 + \epsilon)|L|$ *for some* $\epsilon > 0$, *where* OPT *is the maximum feasible subset of* L *using* P. *Then there is a polynomial time randomized algorithm to find a feasible set of size* $\Omega(\epsilon|L|)$, *with probability* $1 - o(1)$.

We do this by means of a semi-definite programming relaxation, which we show how to successfully round if the condition $|OPT| > \frac{1}{2}(1+\epsilon)|L|$ holds. In addition, we discuss numerical experiments we have performed. These experiments show that the algorithm appears to work quite well on random instances, even better than the guarantees of Thm. 1.

Semi-definite programming has been a staple in designing approximation algorithms for NP-hard problems ever since the seminal work of Goemans and Williams on the Max-CUT problem [7]. It is interesting to note that the discrete "classical" problems closest to wireless capacity, namely the independent set problem and the graph coloring problem, have been fruitfully studied using semi-definite programming [15,18]. The vertex cover problem, also relevant via its connection to the independent set problem, also has SDP-based approximation algorithms [14,17]. Given this background, one may expect some of the techniques to easily carry over to the capacity problem. Yet that does not appear to be the case, at least not in a straightforward manner. A study of the aforementioned papers reveal that the discreteness of the problem plays an important role in the bounds. For example, in [18], the analysis proceeds by bounding the probability of vectors representing edges not being cut by a random hyperplane.

Given the additive nature of the SINR model, it is not obvious how to extend that analysis to this case. There have also been a number of results for these problems on hypergraphs [21,2,3]. Though hypergraphs appear to be closer in spirit to the additive wireless model, they are still different, because the effect of each node on any other node doesn't change in the SINR model (as opposed to in a hypergraph, where it can be different based on which edge they are in). Thus, the (sophisticated) methods on hypergraphs do not appear to translate immediately to the SINR model either. Our SDP relaxation and rounding algorithms are quite simple in contrast to some of the previously mentioned work. Whether or not advanced techniques can be extended to the SINR model remains to be seen.

1.1 Related Work

Moscibroda and Wattenhofer [24] were the first to study of the *scheduling complexity* of arbitrary set of wireless links. Early work on approximation algorithms produced approximation factors that grew with structural properties of the network [27,25,1].

The first constant factor approximation algorithm was obtained for capacity problem for uniform power in [8] (see also [13]) in $\mathbf{R}^2$ with $\alpha > 2$. Fanghänel, Kesselheim and Vöcking [6] gave an algorithm that uses at most $O(OPT + \log^2 n)$ slots for the scheduling problem with *linear* power assignment $P_v = d(s_v, r_v)^\alpha$, that holds in general distance metrics.

Kesselheim obtained a $O(1)$-approximation algorithm for the capacity problem with power control for doubling metrics [19]. Around the same time, the first constant factor algorithm for all sub-linear, length monotone power assignments was achieved on general metrics [12]. Other recent studies in the SINR model include work on topological maps [16], distributed algorithms for scheduling [11], distributed power control [4] and auction based spectrum allocation [23].

2 SDP-Based Algorithm

First, some notation. Vectors are denoted by $\boldsymbol{x}, \boldsymbol{s_w}$ etc. The standard 2-norm of the vector $\boldsymbol{x}$ is $\|\boldsymbol{x}\|$. The ith entry of $\boldsymbol{x}$ is $\boldsymbol{x}(i)$. The inner product of vectors $\boldsymbol{x}$ and $\boldsymbol{y}$ is denoted $(\boldsymbol{x} \cdot \boldsymbol{y})$. Define $g_{vv} = P_v G_{vv} - \beta N$ and $g_{vw} = P_w G_{vw}$ for $v \neq w$. Note that we can assume without loss of generality that $g_{vv} \geq 0, \forall v$. Let OPT be a feasible subset of L of maximum size. Note that $n = |L|$.

Consider the following program.

$$\max \sum_v (\boldsymbol{s_v} \cdot \boldsymbol{s}), \text{ subject to}$$

$$(\boldsymbol{s_v} \cdot \boldsymbol{s}) g_{vv} \geq \beta \left(\sum_{w \neq v} (\boldsymbol{s_v} \cdot \boldsymbol{s_w}) g_{vw} \right), \forall v$$

$$(\boldsymbol{s_v} \cdot \boldsymbol{s}) \geq 0, \forall v$$

$$(s_v \cdot s_w) \geq 0, \forall v, w$$
$$(s_v \cdot s_w) \geq (s_v \cdot s) + (s_w \cdot s) - 1, \forall v, w$$
$$\|s_v\|^2 = 1, \forall v \text{ and } \|s\|^2 = 1 .$$

where $s_v, s \in \mathbb{R}^{n+1}$. Each link ℓ_v has a vector variable s_v associated with it. The dot product of s_v with a vector s denotes the (fractional) extent to which ℓ_v is selected in the solution.

Since the objective function and constraints are all linear functions of vector inner products, this problem is a SDP. Thus the program can be solved up to an additive error of $\varepsilon > 0$ in time that is polynomial in n and $\log \varepsilon$ [28]. Since ε can be made small enough to not matter, we will simply assume that the problem can be solved exactly.

We can rotate the vectors to fix $s = \{1, 0 \ldots 0\}$, thus the above program is equivalent to:

$$\max \sum_v s_v(1), s.t.$$

$$s_v(1)g_{vv} \geq \beta \left(\sum_{w \neq v} (s_v \cdot s_w) g_{vw} \right), \forall v \tag{2}$$

$$s_v(1) \geq 0, \forall v \tag{3}$$

$$(s_v \cdot s_w) \geq 0, \forall v, w \tag{4}$$

$$(s_v \cdot s_w) \geq s_v(1) + s_w(1) - 1, \forall v, w \tag{5}$$

$$\|s_v\|^2 = 1, \forall v . \tag{6}$$

Let us verify that this program is a relaxation of the maximum capacity problem.

Lemma 1. *The SDP is a relaxation of the original problem.*

Proof. Consider any optimal solution OPT to the capacity problem. For all $\ell_v \in OPT$, set $s_v = s = \{1, 0, 0, 0 \ldots 0\}$. If $\ell_v \in L \setminus OPT$ set

$$s_v(i) = \begin{cases} 1 \text{ if } i = v + 1 \\ 0 \text{ otherwise} \end{cases}$$

In other words, we make sure that each unselected link chooses a different position for the single 1 in the vector.

Given these assignments, Equations 3, 4 and 6 can easily seen to hold.

To show that Eqn. 2 is satisfied, first assume $\ell_v \in OPT$. The following observation is immediate:

Claim. If $\ell_v, \ell_w \in OPT$ then $s_v(1) = s_w(1) = (s_v \cdot s_w) = 1$. If $\ell_v \in L \setminus OPT$ then $s_v(1) = 0$ and $(s_v \cdot s_w) = 0$ for any $\ell_w \neq \ell_v$.

Since $\ell_v \in OPT$,

$$s_v(1)g_{vv} = g_{vv}$$

And,

$$\beta \left(\sum_{w \neq v} (s_v \cdot s_w) g_{vw} \right)$$

$$= \beta \left(\sum_{w \in OPT \setminus \{v\}} (s_v \cdot s_w) g_{vw} \right) + \beta \left(\sum_{w \in L \setminus (OPT \cup \{v\})} (s_v \cdot s_w) g_{vw} \right)$$

$$= \beta \left(\sum_{w \in OPT \setminus \{v\}} g_{vw} \right)$$

where the second equality follows from the claim above.

Now, since $\ell_v \in OPT$, $g_{vv} \geq \beta \left(\sum_{w \in OPT \setminus \{v\}} g_{vw} \right)$ (by Eqn 1). Thus, the above two equations show that Eqn. 2 is satisfied when $\ell_v \in OPT$. The case where $\ell_v \notin OPT$ is similar.

For Eqn. 5, the following observations suffice:

- If $\ell_v, \ell_w \in OPT$, $(s_v \cdot s_w) = 1 = s_v(1) + s_w(1) - 1$
- If $\ell_v, \ell_w \notin OPT$, they have 1s in different positions and $(s_v \cdot s_w) = 0 \geq 0 + 0 - 1$
- If $\ell_v \in OPT, \ell_w \notin OPT$, they have 1s in different positions and $(s_v \cdot s_w) = 0 = 1 + 0 - 1$

□

Now we present our algorithm and the proof of Thm. 1. We need two related definitions. Let $\delta_v = \max\{s_v(1) - \frac{1}{2}, 0\}$ for all $\ell_v \in L$. Further, define $L^+ = \{\ell_v \in L : \delta_v > 0\}$. The algorithm is as follows.

Algorithm 1. Capacity1

1: Solve the SDP
2: Select each link $\ell_v \in L^+$ with probability $\frac{\delta_v}{2}$ in to a set R
3: Output $\{\ell_v \in R : \ell_v \text{ is feasible in } R\}$

Lemma 2. If $|OPT| \geq (1 + \epsilon)n/2$, then $\sum_{\ell_v \in L^+} \delta_v \geq \frac{n\epsilon}{2}$.

Proof. Since $|OPT| \geq (1+\epsilon)n/2$, it follows that $\sum_v s_v(1) \geq (1+\epsilon)n/2$ (since the SDP is a relaxation of the original problem). Now by definition of δ_v, $\delta_v + \frac{1}{2} \geq s_v(1)$. Thus,

$$\sum_{\ell_v \in L} \left(\frac{1}{2} + \delta_v \right) \geq (1 + \epsilon)n/2$$

$$\Rightarrow \sum_{\ell_v \in L} \delta_v \geq (1 + \epsilon)n/2 - |L|/2 = (1+\epsilon)n/2 - n/2 = \frac{\epsilon n}{2}$$

Observing that $\delta_v = 0$ for $\ell_v \notin L^+$ completes the proof.   □

We can now prove the main Theorem.

Proof. of Thm. 1

Assume that the random binary variable X_v describes whether or not $\ell_v \in L^+$ is chosen into R. We observe that $\mathbb{E}(X_v) = \frac{\delta_v}{2}$, according to the algorithm.

Then for any ℓ_v,

$$\mathbb{E}\left(\beta\left(\sum_{w \in R \backslash \{v\}} g_{vw}\right)\right) = \mathbb{E}\left(\beta\left(\sum_{w \in L^+ \backslash \{v\}} g_{vw} X_w\right)\right)$$

$$= \beta\left(\sum_{w \in L^+ \backslash \{v\}} g_{vw} \mathbb{E}(X_w)\right) = \beta\left(\sum_{w \in L^+ \backslash \{v\}} g_{vw} \frac{\delta_w}{2}\right)$$

$$\Rightarrow \mathbb{E}\left(\beta\left(\sum_{w \in R \backslash \{v\}} g_{vw}\right)\right) = \frac{1}{2}\beta\left(\sum_{w \in L^+ \backslash \{v\}} g_{vw} \delta_w\right) \qquad (7)$$

Now, by Eqn. 2,

$$s_v(1) g_{vv} \geq \beta\left(\sum_{w \neq v} (s_v \cdot s_w) g_{vw}\right), \forall v \in L^+$$

Since $s_v(1) \geq \frac{1}{2}$ for $v \in L^+$ and $(s_v \cdot s_w) g_{vw}$ is always non-negative, we get for $\ell_v \in L^+$,

$$g_{vv} \geq \beta\left(\sum_{w \in L^+ \backslash \{v\}} (s_v \cdot s_w) g_{vw}\right)$$

$$\geq \beta\left(\sum_{w \in L^+ \backslash \{v\}} (s_v(1) + s_w(1) - 1) g_{vw}\right) = \beta\left(\sum_{w \in L^+ \backslash \{v\}} (\delta_v + \delta_w) g_{vw}\right)$$

$$\geq \beta\left(\sum_{w \in L^+ \backslash \{v\}} \delta_w g_{vw}\right) \qquad (8)$$

where the second inequality follows from Eqn. 5, and the first equality follows from observing that $\delta_v = s_v(1) - \frac{1}{2}$ for $\ell_v \in L^+$.

Then, for $\ell_v \in L^+$,

$$\mathbb{P}(\ell_v \text{ is infeasible in } R) = \mathbb{P}\left(\beta\left(\sum_{w \in R \backslash \{v\}} g_{vw}\right) > g_{vv}\right)$$

$$\leq \frac{\mathbb{E}(\beta(\sum_{w \in R \backslash \{v\}} g_{vw}))}{g_{vv}} \leq \frac{1}{2} \qquad (9)$$

The first equality is the definition of infeasiblity. The first inequality is Markov's inequality. The last inequality follows from Equations 7 and 8.

Now the expected size of the output is

$$\mathbb{E}\left(|\{\ell_v \in R : \ell_v \text{ is feasible in } R\}|\right) = \sum_{\ell_v \in L^+} \mathbb{P}(\ell_v \in R \text{ and } \ell_v \text{ is feasible in } R)$$

$$= \sum_{\ell_v \in L^+} \mathbb{P}(\ell_v \text{ is feasible in } R)\mathbb{P}(\ell_v \in R)$$

$$\geq \sum_{\ell_v \in L^+} \frac{1}{2}\frac{\delta_v}{2} = \frac{1}{4}\sum_{\ell_v \in L^+} \delta_v \geq \frac{n\epsilon}{8}$$

The second equality follows from the independence of the events concerned. The first inequality follows from Eqn. 10. The last inequality follows from Lemma 2. Thus the expected size of the feasible output is $\Omega(\epsilon n)$. It is not difficult to boost the probability of getting a $\Omega(\epsilon n)$ size subset to complete the proof of the theorem.   □

3   Numerical Experiments

We ran simulations to test how well the algorithm does in practice. We used CVX, a package for specifying and solving convex programs using MATLAB [9]. We ran it on version 7.8 of MATLAB running on a Macbook with a 2 GHz Intel Core 2 Duo Processor and 2 GB of RAM.

We generated a number of problem instances where $n = 61$ and $|OPT| = 21, 26, 31, 36$ and 41. The instances were generated as follows. To generate the feasible subset a large random instance M of links on the 2d plane was generated. Each sender $s_v = (s_v(x), s_v(y))$ is a random point in a 450×450 box. The receiver r_v is defined by $(s_v(x) + \text{random}_v(x), s_v(y) + \text{random}_v(y))$ where $\text{random}_v(x)$ and $\text{random}_v(y)$ are sampled uniformly at random from $[-20, 20]$. We generated corresponding gain matrices using the geometric SINR model setting $\alpha = 2.5$ (thus $G_{vw} = \frac{1}{\|s_w - r_v\|^\alpha}$). We used both uniform (P_v is a constant) and mean power assignments ($P_v = \|s_v - r_v\|^{\alpha/2}$) to generate the gain matrix. We set the noise $N = 0$ throughout the experiments.

To generate the input instance G (which is a $n \times n$ matrix), we combined a subset of M with random entries. More specifically, first we retrieved a random feasible subset R of M (found greedily). This defined a $R \times R$ submatrix of G. The remaining entries were chosen iid randomly from $[0, \kappa]$, where κ was chosen large enough so that the remaining $n - |R|$ links would not contain a large feasible subset, thus R would be OPT for the instance.

Though computationally slow (for $n = 60$ the SDP took a few minutes to be solved), the algorithm performed extremely well. Indeed, it took some time to come up with instances where the algorithm didn't have a perfectly integral solution. If the random entries of G corresponding to $L \setminus OPT$ were too large (corresponding to a large κ, meaning that $L \setminus OPT$ contained only very small subsets that were feasible) or if OPT was too *loosely* feasible (ie, Eqn. 2 was far from being tight for most of the links), the algorithm did exceedingly well.

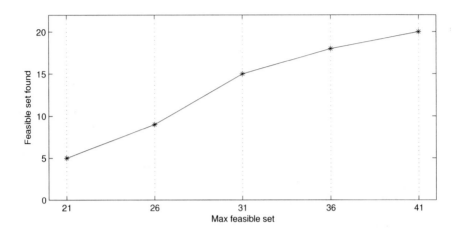

Fig. 1. OPT vs the average size of the set found by the SDP algorithm. In each case $n = 61$.

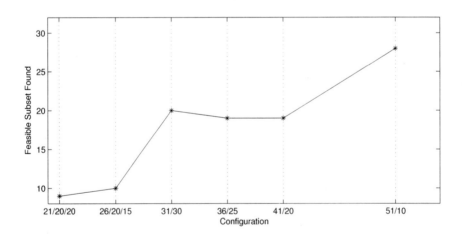

Fig. 2. OPT vs the average size of the set found by the SDP algorithm. In each case $n = 61$ and the links in OPT were generated using mean power. The labels in the x-axis describe the configuration of the instances. Thus, in the first case, the instance is an union of 3 feasible sets of size 21, 20 and 20, respectively, where the latter two are copies of subsets of the first one.

Even after trying to make the problem more difficult, the algorithm did quite well, only degrading when $OPT < n/2$, for which we claim no theoretical guarantee anyway, though even in these cases the output was not unsatisfactory. Indeed, in all these cases, using the simple filtering $(s_v \cdot s) > 0.51$ identified OPT almost exactly. Our sampling algorithm, by design cannot achieve better than a factor 2 approximation in general, and that is almost what we achieved in all cases, as illustrated in Figure 1 for uniform power (the results for mean power were essentially identical).

As we have mentioned, in the above experiments, the algorithm sharply identified OPT. To create more ambiguous instances, we also tried the following. In this setting, we took a feasible set, and added copies of subsets of it. Thus the instance would be of the form $L_1 \cup L_2$ or $L_1 \cup L_2 \cup L_3$ where L_1 is feasible, and L_2, L_3 are copies of subsets of L_1. One expects the solution to be more "spread out" in this case, and that is exactly what we found. The algorithm still performed rather well, even below theoretically guaranteed levels, though the behavior is somewhat different. Figure 2 demonstrates the case for mean power.

4   Conclusion

We have shown how to use semi-definite programming to approximate the wireless capacity problem in cases where the capacity is known to be large. It is an interesting question whether or not these results can be further improved, potentially using the power of geometric SINR model. Questions about the integrality gap and hardness of the problem (apart from what is known via the fact that the problem generalizes max independent set) also deserve attention. Though we have performed some preliminary numerical experiments, the efficacy of this method both in terms of accuracy and computational efficiency also is an interesting avenue of further investigation.

References

1. Chafekar, D., Kumar, V., Marathe, M., Parthasarathy, S., Srinivasan, A.: Cross-layer Latency Minimization for Wireless Networks using SINR Constraints. In: Mobihoc (2007)
2. Chlamtac, E.: Approximation algorithms using hierarchies of semidefinite programming relaxations. In: FOCS, pp. 691–701. IEEE Computer Society (2007)
3. Chlamtac, E., Singh, G.: Improved Approximation Guarantees through Higher Levels of SDP Hierarchies. In: Goel, A., Jansen, K., Rolim, J.D.P., Rubinfeld, R. (eds.) APPROX and RANDOM 2008. LNCS, vol. 5171, pp. 49–62. Springer, Heidelberg (2008)
4. Dams, J., Hoefer, M., Kesselheim, T.: Convergence Time of Power-Control Dynamics. In: Aceto, L., Henzinger, M., Sgall, J. (eds.) ICALP 2011, Part II. LNCS, vol. 6756, pp. 637–649. Springer, Heidelberg (2011)
5. Fanghänel, A., Kesselheim, T., Räcke, H., Vöcking, B.: Oblivious interference scheduling. In: PODC, pp. 220–229 (August 2009)

6. Fanghänel, A., Keßelheim, T., Vöcking, B.: Improved Algorithms for Latency Minimization in Wireless Networks. In: Albers, S., Marchetti-Spaccamela, A., Matias, Y., Nikoletseas, S., Thomas, W. (eds.) ICALP 2009. LNCS, vol. 5556, pp. 447–458. Springer, Heidelberg (2009)

7. Goemans, M.X., Williamson, D.P.: Improved approximation algorithms for maximum cut and satisfiability problems using semidefinite programming. J. ACM 42, 1115–1145 (1995)

8. Goussevskaia, O., Halldórsson, M.M., Wattenhofer, R., Welzl, E.: Capacity of Arbitrary Wireless Networks. In: INFOCOM, pp. 1872–1880 (April 2009)

9. Grant, M., Boyd, S.: CVX: Matlab software for disciplined convex programming, version 1.21. (April 2011), http://cvxr.com/cvx

10. Grönkvist, J., Hansson, A.: Comparison between graph-based and interference-based STDMA scheduling. In: Mobihoc, pp. 255–258 (2001)

11. Halldórsson, M.M., Mitra, P.: Nearly Optimal Bounds for Distributed Wireless Scheduling in the SINR Model. In: Aceto, L., Henzinger, M., Sgall, J. (eds.) ICALP 2011, Part II. LNCS, vol. 6756, pp. 625–636. Springer, Heidelberg (2011)

12. Halldórsson, M.M., Mitra, P.: Wireless Capacity with Oblivious Power in General Metrics. In: SODA (2011)

13. Halldórsson, M.M., Wattenhofer, R.: Wireless Communication Is in APX. In: Albers, S., Marchetti-Spaccamela, A., Matias, Y., Nikoletseas, S., Thomas, W. (eds.) ICALP 2009. LNCS, vol. 5555, pp. 525–536. Springer, Heidelberg (2009)

14. Halperin, E.: Improved approximation algorithms for the vertex cover problem in graphs and hypergraphs. In: SODA, pp. 329–337 (2000)

15. Halperin, E., Nathaniel, R., Zwick, U.: Coloring k-colorable graphs using relatively small palettes. J. Algorithms 45, 72–90 (2002)

16. Kantor, E., Lotker, Z., Parter, M., Peleg, D.: The Topology of Wireless Communication. In: STOC (2011)

17. Karakostas, G.: A better approximation ratio for the vertex cover problem. ACM Trans. Algorithms 5, 41:1–41:8 (2009)

18. Karger, D., Motwani, R., Sudan, M.: Approximate graph coloring by semidefinite programming. J. ACM 45, 246–265 (1998)

19. Kesselheim, T.: A Constant-Factor Approximation for Wireless Capacity Maximization with Power Control in the SINR Model. In: SODA (2011)

20. Kesselheim, T., Vöcking, B.: Distributed Contention Resolution in Wireless Networks. In: Lynch, N.A., Shvartsman, A.A. (eds.) DISC 2010. LNCS, vol. 6343, pp. 163–178. Springer, Heidelberg (2010)

21. Krivelevich, M., Nathaniel, R., Sudakov, B.: Approximating coloring and maximum independent sets in 3-uniform hypergraphs. In: SODA, pp. 327–328 (2001)

22. Maheshwari, R., Jain, S., Das, S.R.: A measurement study of interference modeling and scheduling in low-power wireless networks. In: SenSys, pp. 141–154 (2008)

23. Hoefer, M., Thomas Kesselheim, B.V.: Approximation Algorithms for Secondary Spectrum Auctions. In: SPAA (2011)

24. Moscibroda, T., Wattenhofer, R.: The Complexity of Connectivity in Wireless Networks. In: INFOCOM (2006)

25. Moscibroda, T., Oswald, Y.A., Wattenhofer, R.: How optimal are wireless scheduling protocols? In: INFOCOM, pp. 1433–1441 (2007)

26. Moscibroda, T., Wattenhofer, R., Weber, Y.: Protocol Design Beyond Graph-Based Models. In: Hotnets (November 2006)

27. Moscibroda, T., Wattenhofer, R., Zollinger, A.: Topology Control meets SINR: The Scheduling Complexity of Arbitrary Topologies. In: MOBIHOC, pp. 310–321 (2006)

28. Vandenberghe, L., Boyd, S.: Semidefinite programming. SIAM Review 38, 49–95 (1994)

On the Capacity of Oblivious Powers

Tigran Tonoyan

TCS Sensor Lab, Centre Universitaire d'Informatique
Route de Drize 7, 1227 Carouge, Geneva, Switzerland
tigran.tonoyan@unige.ch

Abstract. We consider the problem of capacity in wireless networks in the physical model. The goal of this paper is to compare different power assignments and models from the perspective of this problem. We show a family of power assignments, including the mean power assignment, which yield larger capacity than uniform and linear power assignments, for each network instance. On the other hand, uniform and linear power assignments are not worse (in the same sense) than any power assignment, which is decreasing as a function of link-length, or increasing faster than linear power assignment. We also compare the directed and bidirectional communication models, and show upper and lower bounds on the gap between optimal capacities using any power assignment in these communication models.

1 Introduction

The *capacity problem* in wireless networks is the following. Given is a network of wireless nodes, with a set of links, each a pair of nodes, a sender and a receiver. The nodes are assigned power levels. The aim is to find a maximal (by the number of links) subset of links, such that all the communications corresponding to these links could be done simultaneously. The *physical model* of signal propagation is adopted, and for the signal interference the *SINR model* is considered, i.e. the number of links in the mentioned subset should be maximized subject to the *SINR-constraint*. This problem is considered in two theoretical communication models: in the *directed model* only one node in each link is transmitting (the sender node) and the other one should receive, and in the *bidirectional model* both nodes in a link may be transmitting with the same power (e.g. performing a handshake protocol), which implies stronger constraints in SINR formula. By definition the directed model should yield a better (at least not worse) performance in the sense of the problems considered here, but apparently the bidirectional model describes the current notion of ad-hoc networks more realistically.

The solution of the capacity problem depends also on the powers assigned to the nodes, as with one power assignment one could get larger SINR-feasible sets than with another assignment. The present work deals with a non-algorithmic, comparative analysis of different power assignments, keeping the focus on the power assignments which are *local*, i.e. they don't depend on the global network structure. Such power assignments are called *oblivious*, and represent a special

T. Erlebach et al. (Eds.): ALGOSENSORS 2011, LNCS 7111, pp. 225–237, 2012.

interest due to the distributed nature of wireless networks. Examples of oblivious power assignments include *uniform, linear, square-root or mean* power assignments, which are the most popular in the literature. Let us note that each of those power assignments optimizes a different parameter of a wireless network. For using the uniform power assignment one doesn't need the capability of power control, hence making the wireless nodes simpler (hence possibly cheaper). Although the linear power assignment requires a capability of power control, it has the valuable property that it spends the minimum energy for a transmission. The mean power assignment, as we will see below, performs better from the point of view of capacity. This all emphasizes the importance of comparing these power assignments from the point of view of capacity, since in a wireless network one usually has to find a good tradeoff between different parameters, such as the energy dissipation and quality of service in terms of the throughput, depending on the capabilities of the nodes and the purposes of the network.

We consider general families of power assignments, which includes the examples above, and try to explore connections between the optimal capacities when using different power assignments, as well as evaluate the difference between the performance of different communication models.

In particular, we show that for any network instance, the optimal capacity w.r.t. uniform power assignment can differ from the capacity w.r.t. linear power assignment by at most a constant factor. Using this relation we are able to prove the main result of this work: there is a family of *sublinear* power assignments, including mean power assignment, which dominate uniform and linear power assignments with respect to capacity problem, in the sense that for any network instance the optimal capacity when using such a power assignment is worse than the optimal capacity when using uniform (linear) power assignment by at most a constant factor, but can be arbitrarily greater than the latter. On the other hand, uniform and linear power assignments dominate any power assignment, which is a non-increasing function of link-length, or grows faster than the linear power assignment. We also try to find connections between two different communication models (the directed model and the bidirectional model) which have been considered in the related work. We show that for any given network instance, the best capacity (using any power assignment) calculated in the bidirectional model can be worse than the best capacity calculated in the directed model by no more than a factor of $O(\log \log \Delta + \log n)$, where Δ is the ratio between the lengths of the longest and the shortest links, and n is the number of links.

Related Work. The problem of capacity is often considered in conjunction with the *scheduling problem*, where the goal is to split a set of links into the minimum number of SINR-feasible subsets. The study on capacity and scheduling problems in physical model got increased attention, when it was shown that in the SINR model one could do better spatial reuse than in traditional graph-based models, thus getting more links to transmit simultaneously without interfering (see [10] and [21] for example). The problem of scheduling for networks arbitrarily located on the Euclidean plane, as opposed to the network instances with nodes uniformly scattered on some area of plane is considered in [22], [19]. They design centralized algorithms for assigning power of the nodes and scheduling a given set of links, but no approximation guarantees are proven. There is a series of papers considering scheduling and capacity problems for given powers. The case of uniform power assignment is considered in [23], [9], [8], [1], whith a constant factor approximation algorithm (centralized) designed in [15]. In [4], [7] and [24] scheduling with linear power assignment is considered, obtaining a constant factor centralized algorithm and a distributed algorithm with a good approximation guarantee. In [18] $O(\log^2 n)$-approximation randomized distributed algorithms are designed dealing with the scheduling problem for the family of *sub-linear* power assignments, while in [13] it is shown that a stronger, $O(\log n)$ approximation guarantee holds. In [14] constant factor approximation algorithms (centralized) are designed for the capacity problem for the same class of power assignments. There is also a considerable effort towards finding power assignments, which would yield better results for scheduling and capacity problems (the problem of *PC-scheduling*). In [6] the bidirectional version of PC-scheduling problem is considered, and it is shown that the mean power assignments yields a poly-logarithmic (in the number of links n) approximation factor. In [11], [25], [12] it is shown that when using the mean power assignment, one can get a $O(\log n)$-approximation for PC-scheduling in the bidirectional model, and a $O(\log n \log \log \Lambda)$-approximation in the directed model, where Λ is the ratio between the longest and the shortest link-lengths. In [17] a constant factor approximation algorithm is given for capacity maximization problem (with power control), which uses non-local power assignments. In fact it is shown [6], that in the directed model for each oblivious power assignment P there is a network instance, which is SINR-feasible with some power assignment, but yields an unefficient schedule using P. An interesting variation of scheduling problem, modeling also *multicast* transmissions, is considered in [5].

2   Problem Formulation

Given is a set $T = \{1, 2, \ldots, n\}$ of links, where each link v represents a communication request between a sender node s_v and a receiver node r_v. The nodes are located in a metric space with distance function d. The *asymmetric distance* d_{vw} from a link v to a link w is defined in two ways, depending on which communication model is used:

$$d_{vw} = \begin{cases} d(s_v, r_w) & \text{directed model} \\ \min\{d(s_v, r_w), d(s_v, s_w), d(r_v, r_w), d(r_v, s_w)\} & \text{bidirectional model} \end{cases}$$

Note that in the latter case $d_{vw} = d_{wv}$ (i.e. the distance is actually symmetrical), but in the former case for some pairs v,w it can be $d_{vw} \neq d_{wv}$.

The length of a link v is $l_v = d(s_v, r_v)$. There is a power assignment $P : L \to R_+$, which assignes a positive number $P(v)$ to each link v. This value determines the power of transmission of a transmitting node of v. In the directed model only the sender node is transmitting, so the power assignment means assigning powers to the sender nodes. In the bidirectional model the communication is bilateral, so both sender and receiver nodes of a link are assigned the same power. We adopt the *path loss radio propagation* model for the reception of signals, where the signal received from a node x of the link v at some node y is $P(v)/d(x,y)^\alpha$, where $\alpha > 2$ denotes the *path loss exponent*. We adopt the *physical interference model*, where a communication v is done successfully if and only if the following condition holds:

$$SINR_P(S,v) = \frac{P(v)/l_v^\alpha}{\sum_{w \in S \setminus v} P(w)/d_{wv}^\alpha + N} \geq \beta, \tag{1}$$

where N is the ambient noise, S is the set of concurrently scheduled links in the same *slot*, and $\beta \geq 1$ denotes the minimum SINR (signal-to-interference-plus-noise-ratio) required for the transmission to be successfully done. We say that S is *SINR-feasible* if $SINR_P(S,v) \geq \beta$ for each link $v \in S$.

In the problem of *capacity*, given the set T of links and a power assignment P, one needs to find a maximal (in the number of elements) SINR-feasible subset of T. The number of links in such a set is called the *capacity* of T with respect to P. A related problem is the problem of *scheduling*, where given a set T of links and a power assignment P, one needs to partition T into a minimal number of SINR-feasible subsets. Such a partition is called *a schedule*, the subsets are called *slots*, and the number of slots is called *the length* of the schedule.

These problems are usually stated for directed and bidirectional models, but some of the results we obtain hold in a more abstract setting. Each link v is just a couple of symbols (s_v, r_v), and L is the set of these links. The lengths of links are given by an arbitrary positive function $l : L \to R_+$, and the asymmetric distances are given by a function $d : L \times L \to R_+$. The only constraint we need is that for each couple of links v, w, the following holds:

$$d_{vw} \leq d_{wv} + l_v + l_w. \tag{2}$$

It is not hard to check that both models above are special cases of this abstract model, but other special cases could also make sense in a real network setting.

We use the notation $OPT_P^D(S)$ for the optimum capacity of a link set $S \subseteq L$ with respect to the power assignment P in the directed model, and $OPT_P^B(S)$ for the capacity in the bidirectional model. When using notation $OPT_P(S)$, we assume that any communication model from the general family above is used. In some cases we will not mention the set S, by assuming that the statement holds for any set, e.g. $OPT_{P_1} = O(OPT_{P_2})$ would mean that there is a constant $c > 0$, such that $OPT_{P_1}(S) \leq c \cdot OPT_{P_2}(S)$ holds for each set S, where two capacities are calculated in the same communication model.

For simplicity of the argument at first we assume that there is no ambient noise, i.e. $N = 0$. In this case the SINR formula becomes simpler to deal with. With this assumption, we consider the inverse of the left side of SINR condition:

$$A_P(S,v) = \frac{1}{SINR_P(S,v)} = \sum_{w \in S \setminus v} \frac{P(w)/d_{wv}^\alpha}{P(v)/l_v^\alpha},$$

which is called *affectance* of link v by set S [15]. With this definition the SINR condition becomes

$$A_P(S, v) \leq 1/\beta.$$

Note that A_P is additive, i.e. if there are two disjoint sets S_1 and S_2, then $A_P(S_1 \cup S_2, v) = A_P(S_1, v) + A_P(S_2, v)$.

If for each link v of a set S $A_P(S, v) \leq 1/p$, then S is called a *p-signal set*. Note that a set is SINR-feasible if and only if it is a β-signal set.

The following theorem is a useful tool in dealing with the SINR condition. We assume the power assignment of the nodes is given. The theorem holds for the general model of communication.

Theorem 1. *[15] There is a polynomial-time algorithm that takes a p-signal schedule and refines into a p'-signal schedule, for $p' > p$, increasing the number of subsets by a factor of at most $\lceil 2p'/p \rceil^2$.*

Among others, we will consider power assignments L_t, for $t \in R$, where the power of each link v is $L_t(v) = c l_v^{t\alpha}$, with $c > 0$ a constant. L_0 is called *uniform power assignment*, L_1 is called *linear power assignment*, and $L_{1/2}$ is called *mean power assignment*, or *square-root power assignment*.

3   Conjugate Power Assignments

For a set of links T we say that *link distances are almost symmetric*, if there is a constant $c > 0$, depending only on α and β, such that $d_{vw} \leq c d_{wv}$ for all (ordered) pairs of links $w, v \in T$.

Consider a power assignment P. We denote by P^* the *conjugate* of P, which is given by the formula $P^*(v) = l_v^\alpha / P(v)$. Obviously, $P^{**} = P$ holds. Some instances of conjugate pairs of power assignments are the pairs $\{L_t, L_{1-t}\}$: it is trivial to check that $L_t^* = L_{1-t}$. In particular, the conjugate of linear power assignment is uniform power assignment ($L_0^* = L_1$), and the conjugate of mean power assignment is itself ($L_{1/2}^* = L_{1/2}$). The following results exhibit a connection between conjugate power assignments.

Lemma 1. *Suppose that for a set $T \subseteq L$ the link distances are almost symmetric with a constant $c > 0$. Then for each power assignment P,*

$$OPT_{P^*}(T) = \Theta(OPT_P(T)).$$

Proof. Let $S \subseteq T$ be a maximum SINR-feasible subset of T with respect to P. Then for each $v \in S$ we have

$$A_P(S, v) = \sum_{w \in S \setminus v} \frac{l_v^\alpha P(w)}{d_{wv}^\alpha P(v)} \leq 1/\beta. \qquad (3)$$

It is not hard to check that A_{P^*} for the pair S, v has the following form:

$$A_{P^*}(S, v) = \sum_{w \in S \setminus v} \frac{l_w^\alpha P(v)}{d_{wv}^\alpha P(w)} \leq c^\alpha \sum_{w \in S \setminus v} \frac{l_w^\alpha P(v)}{d_{vw}^\alpha P(w)},$$

where the equality follows from the definition of P^*, and the inequality holds because the distances are almost symmetric. Since (3) holds for all $v \in S$, we can write

$$\beta|S| \geq \sum_{v \in S} A_P(S, v) = \sum_{v \in S} \sum_{w \in S \setminus v} \frac{l_v^\alpha P(w)}{d_{wv}^\alpha P(v)} =$$

$$= \sum_{w \in S} \sum_{v \in S \setminus w} \frac{l_v^\alpha P(w)}{d_{wv}^\alpha P(v)} \geq c^{-\alpha} \sum_{w \in S} A_{P^*}(S, w),$$

Thus we have $\sum_{v \in S} A_{P^*}(S, v) \leq c^\alpha \beta|S|$, which implies that at least the half of the numbers $\{A_{P^*}(S, v) | v \in S\}$ are not greater than $2\beta c^\alpha$, i.e. the subset $S' = \{v \in S | A_{P^*}(S, v) \leq 2\beta c^\alpha\}$ of S is a $1/(2\beta c^\alpha)$-signal set with respect to P^*, and $|S'| \geq |S|/2$. According to Theorem 1, S' can be split into $k = \lceil 4\beta^2 c^\alpha \rceil^2$ subsets $S_1', S_2', ..., S_k'$, each a β-signal set. Obviously, there is an $i \in \{1, 2, ..., k\}$, such that $|S_i'| \geq |S'|/k \geq |S|/2k$. This completes the proof, as we have $OPT_{P^*}(S) \geq |S_i'| \geq |S|/(2\lceil 4\beta^2 c^\alpha \rceil^2)$. The theorem is proven, since c is assumed to be a constant.   □

An immediate application of Lemma 1 is the following theorem.

Theorem 2. *For each power assignment P, $OPT_{P^*}^B = \Theta(OPT_P^B)$. In particular, $OPT_{L_t}^B = \Theta(OPT_{L_{1-t}}^B)$ for each $t \in R$.*

3.1   Non-increasing and Super-Linearly Increasing Power Assignments

We call a power assignment P *non-increasing*, if it is a monotonically non-increasing function of the link-length, i.e. for any two links v, w, such that $l_v \geq l_w$, $P(v) \leq P(w)$.

    We say a power assignment P is *super-linearly increasing*, if P is a monotonically increasing function of the link-length, and for each two links v, w, such that $l_v \geq l_w$, $P(v) \geq P(w)l_v^\alpha/l_w^\alpha$.

Remark. Note that for each $t \leq 0$, L_t is a non-increasing power assignment, and for each $t \geq 1$, L_t is super-linearly increasing. It is also easy to check that if a power assignment is non-increasing, then its conjugate is super-linearly increasing (and vice versa).

The following lemma is proven in the full version of this paper.

Lemma 2. *If a set of links S is a 3^α-signal set with a power assignment P, which is non-increasing or is super-linearly increasing, then the distances in S are almost symmetric with the constant $c = 3$.*

From Lemma 2 and Lemma 1 we immediately get the following theorem.

Theorem 3. *If a power assignment P is non-increasing or is super-linearly increasing, then $OPT_P = \Theta(OPT_{P^*})$.*

Remark. In particular, for numbers $t \notin (0,1)$, $OPT_{L_t} = \Theta(OPT_{L_{1-t}})$. This means that the linear and uniform power assignments, which are much considered in the literature, yield similar capacities for each network instance. It follows that the optimal schedule lengths for these power assignments differ only by a $O(\log n)$ factor, which can be used to find an approximate expression for the optimal schedule length for uniform power assignment, using the approximation for the linear power assignment, e.g. [7] [24].

4   The Capacity of L_0

Here we compare L_0 with the class of power assignments considered before in this work. In particular, each non-increasing power assignment and each super-linearly increasing power assignment perform not better than L_0. On the other hand, we show that any L_t with $t \in (0,1)$ (i.e. *sub-linear* power assignments L_t) performs not worse than L_0.

Theorem 4. *If a power assignment P is non-increasing or is super-linearly increasing, then $OPT_{L_0} = \Omega(OPT_P)$.*

Proof. Since we have Theorem 3, it suffices to prove this theorem only for non-increasing P. Suppose that S is a set of links which is SINR-feasible with respect to P. Then, according to Lemma 2 and Theorem 1, there is a subset $T \subseteq S$, such that T is a constant fraction of S, and T is a 3^α-signal set with respect to P, and the distances in T are almost symmetric with constant $c = 3$. Consider two links $v, w \in T$, and suppose that $l_v \geq l_w$. Then we have

$$A_P(\{w\}, v) = \frac{l_v^\alpha P(w)}{d_{wv}^\alpha P(v)} \geq \frac{l_v^\alpha}{d_{wv}^\alpha} = A_{L_0}(\{w\}, v), \tag{4}$$

since P is non-increasing. Since the distances are almost symmetric, and $l_w \leq l_v$, then using (4), we have

$$A_{L_0}(\{v\}, w) = \frac{l_w^\alpha}{d_{vw}^\alpha} \leq 3^\alpha \frac{l_w^\alpha}{d_{wv}^\alpha} \leq 3^\alpha A_P(\{w\}, v). \tag{5}$$

Consider the sum of affectances with respect to L_0:

$$\sum_{v \in T} A_{L_0}(T, v) = \sum_{\{v,w\}} A_{L_0}(\{w\}, v) + A_{L_0}(\{v\}, w) \leq$$

$$\leq (3^\alpha + 1) \sum_{\{v,w\}} A_P(\min\{w, v\}, \max\{w, v\}) \leq$$

$$\leq (3^\alpha + 1) \sum_{v \in T} A_P(T, v) \leq (3^{-\alpha} + 1)|T|,$$

where we denote by $\max\{v, w\}$ the link with the greater length and by $\min\{v, w\}$ the other one. The second and third summations are over all non-ordered pairs of links. The first inequality above follows from (4) and (5), and the third inequality follows from the 3^α-signal property of T with respect to P.

Having this, we can conclude, that there is a subset $T' \subseteq T$, such that $|T'| \geq |T|/2$, and for each link $v \in T'$,

$$A_{L_0}(T', v) \leq 2(3^{-\alpha} + 1),$$

and applying Theorem 1 to the set T', we get the claim of the theorem.   □

We will use the following form of Hölder's inequality, which can be found proven, for example, in [16].

Lemma 3. *Suppose that k and k' are real numbers, such that $k > 1$ and $1/k + 1/k' = 1$. Then for positive real numbers $a_1, a_2, \ldots, a_m$ and $b_1, b_2, \ldots, b_m$ the following inequality holds:*

$$\sum_{i=1}^{m} a_i b_i \leq \left(\sum_{i=1}^{m} a_i^k \right)^{1/k} \left(\sum_{i=1}^{m} b_i^{k'} \right)^{1/k'}. \tag{6}$$

Theorem 5. *For each $t \in (0,1)$, $OPT_{L_t} = \Omega(OPT_{L_0})$.*

Proof. Let S be a set of links. Suppose $t \in (0,1)$. Let us consider the following notation: $k = 1/t$, $a_w = l_w^{t\alpha}/d_{wv}^{t\alpha}$ and $b_w = l_v^{(1-t)\alpha}/d_{wv}^{(1-t)\alpha}$, for $w \in S \setminus \{v\}$. Then (6) holds, as $k = 1/t > 1$:

$$\sum_{w \in S \setminus v} \frac{l_w^{t\alpha}}{d_{wv}^{t\alpha}} \cdot \frac{l_v^{(1-t)\alpha}}{d_{wv}^{(1-t)\alpha}} \leq \left(\sum_{w \in S \setminus v} \left(\frac{l_w^{t\alpha}}{d_{wv}^{t\alpha}} \right)^{1/t} \right)^t \left(\sum_{w \in S \setminus v} \left(\frac{l_v^{(1-t)\alpha}}{d_{wv}^{(1-t)\alpha}} \right)^{1/(1-t)} \right)^{1-t}$$

because we have $k' = 1/(1 - 1/k) = 1/(1 - t)$. Note that the left-hand side of this inequality is exactly $A_{L_t}(S, v)$, and the first factor of the right-hand side is $A_{L_1}(S, v)^t$ and the second one is $A_{L_0}(S, v)^{1-t}$, so we have

$$A_{L_t}(S, v) \leq A_{L_1}(S, v)^t A_{L_0}(S, v)^{1-t}. \tag{7}$$

Let $T \subseteq S$ be a maximum subset of links which is SINR-feasible with respect to L_0. Then from Theorem 3 we have that there is a constant $c > 0$ and a subset $T' \subseteq T$, such that $|T'| \geq |T|/c$, and T' is SINR-feasible with respect to L_1 too. We show that T' is SINR-feasible with L_t as well. According to (7) we have that for each link $v \in T'$,

$$A_{L_t}(T', v) \leq A_{L_1}(T', v)^t A_{L_0}(T', v)^{1-t},$$

and since for T' we have that $A_{L_0}(T', v) \leq 1/\beta$ and $A_{L_1}(T', v) \leq 1/\beta$, then we have

$$A_{L_t}(T', v) \leq (1/\beta)^t (1/\beta)^{1-t} = 1/\beta,$$

which means that T' is SINR-feasible with respect to L_t.   □

Remark. In relation to Theorem 5 it is worth to mention that in [11] it is shown that when the link-lengths don't differ much, then uniform power assignment and L_t for any t yield almost the same optimal schedules and capacities (with only difference in a constant factor). On the other hand, it is known [11] [12] [20], that there are network instances, for which $L_{1/2}$ yields poly-logarithmic schedule, while for L_0 the optimal schedule length is $\Theta(n)$.

5   Comparing the Two Communication Models

An interesting consequence of Lemma 2 is that each non-increasing or super-linearly increasing power assignment yields similar results in the directed and bidirectional communication models. To show this we first prove the following lemma. Let d_{vw} denote the distance between v and w in the directed model, and d'_{vw} denote the distance between those links in the bidirectional model.

Lemma 4. *Suppose that in a set of links S, for each pair of links v, w it holds that $\max\{d_{vw}, d_{wv}\} \geq 3\max\{l_v, l_w\}$. Then for each power assignment P, the following holds:*

$$OPT_P^B(S) = \Theta(OPT_P^D(S)) \text{ and } OPTS_P^B(S) = \Theta(OPTS_P^D(S)),$$

where the constants depend only on α, β.

Proof. It is obvious that for each pair of links w, v, $d_{vw} \geq d'_{vw}$ and $d_{wv} \geq d'_{vw}$ hold, hence $OPT_P^B(S) \leq OPT_P^D(S)$ and $OPTS_P^B(S) \geq OPTS_P^D$, so what we need to show is $OPT_P^B(S) = \Omega(OPT_P^D(S))$ and $OPTS_P^B(S) = O(OPTS_P^D(S))$. Let S' be any subset of S, which is SINR-feasible with respect to P in the directed model. Consider any pair of links $v, w \in S'$. Suppose that $d_{vw} \geq d_{wv}$ and $l_v \geq l_w$. Then according to the condition of the lemma we have $d_{vw} \geq 3l_v$. Using the triangle inequality, we have $d(s_v, s_w) \geq d_{vw} - l_w \geq 2d_{vw}/3$, $d(r_v, r_w) \geq 2d_{vw}/3$ and $d_{wv} \geq d(r_v, r_w) - l_w \geq d_{vw}/3$. This implies that $d'_{vw} \geq \max\{d_{vw}/3, d_{wv}/3\}$, which in turn implies that S' is a $3^\alpha\beta$-signal set with respect to P, in the bidirectional model. According to Theorem 1, S' can be split into a constant number of subsets, which are SINR feasible in the bidirectional model. This completes the proof.   □

Theorem 6. *If P is a non-increasing or super-linearly increasing power assignment, then $OPT_P^B = \Theta(OPT_P^D)$ and $OPTS_P^B = \Theta(OPTS_P^D)$.*

Proof. Suppose P is a non-increasing power assignment, and S is a 3^α-signal set with respect to P in the directed model (we use Theorem 1). Then for each pair of links $v, w \in S$, such that $l_v \geq l_w$, we have

$$P(v)/l_v^\alpha \geq 3^\alpha P(w)/d_{wv}^\alpha,$$

so $d_{wv} \geq 3l_v \sqrt[\alpha]{P(w)/P(v)} \geq 3l_v$, and the condition of Lemma 4 holds for the set S. This implies the theorem, as the constants involved in the formula of Lemma 4 depend only on α and β.

The proof for the case when P is a super-linearly increasing power assignment can be done by a similar argument.   □

It turns out that the property described in Theorem 6 partially holds also for the power assignment $L_{1/2}$.

Theorem 7. $OPT^B_{L_{1/2}} = \Theta(OPT^D_{L_{1/2}})$.

Proof. As in the previous lemma, we need to show only the following

$$OPT^B_{L_{1/2}} = \Omega(OPT^D_{L_{1/2}}).$$

Suppose that a set of links S is a 2^α-signal set with respect to $L_{1/2}$ in the directed model. Then for each two links v, w we have

$$l_v^{\alpha/2}/l_v^\alpha \geq 2^\alpha l_w^{\alpha/2}/d_{wv}^\alpha \text{ and } l_w^{\alpha/2}/l_w^\alpha \geq 2^\alpha l_v^{\alpha/2}/d_{vw}^\alpha,$$

so $d_{wv} \geq 2\sqrt{l_v l_w}$ and $d_{vw} \geq 2\sqrt{l_v l_w}$. Let v be shorter than w, i.e. $l_v \leq l_w$. Then we have that

$$d_{wv} \geq 2l_v \text{ and } d_{vw} \geq 2l_v. \tag{8}$$

From the triangle inequality we have $d(s_v, s_w) \geq d_{wv} - l_v$ and $d(r_v, r_w) \geq d_{vw} - l_v$, which combined with (8) yields

$$d(s_v, s_w) \geq d_{wv}/2 \text{ and } d(r_v, r_w) \geq d_{vw}/2,$$

so we have $d'_{vw} \geq 1/2 \min\{d_{vw}, d_{wv}\}$. The latter implies that

$$A'_{L_{1/2}}(\{v\}, w) = A'_{L_{1/2}}(\{w\}, v) \leq 2^\alpha \max\left\{A_{L_{1/2}}(\{w\}, v), A_{L_{1/2}}(\{v\}, w)\right\},$$

which can be used to estimate the total affectance of the set S in the bidirectional model:

$$\sum_{v \in S} A'_{L_{1/2}}(S, v) = \sum_{\{v,w\}} 2A'_{L_{1/2}}(\{w\}, v) \leq$$

$$\leq 2^{\alpha+1} \sum_{\{v,w\}} \max\left\{A_{L_{1/2}}(\{w\}, v), A_{L_{1/2}}(\{v\}, w)\right\} \leq$$

$$\leq 2^{\alpha+1} \sum_{v \in S} A_{L_{1/2}}(S, v) \leq 2|S|,$$

so there is a subset $S' \subseteq S$, such that $|S'| \geq |S|/2$, and $A'(S, v) \leq 4$ for each $v \in S'$. Applying Theorem 1, we complete the proof. □

The results obtained so far can be used to bound the gap between the optimal schedule lengths and capacities of directed and bidirectional models.

The following result has been proven in [14].

Theorem 8. *[14]*

$$OPT^B_{L_{1/2}} = \Theta(OPT^B) \text{ and } OPT^D_{L_{1/2}} = \Omega(OPT^D/(\log\log\Delta + \log n)).$$

Using Theorem 7 we get the following corollary, which bounds the gap between the two models.

Theorem 9. $OPT^B = \Omega(OPT^D/(\log\log\Delta + \log n))$.

In [11] and [12] a family of networks and sets of links T is presented, for which $OPT^D_{L_{1/2}}(T) = O(OPT^D_{LOG^*}(T)/\log\log\Delta)$, where LOG^* is the power assignment, which is given by $LOG^*(v) = l^\alpha_v/\log l_v$. This implies the following corollary, which shows that the gap between the two models can actually be at least $\log\log\Delta$ for some network instances.

Theorem 10. *There is a network instance and a set of links T, such that*

$$OPT^B(T) = O(OPT^D(T)/\log\log\Delta).$$

6   Noise Factor

Here we show how to extend our results for the case of a non-zero noise. First let us notice that if there is a noise N, then if v is a link contained in a set S, which is SINR-feasible with respect to power assignment P, and contains at least two links, then it follows that $P(v)/l^\alpha_v \geq \beta N$, for each link v. We put a slightly stronger assumption on the power level: $P(v)/l^\alpha_v \geq 2\beta N$. Then, if a set S is SINR-feasible with respect to P without noise factor and with $\beta' = 2\beta$, we have $P(v)/l^\alpha_v \geq \beta' \sum_{w\in S\setminus v} P(w)/d^\alpha_{wv}$, so

$$P(v)/l^\alpha_v \geq \beta \sum_{w\in S\setminus v} P(w)/d^\alpha_{wv} + P(v)/2l^\alpha_v \geq \beta \sum_{w\in S\setminus v} P(w)/d^\alpha_{wv} + \beta N,$$

which is the SINR-condition including the noise factor. This shows that if our assumption on coefficients holds $(P(v)/l^\alpha_v \geq 2\beta N)$, then we can consider the problem of scheduling (or capacity) without noise, transform the resulting schedule into a schedule with $\beta' = 2\beta$, then the result will be SINR-feasible schedule even with the noise factor N, and will contain at most a constant times more slots, according to Theorem 1, so all our results hold with a non-zero noise factor: the only change is in constant factors.

7   Future Work

As it is noted in the introduction, one often has to find a tradeoff between different parameters in wireless networks. Two of these parameters are the energy dissipation and throughput. As it has been shown, there are sub-linear power assignments, such as the mean power, which seem to provide a better throughput on all networks, than the uniform or the linear power assignments. We consider it an interesting problem to find sub-linear power assignments (preferably oblivious), which perform good (e.g. as good as the mean power) from the capacity point of view, and are more energy efficient than the mean power assignment.

Acknowledgements. The author thanks the referees and M.M. Halldórsson for valuable comments and advices on the exposition of the paper. This work is partially supported by the EU project HOBNET - ICT/FIRE STREP 257466.

References

1. Andrews, M., Dinitz, M.: Maximizing capacity in arbitrary wireless networks in the SINR model: Complexity and game theory. In: Proc. of 28th Annual IEEE Conference on Computer Communications, INFOCOM (2009)
2. Avin, C., Emek, Y., Kantor, E., Lotker, Z., Peleg, D., Roditty, L.: SINR Diagrams: Towards Algorithmically Usable SINR Models of Wireless Networks. In: Proc. of 28th Annual Symposium on Principles of Distributed Computing, PODC (2009)
3. Avin, C., Lotker, Z., Pasquale, F., Pignolet, Y.-A.: A Note on Uniform Power Connectivity in the SINR Model. In: Dolev, S. (ed.) ALGOSENSORS 2009. LNCS, vol. 5804, pp. 116–127. Springer, Heidelberg (2009)
4. Chafekar, D., Kumar, V., Marathe, M., Parthasarathi, S., Srinivasan, A.: Cross-layer Latency Minimization for Wireless Networks using SINR Constraints. In: Proc. of ACM International Symposium on Mobile Ad Hoc Networking and Computing, MobiHoc (2007)
5. Erlebach, T., Grant, T.: Scheduling Multicast Transmissions under SINR Constraints. In: Scheideler, C. (ed.) ALGOSENSORS 2010. LNCS, vol. 6451, pp. 47–61. Springer, Heidelberg (2010)
6. Fanghänel, A., Kesselheim, T., Räcke, H., Vöcking, B.: Oblivious interference scheduling. In: Proc. 28th Symposium on Principles of Distributed Computing, PODC (2009)
7. Fanghänel, A., Keßelheim, T., Vöcking, B.: Improved Algorithms for Latency Minimization in Wireless Networks. In: Albers, S., Marchetti-Spaccamela, A., Matias, Y., Nikoletseas, S., Thomas, W. (eds.) ICALP 2009. LNCS, vol. 5556, pp. 447–458. Springer, Heidelberg (2009)
8. Goussevskaia, O., Halldórsson, M.M., Wattenhofer, R., Welzl, E.: Capacity of Arbitrary Wireless Networks. In: Proc. of 28th Annual IEEE Conference on Computer Communications, INFOCOM (2009)
9. Goussevskaia, O., Oswald, Y.A., Wattenhofer, R.: Complexity in geometric SINR. In: Proc. of 8th ACM International Symposium on Mobile Ad Hoc Networking and Computing, MobiHoc (2007)
10. Gronkvist, J., Hansson, A.: Comparison between Graph-Based and Interference-Based STDMA scheduling. In: Proc. of ACM International Symposium on Mobile Ad Hoc Networking and Computing, MobiHoc (2001)
11. Halldórsson, M.M.: Wireless Scheduling with Power Control. In: Fiat, A., Sanders, P. (eds.) ESA 2009. LNCS, vol. 5757, pp. 361–372. Springer, Heidelberg (2009)
12. Halldórsson, M.M.: Wireless Scheduling with Power Control, http://arxiv.org/abs/1010.3427
13. Halldórsson, M.M., Mitra, P.: Nearly Optimal Bounds for Distributed Wireless Scheduling in the SINR Model. In: Aceto, L., Henzinger, M., Sgall, J. (eds.) ICALP 2011, Part II. LNCS, vol. 6756, pp. 625–636. Springer, Heidelberg (2011)
14. Halldórsson, M.M., Mitra, P.: Wireless Capacity with Oblivious Power in General Metrics. In: Proc. of ACM-SIAM Symposiun on Discrete Algorithms, SODA (2011)
15. Halldórsson, M.M., Wattenhofer, R.: Wireless Communication Is in APX. In: Albers, S., Marchetti-Spaccamela, A., Matias, Y., Nikoletseas, S., Thomas, W. (eds.) ICALP 2009. LNCS, vol. 5555, pp. 525–536. Springer, Heidelberg (2009)
16. Hardy, G.H., Littlewood, J.E., Pólya, G.: Inequalities. Cambridge University Press (1934)
17. Kesselheim, T.: A Constant-Factor Approximation for Wireless Capacity Maximization with Power Control in the SINR Model. In: Proc. of 22nd ACM-SIAM Symposium on Discrete Algorithms, SODA (2011)

18. Kesselheim, T., Vöcking, B.: Distributed Contention Resolution in Wireless Networks. In: Lynch, N.A., Shvartsman, A.A. (eds.) DISC 2010. LNCS, vol. 6343, pp. 163–178. Springer, Heidelberg (2010)

19. Moscibroda, T., Oswald, Y.A., Wattenhofer, R.: How optimal are wireless scheduling protocols? In: Proc. of 26th Annual IEEE Conference on Computer Communications, INFOCOM (2006)

20. Moscibroda, T., Wattenhofer, R.: The Complexity of Connectivity in Wireless Networks. In: Proc. of 26th Annual IEEE Conference on Computer Communications, INFOCOM (2006)

21. Moscibroda, T., Wattenhofer, R., Weber, Y.: Protocol design beyond Graph-Based models. In: Hot Topics in Networks, HotNets (2006)

22. Moscibroda, T., Wattenhofer, R., Zollinger, A.: Topology Control meets SINR: The Scheduling Complexity of Arbitrary Topologies. In: ACM International Symposium on Mobile Ad Hoc Networking and Computing, MobiHoc (2006)

23. Brar, G., Blough, D., Santi, P.: Computationally Efficient Scheduling with the Physical Interference Model for Throughput Improvement in Wireless Mesh Networks. In: Proc. of the 12th ACM Annual International Conference on Mobile Computing and Networking, MobiCom (2006)

24. Tonoyan, T.: A constant factor algorithm for scheduling with linear powers. In: Proc. of 2010 International Conference on Intelligent Network and Computing, ICINC (2010)

25. Tonoyan, T.: Algorithms for Scheduling with Power Control in Wireless Networks. In: Marchetti-Spaccamela, A., Segal, M. (eds.) TAPAS 2011. LNCS, vol. 6595, pp. 252–263. Springer, Heidelberg (2011)

Author Index